GW00644964

FUTURE WAR AND THE
DEFENCE OF EUROPE

FUTURE WAR

AND THE

DEFENCE OF

EUROPE

GENERAL JOHN R. ALLEN, USMC (RET.)

LIEUT. GEN. F. BEN HODGES, USA (RET.)

PROFESSOR JULIAN LINDLEY-FRENCH

OXFORD
UNIVERSITY PRESS

OXFORD
UNIVERSITY PRESS

Great Clarendon Street, Oxford, OX2 6DP,
United Kingdom

Oxford University Press is a department of the University of Oxford.
It furthers the University's objective of excellence in research, scholarship,
and education by publishing worldwide. Oxford is a registered trade mark of
Oxford University Press in the UK and in certain other countries

© John R. Allen, F. Ben Hodges, and Julian Lindley-French 2021

The moral rights of the authors have been asserted

First Edition published in 2021

Impression: 4

All rights reserved. No part of this publication may be reproduced, stored in
a retrieval system, or transmitted, in any form or by any means, without the
prior permission in writing of Oxford University Press, or as expressly permitted
by law, by licence or under terms agreed with the appropriate reprographics
rights organization. Enquiries concerning reproduction outside the scope of the
above should be sent to the Rights Department, Oxford University Press, at the
address above

You must not circulate this work in any other form
and you must impose this same condition on any acquirer

Published in the United States of America by Oxford University Press
198 Madison Avenue, New York, NY 10016, United States of America

British Library Cataloguing in Publication Data
Data available

Library of Congress Control Number: 2021930461

ISBN 978–0–19–885583–5

Printed and bound by CPI Group (UK) Ltd,
Croydon, CR0 4YY

Links to third party websites are provided by Oxford in good faith and
for information only. Oxford disclaims any responsibility for the materials
contained in any third party website referenced in this work.

This book is dedicated to Joseph Kindle Allen, United States Navy, George Scott Davis, US Coastguard, Katherine Jolliffe, US Army Nurse Corps, Clifford Lindley-French, Royal Navy, and Walter Saunders, Royal Navy. They fought for Europe's freedom and a just peace in the fervent hope that it would be defended and never have to be fought for again.

Preface

There are two theses central to this book. Firstly, the defence of Europe in the face of future war will require a new comprehensive concept of security in which human security and national defence are not only harmonized but seen as central to a new kind of deterrence that stretches across a complex and interlocking mosaic of hybrid, cyber, and hyper-warfare. Secondly, the impact of emerging technologies on future high-end warfare and by extension European defence will be profound.

The 2018 commemoration of the Armistice at the end of the 'war to end all wars' prompted questions that Plato inspired when he is believed to have suggested that only the dead have seen the end of wars.[1] Could Europe again face a major war; if so, what would it look like; and, above all, how could it be prevented and, if needs be, fought? How would such a war unfold? Could Europe withstand the shock of war?

The 2020–1 COVID-19 crisis would suggest there is much work to be done to make European states and their institutions more resilient if the peace to which so many Europeans have become accustomed is to be preserved in the face of emerging threats and natural hazards. If nothing else, COVID-19 has reminded Europeans that shock happens, even if many seem to be in denial. In August 1919 the British government initiated the Ten-Year Rule by which London assumed it would not be involved in a major war for at least a decade and could plan accordingly. In March 1932 Britain scrapped the Rule as war clouds began to appear again in the midst of the Depression. Strategic uncertainty has grown exponentially since the COVID-19 crisis began and such uncertainty is likely to worsen with the economic crisis but, locked into a kind of perpetual and virtual Ten-Year Rule, much of Europe seems unwilling to consider the eloquence of history

---

1. Colin S. Gray (2005) *Another Bloody Century: Future War* (London: Weidenfeld and Nicolson), front cover.

and just how dangerous such moments can be in the eternal struggle between peace and war.

Future War and the Defence of Europe is thus set against a backdrop of crisis and contemporary history, and the rapidly changing strategic, political, and technological environment with which Europeans, and those charged with defending them, must contend. The book also questions contemporary assumptions about the transatlantic relationship and its future, as well as the respective roles of both the North Atlantic Treaty Organization (NATO) and the European Union and the maintenance of peace and stability in Europe.

The focus of the book is thus the future military defence of Europe and, specifically, the future military art, science, and structure sound European defence and deterrence will demand. At its heart, the book is a consideration of the impact of what some have called the Fourth Industrial Revolution on the defence of Europe, and the sweeping changes that are unfolding in civil–military technologies across the globe.[2] Put simply, this book is European defence re-envisioned by three authors with over one hundred years of professional knowledge and experience combined.

John R. Allen
F. Ben Hodges
Julian Lindley-French

2. Min Xu, Jeanne David, and Suk Kim state, 'The fourth industrial revolution, a term coined by Klaus Schwab, founder and executive chairman of the World Economic Forum, describes a world where individuals move between digital domains and offline reality with the use of connected technology to enable and manage their lives...The first industrial revolution changed our lives and economy from an agrarian and handicraft economy to one dominated by industry and machine manufacturing. Oil and electricity facilitated mass production in the second industrial revolution. In the third industrial revolution, information technology was used to automate production. Although each industrial revolution is often considered a separate event, together they can be better understood as a series of events building upon innovations of the previous revolution and leading to more advanced forms of production'. See Min Xu, Jeanne David, and Suk Kim (2018) 'The Fourth Industrial Revolution: Opportunities and Challenges'. *International Journal of Financial Research*, vol. 9, p. 90.

Acknowledgements

The authors would like to thank the many people who have contributed to the writing of this book. Three people stand out for special mention. Paul Cornish, William Hopkinson, and Jim Townsend gave both their time and expertise to render this book a far better work than it otherwise might have been. With many years of experience working at the highest levels of both the British and American governments on matters germane to this book, they not only have a deep knowledge of the issues at hand, but were also instrumental in helping to shape many of them.

JRA, FBH, JLF
January 2021

Contents

About the authors

General John R. Allen, USMC (Ret.)

John Rutherford Allen assumed the presidency of the Brookings Institution in November 2017, having most recently served as chair of security and strategy and a distinguished fellow in the Foreign Policy programme at Brookings. Allen is a retired US Marine Corps four-star general and former Commander of the NATO International Security Assistance Force (ISAF) and US forces in Afghanistan.

Allen served in two senior diplomatic roles following his retirement from the Marine Corps: first, for fifteen months as Senior Advisor to the Secretary of Defense on Middle East Security, during which he led the security dialogue for the Israeli/Palestinian peace process. President Barack Obama then appointed Allen as special presidential envoy to the Global Coalition to Counter ISIL, a position he held for fifteen months. Allen's diplomatic efforts grew the coalition to sixty-five members, effectively halting the expansion of ISIL. In recognition of this work, he was presented with the Department of State Distinguished Honor Award by Secretary John Kerry and the Director of National Intelligence Distinguished Public Service Award by Director James Clapper.

During his nearly four-decade military career, Allen served in a variety of command and staff positions in the Marine Corps and the Joint Force. He commanded 150,000 US and NATO forces in Afghanistan from July 2011 to February 2013. Allen was the first Marine to command a theatre of war. During his tenure as ISAF Commander, he recovered the 33,000 US surge forces, moved the Afghan National Security Forces into the lead for combat operations, and pivoted NATO forces from being a conventional combat force into an advisory command.

Allen's first tour as a general officer was as the Principal Director of Indo-Pacific Policy in the Office of the Secretary of Defense, a position he held for nearly three years. In this assignment, he was involved extensively with policy initiatives concerning China, Taiwan, Mongolia, and Southeast Asia. Allen also participated in the Six-Party Talks on the denuclearization of the Korean Peninsula and played a major role in organizing the relief effort during the South Asian tsunami from 2004 to 2005.

Beyond his operational and diplomatic credentials, Allen has led professional military educational programmes, including as Director of the Marine Infantry Officer Program and commanding officer of the Marine Corps Basic School. He twice served at the United States Naval Academy, first as a military instructor, where he was named instructor of the year in 1990, and later as commandant of midshipmen, the first Marine Corps officer to hold this position. Allen was the Marine Corps fellow to the Center for Strategic and International Studies and the first Marine officer to serve as a term member of the Council on Foreign Relations, where today he is a permanent member.

Among his other affiliations, Allen is a Senior Fellow at the Merrill Center of the Johns Hopkins School of Advanced International Studies and a Senior Fellow at the Johns Hopkins Applied Physics Laboratory. He is an 'Ancien' of the NATO Defense College in Rome, and a frequent lecturer there.

Allen is the recipient of numerous US and foreign awards. He holds a Bachelor of Science in operations analysis from the US Naval Academy, a Master of Arts in national security studies from Georgetown University, a Master of Science in strategic intelligence from the National Intelligence University, and a Master of Science in national security strategy from the National Defense University.

Lieutenant–General USA F. Ben Hodges (Ret.)

A native of Quincy, Florida, Lieutenant-General Ben Hodges (retired) graduated from the United States Military Academy in May 1980 and was commissioned in the Infantry.

After his first assignment as an Infantry Lieutenant in Germany, he commanded Infantry units at the Company, Battalion, and Brigade levels in the 101st Airborne Division and in Operation IRAQI FREEDOM. He also served in an operational assignment as Director of Operations, Regional Command South, in Kandahar, Afghanistan.

Lieutenant-General Hodges (retired) has also served in a variety of Joint and Army Staff positions to include Tactic Instructor at the Infantry School; Chief of Plans, 2nd Infantry Division in Korea; Aide-de-Camp to the Supreme Allied Commander Europe; Army Congressional Liaison Officer; Task Force Senior Observer-Controller at the Joint Readiness Training Center, Fort Polk, LA; Coalition/Joint—3 (CJ3) of Multi-National Corps-Iraq in Operation IRAQI FREEDOM; Chief of Staff, XVIII Airborne Corps at Fort Bragg; and Director of the Pakistan Afghanistan Coordination Cell on the Joint Staff, Chief of Legislative Liaison for the United States Army, and Commander, NATO Allied Land Command. His last military assignment was as Commander, United States Army Europe from 2014 to 2017.

Lieutenant-General Hodges (retired) currently holds the Pershing Chair in Strategic Studies at the Center for European Policy Analysis (CEPA).

Professor Julian Lindley-French

Educated at the University of Oxford, University of East Anglia, and the European University Institute in Florence, Italy, Professor Dr Julian Lindley-French (PhD, MA (Dist.), MA (Oxon.)) is a leading advisor, strategist, and author with many published books and articles to his name. He has three advanced degrees and has held three professorial chairs (Professor of Military Art and Science and Eisenhower Professor of Defence Strategy, Netherlands Defence Academy, and Special Professor of Strategic Studies, Leiden University).

Vice-President of the Atlantic Treaty Association in Brussels until 2017, he is a Distinguished Visiting Research Fellow at the National Defense University in Washington, Senior Fellow at the Institute for Statecraft in London, Director of Europa Analytica in the Netherlands, and a Fellow of the Canadian Global Affairs Institute. He is also founder and chair of The Alphen Group, a high-level strategic 'do-tank' (https://thealphengroup. home.blog).

In 2015 he was made an Honorary Member of the Association of Anciens of the NATO Defense College in Rome. He also served General Sir David Richards and General Sir Nicholas Houghton on the Chief of Defence Staff's Strategic Advisory Group and as Head of the Commander's Initiative

Group for Lt.-General Sir Richard Shirreff, Commander of the Allied Rapid Reaction Corps.

In November 2017 he co-published *The Future Tasks of the Adapted Alliance* (The GLOBSEC NATO Adaptation Reports), for which he was lead writer, with (inter alia) General John R. Allen, Admiral Giampaolo di Paola, and Ambassador Sandy Vershbow. This major senior leader project considers NATO adaptation and the future role of the Alliance in a changing strategic environment. The final report was presented to the NATO Secretary-General and can be downloaded at https://www.globsec.org/news/globsec-nato-adaptation-initiative-final-report.

His influential books and high-level reports combine policy experience and academic expertise. In early 2018 he was made a member and Senior Counsellor to the high-level US–German Loisach Group set up by the George C. Marshall Center and the Munich Security Conference. In October 2018 he received the distinct honour of giving the Trafalgar Night dinner speech to the Royal Navy on board HMS Nelson at HM Naval Base Portsmouth entitled 'Nelson and the Pursuit of Victory'.

The Ten-Year Rule

'It should be assumed, for framing revised Estimates, that the British Empire will not be engaged in any great war during the next ten years, and that no Expeditionary Force is required for this purpose'.

In 1928 the Ten-Year Rule became a rolling rule and was not abandoned until 1932. As such, the Rule has become a metaphor for British strategic complacency during the Interbellum.[3]

---

3. War Cabinet 616A, Minutes of a Meeting of the War Cabinet at 10 Downing Street, Friday 15 August 1919. The Cabinet Papers, Defence Policy 1919–32, www.nationalarchives.gov.uk.

Scenario 1

Europe defeated

COVID-29

It all started with COVID-29. Early in 2029 a new pandemic spread across the world. It was similar to COVID-19, which had locked Europe down in 2020 and brought healthcare systems close to collapse. A decade on and Europe's economy has yet to recover from the extended post-crisis U-shaped depression which followed COVID-19. Throughout the 2020s Europe's overstretched and underfunded armed forces saw their already meagre budgets raided by governments desperate to build more capacity into their healthcare and social care systems.

In 2029 many Western sailors, soldiers, and airmen contract COVID-29. Exercises and training are cancelled, including NATO's massive and hurriedly scheduled Defender 29 exercise. Strangely, Chinese and Russian forces seem far less affected. There is a reason.

It was mid-April 2030 when Jim received a text message during leave to immediately report back to Fort Hood. For days now Jim had been recovering from COVID-29, having contracted the illness during an exercise with British forces. He had been vaguely aware that something was 'up', because the newspapers, TV, and internet were full of 'experts' warning about the build-up of Russian forces in Europe on NATO's eastern border. The Middle East was also in chaos . . . as usual. Still, it was all far away and as far as Jim was concerned, it was somebody else's problem. In any case, this was not the first time he had heard such 'stuff' so Jim had let any clouds of concern he might have drift on by. He had other things on his mind. Unlike COVID-19, COVID-29 also affected young people in huge numbers. It did not kill them, but laid them low. Jim worried for his wife and kids.

Still, as he slowly recovered, something nagged at Jim. He was a member of the elite US Army's 'Ironhorse' Brigade and had twice been deployed to Europe as part of an armoured Brigade Combat Team. For months now American forces had been in a stand-off with the Chinese in the Indo-Pacific. As a frontline combat soldier, and an experienced non-commissioned officer, Jim also knew that in another European emergency he would be one of the first to go, and right in the firing line. During all of those great NATO exercises, Defender 22 (Defender 20 had been cancelled because of COVID-19), Defender 24, and Defender 28, Jim had been at the spear-tip of danger alongside the Marines of Regimental Combat Team 2.

Even though he was only barely fit, Jim left his now concerned wife with the usual assurances that it was just another scare and, like before, he would soon be home. However, deep in Jim's gut something felt different. When he got back to Fort Hood it was clear just how different it was. This was no 'keep the generals happy, tick the box, go through the motions, and get back to business as quick as usual' exercise. There was a real sense of purpose. Jim's force was soon joined by other formations rapidly preparing for enshipment to Bremerhaven in Germany. Jim also quickly learnt that the plan was then to trans-ship across Europe by rail, which worried him. From past experience Jim knew that Europe's rail system, even in ideal circumstances, was simply not up to the task of getting his force forward and deployed quickly enough or anything like secure enough. Now, with much of the workforce ill? Nor was he entirely confident about crossing the Atlantic safely. He had read about Russian nuclear-powered hunter-killer submarines and their scary missiles and, more disturbingly, their super-quiet, extended-range, improved Kilo-class diesel submarines, which had even been reported off the eastern US seaboard. The decision had been taken by the 'brass' to use requisitioned civilian ships and escort them across the Atlantic to Bremerhaven for onward despatch. However, by 2029 less than 1 per cent of US goods were carried by US-flagged merchant ships and assembling such a fleet proved challenging. Still, it had worked for his great-grandfather back in 1943, and who was he to quibble?

In fact, Jim's concerns were reasonable. With tensions so high, shipping any army across the Atlantic in the face of the renewed Russian threat was a risky course of action should a fighting war break out mid-crossing. The US Air Force was moving what squadrons and critical support it could across the Atlantic in force—both regular and National Guard formations, whilst at the same time deploying critical early-deployment formations through the rapidly mobilized Civilian Reserve Air Fleet. However, Washington had a delicate balancing act to perform. If the Americans moved too quickly, far from preventing a war, they could actually trigger one, like the mass force mobilizations that had taken place on the eve of World War One. That is why the decision had been taken to move the bulk of US ground forces across the North Atlantic through a mix of US military fast sealift and civilian ships, even though such a course of action was risky. Such a move would have been a challenge for US planners *if Europe was the only threat the Americans faced. It was not. The situation in the East China Sea was also dire. It was no accident.*

Jim had probably spent too much time watching TV and the seemingly endless parade of retired senior officers who expressed their stony-faced concern about the risks Jim and his comrades faced. 'Don't these guys have anything better to do?' he once exclaimed. Still, he could not stop himself from watching. For almost a decade the Americans had been embroiled in an on-off crisis with the powerful Chinese. Consequently, the US Navy was overstretched and tired, with the bulk of its forces in the Indo-Pacific region. There were other problems. The Navy had been hard-pressed to find the ships or officers who had any idea how to run a convoy in wartime. In spite of the impressive firepower on the ships that surrounded him once Jim had embarked, in reality the force lacked the anti-submarine and air defence capabilities needed to properly defend such a large, vital, and cumbersome convoy against Russia's latest anti-ship weapons. Worse, some of America's 'mighty' aircraft carriers of the Gerald R. Ford class were deemed by some in government as so vulnerable (and expensive) that they were not to be risked. The simple strategic truth faced by those far above Jim's pay grade was that the Navy could either escort the convoy or the carriers, but not both. The days of the 600-ship navy had long gone.[1]

At least the politicians were still talking and, as ever, the US would again come to the rescue of the Europeans, as it always had, or so Jim thought. Still, in his meaner moments Jim did wonder why he was trudging off to Europe again, as his father and grandfather had before him. Surely Europeans could find a way to defend themselves? But Jim was a soldier, and those were issues for others with gold braid on their shoulders to worry about.

---

1. *Defense News* reported in October 2019 that the United States Navy was being forced to reconsider its long-stated goal of a 355-ship navy. 'As it stands now, the Navy has 290 ships, and will hit 300 by next fall. But as Navy leadership tries to build more ships, it has to confront two significant problems: keeping the ships it has in good condition, and wrestling with what are expected to be flat or declining budgets in the coming years. Only about 30 percent of the Navy's destroyer fleet can leave port on time after repairs, while six of the service's 11 aircraft carriers are in dock under repair, including the USS Harry S. Truman, which was supposed to deploy to the Middle East last month but has been hobbled by electrical problems'. The problem of readiness is also shared by the Royal Navy. In October 2019 UK Defence Secretary Ben Wallace suggested the priority was to end the 'hollowing out' of UK armed forces. With particular reference to the Navy, he suggested the priority was to make the ships the Royal Navy already has work. The impact of the COVID-19 crisis on such ambition has yet to become evident. See Paul McCleary, 'Navy May Scrap Goal of 355 Ships; 310 Is Likely', *Defense News*, 25 October 2019, https://breakingdefense.com/2019/10/navy-may-scrap-goal-of-355-ships-310-is-likely/?utm_campaign=Breaking%20News&utm_source=hs_email&utm_medium=email&utm_content=78568134&_hsenc=p2ANqtz-_eq-lYtN5bBNPU3EXDLujq-H56WYp9HWRmeEF5ifq3yDK4pRpggi6PfrYF5zqJOHr3x0Qekvnea2Z9bv3bkztX9HEpig HEpigg&_hsmi=78568134.

It also took time for the force to be marshalled and embark on its perilous journey. The US had done nothing on this scale since 1945. It was not until mid-May that Jim finally got underway. Once underway Jim and his men settled down into a sort of routine, which helped shield them from their many fears and doubts. Constant weapons checks and seemingly endless deck exercises were only interrupted for operation ration packs, or air and sea defence drills. They also engaged in friendly and occasionally not-so-friendly banter with the Marines on board. For all the bravado, Jim could smell the apprehension, even among the Marines who Jim regarded as too dumb to be scared. Some men talked too much; others too little. In fact, the voyage to Bremerhaven went surprisingly smoothly. From time to time he would hear large explosions far off to the north, as the Navy exercised, but nothing close. Like so many American soldiers before him, Jim even enjoyed seeing the white cliffs of Dover, that traditional symbol of British defiance which had stood proud against the Armada, Napoleon, the Kaiser, and, of course, the Nazis so many years before.

Far, far away . . .

At 0925 hours on 10 August 2030, the USS John C. Stennis, a 103,000-ton nuclear-powered American fleet aircraft carrier, entered the disputed South China Sea, the command core of a US carrier strike group. The mission was to conduct a freedom of navigation operation in strength, even though half the crew were either suffering from COVID-29 or showing symptoms.

As recently as June 2016 the US and Chinese navies had conducted a joint tactical manoeuvre exercise in the North Pacific. How times had changed. In 2018, a ruling by the International Tribunal for the United Nations Convention on the Law of the Sea had found in favour of the Philippines and against Beijing's claim that China had exclusive territorial rights to over 80 per cent of the South China Sea. In 2019, President Trump had imposed trade tariffs on Chinese goods entering the United States, and the Chinese had retaliated. Apart from the odd false dawn of hope, Sino-American relations had been difficult ever since, particularly in the wake of the COVID-19 crisis and China's 2021 military occupation of Hong Kong. Throughout the 2020s relations between Beijing and Washington had steadily deteriorated as China redoubled its efforts to impose itself over the entire region, increasingly through the threat of force.

Beijing's strategic aims were sixfold: to create a military capability on the disputed Spratly Islands that would at a stroke end sovereignty disputes in its favour; to control the oil and gas resources believed to lie under the Spratly Islands; to reinforce China's self-proclaimed Air Defence Identification Zone; to extend Beijing's self-proclaimed Exclusive Economic Zone right across the South China Sea; to end the 'Two Systems, One China' policy, intimidate Taipei, and in time force Taiwan under Beijing's yoke; and to tip the strategic balance in the region against the US and Japan, and any other state foolish enough to challenge China's assertions of sovereignty.

In 2029, China's specific military goal was to finally control the South China Sea. The Stennis was ordered to stop it. Since 2025 tensions had become steadily more acute when China had begun reinforcing its forces on several of the artificial islands it had constructed along the Nine-Dash Line. Completed in 2017, one such facility, Fiery Cross Reef, boasted a military airstrip, together with a 5,000-ton sea-berth and an arsenal of hypersonic anti-ship missiles in hardened bunkers. China also had ambitions that stretched far beyond the South China Sea. In the wake of the COVID-19 chaos, China had sought to project Chinese power across the Indian Ocean to East Africa.

At 0425 hours on 11 August, twenty-five Chinese J-31 fighters armed with advanced anti-ship technology approached the US force with orders to engage. After repeated warnings to turn away, the US commander ordered the Chinese aircraft to be engaged and 'downed'. Ten of them were quickly shot down by 'active countermeasures', whilst a further two were badly damaged. However, eight aircraft continued their attack and, before they could be destroyed, an ageing AEGIS-class cruiser, the USS Mobile Bay, was struck by several missiles. She sank with heavy loss of life, throwing the Indo-Pacific into full-blown crisis. The Stennis was also hit by a Chinese projectile fired from a shipborne hypersonic gun which had flown at more than 5,000 mph/8,000 kph for over 100 miles.

Washington warned Beijing of the consequences, but China was in no mood to back down. For an ageing President Xi, this was China's moment of destiny. The action had been carefully planned. Its ultimate aim was to force the reunification of Taiwan with mainland China after the new Taiwanese president had called a plebiscite on permanent independence. Beijing was also determined to become the dominant strategic power in East and quite possibly South Asia, and sensed weakness in Washington. Having helped foment growing crises in Europe and the Middle East, China was also simply ready for 'this supreme test of national destiny', in the words of President Xi. Russia had also proven a useful surrogate for Beijing's ambitions. Indeed, in the face of growing Chinese and Russian military might, US forces were simply unable to engage in strength simultaneously in the Indo-Pacific, the Middle East, and Europe. Knowing this, Beijing had built up its military power patiently and relentlessly, seducing, intimidating, and coercing its neighbours, and buying the sullen compliance of many beyond, even in Europe, through the Belt and Road Initiative and the siren song of cheap but very capable Chinese technology. China and

Russia had also begun a sustained campaign of information warfare to prepare the 'ground' for military action, using 'information shock' to engineer disinformation, deception, destabilization, and growing disruption that reinforced coercion and the implied threat of destruction. On this summer's day in 2030 the world stared down the many 'barrels' of global hyperwar. Realpolitik was back, red in tooth and claw.

China was, of course, also fully aware of what Putin, now President-for-Life, planned next. As the crisis in Indo-Pacific deepened, the US was forced to respond in force. However, American action was only likely to prevail if Washington could commit the bulk of its forces to the Indo-Pacific. That meant withdrawing its pre-positioned forces in Europe, many of which had been earmarked for the defence of Europe. In mid-July 2030 Russia had begun Zapad 2030 (West 2030), a massive military exercise that stretched from the Mediterranean through the Black and Baltic Seas to the Arctic, along the borders of Moscow's Southern and Western Military Districts (Strategic Commands). Europe? Exhausted and worn down by years of austerity, the social and economic consequences of COVID-19, terrorist attacks, relative economic decline, populism, and Brexit, Europe was too divided and too weak to defend itself from war at the seams of its complex societies and at the margins of its fading institutions. Sadly, COVID-29 was decimating the few ranks European forces could muster.

Chaos in the south

Worse, a significant portion of Europe's underequipped and undermanned armed forces had for some time been engaged in Algeria, Libya, and Tunisia trying to shore up states from a series of Salafist insurrections, partly fomented by Moscow and Tehran. Libya was of particular concern as it was the main jumping-off point for millions of desperate refugees and irregular migrants who had embarked on a desperate march of misery towards what they hoped would be a better life in Europe. The wider Middle East and North African region was a powder keg of regional strategic competition between states, exacerbated by the ever-present threat of state collapse. In a kind of grotesque twenty-first-century homage to the Great Game, China, Russia, and the West were competing through a host of proxies for regional dominance.[2]

---

2. The Great Game was the grand strategic struggle between the British Empire and Russia for dominance in Central and Southern Asia during the nineteenth century. The 1901 novel *Kim* by Rudyard Kipling popularized the term and the idea and nature of Great Power rivalry.

The threat of war was ever-present. The proxy fighting that so disfigured Syria had steadily given way to a series of full-on confrontations between a Russian-backed Iran and a Saudi- and Egyptian-led coalition. In 2021 Turkey had seized and held a 60-kilometre strip that now extended along the entirety of its border with Iraq and Syria—an armed buffer zone between Kurds and Turks. Ankara and Tel Aviv were also settling old scores, and Israel was becoming steadily more concerned about the stability of Jordan, as the Iranian Revolutionary Corps of Guards in Syria edged ever closer to the Israeli border and the Golan Heights.

By 2029, the situation in North Africa was close to chaos as many of the states therein existed in name only. Daesh had risen from the ashes of its 2018 defeat in Syria following President Trump's 2019 withdrawal of 2,000 US Special Forces in north-west Syria, and the series of Kurdish–Turkish wars that had ensued. Consequently, and in part aided by China and Russia, both al-Qaeda and Daesh had increased their influence markedly in North Africa throughout the 2020s. The small European force that had landed in Libya in June 2029 in an effort to stabilize the situation was beaten back with significant loss of life by a mix of local militias and Salafist Jihadis, with support and training provided by the Russian 'private' Security Company, the Wagner Group. Hundreds of European nationals also remained trapped in Tunisia and Morocco, where the situation was little better than in Libya. Some were held hostage by criminal gangs which threatened to sell them on to mushrooming Salafist Jihadi groups, steadily being reinforced by battle-hardened foreign Jihadis. Beheadings of captured Westerners began again. Algeria was holding together, but only barely with some 800,000 Ethiopians, Somalis, Nigerians, and people from a host of Sub-Saharan states trapped therein seeking to gain illicit entry into the European Union (EU). As the last vestige of state authority collapsed around them, these already desperate people were driven even deeper into despair as COVID-29 decimated people already weakened by hunger and poverty. They were slaves . . . and pawns.

In February 2030, as the pandemic intensified, migration flows towards Europe suddenly surged. Hundreds of thousands of people were put in horribly overcrowded boats along the North African coast and forced to set out for Europe. For month after month the BBC, CNN, France 24, and DW reported on the tens of thousands of drowned souls being washed around the Mediterranean. The EU's lamentably understrength external border force Frontex was soon overwhelmed, whilst Western navies in the region fared little better. The French Navy, the strongest European navy in the Mediterranean, soon discovered that years of underfunding had left it with far too few ships to cover a sea space filled with the bodies of drowned migrants, some of whom were washing up on European beaches—a ghostly flotsam bearing the spectres of their fears and aspirations.

The post-COVID-19 economic slump had made matters far worse. And since the June 2025 Daesh attack on Istanbul Airport, Ankara had also become steadily more aware that NATO and its Allies were in no fit state to assist Turkey. NATO had been effectively paralysed by the ongoing dispute between Europeans and Turkey's President-for-Life Erdogan over his decision in 2024 to push all refugees and irregular migrants in his country into the EU. Huge numbers of additional migrants had begun arriving on the Greek island of Lesbos and sent to already overcrowded detention centres and holding camps in which crime was rampant. The hopelessly overstretched Greek authorities were soon overwhelmed. Reports also quickly emerged that armed Jihadi gangs had taken command of a large number of camps and begun the systematic murder of local officials, as well as EU and United Nations (UN) personnel.

North Cape

By mid-August 2030 Britain's 70,000-ton heavy aircraft carrier HMS Queen Elizabeth was sailing off Norway's North Cape. These were historic waters for the Royal Navy as 'Big Lizzie' was not far from where, on the late afternoon of 26 December 1943, in the murk of an Arctic twilight, the British battleship HMS Duke of York had sunk the German battlecruiser, KM Scharnhorst. The First Battle of North Cape had not simply been another naval battle. It was at one and the same time the opening engagement of the computer/missile age and one of the last dreadnought-to-dreadnought duals in naval history in which no aircraft played any significant part.[3]

By the standards of the age, HMS Duke of York was a floating electronics platform armed with state-of-the-art sensors and several layers of radar capability that gave her eyes in the dark.[4] Type 284M(3) main gunnery radars were at the centre of an advanced fire control system that was in turn linked to a rudimentary computer that trained her ten 14-inch (35-cm) calibre guns remorselessly onto her German target. Unheard of in any prior battleship-to-battleship engagement, the KM Scharnhorst was straddled and hit by the initial salvo, with one of her main gun turrets immediately

---

3. The last such engagement was the Battle of Surigao Strait which took place on 24–25 October 1944 between forces of the US Navy and the Imperial Japanese Navy.
4. Angus Konstam writes that as well as 'the radars, the battleship [HMS Duke of York] was also fitted with an extensive suite of electronic equipment, designed to detect aircraft, radio or radar transmissions, IFF (Identification of Friend or Foe) transmissions from friendly aircraft or ships, and radar detection equipment. The battleship was buzzing with electronics, and although these were fairly rudimentary by modern standards, in late 1943 they were "state-of-the-art", and that afternoon they were all working perfectly'. See A. Konstam (2009) *The Battle of North Cape: The Death Ride of the Scharnhorst, 1943* (Barnsley: Pen and Sword), p. 113.

disabled. The eventual sinking of the KM Scharnhorst, some three hours later, ended the threat posed by Nazi surface raiders to Allied convoys en route to Murmansk, Russia. It was a decisive turning point in the Battle of the Atlantic—the only battle of World War Two which Churchill claimed ever truly worried him.[5]

Over eighty years later the Second Battle of the Atlantic was about to begin; a struggle to control the strategic lines of communication above, on, and below the surface. Irrespective of China's ambitions, tensions with Russia had been building for months. An ageing and increasingly erratic President Putin, faced with deep economic and societal challenges in the wake of the COVID-19 crisis, had become steadily more aggressive as his popularity declined. For years the regime had relied on the income from oil and gas exports to Europe. For a time, the derived income sustained the regime and its martial ambitions. However, the income had collapsed during the COVID-19 crisis and had yet to recover. In late 2028, led by the powerful German car industry, the EU had also made the historic decision to abandon all petrol- and diesel-powered cars by 2035 in favour of new long-range electric vehicles. This decision took place in concert with another pivotal EU decision to import massive amounts of liquid natural gas from the US, cementing and ensuring Europe's energy independence from Russia. The tradeable value of the rouble collapsed, adding another layer of anti-Western grievance to the many the Kremlin harboured. In the face of growing social and political unrest, overburdened by a security and military deep state far too large for the Russian economy to sustain, and having failed to implement any meaningful reforms to either society or economy, in early 2030 Russia had tipped rapidly into domestic crisis.

In June 2030 Moscow had begun to lash out. First, it implemented what it called its '5D War Plan'. Disinformation, deception, disruption, and destabilization were combined with the implied threat of mass destruction to intimidate Russia's immediate European neighbours. Now, a sixth 'D' was added—engineered disease. COVID-29 was a manmade mutation of COVID-19 that had been developed at a Wuhan laboratory, of all places. Both Beijing and Moscow saw NATO as a kind of twenty-first-century Maginot Line that might appear impressive in 'glossy' public diplomacy films but which in reality was fragile—a cracked eggshell of a defence. If they could reduce its efficiency by no more than 15 per cent, it would fail the moment it was attacked. COVID-29 did just that. The Chinese and Russians also had an antidote.

---

5. Winston Churchill wrote, 'The Battle of the Atlantic was the dominating factor all through the war. Never for one moment could we forget that everything happening elsewhere, on land, at sea, or in the air, depended ultimately on its outcome, and amid all other cares we viewed its changing fortunes day by day with hope and apprehension'. From Jonathan Dimbleby (2015) *The Battle of the Atlantic: How the Allies Won the War* (London: Penguin), p. xx.

As Europeans fell ill and a new lockdown was ordered, EU and NATO members in Central and Eastern Europe began to face regular Russian-inspired cyber-attacks, as banking, transportation, and even healthcare systems were effectively shut down for days at a time. RT, Sputnik, and other Kremlin-controlled Russian media organs pumped out increasingly hysterical fake news stories about Western aggression and the alleged mistreatment of Russian minorities in Europe. Putin also regaled the Russian population with exaggerated nationalist tales of Soviet-era superiority and the national selflessness and sacrifices that had been made by the Russian population during the Great Patriotic War.

Zapad 2029 saw Russia's Western Military District (Oblast) steadily and quickly reinforced with several newly reconstituted Soviet-sounding Guards Divisions which now threatened much of NATO's eastern borders. Worse, Russia significantly increased both the number and type of nuclear and long-range hypersonic weapons deployed to its Kaliningrad enclave between Poland and Lithuania, and markedly stepped up its air defence capabilities.

In late June 2030, the Russian Northern Fleet had also begun to patrol aggressively with aircraft, ships, and submarines regularly intimidating NATO naval forces far out into the North Atlantic. The most dangerous encounters took place in and around the so-called Greenland–Iceland–UK gap close to Norway's North Cape. Such confrontations were not just at sea. Russian Naval Infantry appeared in ever-growing numbers close to Kirkenes on the Russian border with Finnmark. Finnish and Swedish forces were placed on full alert, and when Russian equipment was discovered on a Norwegian beach, rumours of Russian Special Forces operating inside Norway also began to spread. In early July 2030, Russia had also moved a particularly large formation of its recently upgraded Naval Infantry (Marines) to Pechanga, close to Russia's short border with Norway. An alarmed Oslo had immediately called for Alliance support.

In July 2030, as tensions ratcheted up in the South China Sea, the North Atlantic Council (NAC) had ordered the Supreme Allied Commander Europe (SACEUR) to take 'all necessary steps' to demonstrate to Moscow the Alliance's determination and resolve to defend its borders, and the vital sea and air lines of communication around them. Unfortunately, few first-rate US ships were available to the Alliance because of the mounting tensions in the Indo-Pacific as US forces were moved to counter the impressive Chinese People's Liberation Navy.[6] Worse, as the fighting increased in

---

6. At the Battle of Trafalgar in October 1805, Admiral Lord Nelson's wooden battleships were divided into first-, second-, and third-rate ships depending on their age, firepower, and the quality of their crews.

Libya, hundreds more poorly equipped boats and dinghies, all in an appalling state of repair and packed full with migrants, suddenly appeared in the Gulf of Sirte, all heading towards Italy. The hard-line government in Rome demanded EU action, or else it would paralyse NATO.

In spite of the pressures Washington was facing, and the three simultaneous major crises with which it had to contend, the Americans began to airlift US Marines into Norway, alongside their British and Dutch counterparts. It was a small force, barely more than a brigade, but they rapidly established a defensive line. They were a tripwire force with a clear mission: to deter Russia from taking any aggressive action. They settled in rapidly, making use of Marine Expeditionary Brigade equipment that had been wisely 'pre-positioned' in caves. At least some Allied forces were moving.

During the first week of August a hastily arranged NATO maritime task group was formed, organized around HMS Queen Elizabeth, and despatched to North Cape. On paper, NTM-1 was a mighty show of NATO strength designed to deter the Russian Northern Fleet. It included ships, aircraft, and submarines from some twelve NATO allies including Britain, Canada, France, Germany, the Netherlands, Belgium, Denmark, and Norway. Unfortunately, it was more show than strength. Many of the ships lacked vital protected communications, surveillance, and data systems. And, critically, they all lacked offensive and defensive weapons critical to the fighting power of any such force. In the wake of the COVID-19 crisis, defence equipment budgets had been savagely slashed in Europe, with many programmes cancelled.

War!

On 11 August 2030, as the USS John C. Stennis was being attacked in the South China Sea, the Second Battle of North Cape began. One hundred and fifty nautical miles west-northwest of North Cape, weapons, communications, and defence systems on board HMS Queen Elizabeth suddenly crashed as the task group flagship suffered a sustained cyber-attack, along with much of the rest of the force. Almost simultaneously the huge ship was attacked by a swarm of autonomous, advanced, lethal artificial intelligence (AI) aerial robots, with each 'bot' equipped with tailored anti-ship technology programmed to seek out and destroy specific parts of the mighty ship's defences. Terrifyingly, these new-generation robots were also able to learn from each other as they probed the defences of the NATO task group.

As the Second Battle of North Cape unfolded, high above the ships space also became a battlefield as US and European reconnaissance satellites were first blinded *and then destroyed. Simultaneous attacks also took place on European command and control systems, and dual-use civil–military commercial communications satellites, such as Skynet V. Galileo and GPS, also failed. NATO was effectively blind over the North Atlantic at a critical moment. Something similar was happening to Allied forces over the Eastern Mediterranean and, critically, the South China Sea. Indeed, the only thing that was clear was that Beijing and Moscow were closely coordinating their efforts. It may not have been the War of the Worlds, but it was clearly two worlds at war.*

At 0331 hours the situational awareness of the NATO fleet commander on board HMS Queen Elizabeth was effectively and suddenly reduced to nil. The other NATO commanders also found their ability to respond was drastically reduced, with the command response time of the HMS Queen Elizabeth's captain down to less than a second. Suddenly, the NATO commodore lost all communications and command and control links to the task group. The attack drone swarm then split up and began to attack specific systems in the operations centre of HMS Queen Elizabeth. By 0332 hours internal communications on 'Big Lizzie' were disabled as the damage control system failed. Worse, the ship suddenly stalled as the engines were thrown into full reverse. Chaos ensued with the captain no longer in effective command of her ship.

Some way off the NATO fleet, two Russian Yasen-class nuclear attack submarines had successfully exploited the complex layers of water at different temperatures and densities that are common in the frigid waters of the North Atlantic and avoided detection by the ageing 3G and 4G defensive systems of the NATO task group. At 0333 hours, the two Russian submarines each launched a Zircon hypersonic anti-ship missile, both of which came in behind another autonomous swarm which was systematically attacking and confusing the ship's anti-missile defensive weapons. The Sea Ceptor 2 missile defence system, with which 'QE' was armed, had taken out one of the Zircons, but only one. The subsequent explosion was enormous, the damage to HMS Queen Elizabeth devastating, and in an instant Britain's flagship, the pride of the Royal Navy, was crippled.

By 0335 hours the ship had begun to rapidly take on water and began listing heavily to starboard. With the automated damage control system down, the ship was unable to pump or counter flood to correct the list. Fires were soon burning out of control all over the ship and spreading towards the Avgas fuel tanks. The surviving crew rushed to the upper decks in a desperate attempt to escape the doomed ship. After another enormous internal explosion, a shocked captain finally gave an order she never thought she would have to issue— 'abandon ship—everyone for themselves!' Those 'lucky' enough to make it onto the rapidly tilting flight deck were forced to jump into the freezing North Atlantic and died within minutes as hypothermia wrapped its cold tentacles of death around them. Even those wearing survival suits did not last much longer.

At 0353 hours, twenty minutes after the attack began, a burning HMS Queen Elizabeth, the largest ship ever to have served in the Royal Navy, capsized and sank by the bow, propellers churning towards oblivion in the cold, dark light of an Arctic dawn. Much like HMS Hood, which blew up in the Denmark Strait in May 1941 not so far from the scene of the Royal Navy's latest disaster, there were only three survivors from a crew of 1,500. 'Big Lizzie's' powerful complement of F-35 Lightning II/5 (Enhanced-Range) fast jets, and Merlin 7 ASW helicopters? They never even got off her decks.

At 0454 hours the Russian submarine Novosibirsk flashed a success signal to Moscow. It contained just one word: 'Kursk'.

Crash!

As 'Big Lizzie' sinks, vulnerable civilian critical infrastructures across Europe crash as telephone and computer systems fail, and air and rail transportation is brought to a halt. TV and social media are hacked, and because of the interconnectedness of new 5G civilian networks, much of it furnished by China, and much of it enabling Europe's much-vaunted AI Internet of Things, some domestic appliances even explode. Europeans, many of them struggling with COVID-29, awake to chaos and are disoriented and in shock. They search for reassuring news only to find TV, radio, and social media seized with apocalyptic messaging warning of impending nuclear, biological, and chemical attacks on major European cities. No-one had prepared the European people for this, especially deep fake news reports about bio-weapons and the outbreak of an extremely virulent and highly communicable fatal haemorrhagic plague, of which COVID-29 is allegedly but the first phase!

Off the coast of Northern Scotland, some 80 nautical miles north of Cape Wrath, a Russian Belgorod-class submarine has systematically destroyed critical undersea cables—vital sea lines of communication. This is just the beginning.

If only . . .

Whilst there was much talk among leaders in the wake of the COVID-19 crisis, particularly in Europe, about the need for more robust and resilient infrastructure able to cope with just such an emergency, little was actually done. And, in spite of tentative efforts to 'fuse' new big data-based intelligence analysis which could have given European leaders some forewarning of the combined cyber- and AI attacks, no such system was in place. Comprehensive European AI-powered intelligence analysis could have provided clear indications of final preparations for a series of attacks some time before they were launched and was, indeed, being built, but like much to do with European defence, it was late, underfunded, and far from completion when the attack came. As the attacks unfolded, the many seams within Western societies also revealed the extent of the systemic vulnerabilities in food, health, and transportation systems from which Europe suffered. All over Europe, hospitals were deluged with hysterical people claiming to be suffering from a new plague. Unfortunately, health professionals had been locked out of their respective healthcare systems because patients' medical records had been permanently encrypted by a form of strategic ransomware, albeit without any ransom demand. This was war, future war.

Panic rapidly grew and mass hysteria ensued in European mega-cities already hard-hit by the pandemic. Worse, given those same cities were also the seat of government in many European countries, authority rapidly collapsed. The chaos had been made worse by simultaneous terrorist attacks upon groups of bewildered people by sleeper cells carefully implanted over time in the EU, most notably in Brussels, where crisis response rapidly collapsed. The deep fake reports of plague that were spread by the seemingly credible and familiar in several European countries only complicated an already dire situation and hindered the movement of both first responders and security and defence forces. Insufficiently hardened critical national infrastructures, overly reliant on a vulnerable net—transport, healthcare, policing—simply evaporated or ceased to function at all, as devastating well-placed and coordinated cyber- and physical attacks maintained the momentum of engineered mayhem. As people began to flee Europe's cities, transportation arteries vital to any Allied civil or military mobility rapidly became clogged up. However, as shocking as the chaos was, equally shocking was how easily and quickly Europe's long-established political order had collapsed.

Political and military command in many NATO countries was rapidly decapitated by a series of well-coordinated cyber-attacks on insufficiently robust government and military communications systems. In any case, it was an open door for the enemy as many of Europe's leaders were laid low by COVID-29, in much the same way as British Prime Minister Boris Johnson had been during the COVID-19 crisis. The NATO Cyber Ops Centre soon became overstretched and then overwhelmed before it failed. Leaders and commanders simply did not know where the attacks were coming from because they lacked the indicators and expertise that would have provided such a picture. Very quickly, the response of both the EU and the Alliance descended into little more than a series of poorly coordinated local actions.

Jim? His problems began when he arrived off Bremerhaven. First, he felt like shit. Second, whilst the British had mustered what force they could, much of their fighting power had also been reduced by COVID-29. The British force had also arrived at the mouth of the River Weser just before the Americans, which overwhelmed the bespoke military reception facilities. Whilst the British were fortunately under American command, the rest of the port was not and the German officials charged with trying to manage the snarl-up were inexperienced stand-ins for ill colleagues. Faced with a collapsed IT system, they were trying to manage the movements of a large number of vessels packed with troops in a very confined space, working with people they did not know—civilian and military—in several languages using old-fashioned manual methods. Whilst the delay was eventually resolved, it still created in Jim's mind the sense that this was going to be a serious 'shit show'.

In fact, Washington had made it perfectly clear to the Europeans that such were the pressures faced by US forces, and the dangerous nature of the crisis, that 'no way' would the Americans rely on that 'talking shop NATO', as the American president had called it. Washington had simply assumed command, and in spite of a few 'chirps' from the French, the Europeans had meekly accepted it.

And yet, for two days Jim and his ill mates had sat off Bremerhaven waiting to disembark and move forward to where the force's Polish-based pre-positioned equipment was waiting for them. Sitting ducks. When they finally got ashore, they waited a further two days before they set off eastwards across Northern Germany towards Poland. Once in Poland, they made their stuttering way along a shiny new railway festooned with large signs saying it had been built with money from the EU. However, few of these new lines had been designed with military mobility in mind and foul-up after foul-up ensued. Jim's mood darkened further as news reached him that this was now a full-blown crisis with a full-scale European war imminent.

Would it happen? Could it happen? Will I survive? What about my family? Above all, will I let myself and my fellow soldiers down—the men and women whose lives depend on me? Over and over again Jim's mind mulled the eternally mullable. Faced with such gnawing uncertainty, it was a relief simply to go through another drill or weapons check. For all the problems, Jim still had faith that his training, equipment, and American know-how would somehow get him through. Still, every now and then Jim would linger on images of his wife and kids and wonder.

Somewhere in Western Poland the train suddenly stopped. It never moved again. Jim never saw or heard the Kh-47M2 Kinzhal hypersonic missile that destroyed his column. The MiG 31 that fired it never even left Russian airspace. His Bradley Armoured Fighting Vehicle was still on the train in Western Poland when the missile hit. Somehow Jim survived, amidst the chaos and carnage all around him. Where and why had it all gone so wrong?

Meanwhile . . .

The bulk of NATO's main defence forces had been covering the Baltic States and Poland when Jim was attacked, along with the few available US forces in Europe, all of which were priority Russian targets. In Southeastern and Southern Europe, with the crisis in North Africa getting worse, what forces had been assigned to the Alliance or EU were rapidly placed back under what little national control still existed. Paradoxically, Europe's more 'analogue' societies somehow seemed more robust and better able to instigate some kind of attack mitigation and consequence management than their richer Northern and Western European neighbours.

Far to the north of Europe, as the Second Battle of North Cape unfolded, and with Russian nuclear forces on high alert, Russian Naval Infantry and Spetsnaz rapidly seized Norway's North Cape, the Svalbard Archipelago, and all non-Russian forces within the Arctic Circle. It slowly became clear that the chaos in the heart of Europe had merely been a feint to mask Russian forces at their most vulnerable—as they concentrated to attack. Moscow's war aims had also become clear. First, Russian forces seized the new Northeast Passage between Asia and Europe, and secured by force all the oil and gas believed to lie under the Arctic Circle. Second, as chaos ensued, Russian forces had moved to cut the Baltic States off from the Alliance. Put simply, President Putin had bet everything on the inability of NATO to effectively resist Russia's first attack and that thereafter the NAC would never agree to commit the Alliance to fight for the recovery of any lost allies. He was right.

War in the East

The Russians had quickly moved from what they call 'non-linear warfare' to full-scale kinetic warfare as the equivalent of four army corps or 120,000 troops had moved over the border from the Western Military District into NATO territory. The NAC met in emergency session and reluctantly put both the Very High-Readiness Joint Task Force (VJTF) of some 5,000 troops and the enhanced NATO Response Force (eNRF) of some 40,000 troops on five days' Notice to Move. They had also ordered the nine high-readiness corps headquarters to stand by, including the British-led Allied Rapid Reaction Corps.[7] However, the hard military-strategic truth was that the

---

7. The Allied Rapid Reaction Corps is one of nine multinational NATO Rapidly Deployable Corps headquarters designed to command Allied forces in the field. The ARRC emerged from I British Corps in October 1992.

VJTF required some five to seven days to move, whilst the eNRF needed at least thirty to forty-five days. And whilst on paper NATO had some 180 battalions to call on as part of its wider force structure, many of them were ill equipped, and almost all of them lacked critical logistics capabilities, or were simply unable to move. Because of the post-COVID-19 economic crisis, they had been maintained for too long at too low a level of readiness and had atrophied, only exercising occasionally with other NATO forces. Even the most optimistic of Alliance planning scenarios had suggested that the bulk of NATO's defence forces would take between 60 and 180 days to move, if at all, with an even longer time lag between Notice to Move and Notice to Action—something the Russian Armed Forces had noted. In any case, the Southern Allies had had their eyes firmly fixed on the deteriorating situation to the south of the Mediterranean. To them, the High North and NATO's eastern front with Russia had always seemed a very long way away indeed. Russia's information operations had been effective cynically accusing NATO of entirely fictitious violations of Russian air, sea, land, and cyber space. Completely fabricated stories of 'outrages' against ethnic Russians living in the Baltics had also become a staple.

At dawn on 11 August 2030, the 6th Combined Arms Army, augmented by a Russian airborne/air assault division, and with a Spetsnaz brigade fomenting civilian and military chaos, had begun to overrun Estonia and take control of the Gulf of Finland which gave access to St Petersburg. The 1st Guards Tank Army, with a second airborne division attached, had struck south for Kaliningrad via Vilnius to avoid contact with Polish forces before turning north to cut off the Baltic States. As Russian forces entered Estonia, NATO's Multinational Division North headquarters at Adazi in Latvia had simply ceased, simultaneously struck by several hypersonic missiles.

Critically, NATO airpower, whilst superior on paper, was markedly inferior where it mattered. With the Americans only just beginning a limited tactical air push to Europe, NATO air forces took far too long to concentrate, partly because of COVID-29. Consequently, Russian airpower and air defences quickly established local air superiority over the area of operations for the duration of the campaign. NATO's conventional air power was, in any case, unable to overcome Russian anti-access/area-denial capabilities that had been strengthened immeasurably by the 2024 stationing of the Voronezh 2 radar system in Kaliningrad and the 2021 deployment of the S-500 anti-aircraft missile system.

End-game

At the United Nations Security Council Moscow had stalled, citing the failure of both Vilnius and Warsaw to guarantee Russian land access to Kaliningrad along the

Suwalki Corridor as a reason for what it quickly called a 'corrective action'. The NAC had again met in emergency session, and at Poland and Lithuania's insistence invoked Article 51 of the UN Charter and the right to collective self-defence. However, some of the Southern Allies had balked at declaring Article 5 collective defence and had only agreed to the issuing of an ultimatum; unless Russian forces were withdrawn from NATO territory in forty-eight hours, the Alliance would then declare a breach of Article 5 and finally invoke collective defence.

Russia had immediately responded by putting its Iskandr M, Kalibr, and Novator short- and medium-range nuclear weapons on full alert, and threatened a nuclear attack on European cities. However, Moscow was careful not to place all of its Strategic Rocket Forces on alert as that would have implied an impending strike against continental North America. In the wake of the NAC meeting the Kremlin also cited a 'vital' Russian need to consolidate a 'peace buffer' between Russia and an 'overtly aggressive NATO'. It had soon become clear that Allied conventional deterrence has failed as Russian forces consolidated their grip on the three Baltic States. Estonian, Latvian, and Lithuanian forces, together with the few forces their NATO allies had deployed forward, put up a brief, effective, and deadly fight, but it soon became clear that with Russian forces massing in strength, neither the Alliance's enhanced Forward Presence battlegroups, the VJTF, nor even the eNRF would ever be in anything like sufficient strength to rescue the Baltic Allies, even if they were a match for Russian forces, which, in the absence of US reinforcements, they were not.

The Western democracies had thus found themselves facing the same dilemma Hitler had forced on them in 1939: do they trade space for time, or simply give up? The US president, in characteristically blunt language, told the Europeans: 'We Americans are busy. We have sent you all we can'. Unfortunately, by 2030 European forces had become too hollowed out; they lacked too many key enablers and vital logistics to have any chance of prevailing. In any case, with much of the population ill, their focus was elsewhere and their leaders lacked the political will to respond in force. Putin knew full well that having overcome NATO's conventional deterrent, the Alliance would face a long war to recover the Baltic States. At this point, Putin pulled off his masterstroke. He offered his enemies a way out of their misery.

America overstretched, Europe defeated

On 3 September 2030, having achieved his military objectives, Putin called a halt to the Russian advance in what was rapidly dubbed the Thirteen-Day War. Putin then called the German Chancellor. He told her that his 'limited correction' was over, and that Russia was now content with the new strategic 'balance' in Europe. Moscow, he insisted, had no further territorial ambitions and he lamented the fact that European leaders had not heeded his many warnings about the threat the twin enlargements of NATO and the EU had posed to Russia. He even offered to compensate the families of the 724 NATO force members killed during Russia's 'corrective' operation, although he pointedly offered nothing to the Americans or British.

President Putin had also presented the Bundeskanzlerin with a stark choice. Did she really want to fight a war to recover the Baltic States? The consequence was a strategic and political dilemma for which neither she nor contemporary Germany was prepared. London and Paris obfuscated and blustered but did little. With US forces committed to the Indo-Pacific, and Southern Europeans either impotent or desperately trying to manage the deteriorating situation in the Middle East and North Africa, Washington was too overstretched to respond in force in all three theatres in which major conflict had broken out. 1939 redux?

The hard truth in 2030 was that NATO Europeans were too weak and divided to act as effective first responders, and in any case the White House would not risk a nuclear confrontation with Russia over the Baltic States. After all, they were small countries far away about which most Americans knew next to nothing. The EU's European Council went into one of its long emergency sessions to impose punitive sanctions on Russia, but in reality it too was divided and in the end could not agree even to invoke Article 42.7 of the Treaty on European Union, the mutual defence clause. For NATO it was the end. President Putin had achieved his long-held dream of consigning the Alliance to history and in so doing consolidating his regime, his legacy, and above all his family. He was a hero of Russia. With its bluff well and truly called, NATO had been shown to be little more than a paper tiger. From Putin's perspective, any EU sanctions had been a price worth paying given the surge of popularity he had suddenly enjoyed in Russia, and he was sure the supine Europeans would soon look to 'normalize' relations with a victorious Russia, no doubt masked by some suitably pompous political metaphors to mask their defeat. He was proved right again.

Critically, there is something else that both the Chinese and Russians knew that the West at the time did not. COVID-29 had been their invention—an engineered pathogen they released at a time and in places of their choosing for which they had an antidote. Given the stakes, they were even prepared for the disease to reap its harvest even of their own old and sick. In fact, in the grim Russian econometric of death, the loss of so many old Russians actually paid for the offensive, and in any case, Putin declared them all heroes of Russia. Having inoculated both their officials and their fighting men and women against the disease, in victory they had also suddenly claimed to have found a cure which they had 'magnanimously' offered to Europe's suffering peoples. Western intelligence had picked up some indicators of such a programme before the war but had failed to make the link between disease and war before it was too late. Welcome to future war!

Introduction

The hinge of history

COVID-19, and the crisis of economy, governance, society, security, and defence it has spawned, highlights the fundamental dilemmas at the heart of European defence: what and whom to defend against and with what? Above all, where to strike a balance between human security on the one side, and all the advanced healthcare and social security demands from an ageing, vulnerable population and national defence on the other? What trade-offs are required to defend against another such civil emergency and at the same time prevent future state-on-state conflict?

The central contention of this book is that the COVID-19 crisis will have a major impact on Europeans and how they are defended, but it will do so by accelerating trends already apparent prior to the crisis, and in so doing intensify strategic consequences as political leaders on both sides of the Atlantic search for a sustainable and credible balance between security and defence in a rapidly changing world. There is a caveat: the extent to which COVID-19 will impact Europe's future defence choices will depend largely on the extent and length of the economic crisis it triggered—recession or depression. In the midst of the crisis, COVID-19 looked to some like some latter-day Black Death, but for a host of reasons the parallels are only few. Equally, history has several examples of how such ruptures accelerate the descent into war—none more terrifyingly eloquent than the rise of Fascist Italy, Nazi Germany, and militarist Japan in the wake of the 1929 Wall Street Crash and the Great Depression. Therefore, perhaps the biggest strategic mistake Europe's leaders could now make is to believe that COVID-19 and its economic impact has lessened the likelihood of future war.

This book is thus a wake-up call—a book about dangerous futures, European futures. It is also a book about American and global futures with two big ideas at its core. First, whilst, as Thomas Hobbes once wrote, 'Covenants with the sword are but words, and of no use to any man', credible 'covenants' in the form of international norms and institutions matter, and will matter more if peace is to be preserved in the post-COVID-19 world.[1] Indeed, such instruments are the essence of the West and the transatlantic relationship that is and must remain its core. The European Union (EU), North Atlantic Treaty Organization (NATO), United Nations (UN), and even the transatlantic security relationship itself are the stuff of how the West—old, now, and into the future—must continue to view the essence of international relations and the maintenance of peace. This is not just because 'togetherness' is good in and of itself, or cheaper and more efficient, but because membership of such covenants prevents extreme state behaviour and the threat to peace that is the anarchy of *Machtpolitik*. Second, such covenants need defending and upholding against those that seek a return to anarchy for the purposes of narrow nationalist or autocratic interests and values. However, given that challenge, Europe's twenty-first-century defence is in need of a radical overhaul because words are no longer enough if such a war is to be deterred and defended against, and if the very idea of a freedom-enshrining 'West', an increasingly global idea rather than a place, is to be preserved and adapted.

Such a defence will necessarily be focused on the European nation-state, but to be credible it will also need far greater efficiency of effort and effectiveness of action, with Europe's two primary security and defence institutions—the EU and NATO—to the fore. Any such architecture will only be afforded if European states become far more coherent in their understanding of what such a defence will entail, and far more cohesive in their collective efforts to defend their citizens in the twenty-first century. Above all, any such defence will require a new form of European grand strategy, and the organization and application of immense public and private means in pursuit of legitimate defence ends via a host of new, radical, and technology-driven ways. Europe's future defence must embrace a new strategic public–private partnership in which technology plays an ever larger role in driving security and defence policy and strategy. In other words, all

1. See Richard Tuck (ed.) (1991) *Hobbes' Leviathan* (Cambridge: Cambridge University Press), p. 117.

the strategic and political assumptions underlying Europe's current defence effort must change. That is why, to make its case, this necessarily ambitious book stretches across strategy, policy, history, and technology, with even a bit of philosophy thrown in for good measure.

In a June 2017 speech, whilst paying tribute to General George C. Marshall at the George C. Marshall Center in Garmisch-Partenkirchen, Germany, former US Secretary of Defense James N. Mattis said, 'Our hands rest purposely on history's door and it depends on us to push it in the right direction'.[2] Power is relative and purposive, although many Europeans seem to have forgotten that. Consequently, Europeans lack the policy cohesion and diplomatic, military, and other capabilities to assure their own security and defence in the twenty-first century, even in their own strategic neighbourhood. At the same time, Europe's long-time defence guarantor, the United States, not only faces challenges the world over that stretch its forces and resources thin, but American domestic, foreign, and security policy is also changing as America itself changes. The defence of Europe is at another hinge of history.

Future War and the Defence of Europe is thus a necessarily hard-hitting book which seeks to answer two profound policy questions. First, how can credible deterrence be maintained in the face of a new kind of warfare that stretches across 5Ds through the simultaneous, planned, and applied use of disinformation, deception, disruption, and destabilization, reinforced by coercion through implied or actual destruction? 5Ds to which a sixth might be added—disease. Second, how can another major war be prevented in Europe when so many Europeans no longer believe war is possible despite history, and indeed reality, suggesting otherwise?

COVID-19 or no, European defence must be radically modernized, or it could fail suddenly and catastrophically, as it did in both 1914 and 1939. However, Europe's future defence is not simply a question of force modernization. The problem back in 1914 was not that European forces were unmodernized, nor did they fail. The German Army was in fine fettle, as was Britain's Royal Navy, whilst the French and Russian Armies appeared to offset a lack of capability and organization with either *élan* or simple brute mass. World War One was a failure of diplomacy and politics. Even in 1939, what failed catastrophically was deterrence, and in 1940 the French Army and British Expeditionary Force. European forces certainly need to be radically improved, but without a concomitant strengthening of European political will, they could still fail in the absence of resolve. Such a transformation will not be easy. During the thirty or so years since the end of the Cold War, the assumption that a major war will never happen again in Europe has also become firmly established at the highest levels of the European body politic. War is simply *passé* in the salons of European power. In any case, Europeans have legislated such danger away, or so the mantra goes. In the wake of Russia's seizure of Crimea, repeated cyber-attacks, Moscow's sustained interference in elections and the democratic process, the July 2014 shooting down of Malaysian Airlines Flight MH17, the murder of almost 300 people allegedly by the Russian Army, and the poisoning of Sergei and Yulia Skripal in Salisbury, some form of warfare is never far from Europe's reality. Moreover, with the revolution in military technology underway and with hypersonic weaponry, artificial intelligence (AI), super-computing, and in time quantum-computing steadily marching onto the battlefield, hopes for an eternal European *belle époque* seem fancifully and dangerously quaint. There are practical consequences. For example, in spite of the 2003 SARS epidemic, many European countries failed to plan adequately for a recurrence of a SARS-like pandemic. The decoupling of risk assessment, policy, and planning has become common across European security and defence.

With hard geopolitics returning red in tooth and claw, such a failing is particularly dangerous. Today, China and Russia, the power autocracies of the twenty-first century, are systematically and subtly (and not so subtly) undermining Western institutions and regimes in favour of a new form of strategic anarchy that Beijing and Moscow believe favours them through a revised balance of power and new spheres of influence. China is fast emerging as a world power determined to challenge the US across the Indo-Pacific, and developing new forms of warfare to do it. Europe is not immune. The war in Syria has also pushed the Middle East towards a twenty-first-century version of the Great Game in which Sunni and Shia fundamentalists fight with each other, whilst Middle Eastern states vie for regional-strategic supremacy. Worse, a proxy war is underway between Russia, China, and the West which further complicates the myriad of existing complexities in a Middle East that teeters on the brink of political and societal collapse with profound implications for the security of Europe. The 'threat' of huge numbers of irregular refugees and migrants heading towards a Europe already weakened by years of post-crisis austerity and

COVID-19 adds to the array of 'no obvious solution' challenges with which European leaders must contend.

The transatlantic relationship? The commitment of the US to the defence of Europe remains generally firm. Both President Obama and President Trump increased military aid to Europe under the European Deterrence Initiative (EDI).[3] However, the *status quo ante* is fast becoming unsustainable. The real challenge to any sustained US commitment to the defence of Europe comes not from uncertainty about the political commitment, but rather growing pressures on America's armed forces as they face a range of threats the world over. Tensions in the transatlantic relationship primarily concern the sharing of risk and burdens between the Americans and their European allies, but it is ultimately a question of relative cost. During the Cold War the European allies provided some 50 per cent of the military capability and capacity committed to the defence of Europe at a time when the geographical area to be defended was far smaller and the number of allies far fewer. Today, Europeans provide only some 25 per cent of military capabilities to cover a much larger defended space, and almost all are fast falling behind US, Chinese, and Russian forces in terms of quality and technical capability.[4]

Even if Europe's long post-Cold War strategic vacation is clearly over as Europe and much of the world beyond returns to some form of *Realpolitik*, Europeans are finding it hard to adjust.[5] It is only a minor exaggeration to suggest Europe could again be facing all the dangerous uncertainties and strategic vicissitudes that were evinced during the descent into conflict in August 1914 and the catastrophe of World War One. Russia's willingness in 2014 to change European borders by force and flout the UN Charter came as a profound shock to many Europeans long used to a legalistic view of international relations enshrined in the EU ever since its 1950 inception as

---

3. See European Deterrence Initiative, Department of Defense Budget, Fiscal Year 2019, Office of the Under Secretary of Defense (Comptroller), February 2018, https://comptroller.defense.gov/Portals/45/Documents/defbudget/fy2019/fy2019_EDI_JBook.pdf.

4. See GLOBSEC (2017) *Globsec NATO Adaptation Initiative, One Alliance, the Future Tasks of the Adapted Alliance* (Bratislava: GLOBSEC), p. 22, para 6.2.

5. Henry Kissinger wrote of *Realpolitik*, 'Realpolitik—foreign policy based on calculations of power and the national interest—brought about the unification of Germany. And the unification of Germany caused Realpolitik to turn in on itself, accomplishing the opposite of what it was meant to achieve. For the practice of Realpolitik avoids armaments races and war only if the major players of an international system are free to adjust their relations in accordance with changing circumstances or are restrained by a system of shared values, or both'. Henry Kissinger (1994) *Diplomacy* (New York: Simon & Schuster), p. 137.

the European Coal and Steel Community (ECSC). For Moscow, *Realpolitik* reflects the contemporary world-view of the Russian state, even if technology affords such policy far more sophistication than hitherto in the manner by which it conducts complex strategic coercion against its neighbours. Russia's ability to exploit open Western societies through the sophisticated use of the internet and social media marks a new departure in the idea of conflict. Moscow's open and unyielding support for an active separatist insurgency in the Donbas region has emaciated Ukraine to the point of dysfunction. There is now clear evidence that Russia is also seeking to expand the struggle with the West into the Arctic Circle, where China is also showing significant interest. Some EU and NATO states, sorely pressed in the wake of the 2008–10 banking and financial crises, and under intense economic pressure in the wake of the COVID-19 pandemic, seem only too eager to seek Chinese investment, even if the debt that ensues comes with very long and onerous strategic strings attached.

For much of the Cold War the US-led policy of the West was to contain the then Soviet Union. It could be that China and Russia are beginning to contain Europe, if not the wider West, as the reality and consequence of Europe's vertiginous decline since 2010 becomes strategically apparent.

Great Power strategic peer competitors are not the only threats to Europe. NATO leaders talk long and often about a 360-degree Alliance capable of dealing with all and any threats, from all and any strategic direction.[6] In reality, the Alliance is deeply divided between those to the east of NATO, who see Russia as the main threat, and those to the south of the Alliance, who see Salafist Jihadism, and the endemic instability of weak states across the Middle East, North Africa, and the Sahel, as the main threat. Alliance contention takes place at a time when the US is moving to master the hyperwar of the future: ultra-fast warfare that combines a myriad of systems to wreak havoc in an instant. Europe is not. Of Europe's 'Great' Powers, Germany is deeply uncomfortable with the call to leadership its economic power demands and too often confuses leadership with short-term political

---

6. NATO defines the '360-degree' approach thus: 'The Alliance is determined to implement a 360-degree approach to security. In addition to measures to reinforce the Alliance's Eastern Flank, NATO has also strengthened its efforts in projecting stability and the fight against terrorism. It contributes to the Global Coalition to Defeat ISIS with AWACS intelligence flights and training for Iraqi forces'. See 'Mediterranean Dialogue Partner Countries Discuss Intelligence with NATO', Communiqué, 18 November 2018, https://www.nato.int/cps/en/natohq/news_160671.htm.

control. This is because Germany still continues to be mistrustful of itself over such matters and has avoided a serious, and critical, internal debate about Germany's strategic role in the twenty-first-century world. Moreover, Germany has a different strategic concept from the US. Berlin's impressive performance during the COVID-19 crisis shows a preference for investing in human security rather than national defence. France has a 'grand' vision for European defence, but is mired in debt and internal (and intra-European) political friction. The UK, that one-time European bastion of the Alliance, has simply been hollowed out over time by austerity and the obsession with outsourcing hitherto vital state functions.

The character of warfare is changing, as it always has. However, the desire of Europeans to understand that change seems dangerously limited. Spurred on by a revolution in civilian technology, a whole host of 'applications' are finding their way into the battlespace. However, as warfare becomes increasingly digitized across enormous 'architectures', European ideas of warfare remain distinctly analogue and small, a little like what happened during the Interbellum. AI, deep learning, natural language processing, computer vision, and other related characteristics; super-computing, eventually quantum-computing, and nano and bio technologies; advanced big data analytics; and other emerging technologies are beginning to offer an entirely new way of war, and at command speeds hitherto unimaginable. The revolution in sensor and command technologies is matched only by developments in long-range, hypersonic 'intelligent' weaponry and new swarms of killing machines allied to a range of directed-energy weapons. Such a potentially revolutionary change in the character and conduct of war must necessarily impose entirely new ways of defence. If not, technology-driven change will critically undermine any understanding of 'defence' if new arms control architectures fail to slow the pace of such change. Whither European defence?

Contemporary 'defence' also demands force and resource across a wide spectrum of technologies and infrastructures. What would be the implications for the North Cape scenario if Europe and NATO had invested more intensively in, for example, AI-based cyber defensive and offensive capabilities, and/or invested far more in civil critical infrastructure protection? There is, after all, a precedent for such attacks. The Notpetya malware attack by the Russians on Ukraine prior to the seizing of Crimea could well have been a trial run for a possible devastating cyber-attack against Europe as a prelude to the kind of major war envisaged in Scenario 1 that opened this book.[7] Had *HMS Queen Elizabeth* and her task force been equipped with state-of-the-art cyber protection, would she have been able to protect herself from Russia's 'preparatory cyber fires', and could Europe become cyber-proof from the socially debilitating results of the Russian attacks on the civil infrastructure of Europe?[8]

The striking of such a new balance between security and defence will also demand serious thinking about what would constitute an attack on NATO, and thereafter the nature of any response. Given the interlocking nature of 5D warfare and the intimate strategic relationship that exists between paralysis of action and destruction and defeat, the enhanced cyber threat at the heart of future war calls for a redefinition of how NATO's Article 5 collective defence is understood, and such a shift communicated clearly to both Allies and adversaries. For example, how should and would the Alliance respond to a devastating cyber-attack on Warsaw or Brussels? Article 5 states,

> The Parties agree that an armed attack against one or more of them in Europe or North America shall be considered an attack against them all and consequently they agree that, if such an armed attack occurs, each of them, in exercise of the right of individual or collective self-defence recognised by Article 51 of the Charter of the United Nations, will assist the Party or Parties so attacked by taking forthwith, individually and in concert with the other Parties, such action as it deems necessary, including the use of armed force, to restore and maintain the security of the North Atlantic area.[9]

7. For a frightening analysis of the damage done by the Notpetya attack see Andy Greenberg's piece for *Wired*. The Danish Maersk Shipping Line was effectively shut down for weeks and lost millions of Euros because of a Russian cyber-attack that was actually targeting Ukraine. It is a salutary lesson of what could happen to Europe's transportation networks in the event of such an attack. See Andy Greenberg, 'The Untold Story of Notpetya: The Most Devastating Cyberattack in History', *Wired*, 22 August 2018, https://www.wired.com/story/notpetya-cyberattack-ukraine-russia-code-crashed-the-world.

8. In a 2017 piece for the United States Naval Institute, John R. Allen and Amir Husain gave a flavour of a future war cyber-attack in the battlespace. 'The battle damage was devastating and constituted the leading edge of what the United States soon would discover was a widespread, strategic attack. The guided-missile destroyer had not "seen" the incoming swarm because it had not recognized that its systems were under cyber-attack before things turned kinetic. The undetected cyber activity not only compromised the destroyer's sensors, but also "locked-out" its defensive systems, leaving the ship almost helpless. The kinetic strikes came in waves as a complex swarm. The attack appeared to be conducted by a cloud of autonomous systems that seemed to move together with a purpose, reacting to each other and to the ship'. Amir Husain and John R. Allen, 'On Hyperwar', *Naval Institute Proceedings*, July 2017, https://www.usni.org/magazines/proceedings/2017/july/hyperwar.

9. See 'The North Atlantic Treaty', https://www.nato.int/cps/en/natohq/official_texts_17120.htm.

Would such an attack even constitute an 'armed attack', and would the Allies agree?[10]

NATO is clearly considering these questions. In August 2019, the UK's *Daily Telegraph* reported that,

> [NATO Secretary General] Jens Stoltenberg cited the WannaCry ransomware attack as an example of a 'serious cyber-attack' that would be viewed by NATO as requiring a response from all members of the alliance . . . The US and UK have publicly accused North Korea of being behind the attack. But other state actors including Russia, China and Iran have been blamed for other cyber-attacks in the West. Stoltenberg said a similar attack could in the future trigger Article 5 of the NATO founding treaty, which commits member nations to treating an attack on one member as an attack against all.[11]

Stoltenberg's aim was to bolster Alliance deterrence because deterrence, far more than defence, is NATO's real business. To that end, NATO Summit communiqués are important statements of deterrence, but they must be underpinned by the demonstrable capacity to act if they are to shore up the Alliance's critical deterrence mission. Steps have been taken, such as the establishment of the NATO Cyberspace Ops Centre, but far more needs to be done to better assure deterrence. Given the broad bandwidth of contemporary deterrence, there is a clear need for significantly greater political and strategic ambition to be invested in NATO's strategic partnerships, most notably with the EU. Indeed, the very pan-society nature of future war calls upon both NATO and the EU to develop in parallel the kinds of capabilities that could not only 'sense' evolving cyber-attacks, but also respond across the multi-domains of future war and climb a spectrum of escalation against potential perpetrators—and do it extremely quickly. Interestingly, there is a significant debate about escalation control within the cyber community which could form the basis for a new concept of Allied deterrence. Are either the Alliance or the EU at all structured to respond in such a way? Would the North Atlantic Council (NAC) be willing to devolve command authority to the Supreme Allied Commander Europe (SACEUR) even prior

---

10. There is actually an extensive debate on this and some substantial literature; for example, Michael N. Schmitt (ed.) (2017) *The Tallinn Manual 2.0 on the International Law Applicable to Cyber Operations* (Cambridge: Cambridge University Press). The problem is finding agreement amongst all the Allies in time for appropriate action.
11. Robert Mendrick, 'Cyber-Attack on NHS Would Trigger Full NATO Response, Says Alliance's General Secretary', *Daily Telegraph*, 27 August 2019, www.telegraph.co.uk/news/2019/08/27/cyber-attack-nhs-would-trigger-full-nato-response-says-alliances.

to an attack? Given the speed of future war, demonstrable speed of command will be central to both credible deterrence and warfighting.

For example, the August 2019 decision of London to reconstitute the British Army's 6th Division as an offensive and defensive digital warfighter highlights both the opportunity and the dilemma faced by Europeans.[12] It affords Europeans a chance to invest now in the capabilities and capacities needed to prepare a future war defence across the 5D spectrum of deception, disinformation, destabilization, disruption, and destruction, but it is likely to come only by scrapping many of the existing platforms and systems and their replacements. In other words, Europeans have something of a defence clean sheet, but only if they act quickly and together. COVID-19?

The implications for a future war European defence would certainly be profound if Europe, and by extension the Alliance, properly invested in AI-based cyber defensive and offensive military capabilities.[13] Again, there are steps being taken in such a direction, such as the 2016 Grand Challenge set by the US Defense Advanced Research Projects Agency (DARPA) and the importance accorded AI in the 2018 US Cyber Strategy. Such investments would by their very nature also create much-needed synergies between NATO and EU military power projection capabilities and critical civilian infrastructure protection, and thus endow deterrence with much greater robustness and critical systems redundancy. Innovative thinking, and the generation of new partnerships vital to such systems and subsequent action, would also be encouraged and will be vital across the hybrid–cyber–hyper spectrum of future war. To that end, the US and its European allies will also need to explore more systematically a far closer relationship with those private-sector providers who best understand the mix of advanced technologies such a defence would demand, which would also probably profoundly change the relationship between government, armed forces, and much of the private sector. Such a change would also require Europeans, in

---

12. As a sign of how quickly technology is revolutionizing warfare, on 1 August 2019 it was announced the British Army would reactivate its 6th Division. According to Lt.-Gen. Ivan Jones, '6 Div' will focus on 'Cyber, Electronic Warfare, Intelligence, Information Operations and unconventional warfare through niche capabilities such as the Specialised Infantry Battalions'. Jones went on, 'The speed of change is moving at a remarkable rate and it will only get faster and more complex'. See 'Army Restructures to Confront Evolving Threats', 1 August 2019, *Army News*, https://www.army.mod.uk/news-and-events/news/2019/08/army-restructures-to-confront-evolving-threats.

13. In 2016 the US Defense Advanced Research Projects Agency created the Cyber Grand Challenge. The aim was to stimulate the development of automated defence systems able to rapidly discover, prove, and correct software flaws in real time.

particular, to reassert far more control over supply chains far beyond the traditional defence sector which are deemed critical to national/European defence. One way forward could be to build on the old Smart Defence and Smart Procurement projects that NATO proposed at the 2012 Chicago Summit by establishing a new kind of strategic public–private partnership with corporate technology giants.[14] In the wake of the COVID-19 crisis, some of them might be more open to such partnerships, given tensions with China.

Megatrends, technology, and European decline

COVID-19 will also advance structural change in the global megatrends with which European defence must contend, and which could combine to create the conditions and opportunities for the use of complex strategic coercion and 5D warfare against Europe. There are four major global megatrends relevant to Europe's defence that magnify and leverage technology change and Europe's relative decline: climate change, rapidly changing demographics, water scarcity beyond Europe's borders, and a structural shift in economic and military power from West to East.[15] Such changes already have strategic consequences for Europeans as competing groups within countries further undermine state structures, and competition and consequent friction between states increase.

Climate change will place ever more, ever larger populations under ever greater stress, which in turn could help trigger systemic migrations far greater than those witnessed in Europe during 2015 and 2016. In future population

14. NATO defines Smart Defence as follows: 'In these times of austerity, each euro, dollar or pound sterling counts. Smart Defence is a cooperative way of thinking about generating the modern defence capabilities that the Alliance needs for the future. In this renewed culture of cooperation, Allies are encouraged to work together to develop, acquire, operate and maintain military capabilities to undertake the Alliance's essential core tasks agreed in NATO's Strategic Concept. That means harmonising requirements, pooling and sharing capabilities, setting priorities and coordinating efforts better'. See 'Smart Defence', https://www.nato.int/cps/en/natohq/topics_84268.htm.
15. The '2017 GLOBSEC NATO Adaptation Initiative' states, 'There are a range of global megatrends that will necessarily form the strategic backdrop to [NATO] Adaptation that can be roughly divided into four linked change-driving factors, all of which have profound implications for the Alliance and the security and defence of NATO nations: climate change, rapidly-changing demography, resource-scarcity, and a structural shift in economic and military power from the West to the East'. See GLOBSEC (2017) *Globsec NATO Adaptation Initiative, One Alliance, the Future Tasks of the Adapted Alliance* (Bratislava: GLOBSEC), p. 53.

stress could well grow exponentially in both scale and intensity as rising sea levels and accelerating desertification render large swathes of the globe untenable, much of it the result of human intervention. The mass movement of peoples will also be aided and abetted by the mass messaging of global communications, which in large part defines globalization. Mass immigration is also changing the nature of European societies, making it far harder to maintain the social cohesion upon which defence has traditionally been established. The entry into Western societies of people with often very different beliefs and practices does not necessarily mean the collapse of social cohesion, as most immigrants wish to be productive members of their new societies, but it does complicate the ability of a state to organize in a crisis. It also creates seams within society that enemies can exploit, mainly through technology. The resurgence in a form of ideological friction and struggle is reinforced by social media, the internet, and the 'dark web', all of which provide platforms for radicalization and recruiting for the likes of al-Qaeda and Daesh, and against which it is very hard to defend without undermining liberty itself. For example, Russia's use of hybrid warfare and its exploitation of disinformation and concerted influence operations are all driven by new technologies. Such efforts might well also be the harbinger of further efforts by ostensibly weaker states and highly coherent non-state actors and criminal networks to destabilize stronger but less cohesive states, and perhaps permanently.

For European societies it is the combination of globalization, urbanization, and mass technology that both enables its people and threatens them in equal measure. The growth of mega-cities also points to the emergence of competing poles of power within states, and makes them vulnerable to the rapid spread of pandemics such as COVID-19. The UK is a case in point. Once, Westminster reigned supreme over what was thought to have been one of the world's most stable states. Today, Westminster must contend with competing poles of power in Scotland, Wales, Northern Ireland, and, interestingly, London. Urbanization and technology change will also go hand in hand with the further concentration of large numbers of skilled people as states, at one and the same time, become more advanced, more diverse, and more vulnerable.

Urbanization and technology will also exacerbate the perception of inequality as relatively wealthy, educated, technology-savvy people live cheek by jowl with less wealthy, relatively uneducated, technology-poor populations. Such friction could further polarize politics and fuel frictions and tensions within fast-change, high-tension societies and communities in which technology transcends borders, creating new communities and identities that challenge traditional ideas of citizenship and obligation. European forces may well have to endeavour to project stability into such distant mega-cities, and draw recruits from their streets.

For Europeans, such change will also force new concepts, balances, and relationships to be forged between policing, armed forces, and intelligence agencies. Critically, as COVID-19 has revealed, European states are unlikely to project power, influence, and stability unless they can protect and control an increasingly fractious and complex home base. Whither liberty? The nature of emerging technologies, allied to their relative affordability and usability, could also promote an inverse and perverse relationship between the small size of dangerous, insurgent groupings and their ability to spread mass disruption and cause mass destruction. What kind and scale of European forces would be needed to both defend a state from without and stabilize a state from within? This is an uncomfortable technology-driven megatrend question with which all European states must contend, not least because of the complex mosaic of rapid, interlocked, and interlocking actions and effects that will define future war. The days of Clausewitzian formality and strategic neatness are long gone. 'Defeat'—an inability to respond or govern—could result at the behest of a skilled enemy (or enemies) employing a range of devastating, sequenced attacks through the hybrid cyber mosaic as a preamble to hyperwar, and to which no European state could respond, and thus have little alternative but to sue for a very unfavourable peace. As COVID-19 has demonstrated, shock happens!

Indeed, it may even be possible to envisage a state being destroyed one day without a shot actually being fired. In such circumstances, the purpose of armed forces would be to deter not simply via the threat of kinetic retaliation, but across an entire range of future war coercions. If COVID-19 is used as an excuse to emphasize human (healthcare) security at the expense of national defence, Europeans will arrive at 2030 with little but an expensive and by and large irrelevant legacy force. Strategic prey there for the taking by strategic predators.

The state of the debate

Given that backdrop, the debate within *Future War and the Defence of Europe* is necessarily wide, even if much of it has yet to grasp the implications of the COVID-19 crisis. For the purposes of this book the focus has been on those works that actually add value to the specific debate on the relationship between future war and European defence. The environmental framework for such a defence is well established in Paul Cornish and Kingsley Donaldson's book, *2020: World of War* (2017), which offers a sobering assessment of the many challenges Europeans face, and the need for a comprehensive relationship between security and defence. General Sir Richard Shirreff's *2017: War with Russia* (2016) is a novel about a future war with Russia. However, Shirreff was also Deputy Supreme Allied Commander Europe for NATO until 2015 and the book offers a compelling insight into how a senior Allied commander would fight such a war, and the challenges they would face.[16] To some extent Shirreff's book is a natural successor to General Sir John Hackett's seminal work, *The Third World War: The Untold Story*, which in 1985 offered an informed insider's analysis of what could well have happened if the Cold War had turned hot. However, perhaps the most noteworthy successor to Hackett was Cornish and Donaldson's *2020: World of War*, which considered a range of possible future war scenarios.

Whilst this book is not the place to conduct a major survey of the enormous body of literature on European defence, there are categories of analysis that could prove useful to the reader. Perhaps the most prevalent area of study is the contest, for that is what it is, between those who champion NATO and those who champion the EU's Common Security and Defence Policy (CSDP) and the Permanent Structured Cooperation (PESCO). In crude terms, and by no means exclusively, those who champion NATO tend to be found in the US, the UK, and Canada, as well as Central and Eastern Europe. Proponents of CSDP tend to be found in parts of Western and Southern Europe, and in at least one district of central Brussels. Within those groups a further divide can be detected between and among those who focus on the challenges to the transatlantic security relationship, those who look specifically at Europe's conventional forces, and those who consider nuclear weapons and policy.

Much of the CSDP 'literature' tends to be focused on political science, with a particular emphasis on international relations theory. Much of the literature on NATO tends to be either policy-oriented and/or military-strategic by nature. There are exceptions to this rule—scholars who seek to bestride camps by combining policy, strategy, and theory. Most notable

---

16. Julian Lindley-French served as Head of Shirreff's Commander's Initiative Group when Shirreff was Commander of the Allied Rapid Reaction Corps.

among this group are Hans Binnendijk, Sven Biscop, Anthony Cordesmann, Paul Cornish, Ivo Daalder, Sir Lawrence Freedman, Jolyon Howorth, Graeme Hurd, Robert Kaplan, Hugo Meijer, Andrew Michta, Christian Molling, Stan Sloan, Julianne Smith, Sir Hew Strachan, Jim Townsend, Anna Wieslander, Rob de Wijk, and Marco Wyss, to name but a few.

Driven perhaps by the recent explosion in books on US corporate strategy, one field of study considers decision-making in complex contingencies. Much of the literature herein also focuses on the evolution of decision-making within institutions, most notably the EU and NATO—specifically, how to generate substantial European resources and apply them to effect across a range of contingencies throughout a crisis conflict cycle. Few, if any, have identified solutions that would enable Europe's institutions to act with speed of effect if faced with a major emergency.

Another swathe of literature considers how to procure and apply future European military capabilities. This body of work tends to be divided between those who consider the command options for pooled and shared equipment, with some calling for a much more integrated command, akin to something like the failed European Defence Community of the early 1950s, and those who consider procurement and fielding of European equipment, and how 'best' to organize the European Defence Technological and Industrial Base. Much of the latter group are focused on the institutional organization of what might be termed defence-equipment generation. The debate is either focused on NATO's Committee of National Armaments Directors and/or the EU's new PESCO and European Defence Fund arrangements. Much of the work considers the specific problems of national armaments acquisition in an environment in which defence-investment budgets have shrunk markedly as the unit cost of ever more complex equipment has risen. Bastiaan Giegerich, Anthony King, Holger Mey, Matthew Uttley, and Richard Whitman are leading European figures in this field.

Another body of literature considers the changing nature of the threat to Europe. Here, a divide exists between the 'Russianists', who consider the extent to which Moscow and its forces are a threat to Europe. Isabelle Facon, Keir Giles, Bobo Lo, Andrew Monaghan, and James Sherr are leading lights in this field. On the other side of the divide there is a vast bulk of post-9/11 literature that considers the threat to the south of Europe posed by Salafist Jihadi terrorism and/or the threat to Europe posed by instability across the Middle East and North Africa. A lot of this literature grew out of the campaigns in Afghanistan and Iraq, much of it devoted to stabilization and reconstruction in war-ravaged societies. David Kilcullen, and his work on unconventional warfare, is a leading authority in this field, but there are a host of others, such as the Oxford Research Group and their work on remote warfare. There are other dimensions to the literature such as growing resource scarcity, climate change, and the effects of climate migration in the south, with truly frightening humanitarian and security implications. Some of the most instructive literature on the threat posed by pandemics can be found in fiction as well as non-fiction. David Quammen's *Spillover* (2012) considers how pandemics spread, in this case Ebola, whilst Philip Ziegler's *The Black Death* (1969) is a sobering analysis of a pandemic that killed up to 40 per cent of the European population in the mid-fourteenth century with profound strategic, political, and economic consequences. Katherine Anne Porter's magisterial *Pale Horse, Pale Rider* (1939) tells the story of the 1918 Spanish flu pandemic and is just as relevant to COVID-19 and its consequences.

What is striking about the major bulk of the literature devoted specifically to European defence is just how parochial it has become. There are a lot of passing references to the globalization of threat, some debate over burden-sharing with the Americans, and some debate about the role of the Fourth Industrial Revolution in European defence. However, much of this debate comes as an afterthought to a seemingly interminable debate about the institutionalization of European defence and how to get the biggest bang out of Europe's very limited (compared to other powers) defence budgets. Little of the literature is seriously devoted to the defence outputs Europeans need to generate in a world which is changing fast, in which US forces are increasingly overstretched, and where a radical 'dreadnought'-style shift in destructive technologies could also radically shift the balance of power in the European security-/battlespace.

It is where grand strategy meets military strategy that the most insightful and useful literature tends to be found, with Hans Binnendijk, Christopher Coker, Anthony H. Cordesmann, Paul Cornish, Chris Donnelly, Andrew Dorman, Francois Heisbourg, Robert Kaplan, Michael O'Hanlon, Julianne Smith, Hew Strachan, Bruno Tertrais, and James Townsend to the fore. Interestingly, the bulk of these authors are American or British, not continental Europeans, whilst none are German!

The structure of the book

The book is divided into two parts. Although the first part of the book commences with an analysis of the possible impact of the COVID-19 crisis on European defence, it is essentially descriptive with some discussion of the contemporary historical roots. The second part of the book is more prescriptive and considers the challenges of realizing a future war, future European defence. The book itself begins with Scenario 1: 'Europe defeated', a worst-case, grand future war scenario designed to challenge the assumptions of the reader.

Chapter 1, 'COVID-19 and the European defence dilemma', considers the immediate impact of the pandemic on Europe's future defence and the trade-offs that will need to be made between people protection and power projection and human security and national defence. The chapter also considers how China and Russia are exploiting the crisis through the use of information shock, either to shift responsibility or to complicate Western responses, and possible future strategic, political, and economic consequences of the pandemic for Europe's future defence.

Chapter 2, 'The end of the beginning?', provides the historical context for the future defence of Europe by considering the evolution of European defence since 1944 and shines a light on the challenge of the contemporary and future as much as the past. The chapter also uses a historical narrative to move the debate away from the idea of the 'Cold War' precisely because it obscures the very different nature of the contemporary threat and constrains much-needed thinking about how to preserve peace in a very different Europe to that which existed between 1945 and 1989.

Chapter 3, 'Russia and Europe's northern and eastern flanks', considers the specific military threat posed by Russia and also poses four questions central to the book: what if deterrence fails? What is deterrence and what is its relationship to the future defence of Europe? How do different Europeans see deterrence and defence? Where does the defence of Europe begin and end?

Chapter 4, 'Demons and dragons: Europe's southern flank', is about the dilemma of Europe's defence. Beyond the Russian military threat, Europe also faces a dangerous mosaic of interacting menace which includes and incorporates elements of hybrid war, cyber war, and hyperwar by state and non-state actors from Daesh to China. The chapter both comprehensively analyses such threats and highlights the new and radical approaches Europeans will need to adopt that must forge security and defence with new shields and arsenals, if Europeans are to successfully balance the protection of Europe's people with the projection of force and power that its contemporary and future defence needs.

Chapter 5, 'China', is in some ways the pivot around which the book turns. The chapter first considers China's role in the COVID-19 crisis and the damage done to its reputation as a responsible actor and its strategic ambitions. It then analyses the impact of growing tensions between the US and China for European defence before discussing the nature and scope of tensions on the Pacific. The chapter concludes by highlighting the extent to which China's rise is driving geopolitics and a twenty-first-century version of *Machtpolitik*.

Chapter 6 is entitled 'Could NATO (still) defend Europe?' The US is to all intents and purposes the defence of Europe. However, as the only global superpower, the US also faces growing pressures the world over which will force Europeans to make hard choices. Since 1949, Europe's defence has been established on the principle that the US is the main European power and, in spite of many tensions, most Europeans have been content to organize their respective national security and defence efforts around the Americans. The chapter explores the strategic implications for European defence if Washington at some point concludes it is unable to maintain the security guarantee it has afforded Europeans since the founding of the Alliance. Central to the chapter is a consideration of the mounting pressures on the US and its armed forces worldwide, as well as the changes underway to US foreign, security, and defence policy.

Chapter 7, 'Could Europe defend Europe?', challenges Europeans to imagine the defence of Europe without the Americans and the true cost of defending Europe. Critically, how would and could Europe defend against complex threats that emerge from instability to Europe's south, as well as to its east and north? The chapter also explores European assumptions about the future defence of Europe and the changing relationship between NATO and the EU. Is NATO still the natural institutional focus for the defence of Europe? The EU? The EU's CSDP implies a much deeper level of European defence integration, and a new balance between defence efficiency and effectiveness. And yet, so many EU defence initiatives are either stillborn or have little impact. Is the EU the future of European defence and is defence integration ever going to happen? Finally, how should Europeans afford their defence?

Chapter 8, 'Hyperwar: Europe's digital and nuclear flanks', is the signature chapter of the book. The core message is succinct: technology will drive policy and strategy in unprecedented ways. Europeans will need to apply a host of new technologies to the future defence of Europe to counter new weapons that threaten to destroy, at a stroke, the vulnerable systems architecture upon which European defence depends. Central to the chapter is consideration of cutting-edge technologies in future war: AI, super-computing leading to quantum-computing, big data, machine-learning, and offensive cyber and nano technologies. Warfare is rapidly being reinvented, with massive implications for how the defence of Europe is conceived. Are Europeans up to the technology challenge? Above all, are Europeans willing to invest in innovative and strategic public–private partnerships to build a future war defence and deterrence architecture?

Chapter 9, 'Defending Europe', brings the book to a climax by considering the policy options facing the Allies in the wake of the COVID-19 crisis, the lessons that must be drawn from this, and the balance to be struck between engagement and defence in managing Russia. At its core is a call for greater European strategic responsibility, a radical European strategic public–private partnership, a future NATO–EU strategic partnership imbued with sufficient strategic ambition to meet the challenge of Europe's future defence, and an Alliance sufficiently adapted to be successful in its core 'business'—the maintenance of deterrence.

The book concludes with Scenario 2: 'Europe defended'. This time the Europeans and Americans prevail, deterrence is assured, and peace is maintained.

Power and defence

Future War and the Defence of Europe is thus about the 'stuff' of Europe's future defence. It is about a Europe that must rapidly reassess the forces and resources its defence will need to mount a credible defence irrespective of COVID-19. It is about the advanced military capability and capacity Europeans will need to maintain peace in a turbulent world in which a new balance will need to be struck between security and defence, people protection and power projection. The mounting of any such defence will also require Europeans and North Americans to adopt not only a new approach to collective defence, but an entirely new level of collective strategic ambition.

To create such a defence, both Americans and Europeans will need to honestly answer several difficult questions. What if deterrence fails? What is deterrence today and what is the relationship between deterrence and defence? How do different Europeans see deterrence and their own defence? Where does the defence of Europe begin and end? Are Europeans in denial about future war and, if so, can the transatlantic relationship survive in its current or indeed any form?

Given that challenge, Europeans must face and overcome a range of dilemmas if the defence of Europe is to be maintained and assured. For example, much is being made of the enhanced cyber threat to Europeans with some calling for a NATO Article 5 response to a devastating cyber-attack at the Warsaw and Brussels summits.[17] Could NATO and the EU even develop the kinds of capabilities needed for such a response, which would need to go well beyond the traditional military realm, and demand a cross-domain response along a spectrum of escalating violence that 5D war would engender? In such circumstances, what capabilities, and at what level of capacity, would be needed to re-establish credible deterrence and mount an effective defence? Are European governments and their military estab-lishments sufficiently nimble of mind to recognize that 'defence' in the twenty-first century requires investment in non-military solutions, and thus avoid the temptation to simply buy more of what will soon become obsolete? Above all, will Europeans even be able to mount a defence in the wake of the COVID-19 crisis?

What about the US? It seems reasonable to assume that if the hard-pressed Americans are to continue to afford the Europeans the relatively 'cheap' defence to which they have become accustomed, Europeans are going to have to become much less 'cheap' about defence and help Americans with their own growing strategic dilemma. Why? The defence of North America

---

17. Paragraph 20 of the NATO Brussels Summit Declaration of 11 July 2018 states, 'Cyber threats to the security of the Alliance are becoming more frequent, complex, destructive, and coercive. NATO will continue to adapt to the evolving cyber threat landscape, which is affected by both state and non-state actors, including state-sponsored. Cyber defence is part of NATO's core task of collective defence. We must be able to operate as effectively in cyberspace as we do in the air, on land, and at sea to strengthen and support the Alliance's overall defence and deterrence posture. We therefore continue to implement cyberspace as a domain of operations'. See https://www.nato.int/cps/en/natohq/official_texts_156624.htm.

can no longer be separated in any defence-meaningful way from the defence of Europe, and vice versa. Given the growing scope and range of the threats faced by the US, Europeans will also need to consider how, and to what extent, they can collectively share the burdens traditionally borne by the US in their defence. The alternative? Europeans might themselves have to consider bearing the true cost of their own future war, future defence.

Frederick the Great once said, 'Diplomacy without arms is like music without instruments' (2020). Pragmatism and ambition are the indispensable partners if Europeans and their American allies are to generate together a critical and credible level of diplomatic, economic, and military power not only to influence the dangerous world in which Europe resides, but to change it for the better.

I

COVID-19 and the European defence dilemma

The defence implications of COVID-19

What are the implications for European defence of COVID-19? One of the greatest challenges any democratic government faces in the midst of crisis is to remember that there will be other threats that must be planned for. Indeed, the preservation of balance in both policy and strategy in the midst of popular clamour is the essence of sound government. As such, the European defence dilemma post-COVID-19 will concern the striking of a political balance between increased human security against such pandemics and the maintenance of national defence given emerging threats and at a time of severe economic constraint.

The economic statistics are chilling. According to the International Monetary Fund (IMF), growth in the so-called Advanced Economy Group contracted by 6.1 per cent in 2020 with the US contracting by 5.9 per cent, Japan 5.2 per cent, UK 6.5 per cent, Germany 7.0 per cent, France 7.2 per cent, Italy 9.1 per cent, and Spain 8.0 per cent. Asia is projected by the IMF to be the only region with a positive growth rate of 1 per cent in 2020, albeit more than five percentage points below its average in the previous decade. In China, there are some indicators that industrial production, retail sales, and fixed asset investment contributed to a contraction of economic activity in the first quarter of some 8 per cent year over year. Even with a sharp rebound in the remainder of the year and sizeable fiscal support, the economy is projected to grow at a subdued 1.2 per cent in 2020.[1]

---

1. See 'IMF Cuts Growth Forecast Following Advanced Economy Slowdown', 10 May 2020, https://www.worldfinance.com/markets/imf-cuts-its-growth-forecast-following-global-economic-stagnation.

It is certainly true that all such shocks to the existing order accelerate change. Between 1914 and 1945, some thirty-one years, World War One, Spanish flu, the Great Depression, and World War Two completely transformed geopolitics. The COVID-19 crisis has been first and foremost a human tragedy, rather than a prelude to war, with the 'enemy' a pathogen, rather than a state or group, and policy and strategy should be shaped accordingly. However, historians of the future will wonder how the virus brought the global economy to its knees so quickly, and with it much of European society.[2] They will also possibly conclude that the twenty-first-century world, far from being a globalized economy, was, in fact, a hybrid interdependent anarchy to which shock was endemic and routinely magnified, making future war more rather than less likely. China was at the epicentre of a pandemic that has the most profound of strategic implications, not least for European defence. And yet, the very strategy Europeans eventually adopt to counter COVID-19 could, if a new working balance is not struck between protection against such pathogens (human security) and national defence, undermine Europe's future defence. Of all European states, only Germany seemed reasonably prepared to cope with a SARS-like pandemic and had both the forward-planning and capacity to deal with it. The inference is that Germany has for some time invested more of its national wealth in human security than national defence compared with, say, the UK, France, or Italy. Certainly, the political agenda will be dominated for the foreseeable future by the need to tackle COVID-19 and make relevant systems less prone to being again overwhelmed by a similar event. More resiliency and redundancy clearly needs to be built into national, intergovernmental, and even globalized systems, as only a properly coordinated global effort is likely to contain such a threat at source and then reduce it. Equally, past pandemics would also suggest there is every chance the aftermath of COVID-19 could see even more intense Great Power competition as states seek to blame each other for its cause, mismanagement, and transmission.

2. There are important questions to be asked about whether comparing death rates across countries is even possible given the array of statistical models. On 24 April 2020, *The Guardian* even asked if such an approach had any worth. See Jennifer Rankin, Stephen Burgen, Kim Willsher, and Shaun Walker, 'Is Comparing Covid-19 Death Rates Across Europe Helpful?', https://www.theguardian.com/world/2020/apr/24/is-comparing-covid-19-death-rates-across-europe-helpful.

Every major pestilence in European history has had profound strategic consequences. For example, between 1347 and 1353 the population of Boccaccio's Florence fell from 110,000 to 50,000, a mortality rate that was reflected across Europe where some 40 per cent of the population perished.[3] Wage inflation and aristocratic debt soared, destabilizing an already fragile European polis and bringing feudalism to an end once and for all. There were profound geopolitical consequences as power shifted tectonically, leading to a series of conflicts, most notably the Hundred Years' War between England and France which was intensified as a consequence of the Black Death. Thankfully, COVID-19 is not the Black Death, but it will have profound economic, political, and strategic consequences, most notably in Europe.

The reckoning, when it inevitably comes, will test to the limit Europe's for-too-long tenuous relationship between rhetoric and structure, the state and the individual, as well as debt and defence, just as it did in the fourteenth century. Many European states devoted huge additional resources to the struggle against COVID-19, worsening already deeply adverse debt-to-GDP ratios. The combination of huge increases in COVID-19-related national debt allied to a reticence of Germany and other richer Northern European states to fully 'mutualize' Eurozone debt left an already vulnerable Euro open to the kind of catastrophic run on the currency last seen in 2010. During the crisis a major row developed between Germany and the richer Northern EU member-states and France, Italy, Spain, and other EU member-states, which further undermined European cohesion already weakened by Brexit and the initial response to the COVID-19 crisis.

The early spread of COVID-19 also seemed to eerily follow the old Silk Road, spreading first within China and then on to Europe via Iran and all over the world, again suggesting parallels with the Black Death or bubonic plague of the fourteenth century. First, COVID-19 was also a trade route pandemic, albeit a very twenty-first-century variant, and, as such, a disease of globalization. Second, like the bubonic plague, there have been several waves of infection. Third, and again like trade, the pandemic spread quickly

---

3. With echoes of today, Boccaccio's *The Decameron* tells the story of how Florence's entrepreneurial society was devastated by the plague. The book offers one hundred stories from people who had to cope with and adjust to life in the wake of the pandemic. *The Decameron* also provided the inspiration for Chaucer's subsequent *Canterbury Tales*. Giovanni Boccaccio (2008 edn) *The Decameron*, edited by Jonathan Usher (Oxford: Oxford University Press).

far beyond its initial path, undermining many of the advanced economies that helped spread it, replacing cooperation with confrontation.

In 2020 the world faced a choice between seeking parochial advantage or working together to confront and deal with a threat common to all. The early signs have not been good, with COVID-19 seeming to reinforce confrontational geopolitics. The very nature of contemporary globalism may well be a factor. Indeed, far from being the community of world citizens its more ideological adherents claim, when under pressure globalism becomes more like a form of interdependent anarchy. Given the fragile and fractious nature of any such international system, a relatively small event or group can create enormous shock, an ever more frequent phenomenon in the twenty-first century. In 2001, al-Qaeda spawned the Global War on Terror by attacking New York and Washington, whilst in 2008 a relatively small group of bankers triggered the worst financial economic and financial shock since the Wall Street Crash of 1929. All such shock also has profound and extended strategic consequences, two of which have been the precipitant relative strategic decline of Europe and the accelerated rise of China as power has shifted from West to East at pace.

The contemporary shift in power can even be measured. At the time of the 2003 SARS pandemic, which also originated in China, the Middle Kingdom represented 4.3 per cent of the world economy, whereas in 2019 it represented some 16.4 per cent.[4] In the past most such contagions also tended to be relatively localized because travel was far more restricted, lockdowns at times of plague were far more common, and people died far more quickly, limiting the ability of any contagion to spread. There were, of course, exceptions, the Black Death being but the most historically noteworthy.

COVID-19 and the shifting balance of power

The test of any system is how it copes with shock. In that light, COVID-19 is as much a warning as a crisis, and unless collective action is taken, a truly

4. See Rob Ibbetson, 'Coronavirus Is Costing the Global Tourism Industry Billions as Big Spending Chinese Travellers Are Stopped from Leaving the Country', *The Daily Mail*, 28 January 2020, https://www.dailymail.co.uk/news/article-7938497/Coronavirus-costing-global-tourism-industry-BILLIONS.html.

mass extinction humanity-culling pandemic could one day come down the same old Silk Road as COVID-19. Conversely, collective action against a common enemy might just help promote a more stable world order. If not, then the 2020–1 COVID-19 crisis will do much to shape international relations in the twenty-first century, and Europe's future defence, and not for the better. And yet, COVID-19 has also shown that globalization as a structure of power is profoundly fragile and that the Western/European ideal is dangerously complacent. The globalized international system is, at best, a virtual interdependent anarchy which, whilst created by state sovereignty, affords such sovereignty very little influence over it, particularly European state sovereignty and particularly at dangerous moments. Its currency remains relative to state power and its ongoing transfer from West to East contains within it an implicit systemic struggle between two powers for dominance: the US and China. In other words, COVID-19 has revealed the world on the cusp between a more cooperative order and a world that looks passably like the contentious dependencies in Europe prior to World War One.

Power, or rather its shift, may even have some responsibility for the outbreak of COVID-19. The West has fuelled China's rise by allowing Europe, in particular, to become like Rome at the height of its powers, which was apparently secure but always dependent on Egypt for its food. Indeed, the threat of famine was never far away from the Eternal City even at the height of its powers. For all the growth in Beijing's power and wealth since 1989, China today remains a huge, populous country full of very poor people. There is thus a profound friction between the twenty-first-century state Beijing likes to project to the world, and the reality of rural and urban poverty from which many millions of its citizens suffer. The average GDP per capita in China is still only around $10,000 per annum (with millions living on incomes far below that) compared with US GDP per capita at $65,000 per annum, whilst living conditions are often appalling by Western standards, with huge numbers of Chinese families crammed together in high-rise poverty.[5] Conspiracies abound suggesting COVID-19 was some form of bio-weapon, even if the evidence suggested the cause was far more prosaic: a lack of food hygiene, allied to the appalling attitudes to animal welfare and hygiene driven by huge demand for fresh meat slaughtered in

5. See 'Lists of Countries by GDP (Nominal) Per Capita', http://statisticstimes.com/economy/countries-by-gdp-capita.php.

the traditional Chinese manner. Indeed, the rapid growth of China's urban poor mega-cities such as Beijing, Shanghai, and, of course, Wuhan, where the contagion is believed to have begun, see many still wedded to traditional practices such as so-called wet (blood) markets. Beijing has tried to an extent to stamp out such practices, but has by and large failed.

The COVID-19 pandemic will also have profound consequences for Europe's future defence and a stable world order. Indeed, there can be little question that over time the consequences will affect all areas of statecraft, from the economic to the military. Neither China nor especially Russia are invulnerable to such consequences. For example, the price of benchmark West Texas crude oil collapsed from \$55 per barrel in December 2019 to below \$0 in April 2020.[6] Russia needs to export its oil at around \$70 per barrel for the Russian economy to be sustained at current levels of income, of which the Kremlin is acutely aware. China is less vulnerable but, nevertheless, the first quarter of 2020 saw Chinese manufacturing production drop by 13 per cent, the fastest and largest fall for fifty years.[7]

Worryingly for Europeans, autocracies tend to share certain characteristics when under such pressures. The primacy of the state over the individual is usually reinforced, with self-serving elites wrapping themselves in nationalism as the very embodiment of the nation and thus indispensable to it. Both Beijing and Moscow are already moving to exert more control domestically. Given their ambitions and the stakes, there is every reason to believe such efforts will be extended externally. Another sign is the entrenchment of those in power. President Xi, China's President-for-Life, has openly stated that his aim is for China to become the dominant world power by 2050. If, as seems likely, President Putin also succeeds in his efforts to remain president at least until 2036, Russia too will likely become more autocratic. That, after all, is the history of 'strongman' rule in which fawning elites not only tell power what it wants to hear, but also fear their own people.

History also plays an important role. Both Xi and Putin were shaped by the collapse of the Soviet Union in 1991 and fear the consequences of a sustained period of post-COVID-19 economic decline and their ability to hold onto power. President Putin is already suffering from falling popularity, with Russia retreating into an even more reflexive, nationalistic, and militaristic

---

6. On 20 April 2020 the benchmark West Texas oil traded at over *minus* \$37.
7. See 'China Economy Skids as Virus Immobilises Factory, Consumer Sectors', *Reuters*, 16 March 2020, https://news.trust.org/item/20200316071843-1rb9t.

posture with the West, the source of most of Russia's foreign-generated income, routinely cited as a threat. China, too, shows signs of becoming far more militarily aggressive, with Taiwan particularly vulnerable. Therefore, the possibility of both power autocracies embarking on some form of military adventurism must not be discounted as a downstream albeit indirect consequence of COVID-19.

There is also the possibility of large-scale re-shoring which would also have profound post-COVID-19 strategic and economic consequences. As China cracks down on internal dissent and the Chinese Communist Party moves to exert even greater control, the legal frameworks that enable Western multinational corporations to operate therein will also likely become more onerous. Many Western companies could well seek to 're-shore' their operations back to the US and Europe, exacerbating the economic crisis in China.[8] At the very least, many such corporations will (and should) likely reconsider their reliance on Chinese supply chains, which are today vulnerable to catastrophic failure, political manipulation, or both.

National distancing?

Social distancing might lead to national distancing as the whole idea of contemporary 'Europe', with its focus on free movement of goods, services, and people, may well need to be reconsidered in light of COVID-19. Faced with the strategic and political choices inherent in the COVID-19 crisis, there are essentially two options for Europe's states: more cohesion or fragmentation. On the face of it, a more cohesive response would appear to be the only possible option because any other approach would simply guarantee lose-lose outcomes for all, and there are some strategic lessons already apparent about the complex crises with which Europe must contend. Europeans were once again major victims of crises made elsewhere as Europe quickly became the epicentre of the pandemic. There is also a profound danger that the COVID-19 crisis will merge with a renewed refugee/migration crisis. A complex set of crises in combination would not only test European solidarity, but also place all European systems of government and governance under the utmost strain, with economic

---

8. Re-shoring is the practice of a company legally domiciled in one country returning productive capacity to that country from offshore.

consequences that would likely endure for at least another decade. Worse, the scale, complexity, and enduring nature of the crisis could well reinforce the attractiveness of extremist political parties.

Much will depend on the efficacy of the initial measures put in place to respond to COVID-19 in which epidemiological strategy and national and European strategy combine with strategic consequences. Brian Doberstyn, the former director of the World Health Organization (WHO) Western Pacific Region's Division for Combatting Communicable Disease, identified three main policy actions: transparency and a willingness of states to admit the scale and pace of early infection; the use of proven past practices in harness with twenty-first-century science; and rapid and effective global scientific collaboration to enable the early mapping of the genome of the virus.[9]

However, any such strategy would require all the responsible European states to craft a complex new strategic agenda that transcended geopolitics and presupposed a level of mutual trust that the crisis revealed to be in short supply, even between Europeans. Moreover, such efforts would need to range across sustained actions from the epidemiological strategy to the use of forces and resources in support of a sustained civilian and military mobilization, and all bound together by vital tight and effective strategic communications. In other words, any such strategy would require a profound change in both the tone and nature of European state behaviour.

As the crisis matures, much of the tone and nature of geopolitics will depend on whether China (and to a lesser extent Russia) seeks to repair its battered post-COVID-19 relationship with the West, or embarks on a path of geopolitical confrontation. The initial Chinese response was not encouraging. First, China embarked on a major propaganda exercise in an attempt to shift the blame for COVID-19 onto the US. China even claimed that the virus had been brought to Wuhan by the US military, which led to a formal complaint from then US Secretary of State Mike Pompeo. In fact, it was Beijing's obsession with control and secrecy that helped turn an outbreak into a global contagion. Second, the March 2020 re-appointment of Zhao Lijian, a particularly feisty Chinese nationalist, as Foreign Ministry Spokesman undermined any real hope that China was willing to act collectively with the US and the wider West. If Beijing adopts such a posture and refuses

9. See World Health Organization (ed.) (2006) *SARS: How a Global Epidemic Was Stopped* (Geneva: World Health Organization).

to acknowledge that two months of Chinese mismanagement during the early stages of COVID-19 dangerously exacerbated the crisis, then it will be hard for many Europeans to treat China as a responsible strategic actor and reliable partner. Third, China sought to coerce others. For example, in late April 2020, Beijing successfully exerted pressure on the EU to water down a report by the European External Action Service (EEAS) into Beijing's aggressive and widespread use of fake news in Europe during the crisis.[10]

Irrespective of China's behaviour, a much tighter relationship is needed in Europe between risk assessment, planning, and capacity-building across Europe's security and defence paradigm, and COVID-19 should provide the impetus. Far greater resiliency and engineered redundancy in critical systems and people is needed, and an end to the 'just-in-time', hollowed-out European security and defence state. Critically, much stronger strategic public–private partnerships need to be forged both to prepare for shock across the spectrum of adverse events and to recover from them. One consequence of globalization has been the progressive decoupling of Western states from Western corporations with the very idea of the multi-national corporation as the antithesis of the Western nation-state. A far stronger partnership between the public and private sectors in states and across states will now be crucial, and not just to limit the effects of systemic shock.

A much closer relationship between assessed risk and concrete planning will also need to be re-established. For example, the UK's 2017 National Risk Register for Civil Emergencies stated that the likelihood of a severe SARS-like pandemic was low, whilst its forerunner had stated quite the opposite. Consequently, little was actually done to prepare the UK for such an event.[11] Similar disconnects between risk assessments, policy prescription, and action are evident across the European security and defence establish-ment. Critically, better intelligence and early warning indicators will also need to be established across the security and defence spectrum. Indeed, the

---

10. Bruno Waterfield, 'China Forces EU to Tone Down Fake News Dossier', *The Times*, 27 April 2020, https://www.thetimes.co.uk/article/china-forces-eu-to-tone-down-fake-news-dossier-zdh5fvkcf.
11. Many European countries deemed the danger of such a pandemic as low risk. For example, the 2017 UK National Risk Register states, 'Emerging infectious diseases could also cause large numbers of people to fall ill. These are diseases which have recently been recognised or where cases have increased over the last 20 years in a specific place or among a specific population (e.g. the Zika virus). The likelihood of an emerging infectious disease spreading within the UK is assessed to be lower than that of a flu pandemic'. See 'The National Risk Register of Civil Emergencies', 2017 edition (London: Cabinet Office), p. 34.

very spectrum of threats European states face must be re-conceptualized. Failure to do so could well lead to zero-sum trade-offs in which, for example, national defence is abandoned in favour of a knee-jerk political reaction to any such crisis as COVID-19. The resources required to maintain both credible human security *and* national defence also suggest a much tighter effort is needed between European states, irrespective of whether they are in the EU, as well as a far more cohesive transatlantic relationship in which both North Americans and their European allies understand precisely what their respective roles would be in any emergency. Above all, the culture of worst-case planning needs to be re-embraced. Security and defence policy has always required strategic judgements to be made along with trade-offs between risk and cost. However, as Scenario 1 at the start of this book envisages, future war could well involve the deliberate and purposeful unleashing of many forms of coercion and destabilization simultaneously. If the transatlantic relationship and flagship Atlantic Alliance at its core is not capable of deterring, defending, and dealing with the worst case future war can generate, then what exactly is it for, beyond platitudes about shared values?

Critically, early and decisive response across the security and defence spectrum needs to be faster, more assured, and better coordinated, healthcare systems (both public and private) need to be better prepared, and critical infrastructures need to be made more resilient, with redundancy built into information networks and government structures. Above all, national defence needs to be re-energized through a reformed NATO and EU because for all its contemporary weakness, it is the still European state that must be central to any future broad-based crisis response if freedom is to be preserved, and it is with the European state that the political legitimacy for action remains.

Comprehensive security and national defence

How can Europe's defence be prepared for future war given the costs of the COVID-19 crisis? A central thesis of this book is that sound national defence in the face of future war will require a new comprehensive concept of security in which human security and national defence are harmonized. However, any such harmonization must not become a political metaphor for the effective abandonment of national defence and the further depressing of defence budgets. At the very least, there are profound implications for Europe's 'welfarized' states as they seek to strike a new balance between the security of the individual and defence of the state. Consequently, the very nature and concept of 'defence spending' needs to change as part of comprehensive security, as will the way Europe's defence is organized and structured. In the wake of the crisis the ends, ways, and means of Europe's future defence must be rethought to ensure greater efficiency and effectiveness of the European defence effort, which is one of the manifold aims of this book. In the short term, the focus should be on the search for synergistic 'crossovers' between COVID-19 crisis response (and an effective response to other hazards) and defence and deterrence in the application of civilian and military resources. Thankfully, improved crisis response and hardened civil defence could at least help point the way towards future defence and deterrence.

A debt–defence paradox is already apparent in the wake of the pandemic, with spiralling public debt a major consequence of COVID-19. Paradoxically, the immediate political reaction of traditionally big-government Europeans has been for more government, but the danger is that bigger government means less defence. Most Europeans spend an average of around 10 per cent GDP on healthcare and 1.2 per cent GDP on defence.[12] Prior to the crisis, collective European defence expenditure was expected to reach $300 billion/€275 billion in 2021, which is now unlikely. For example, the UK's Integrated Security, Defence, and Foreign Policy Review was effectively derailed by the additional borrowing (much of it on the bond markets or from China) London committed to in an attempt to offset the worst economic impacts of the first phase of the crisis.

There is also a danger of a profound 'anti-defence' shift taking place in how European politicians and their citizens perceive 'security', the twenty-first-century equivalent of fighting the last war more effectively. Consequently, whilst more of the European state is being devoted to cocooning the individual and the economy from COVID-19-style risk in the form of reinvested healthcare, more social security, crisis subsidies, and elevated levels of admittedly 'cheap' borrowing, many defence budgets are under renewed pressure. Whilst the individual European citizen might in time have access to more resilient locally provided pandemic protection, the state

---

12. 'Healthcare Expenditure Across the EU: 10% of GDP', *Eurostat*, 31 March 2020, https://ec.europa.eu/eurostat/web/products-eurostat-news/-/DDN-20200331-1.

itself will become progressively more vulnerable to externally generated strategic shock.

Burdened by additional debt, Europeans could become more inward-looking and retreat further from power and influence projection, upon which much of contemporary defence is predicated. The already limited ability of Europeans to project coercive power upon which credible twenty-first-century defence and deterrence depend could well be effectively abandoned in favour of armed forces that are little more than a reserve for domestic civilian crisis management. Critically, research into future defence technologies which could well define peace and war in the twenty-first century will be effectively abandoned by Europeans, with much of Europe's existing defence procurement re-focused in an effort to show concerned publics that their respective states are responding to the specific technology challenges of COVID-19.

In such circumstances, the transatlantic relationship will wither as the burdens on the US for providing a European public good—defence—simply become too high. The US and most of its European allies make roughly the same public investment in healthcare: between 7 and 10 per cent of GDP. However, since the end of the Cold War the US has devoted twice as much of its public national wealth to defence as its European counterparts. That disparity during a time of relative systemic peace enabled Europeans to not only benefit from a so-called 'defence premium', but to effectively free-ride on the US which was still able to reduce its own Cold War defence burden *and* furnish Europeans with a defence guarantee through NATO. However, even before the COVID-19 crisis, US expenditures on healthcare and social security were forecast to rise fast as the post-war 'baby boomer' generation entered old age. China, as an aside, faces an even more acute demographic time-bomb. The US is moving to resolve this tension by investing in advanced defence technologies. Europeans are not, which in time will make it increasingly hard for the US and Europe to work effectively together during high-end military crises. Indeed, so-called 'interoperability' will be one of the major challenges faced by the Alliance in the years to come.

Other synergies must also be sought. Military mobility, or rather crisis mobility, should be improved and accelerated. The ability and capacity to move relevant resources across Europe in sufficient mass to prevent crises, respond to them, and mitigate their consequences is a vital need for both military-supported civilian crisis response and defence and deterrence. As such, work to enhance political, legal, and physical 'infrastructure' across

Europe will be critical to more effective crisis management, alongside an enhanced ability to receive, organize, and manage forces and resources, and move them rapidly, securely, and efficiently to where they are needed. Efforts to increase and enhance military mobility could well provide the model for partnerships between and within states, and between the EU and NATO.

Europeans also need to fully understand the strategic consequences of their post-COVID-19 decisions for the US. Any significant resource-shift by Europeans away from defence will take place just at the moment the US faces growing worldwide pressure on its armed forces and, quite possibly, domestic pressure to withdraw further from its military leadership of the free world, which many Americans see as a cost rather than a benefit. In other words, if Washington is to maintain the security guarantee to Europe through NATO, the European Allies will need to do more, not less, for their own defence. In such circumstances, the effective defence of Europe is likely only to be both possible and credible if a far tighter set of defence relationships is forged between Europeans.

Europeans also need to make far better use of existing structures and systems. NATO and Supreme Headquarters Allied Powers Europe (SHAPE) will (and must) remain the exclusive command hub for the organization of military effect across Articles 4 and 5 high-end contingencies. The effective use of Allied Rapid Air Mobility during the crisis pointed to an expanded role for the Alliance in balancing both enhanced human security and national defence. Any such adaptation would be much enhanced if the Alliance also became far more agile and adaptive across the 5Ds of future war: disinformation, deception, destabilization, disruption, and the tailored destruction.

Russia, 5D warfare, and information shock

Has the COVID-19 crisis changed the behaviour of adversaries such as Russia? Sadly, Russia's strategic response to COVID-19 was mainly confrontational, with Russia employing *dezinformatsiya* extensively to exploit the crisis for political and strategic gain. Moscow's strategic aim is to keep European states permanently off-balance politically and socially, and to exploit all and any divisions between the US and its European Allies to undermine the cohesion of the Atlantic Alliance.

It is not the first time. Operation Infektion, Operation Vorwaerts II, or Operation Denver, as it was variously known, was a joint 'information operation' between the KGB and the East German Stasi. It began in 1983 with the aim of fostering anti-Americanism in those European states hosting US forces at the height of the Euromissiles crisis, during which Moscow sought to decouple the defence of Europe from the US strategic nuclear umbrella. The narrative (all offensive NKVD, KGB, and FSB operations are built around some form of narrative) was that the Americans had 'invented' HIV/AIDS at Fort Derrick in Maryland and had intentionally spread the disease across Europe.

In March 2019 the EU's EEAS identified some eighty Russian COVID-19 disinformation injects over two months, whilst the European Commission has also confirmed a marked increase in Russian disinformation efforts to that end since the outbreak of the pandemic. *The Guardian* newspaper also stated that 'Coronavirus was claimed [by Russian disinformation] to be a biological weapon deployed by China, the US or the UK. Other conspiracy theories contended the outbreak was caused by migrants or was a pure hoax'.[13]

During the COVID-19 crisis Moscow launched a variant of Operation Infektion, much of it through social media, with the aim of undermining the ability of European states to effectively manage the crisis. One Russian strategy during the crisis was to exploit a vulnerable adversary suffering systemic shock by making it worse through applied information shock. As such, COVID-19 was simply the latest variant of the use of long-applied opportunistic disinformation in Russian statecraft. The so-called 'Bronze soldier' campaign in Estonia in 2007, the run-up to the 2014 seizure of Crimea and the destabilization of Eastern Ukraine, as well as a sustained campaign to deflect responsibility for the July 2014 shooting down of Malaysian Airlines Flight MH17 by a Russian Army BUK missile all conform to a pattern of Russian information operations.

The March 2018 poisoning of Sergei and Yulia Skripal in the UK was another such case when two members of the Soviet military intelligence (GRU) Unit 29155 bungled an attempted assassination of a former Russian intelligence officer who had defected to the UK. During 2019 and 2020

13. Jennifer Rankin, 'Russian Media "Spreading Covid-19 Disinformation"', 18 March 2020, https://www.theguardian.com/world/2020/mar/18/russian-media-spreading-covid-19-disinformation.

Moscow also tried to blame Warsaw for the outbreak of World War Two by masking Russia's role in the so-called Secret Protocol to the August 1939 Molotov-Ribbentrop Pact, which carved Poland up between Hitler's Germany and Stalin's Soviet Union. Perhaps most cynically of all, Moscow tried to shift responsibility for the 1940 Soviet massacre of 22,000 Polish officers in Katyn Forest, even though former President Mikhail Gorbachev formally apologized for the war crime in 1990.

What are Moscow's specific aims? According to the EEAS, the specific goal is to undermine popular trust in the ability of European governments to cope with a major crisis. Some of the claims were absurd. For example, in February 2020, Sputnik radio claimed that the UK and certain international organizations were seeking to force China to open its markets through force, in much the same way the British Empire did at the 1842 Treaty of Nanking and thereafter in what the Chinese call the 'unequal treaties'. However, the effectiveness of disinformation does not depend on whether or not the information being peddled is believable, but rather believable where it matters in constituencies critical to the realization of Russia's broader national interest. Russian disinformation is also as much a strategic reflex as a cohesive strategy, reflective of the strategic spoiler role Moscow plays in European and world affairs. Disinformation is also how a future war might well start. Operation Infektion was part of so-called Russian active measures (aktivinyye meroproatia), a broad strategy of offensive influence operations conducted by both the KGB and GRU as part of 5D warfare.

However, for all of President Putin's hard-edged assertiveness, there are also clearly limits to his military ambitions, with significant cuts to planned public investment, including some cuts to the 2018–27 Strategic Armaments Programme.[14] And yet, President Putin shows little or no sign of abandoning an aggressive and at times expansionist foreign and security policy that since 2008 has seen the invasion of Georgia, the illegal 2014 seizure of Crimea and much of Eastern Ukraine, and Russia's incursion into Syria, as well as the seizure of the Kerch Strait.[15] Relative figures on defence

---

14. For an excellent study of Russia's military modernization see Anton Lavrov (November 2018) 'Russian Military Reform from Georgia to Syria' (Washington, DC: CSIS).

15. The Kerch Strait is a strategic waterway connecting the Black Sea with the Sea of Azov which, until the 2014 Russian seizure of Crimea, separated Russia from Ukraine. The Ukrainian port of Mariupol is dependent on access to the Strait. Following seizure of Crimea from Ukraine, the Russians constructed a road bridge across the Strait which opened in May 2018, whilst a rail bridge opened in 2019. In November 2018 the Russians seized three Ukrainian ships which

investment programmes are also telling. For example, whilst the US plans to invest some $700 billion on new equipment over the next ten years, and even the UK some $250 billion, Russia still plans to invest some $300 billion, which is about the same as the rest of Europe spends annually on defence.[16] Given the relatively small size of Russia's economy, Moscow's determination to commit a very significant portion of its relatively modest economic resources to its armed forces remains dangerously high when compared with most European states, COVID-19 or no.[17] In other words, Russian military might remains a far higher political priority for Moscow than for the democracies to its west.

During the crisis China both offered support to Europe's COVID-19 response and sought to exploit it through the use of an increasingly aggressive information and propaganda campaign. Certainly, Russia and China also seemed to have shared 'best practice' about the utility and application of disinformation during the crisis, as both clearly engaged in advanced information operations. Whilst the nature of China's operation fosters uncertainty, which is a strategic end in itself for Beijing, Russia's approach seems to be inherently more adversarial, and the extent to which Beijing and Moscow adopted a joint approach during the crisis remains unclear. However, Europeans should be under no illusion, as a broad strategic information operation continues to exert Chinese and Russian influence in an attempt to divide European states and their ability to respond to crises.

---

claimed to be sailing from Odessa to Mariupol. Twenty-four Ukrainian sailors are being held by the Russians.

16. See Julian Lindley-French (November 2015) 'Shifting the Goalposts: Defence Expenditure and the 2% Pledge', written evidence to the House of Commons Defence Committee, www. parliament.uk.

17. It is hard to specify the actual amount. GlobalSecurity.org wrote: 'Michael Kofman, an analyst of the Center for US Naval Analysis, wrote in Defense News, "The best example of this problem is a recent announcement by the Stockholm International Peace and Research Institute that Russian military spending has fallen to the sixth highest in the world in 2018, at $61.4 billion. Rest assured, or perhaps discomforted: Russian defense spending is several times higher than $61.4 billion, and the Russian defense budget remains the third largest in the world, dwarfing the military expenditures of most European states combined. In reality Russia's effective military expenditure, based on purchasing power parity (Moscow buys from Russian defense manufacturers in rubles), is more in the range of $150–180 billion per year, with a much higher percentage dedicated to procurement, research and development than Western defense budgets"'. See 'Russian Military Spending', https://www.globalsecurity.org/military/world/russia/mo-budget.htm.

The world beyond COVID-19

COVID-19 is also likely to accelerate existing global megatrends that have been driving structural shifts in the global order for some time. Climate change will continue to be exacerbated by a rapidly growing world population and resource scarcity that could well lead to more large flows of peoples from South to North. The profound shift in economic and military power from West to East apparent for the past twenty years or so is likely to continue, if not accelerate further. And, COVID-19 or not, perhaps for the first time in 500 years Europeans will lose the power to shape world events in their interest. To a limited extent the EU has slowed the loss of such influence, but unless significant action is taken by European states, their loss of influence could well now also accelerate. Consequently, in the post-COVID-19 world Europeans are likely to become far more the victims of change rather than its architect.

There are also a range of relatively immediate defence-relevant strategic consequences that go beyond the COVID-19 crisis. Growing populations to Europe's South and East will come under increased pressure, with climate stress a major driver of insecurity. The implications for Europe's future security of resource scarcity, sea-level rise, and changes to weather patterns are at least as dangerous as future pandemics (and perhaps the topic for a second volume of this book).

It is also worth noting that forced migrations are frequently accompanied by widespread radicalization as migrants' hopes and aspirations are dashed and their adopted governments either abandon or attack them. If only one hundredth of 1 per cent of future migrants to Europe are radicalized, then Europe would face some 20,000 potential radical extremists. If that figure were to reach one tenth of 1 per cent, then there would be some 200,000 violent radicals in Europe, a virtually endless supply of extremists and terrorists with which European governments would have to contend. In such circumstances, a resurgence in ideological friction and struggle within European societies could intensify, reinforcing extremist groupings across the political and ideological spectrum.

Such megatrends will also make European states more vulnerable to internal interference and planned dislocation. For example, Russia's use of 5D warfare is already creating difficult dilemmas for European governments and such complex strategic coercion is only likely to intensify.[18] Such a systematic application of manipulation and coercion, in theory at least, could enable a nominally weaker state to exert influence over ostensibly stronger but more fractured and vulnerable neighbours.

Longer-term and more esoteric change (albeit at a relatively fast pace) could well see the twinned megatrends of globalization and urbanization impact Europe and its future defence profoundly. Indeed, COVID-19 could well be the world's first globalization–urbanization pandemic. Mega-cities have already emerged in Europe (e.g. London, Paris, and Moscow all have populations over 10 million people), changing the political balance within European states, and whilst European capitals are likely to grow in relative power and importance within Europe, European states could well decline. One strategic and political consequence of such population shift, growth, and concentration may thus be the emergence of competing poles of power within European states, making their effective governance far more complex, not least because of the reaction of nativist populations to the diversity implicit in the growth of such cities.

Urbanization and the emergence of mega-cities will also go hand in hand with rapid technological change. Relatively rich European mega-cities will attract large numbers of skilled people. States will, at one and the same time, become both more advanced and more vulnerable, requiring the very ideas of 'security' and 'defence' to be reconceived, as will the balance between civilian security and military defence, as any prior boundaries between them evaporate.

Defending this new Europe will also demand new balances and relationships to be forged between police, armed forces, and intelligence. European states are unlikely to be able to project power and influence unless they can protect, and demonstrably so, a fractious and complex home population. Look at the mass disruption evident during the COVID-19 crisis. The alternative would be for Europeans to learn to live with far higher levels of risk of far more 'attacks' in far more and different forms from many actors and events across an expanded horizon of threat escalation. Worse, technology could well create an inverse and perverse relationship between the size of any adversary group and its ability to cause mass disruption and

---

18. For a detailed description of complex strategic coercion see J. Lindley-French (2019) *Complex Strategic Coercion and Russian Military Might* (Ottawa: CGAI).

destruction. At the very least, European states will need to become far more adept at making difficult policy choices during complex crises and forge new relationships between criminal and military intelligence if Europeans are to mount a credible security and defence against such threats. Whither European democracy?

COVID-19, Europe, and military megatrends

The military threats to Europe seemed far distant during the COVID-19 crisis, but they will return, forcing Europeans to contend with already adverse military megatrends. The relative and growing military disparity between Europe's liberal democracies and China and Russia has changed radically over the past decade, a shift in the balance of military power that became marked in the wake of the banking, sovereign debt, and Eurozone crises a decade or so ago. Given COVID-19 and the seeming inability of many European states to properly reform and modernize their respective and collective economies and armed forces, such a shift is likely to continue, particularly if European leaders now prioritize extending expensive European health and social security over national defence.

Defence rarely gets a politician elected in Europe in peacetime, particularly in the wake of a crisis in which armed force played a relatively marginal role. One 'solution' might be deeper defence integration, or even a European Defence Union. And yet, many European states remain unwilling to take radical political steps that would see greater military efficiency and effectiveness at the cost of national sovereign control. Worse, much of the defence-effectiveness of European defence spending is dissipated by the fractured and ill-considered application of defence investment in Europe, a crippling constraint with which China, Russia, and the US need not contend.

Critically, a profound change is now needed in the way defence is viewed in Europe that, given the COVID-19 crisis, will be politically counter-intuitive. Since the economic and financial crises, Europeans have tended to see defence as an area for the national exchequer to cut to reduce their respective national debts and strike a new balance between the kinds of security required to mitigate the threat of violent Jihadi movements and defence in the face of renewed state-generated threats. What choices now in the wake of the COVID-19 crisis?

The critical and determinant factor is that trends in Europe's defence expenditure still reflect a defence of Europe that is becoming relatively weaker year on year compared with the US and potential adversaries, even its 'strongest' military actors. For example, prior to the COVID-19 crisis *Statista* showed that British defence spending fell from £38.6 billion in 2008–9 to £35.1 billion in 2015–16, a real-terms decline of some 9 per cent over that period. And, although the UK is still nominally committed to a substantial defence investment programme over the 2020–24 period, it is open to question to what extent those investments will actually happen, given the burgeoning public debt and economic contraction due to COVID-19. In any case, even prior to the crisis much of the 'growth' in the UK defence budget had been achieved by creative defence accounting, in particular aligning British defence expenditure with NATO criteria to include a coterie of non-defence expenditures. This suggests the British were unlikely to balance the ends, ways, and means of their defence strategy even prior to the crisis.[19] Now?

European defence is thus at a COVID-19 crossroads. Economic austerity has been a major driver of European defence choices for at least a decade and the downward pressure on defence budgets is only likely to intensify. For too long Europeans have been trying to square an impossible defence circle and placed the transatlantic relationship under the most intense strain, not least because budgets were cut in the midst of major military campaigns. For example, between 2006 and 2015 defence expenditure in non-Russian Europe fell by 8.5 per cent, even though most European states were engaged in a major military campaign in Afghanistan for much of that period, with some of them also fighting a war in Iraq. Critically, between 2006 and 2015 US defence expenditure also declined by 3.9 per cent, whilst Chinese and Russian defence expenditure grew strongly year on year over the same period. The Italian defence budget even contracted by a whopping

---

19. A joint July 2016 report by the UK House of Lords and House of Commons captured the British dilemma succinctly: 'We welcome the Government's commitment to meet the NATO target of spending at least 2% of GDP on defence. However, we are concerned that the changed economic climate following the UK's vote to leave the EU will see the defence budget reduced in real terms, reversing the November 2015 decision to make additional funding available for defence. We are also concerned that the NATO minimum spending target would not have been fulfilled in 2015 if UK accounting practices had not been modified, albeit in ways permitted by NATO guidelines'. See 'National Security Strategy and Strategic Defence and Security Review 2015', Joint Report of the Joint Committee of the National Security Strategy, 10 July 2016, https://publications.parliament.uk/pa/jt201617/jtselect/jtnatsec/153/153.pdf.

30 per cent! Only Germany increased its defence budget by 2.8 per cent over that period, albeit from a very low base. Rarely in history do powers prevail in such campaigns whilst cutting their respective defence budgets.

The changing balance of power is also having an adverse impact on US military power, which should be of profound concern to Europeans. Indeed, although the Trump administration took some steps to ease relative and partial American defence decline and US military-strategic overstretch, it has not been stopped.[20] US overstretch could well become more pronounced in the wake of the COVID-19 crisis with profound implications for the future defence of Europe, not least because the nature of future war technology will pose a range of investment challenges, even to the US. In such circumstances, will the US be able to afford its European allies? Indeed, as Justin Bronk has written, 'The largest problem for non-US air forces in trying to prepare for high-intensity warfighting in the future will be the inability to negate the risks posed by significant combat attrition and inadequate combat mass through the pursuit of exquisite platform capabilities within limited budgets'.[21]

In spite of COVID-19, America's uncomfortable reality would suggest Europeans need to become more credible and effective crisis first responders in and around Europe. Instead, rather than confront twenty-first-century strategic change, the danger now is that Europe's defence effort will become even more parochial and backward-looking. COVID-19 or no, the dark side of globalization will endure in some form or another and will require Europeans to place their own defence in a much larger and necessarily global military context. The facts support this. The Stockholm International Peace Research Institute (SIPRI) noted a rise in military spending in Asia and Oceania (Australasia and the surrounding region) of some 64 per cent

---

20. Professor Paul Kennedy in his seminal work *The Rise and Fall of the Great Powers* states: 'if a state overextends itself strategically—by, say, conquest of extensive territories or the waging of costly wars—it runs the risk that the potential benefits from external expansion may be outweighed by the great expense of it all—a dilemma which becomes acute if the nation concerned has entered a period of relative decline. The history of the rise and later fall of the leading countries in the Great Power system since the advance of western Europe in the sixteenth century—that is, of nations such as Spain, the Netherlands, France, the British Empire, and currently the United States—shows a very significant correlation over the longer term between productive and revenue-raising capacities on the one hand and military strength on the other'. See Paul Kennedy (1987) *The Rise and Fall of the Great Powers: Economic Change and Military Conflict from 1500 to 2000* (New York: Random House).

21. Justin Bronk, 'Next Generation Combat Aircraft: Threat Outlook and Potential Solutions', Occasional Paper, November 2018 (London: RUSI), p. 32.

between 2006 and 2015. A significant part of this increase was due to Chinese military expansionism, and a North Korea that became a nuclear power during that period, possibly armed with intercontinental missiles. Important allies of the US, most notably Japan and South Korea, also increased their defence budgets markedly over the same period, as did Taiwan, Indonesia, and the Philippines.[22] Precisely because of its impact on the US, the arms race gathering pace across much of the Indo-Pacific, particularly in East Asia, must also help shape Europe's future defence choices, if Europe's leaders can look beyond COVID-19. This is primarily because such change will have enormous implications for the ability of the Americans to act fast and in strength during a European emergency. This will particularly be the case if the Americans face engineered and simultaneous emergencies in several theatres, including the possible use of tailored pandemics.

The situation in the Middle East and North Africa (MENA) is even harder to gauge and probably just as dangerous given the region sits on Europe's strategic doorstep. The impact of COVID-19 on the so-called developing world was by and large ignored during the crisis and its implications for already fragile states across MENA should remain of great concern. Salafi Jihadist terrorist networks, regional-strategic competition, and civil wars in fragile and failing states, as well as mass, forced, irregular migration, will all continue to pose a significant level of threat to Europe. Equally, defence expenditures across the region are also increasing. Saudi Arabia has emerged as a top five world defence spender, displacing the UK. Indeed, in 2020, Riyadh's spending on defence was double the amount it spent on defence in 2006, which is hardly surprising given that Saudi Arabia is engaged in a costly war in Yemen, as well as a regional cold war with Iran. The implications of the COVID-19 collapse in the oil price have yet to work through and Riyadh is keen to extricate itself from Yemen. Still, the regional cold war with Iran will continue and, quite possibly, intensify.

---

22. As an example of the burgeoning arms race in East Asia in 2018 the Japanese Ministry of Defence submitted a request for a 2.5 per cent increase over fiscal year 2017. Much of the increase was to enhance Japanese air defences, but some of it, such as the request for six additional F-35 strike aircraft, was to enhance Japanese offensive capabilities. The Japanese experience is reflected across the region. See 'What's in Japan's Record 2018 Defense Budget Request', *The Diplomat*, 28 August 2017, https://thediplomat.com/2017/08/whats-in-japans-record-2018-defense-budget-request.

The stress from which European defence suffers is not simply a function of constrained resources; it is also a function of the rapidly expanding bandwidth of warfare, a new mosaic of warfare that stretches across hybrid war, hyperwar, and cyber war that will continue long after the COVID-19 crisis. This rapid and profound change in the character of war demands, in turn, a new kind of European future force that would be capable of operating across the large, multiple domains (5th Domain Operations) of the twenty-first-century battlespace—air, sea, land, space, cyber, and the information and knowledge systems that enable them. Such a force will cost money but only a radically new concept of combined and joint arms will enable Europeans to close this rapidly expanding defence gap, a gap made wider by the poor defence value Europeans generate from their respective defence investments and, of course, COVID-19.

The same challenge also afflicts the US. In May 2018, giving evidence before the US Congress, then US Army Chief of Staff (now Chairman of the Joint Chiefs) General Mark Milley stated, 'I've seen comparative numbers of US defense budget versus China, US defense budget versus Russia. What is not often commented on is the cost of labor. We're the best paid military in the world by a long shot. The cost of Russian soldiers or Chinese soldiers is a tiny fraction'.[23] A senior member of the US government told one of the authors that given military purchasing power parity, the Chinese might already enjoy some 80 per cent of US military capability.[24] China's armed forces are on track to surpass US forces, possibly within the next decade. Critically, the relationship between cost and capability is far worse for Europeans than it is for Americans. Again, Europeans faced hard choices even before the COVID-19 crisis about how to mount a credible future defence. Now? At the very least, the need for innovative thinking, as well as new structures and capabilities, has now grown exponentially. Unfortunately, since the end of the Cold War, whatever 'joint' European mechanisms have been created to help foster more effective European defence have also too often become the political battlefields upon which a struggle is fought over the very purpose of defence and whether the EU or NATO should be in the lead. Worse, many European states and their

23. See Sidney J. Freeberg, Jr, 25 May 2018, 'US Defense Budget Not Much Bigger China, Russia: Gen. Milley', Fact.International, http://fact.international/2018/05/us-defense-budget-not-that-much-bigger-than-china-russia-gen-milley.
24. Conversation on 7 May 2020.

citizens seem no longer to understand why they spend money on defence, with some even suggesting that such expenditures may be 'immoral'—a tendency the COVID-19 crisis will only exacerbate.

In the past, the Americans effectively decided Europe's defence investment choices because during the Cold War Europeans were little more than spokes attached to an American defence hub. Through NATO, Europeans also became progressively more comfortable with defence on the cheap afforded them by US taxpayers. As the importance of defence slid down the domestic political agenda in the wake of the Cold War, European defence spending choices, such as they were, became dictated almost solely by the need to maintain minimum effective military 'interoperability' with US forces during an emergency. Today, whilst the need to maintain interoperability remains a military imperative, it is far less a political imperative.

As the transatlantic relationship creaks under the growing weight of political and strategic divergence, and in the absence of effective American or European leadership, there is now a danger that in the wake of the COVID-19 crisis Europeans will simply abandon defence in the hope that the threat will somehow ignore or pass the Old Continent by. The warning signs have been clear for some time and pre-date the pandemic. For example, a 2018 Deutsche Presse Agentur opinion poll suggested 42 per cent of Germans wanted the complete removal of US bases from Germany.[25]

There are today distinct parallels between the US today and the British at the height of their imperial power. In 1889, in a statement to the House of Commons on the Naval Defence Act, First Lord of the Admiralty, George Hamilton, stated,

> Our supremacy on the sea must, after all, be measured by the number of battleships we can put into line. It is further our duty, as we find other nations pushing forward this particular class of ship, to do the same. I have endeavoured during the past year to study the speeches of those who, in previous years, have held my position and that of Prime Minister, so as to ascertain the paramount idea underlying their utterances when they spoke of the standard of strength upon which our naval establishment should be maintained. I think

25. See Rick Noack, 'As Trump Rattles NATO, 42 Percent of Germans Now Want U.S. Troops Out of the Country', *The Washington Post*, 12 July 2018, https://www.washingtonpost.com/news/worldviews/wp/2018/07/12/as-trump-rattles-nato-42-percent-of-germans-now-want-u-s-troops-out-of-the-country/?noredirect=on.

I am accurate in saying that our establishment should be on such a scale that it should at least be equal to the strength of any two other countries.[26]

In other words, whilst the statement of strategic ambition, and the headline budget to support it, were clear, Hamilton's position also revealed a Britain increasingly concerned about the emerging power of other states and the sheer scope of its strategic responsibilities. Fifty years later, such responsibilities would force Britain to choose between defence of the home base, defence of the Mediterranean, and defence of Britain's Eastern Empire. In 1942, *force majeure* forced the British to effectively abandon the latter with the crippling defeat at Singapore at the hands of the Japanese.[27] America's contemporary global responsibilities might be very different in form to that of the British over a century ago, but the principle of power and overstretch, and the hard choices it inevitably imposes over time, are not.

European defence in the post-COVID-19 world

The need for a credible future military defence of Europe has not evaporated because of COVID-19. If anything, the behaviour of both China and Russia during the crisis has highlighted the need for just such a defence. Europe's future defence cannot be separated from the wider responsibilities of Europeans in the twenty-first-century world. COVID-19 happened because of a failure of policy in China and an absence of safeguards elsewhere, particularly in Europe. The crisis also revealed the extent to which Western democracies have become over-reliant on one autocratic state and strategic competitor for many of the supply chains that sustain their respective economies and societies. However, those who believe time can be rolled back and globalization abandoned have to ask themselves: with what? Contending, hermetically sealed and confrontational blocs? History would advise against such a world.

Clearly, European states need to better protect themselves from crises made elsewhere, but what has been missing for far too long in European

---

26. https://www.globalsecurity.org/military/world/europe/uk-rn-policy2.htm.
27. On 15 February 1942 Lt.-General Percival surrendered some 80,000 British, Indian, and Australian troops to the Japanese. Many would perish in Japanese prisoner-of-war camps. Prime Minister Winston Churchill called the defeat 'the worst disaster and greatest capitulation in British military history'. Christopher M. Bell (2019) *Churchill and the Guns of Singapore, 1941–42: Facing the Wrong Way?* (Hillsdale College, MI: The Churchill Project).

defence is the considered practice of statecraft. The dark side of globalization, of which COVID-19 is a frightening example, must be gripped and structure built to mitigate its risks and dangers. Such structure will and must include sound defence; the 'stuff' of this book. However, globalization must not be abandoned for to do so would cut the very connectedness that mitigates the nationalism and militarism that would doubtless come to dominate both Beijing and Moscow if they were completely denied access to Western markets.

COVID-19 has also revealed the extent to which Europe's leaders have for too long been on 'strategic vacation'. The seeming inability of European leaders to confront Europe's rapidly deteriorating strategic environment and the atomization of security and defence that has been all too apparent over recent years has exaggerated the shock Europeans experience as shock breaks over them. The 'grand strategy' of Europe's future security and defence will thus demand the far more efficient application of great means in pursuit of high political and strategic ends. Unfortunately, the current crisis has once again demonstrated that not only does European solidarity (and with it the EU) tend to fail at such moments, but the concomitant renationalization of response leaves NATO with little or no role. If that happened in a worst-case military crisis, the Americans and a few of their more capable European allies would simply bypass both NATO and the EU.

New European political realities will also need to be faced and accommodated. With the UK outside the EU, the organization and enabling of transatlantic relations and Europeans' security and defence will be increasingly established on two pillars: a NATO-focused 'Anglosphere', in which efficient collective action is the ethos, and a 'Eurosphere' of continental Europeans that is increasingly common; or collective to the point of defence fusion if EU member-states are to close Europe's yawning ends, ways, and means gap that now stretches across the comprehensive security spectrum from human security to national defence. Equally, given that the UK cannot be outside the EU and part of a common EU effort, the more common the EU effort, the less the UK could, or would, play any meaningful role for a whole host of complex political, strategic, and legal reasons. The EU–NATO strategic partnership will become more rather than less important. However, such a partnership will also need to become a real force and resource generator and command and control hub that sits at the juncture between people protection and power projection. In short, in the wake of the COVID-19 crisis, EU member-states must either prove they are committed to a common approach, or abandon it.

Above all, America must learn again to lead the free world, which remains a critical US national interest. That begs a further question: lead where? First, towards a shared understanding that China is as much a (if not *the*) strategic challenge to the world's democracies as it is a partner. Second, a shared Allied recognition that the relationship with China has become dangerously unbalanced with too many Western supply chains now dependent on a country that is as much predator as partner. Third, the future Atlantic Alliance and European defence cohesion need to be seen against the back-drop of such challenges. Fourth, and perhaps most important of all, Europe's intergovernmental institutions need to become far more adept at anticipat-ing shock and far more robust in the face of such shock, and better able to assist Europe's states to strike a realistic balance between human security and national defence.

Where to start? During the Cold War there was a list of prescribed strategic metals that Western powers insisted must remain under their control. One lesson from this crisis given China's behaviour must surely be the need for the West, Europe in particular, to regain control over certain 'strategic' technologies vital to a forward-looking concept of comprehensive security across the human security/national defence spectrum. Faced with such a determination, China may well decide to be less predator and more partner.

European governments must urgently confront the false dichotomy they are fast barrelling towards between disease, debt, and defence. Far better use of the Alliance must be made as a mechanism for the further promotion of transatlantic defence and deterrence effectiveness, alongside, and in parallel to, EU efforts to act as the cradle for high-end aggregated support of civilian authorities. If not, and geopolitics becomes more confrontational whilst Europe's defence becomes progressively weaker, then whilst COVID-19 is not a war, it could well come to be seen as the pivotal battle in a much wider and longer-term strategic struggle for dominance, and quite possibly the prelude to a major future war which can no longer be ruled out.

Therefore, for Europeans the choice between more protection against COVID-19 and its ilk and more defence is not only a false dichotomy, it is a dangerous delusion.

2

The end of the beginning?

D-Day, NATO, and the importance of legitimate military power

There are a raft of lessons contemporary history offers Europe's future war, future defence of Europe spread across eight systemic themes: the need for strategic ambition; the importance of relevant military power for minimum defence and credible deterrence; the importance of demonstrable political cohesion; the need to share burdens equitably; innovation is central to an effective defence; strategic intent must be made clear; for democracies there are no permanent enemies; and the vital importance of leadership in alliance.

The first lesson is that the real bedrock of hard legitimate defence power comes from democracies acting in concert, and being demonstrably willing and able to consider and act in the direst of situations. Indeed, it is for that reason that in many ways NATO was born on the beaches of Normandy. On 6 June 1944, British, American, and Canadian forces stormed ashore along a 50-mile/80-kilometre front on the five landing beaches of Normandy—Gold, Juno, Sword, Omaha, and Utah. 'D-Day' was not simply an Anglo–American–Canadian effort; it was an alliance effort, with forces and personnel from Australia, Belgium, then Czechoslovakia, Greece, the Netherlands, New Zealand, Norway, Poland, and, of course, France. In fact, much of the alliance that was to become the Alliance was forged on those five historic beaches. It was also the beginning of a long story of post-war European defence as D-Day also marked the beginning of a profound shift in the respective power and fortunes of the combatants involved.

Desmond Scott, a New Zealander who commanded a wing of four RAF Typhoon squadrons, said, 'The preparations were staggering. The airborne assaults, the quantity and variety of shipping, the number of army divisions, the tremendous weight of the air offensive. The scale and precision of it all made our past efforts look insignificant'.[1] D-Day also saw the high-water mark of British strategic influence and military strike power. Contrary to much of the narrative that has ensued ever since Operation Overlord, or more specifically Operation Neptune, the naval operation, D-Day was primarily a British-led operation. On that single day, 156,000 troops were landed, of which 73,000 were American, whilst 83,115 were under British command, with 61,715 British and 20,000 Canadian troops. Of the 1,213 principal warships supporting the landing, 892 were Royal Navy ships, while of the 4,126 landing craft deployed, 3,261 were British with only 200 US craft.[2] In total 7,700 ships and craft were deployed in support of the landings, the overwhelming bulk of which were British, as were the two giant floating Mulberry Harbours, without which the landings simply would not have been possible.[3] In the air, some 12,000 aircraft took part, of which some 70 per cent were from the Royal Air Force or Royal Canadian Air Force.

Whilst US General Dwight D. Eisenhower was Supreme Commander of the Allied Expeditionary Force, all of his operational commanders were British. The Deputy Supreme Allied Commander was Air Marshal Sir Arthur Tedder, whilst the Commander-in-Chief, Air was Air Marshal Sir Trafford Leigh Mallory, Commander-in-Chief, Sea was Admiral Sir Bertram Ramsey, and Commander-in-Chief, Land was General Sir Bernard Law Montgomery. The operational plan was mainly British, as was the air campaign to isolate Normandy from German reinforcements (Operation Transportation), as well as the massive deception campaign (Operation Bodyguard) to convince the Nazis that the real objective for any invasion force would be the Pas de Calais.

This in no way downplays the US contribution to D-Day. The two US beaches, Omaha and Utah, were perhaps the hardest objectives to be seized and demonstrated American valour and courage of the highest order. Still, the fact remains that some British forces performed better on D-Day. This can be explained partly by the innovative technology they employed, which is one lesson from D-Day for Europe's future defence. Innovation also

1. Antony Beevor (2009) *D-Day* (New York: Penguin), p. 79.
2. These figures come from 'Exploding the Myths of the D-Day Landings', James Holland, 5 June 2014, https://edition.cnn.com/2014/06/05/opinion/opinion-d-day-myth-reality.
3. See 'D-Day Facts and Stats', Stephen Ambrose Historical Tours, https://stephenambrosetours.com/d-day-facts and 'Ten Things You Need to Know About D-Day', Imperial War Museum, https://www.iwm.org.uk/history/the-10-things-you-need-to-know-about-d-day.

extended to tactics. The British and Canadians deployed their amphibious tanks and landing craft closer in-shore, which better protected them from being swamped by the sea, and ensured combat troops were less seasick when they disembarked. Critically, the British and Canadians deployed in strength specially adapted tanks, known as Hobart's Funnies, which helped clear a path through obstacles and minefields for the invading force.[4] American commanders had, for a range of reasons, by and large eschewed the use of such innovation. British Special Forces were particularly effective, not just in reconnoitring the beaches but also in helping to secure the vital bridgehead. The famous 'Zero Hour' midnight glider assault on what became Pegasus Bridge by Major John Howard and his Oxford and Buckinghamshire Light Infantry was critical to securing the invasion's left flank.

Churchill had once said of Montgomery's 1942 victory over Rommel at El Alamein in present-day Egypt that whilst the battle was most certainly not the beginning of the end, it was, perhaps, the end of the beginning. With Soviet forces advancing from the east, D-Day was certainly the beginning of the end for Hitler, but it was only a beginning. For that reason, D-Day must not be seen in isolation, as it was only one operation at the start of a massive campaign to liberate Northwest Europe. This is critical to any understanding of the story of European defence then, now, and into the future. It is what happens from D+1 onwards that is most significant for Europe's contemporary and future defence, for it began a process of overwhelming American leadership of the defence of Europe that continues to this day. From D-Day on, the Americans poured men and materiel into the fight for Normandy on such a scale that the British were soon reduced to an important but nevertheless junior partner in the Allied effort. By June 1944, after almost five years of systemic war fought across three continents, the British were reaching the limits of their manpower, industrial, and financial capacity and their armed forces were tired. The Americans were only just beginning to exploit their own immense resources, in spite of fighting two major wars simultaneously in the Pacific and Europe. The British never properly recovered from the cost and exertions of World War Two which, in spite of victory,

---

4. Hobart's Funnies were a direct result of the disastrous August 1942 raid on Dieppe during which the Canadians paid a grievous price. Named after Major-General Percy Hobart, they were specially adapted British tanks that could clear minefields and other impedimenta to assist infantry and more standard armour to advance. Hobart's Funnies were the forerunner of the modern combat engineering vehicle.

accelerated Britain's decline from the pinnacle of world power. America's rise was just beginning.

Something else took place on D-Day that was vital to European defence: the building of the foundations for a multinational alliance of democracies that in time became the bedrock upon which the defence of Europe would stand. D-Day, and the campaign to liberate Northwest Europe that ensued, was about the proportionality of effort that would come to define the post-war Atlantic Alliance. For example, the number of Dutch present at D-Day was relatively modest, with many of those who had escaped to Britain in 1940 on the fall of the Netherlands (the so-called Engelandvaarders) embedded in British forces.[5] However, on 6 August 1944, the 2,000-strong Royal Netherlands Motorised Infantry Brigade (Prinses Irene Brigade) landed at Graye-sur-Mer in Normandy. First, under Canadian command, and then under the command of General Dempsey's 2nd British Army, the Dutch fought their way from Normandy back to their homeland, joining in the liberation of Tilburg in October 1944 before entering The Hague in triumph at the very end of the war on 9 May 1945.

The essential message from D-Day is that it succeeded precisely because it was a team effort forged from an alliance that in time forged the Alliance. Often very different and differing cultures and personalities, most notably Bernard Law Montgomery and George S. Patton, learned to work together for the common good under enlightened American leadership and often equipped with American weapons. It established a culture that lay the foundation for the creation of NATO in April 1949. Moreover, its success was not just due to American might, but also the immense investment in political capital as well as the brains, men, and materiel of the British, Canadians, and a host of others. Burdens and risk were shared, the antithesis of nationalism, by force of democracies. Indeed, it was the very democratic nature of that alliance which also enabled former enemies—Italy first, and then the Federal Republic of Germany—to join the Alliance once freed from fascism and Nazism.

Today, the single most important lesson afforded the future defence of Europe by the great citizen armies of D-Day democracies—the Tommies,

---

5. 'Engelandvaarders', or England sailors, was the name the Dutch gave to those who escaped to Britain in the wake of the June 1940 conquest of the Netherlands. Many were killed or died at sea in the attempt to escape. Some 1,700 made it to Britain and continued the fight for liberation alongside, and often in support of, the Dutch resistance.

the GIs, the Canucks et al.—who battled to gain that first foothold on the sweeping sands of Normandy over seventy-five years ago remains poignant. If Europeans do not wish to put young Europeans, men and increasingly women, through the horrors of some twenty-first-century D-Day, somewhere, sometime, and there were horrors and tragedy aplenty on that day, then Europe's leaders must stop appeasing the dangerous reality of today and learn the lessons of Europe's contemporary history. COVID-19 or no, they must face down together the military threats Europeans will face. The price of freedom was heavy, and will continue to be so. On D-Day alone the long march towards a free Europe cost the lives of 6,603 Americans, 2,700 Britons, and 946 Canadians and others who had seen the sun rise on D-Day, but would not live to watch it set. Not only did they forge a path to freedom, they forged on the anvil of unity an enduring Alliance and a free Europe. The legacy of D-Day must not be squandered.

Defence and power

The second lesson is that any sound defence strategy must be informed by power. Winston Churchill once said that when strategy and power are properly aligned, all that then matters is the proper application of overwhelming force. History also offers a range of lessons for Western leaders to consider, particularly European leaders, as they mull over their strategic options in the wake of the COVID-19 rupture. D-Day was a relatively small part of an Allied grand strategy that carried the democracies to victory. The past containment of the Soviet Union, for all its Cold War clunkiness, was also a considered strategy that established the framework for legitimate collective and effective defence and deterrence. Today, Americans and Europeans seem confused, or just plain disagree, about the ends, ways, and means of Europe's defence. As the world becomes steadily more dangerous, and with Europe again a cockpit for contestation and instability, such confusion needs to end fast.

Equally, the injudicious application of history to strategy can lead to false assumptions. The term 'a new Cold War' is often bandied around as if European defence is today heading back to some dangerous future. It is not. If anything, the anachronistic use of terminology actively prevents a proper understanding of the changing nature of today's threats, something the COVID-19 shock bolsters. Thankfully, the threat Europe faces is not, as yet, an existential clash of implacable ideological adversaries backed by mutually annihilating nuclear arsenals, even if the technology for such a threat has never gone away. Precision of description and analysis is thus vital if an understanding of the contemporary history of European defence is to play an important and constructive role in Europe's future. The very idea of a Cold War can lead people to make lazy assumptions about threat that prevent sound strategy and application of limited force and resource and restrain innovative thinking about how best to respond. Precision over the nature of differences between allies, and contestations over policy, strategy, and affordability, should enable both policy-makers and planners to develop a capacity to see more clearly what the remedies might be across a wide spectrum of options, and better define and respond to what is a unique twenty-first-century security environment. There is a big rejoinder to this assertion, particularly in Europe—that European leaders must have the political courage to act on strategic guidance. For example, it would be wrong to assume Russia and the West are now locked into an unavoidable descent into major war, even if it is hard not to conclude, given current strategic and political trajectories, that Russia and the West are heading towards further showdowns. It would be equally wrong to believe that the battle to recover from COVID-19 has ended the threat of war and that defence budgets might be raided accordingly. Strategy, and the security policy it serves, is ultimately about balance.

There are also specific lessons that can be gleaned from Europe's Cold War experience that should inform current strategy. In 1946, US diplomat George Kennan warned that Stalin was merely using ideology as 'a justification for the Soviet Union's instinctive fear of the outside world, for the dictatorship without which they did not know how to rule, for cruelties they did not dare not to inflict, for the sacrifice they felt bound to demand... Today they cannot dispense with it. It is the fig-leaf of their moral and intellectual respectability'.[6] Kennan's famous 1946 dispatch from the US Embassy in Moscow marked the moment that post-war Washington finally began to wipe away the cobwebs of self-delusion and recognize that Churchill was essentially right: Stalin's Soviet Union was no partner of the West and would pose a direct threat to the European democracies. Kennan's

---

6. See George Kennan (1946) 'The Long Telegram', Wilson Center Digital Archive, 22 February 1946, https://digitalarchive.wilsoncenter.org/document/116178.pdf?v=7a7b69bd3c47e05-a3ca88476d232e326.

dispatch was from the right man, writing the right thing at the right time, and from the right place. The subsequent 'Mr X' (Kennan) article in *Foreign Affairs* was a wake-up call. With the work of others, such as Paul Nitze, it led in time to an evidence-based shift in US policy and strategy, the Truman Doctrine, NSC-68, and, of course, NATO.[7] Does contemporary Europe have the will and the instruments to make similar evidence-based shifts of policy and strategy or are Europeans trapped in some latter-day virtual and perpetual Ten-Year Rule? The US-led grand strategy that ensued was ambitious but compelling: Soviet aggression must be contained by strengthened Western institutions and credible military force until Russia's inner contradictions ushered the USSR towards collapse.

For all his many failings, Putin is no Stalin. Equally, Putin's Russian nationalism remains dangerous, paradoxically because of contemporary Russia's far weaker strategic and economic position in the early 2020s compared to that of the Soviet Union in 1946. It is Russia's economic weakness combined with Putin's strategic activism that makes Putin's Russia so dangerous and increasingly prone to extreme and violent action. Moscow's development of advanced military capabilities might give the impression of power and offsetting Russia's own sense of weakness, at least temporarily, but such weapons exacerbate the threat Europeans face and cannot simply be wished away.

European defence and leadership

The third lesson is that Europeans must learn to trust each other and welcome US leadership even as it inevitably and necessarily changes. In March 1946, with President Harry S. Truman in attendance, Winston Churchill made a speech which was a hinge of history.[8] He spoke of an

7. The importance of NSC-68 in realigning US and Western policy cannot be overstated. It proposed a strategy of comprehensive Western rearmament focused upon, and led by, the United States. It also marked the beginning of the so-called Long Haul of confronting and containing Soviet expansionism. As such, NSC-68 was a genuine grand strategy—the organization of immense American means in pursuit of big, strategic ends. Paradoxically, NSC-68 might not have become American policy had North Korea not invaded its southern neighbour in 1950. See Julian Lindley-French (2007) *A Chronology of European Security and Defence 1945–2007* (Oxford: Oxford University Press), p. 25.
8. The 5 March 1946 speech was entitled 'The Sinews of Peace' and was made at President Harry S. Truman's alma mater. At the time Truman was none too pleased Churchill envisioned another entangling war for the United States in Europe. The domestic pressure to 'bring the

'iron curtain' descending across Europe from Stettin in the north to Trieste in the Adriatic. It was a grand visionary statement of grand strategy, calling for the organization of immense Allied means in pursuit of vital Allied ends, which an exhausted Britain was incapable of generating. Put simply, it was a call for the Americans to lead a renewed alliance for the defence of Europe from a new threat that was also in time to lead to German leadership of Europe. A US–German partnership, allied to German leadership, which will be vital if Europe's future defence is to be assured.

In 1948 the First Berlin Crisis galvanized Churchill's words into Allied action, began the slow transformation of Germany from defeated enemy to Europe's leader at the heart of democratic Europe, and cemented the post-war US commitment to European defence.[9] The crisis, like so many before and since, came as a shock when Soviet forces began blockading Berlin by closing the road and rail corridor that linked the American, British, and French occupation zones within the city, with their respective occupation zones in the west of Germany. The response was swift and phenomenal. Between 24 June 1948 and 12 May 1949 the Berlin Airlift saw 441 American and 248 British aircraft fly 277,804 sorties delivering 394,509 tons of essential supplies to the people of Berlin.[10] On 16 April alone the air-bridge delivered more supplies than the combined road and rail link prior to the blockade, with one Allied aircraft landing in Berlin every minute.

The ostensible cause of the First Berlin Crisis was the introduction of the new *Deutschemark* by the Western Allies. For Stalin, the introduction of the currency was a step on the road to the eventual reunion of a Germany that could, and indeed would in time, eclipse three of the four occupying powers—Britain, France, and Russia. For Stalin, the emergence of a democratic Germany was as great a threat as the re-emergence of a functioning and in time independent German state.

---

boys home' was strong in the US. With time, and in conjunction with Kennan's 'Long Telegram', Churchill's seminal post-war speech laid the political foundations for the April 1949 founding of NATO.

9. One needs to be careful not to overstate the pace of Germany's political transformation; as Paul Cornish has argued in his seminal work *British Military Planning for the Defence of Germany 1945–50*, 'Defence of Germany was always a heavily circumscribed notion. Long before German pressure for "forward defence", up to the outbreak of the Korean War the Allies were only ever willing to countenance "defending" Germany on the Rhine'. See Paul Cornish (1996) *British Military Planning for the Defence of Germany 1945–50* (London: Macmillan), p. 167.

10. For an excellent study of the Berlin airlift see John Grehan (2019) *The Berlin Airlift: The World's Largest Ever Air Supply Operation* (Barnsley: Pen and Sword).

Stalin's clumsiness and the 'law' of unintended strategic consequences helped pave the way for both a united Germany and a united (sort of) Europe. Rebuilding Germany, the erstwhile enemy, took great political courage but it was the right strategic thing to do. Throughout 1946 the Americans and the British completed work on the so-called *Bizone* which unified the economies of their respective German occupation zones. On 1 June 1948, the French occupation zone also joined, forming the *Trizone*, establishing the sovereign space for the Federal Republic of West Germany to emerge on 23 May 1949 (a month or so after the Washington Treaty and the founding of NATO). On 7 March 1948, to ensure the Federal Republic would be politically and economically viable, it was also agreed that the Marshall Plan, or European Recovery Program as it was officially called, would be offered to the whole of Germany, something Moscow rejected out of hand for its area of occupation.

Interestingly, much of the preparatory work on the Marshall Plan was undertaken by the Brookings Institution. In January 1948, Brookings had begun work on a twenty-page report that led to the eight recommendations at the heart of the European Recovery Program, and which also led to the creation of a new Cabinet-level post in Washington with direct access to President Truman, together with the appointment of high-level Special Representatives in each recipient country to manage the programme.

By May 1949, it was clear even to Stalin the blockade was not working. He was unwilling to provoke an open conflict with the Americans, who at the time were still the only atomic power (the Soviets did not test their first atomic bomb until 29 August 1949), so finally lifted the blockade on 12 May 1949.

NATO and the importance of alliance

The fourth lesson of history for European defence is that the Atlantic alliance is as much in the American as the European interest, and that the resolve, solidarity, and applied military capability of democracies is the foundation stone of a transatlantic relationship as vital now as it was in the past. A fifth lesson is that no state is a permanent enemy of democracy. On 4 April 1949, NATO was born when its founding instrument, the North Atlantic Treaty, was signed by Belgium, Canada, Denmark, France, Iceland, Italy, Luxembourg, the Netherlands, Norway, Portugal, the United Kingdom, and the United States. As the democracies became stronger NATO was joined (in order) by Greece, Turkey, Germany, Spain, the Czech Republic, Hungary, Poland, Bulgaria, Estonia, Latvia, Lithuania, Romania, Slovakia, Slovenia, Albania, Croatia, and Montenegro.

The sixth lesson of history is that declaratory defence and deterrence matters. At the core of the defence and deterrence of a free Europe, and enshrined in the North Atlantic Treaty, is Article 5 which commits all member nations of the Alliance to consider an attack on one ally as an attack on all. Interestingly, the Second Berlin Crisis between 1960 and 1962 demonstrated just how important such a statement was, and how far the US was prepared to go to uphold its commitment to Europe. In 1960, President Kennedy decided to challenge Soviet attempts to freeze the Western Allies out of Berlin and ordered Chairman of the Joint Chiefs, General Lyman L. Lemnitzer, to send an armoured battlegroup to Berlin to augment US forces therein. This act sent a strong message of US solidarity with Berliners to the Soviets and their East German satellite. Kennedy's decision came in spite of the concerns of Secretary of Defense Robert McNamara who feared that such a move would weaken existing defences in West Germany and add little to the capability of the Berlin garrison. US commanders were equally concerned that they would face Soviet opposition as they transited the corridor between West Germany and Berlin. The Crisis also demonstrated the seventh and eighth lessons for Europeans: US support must never be taken for granted and European military capability matters.

On 13 August 1961 the German Democratic Republic began to construct the infamous Berlin Wall, as Churchill's 'iron curtain' became concrete reality. At 0530 hours on 18 August 1961 the First US Battlegroup, 18th Infantry, 8th Infantry Division moved out from Mannheim and moved to Helmstedt. At 0630 hours the following day the first US vehicles arrived at the Soviet checkpoint at the start of the autobahn which linked Berlin across East German territory. The Soviets made a perfunctory challenge, but eventually let the battlegroup through, which made it to Berlin that after-noon where the force was reviewed by US Vice-President Lyndon B. Johnson. Deterrence had been assured.

Europe and European defence

Lesson nine is that Europeans must also take responsibility for their own defence. On 9 May 1950, French Foreign Minister Robert Schuman stated a truism that should be on the wall of every European leader's office: 'World peace cannot be safeguarded without the making of creative efforts proportionate to the dangers which threaten it'.[11] The Schuman Declaration started Europe on a journey that would eventually lead to the European Union. However, Schuman also created another European defence dilemma that is both simple and enduring: if Europeans want the hard-pressed Americans to maintain their defence guarantee to Europe, then Europeans are going to have to take on more responsibility for their own defence, and build more and better armed forces (COVID-19 or no), and the Americans must not only accept such ambition, but encourage it.

The tenth lesson is that sound Allied planning, allied to sufficient European military capacity and capability, is a vital component of any credible European defence, reinforced by sufficient redundancy to cope with shocks such as COVID-19. A short survey of NATO's strategic concepts since its founding—the what, when, where, why, and how of Alliance action—demonstrates just what a challenge this particular lesson is for Europeans. It also reveals the enduring nature of many of the challenges critical to the effective and efficient defence of Europe. In January 1950, NATO made a sound defence and deterrence posture central to the Alliance mission, built on standardization of forces and equipment, and allied to proportionality of effort and the sharing of risks and burdens. In December 1950, with the outbreak of the Korean War, and with pressures growing on US forces worldwide, the need for much greater Allied efficiency of effort was highlighted by the creation of an integrated command structure. NATO's first Supreme Allied Commander Europe (SACEUR) was General Dwight D. Eisenhower, who oversaw the formation of the Supreme Headquarters Allied Powers Europe (SHAPE), first at Fontainebleau in France, and then later in Mons, Belgium. The choice of Mons was eloquent, for in August 1914 it was where the great set-piece battles of World War One effectively began when British and German troops clashed. It was also at Mons that World War One effectively ended when in November 1918 the Armistice was agreed as British Imperial forces advanced towards Germany.

The years between 1950 and 1954 were, in certain respects, a pivot for the Cold War organization of Europe's defence. The outbreak of the Korean War led Washington to demand that far more Europeans be deployed in

11. See Julian Lindley-French (2007) *A Chronology of European Security and Defence* (Oxford: Oxford University Press), p. 26.

their own defence. The most contentious US demand was for the use of German manpower and limited German rearmament. This led France to attempt the first great *démarche* in European defence integration through the supranational European Defence Community (EDC). Paris agreed to limited German rearmament but only if German forces were deeply embedded in a European command structure. The EDC also triggered a debate over European strategic autonomy from the US that continues to this day, particularly so when in 1954 the implications of Soviet atomic weaponry for European defence became apparent.

An uneasy Alliance

Lesson eleven is that alliances are never easy. Tensions within the Alliance intensified following the failure of Europeans to meet the ambitious force goals set at the 1952 Lisbon Summit which agreed the so-called Lisbon Force Goals on NATO force levels.[12] Under the plan, NATO Europeans were to deploy some twenty-five ready divisions and forty-eight reserve divisions within thirty days of an emergency being declared. With echoes of the contemporary debate over NATO force levels and readiness and with Europeans again under significant economic pressure in the wake of COVID-19, April 1953 saw the North Atlantic Council downgrade the force levels to thirty ready divisions (in fact a marginal increase) but only twenty-six reserve divisions. The decision confirmed a profound mismatch in favour of the Group of Soviet Forces Germany, and was of deep concern to Washington. The strategic concept that emerged enshrined the role of NATO as a nuclear alliance. The subsequent strategic concept, Massive Retaliation, embedded first use of nuclear weapons in Alliance doctrine and was to prove contentious throughout the Cold War.

Lesson twelve is that alliances must constantly adapt. In 1967 NATO moved away from Massive Retaliation to a more nuanced form of defence. Flexible Response enshrined the idea of proportionality and controlled

12. At the North Atlantic Council meeting of 20–25 February 1952 in Lisbon, Portugal Europeans were set a target of raising ninety-six divisions by 1954 at mobilization plus another thirty days for reserves to be called up. At no time did Europeans come close to realizing such a goal and have pretty much been missing Alliance force-level goals ever since. See Julian Lindley-French (2007) *A Chronology of European Security and Defence 1945–2007* (Oxford: Oxford University Press), p. 37.

escalation at the heart of Alliance doctrine, allied to the pursuit of a political settlement with the Soviet Union. Reflective of Germany's growing weight within the Alliance, December 1967 also saw delivery of the Harmel Report, which committed NATO to a new principle: defence and dialogue.[13]

Lesson thirteen is that the Alliance must be capable of contending successfully with political unrest within its ranks and fake news generated by adversaries. The 1967 strategic concept endured for the rest of the Cold War, but only just. The Euromissile controversy of the late 1970s and 1980s tested the transatlantic bond to the limit. The Americans had moved to counter the 1977 Soviet deployment of SS-20 triple-warhead nuclear missiles that could only strike targets in Western Europe by deploying both Cruise and Pershing 2 missiles that could also only hit targets in Eastern Europe and the Western Soviet Union. This decision led to profound domestic political strife in many NATO European countries that threatened to topple several governments. The crisis was fuelled by Soviet information operations that helped incite mass public disobedience. The crisis was only brought to an end with the December 1987 Intermediate Nuclear Forces Treaty, which was abandoned by both the US and Russia in August 2019.

Coping with peace

Lesson fourteen is that both the EU and NATO must align their efforts. The Intermediate-Range Nuclear Forces Treaty was the last throw of the strategic dice by a failing Soviet Union. With the November 1989 fall of the Berlin Wall and the 1991 collapse of the Soviet Union, many believed NATO's job was done and it too should be abolished. However, in 1991 the brief Gulf War saw much of NATO's training and preparation transposed to the sands of Kuwait and Iraq. At the 1991 Rome Summit, and following the withdrawal of Russian forces from much of the Warsaw Pact, the focus of NATO shifted away from Cold War defence and deterrence

---

13. The Harmel Report, entitled 'The Future Tasks of the Alliance: The Report of the Council', was presented to the North Atlantic Council on 13 December 1967. It stated: 'The Alliance is a dynamic and vigorous organization which is constantly adapting itself to changing conditions. Given such changes, people in NATO societies want action/protection and are not seeing it. It has also shown that its future tasks can be handled within the terms of the [Washington] Treaty by building on the methods and procedures which have proved their value over many years'. http://www.bits.de/NRANEU/nato-strategy/Harmel_Report_complete.pdf.

towards building partnerships with former adversaries. The European Allies wanted to make massive savings in their defence budgets by realizing what was euphemistically called 'defence premiums'.

Critically, NATO declared that it no longer had enemies, only friends. And yet, with the deployment of a vast array of new military technologies, much of it revealed to publics on television, the 1991 Gulf War also offered the first tentative steps towards the revolution in military technology that has gathered pace ever since.

The mid-1990s saw an effort to shift the Alliance towards crisis management and 'lighter' peacekeeping forces, particularly by Europeans. The European Allies within the EU enthusiastically embraced the idea that the Union could act collectively without the US, in the areas such peacekeeping and peace-making. However, the so-called Petersberg Tasks came up against hard, tragic reality, as the Balkans descended into an extensive period of blood-letting and genocide during the War of the Yugoslav Succession between 1991 and 1995. Prior to the 1995 Dayton Accord, and in the absence of clear American leadership, the European Allies had neither the capability nor the political will to act militarily in the former Yugoslavia in anything but the most permissive of operations.[14]

Lesson fifteen is that Europeans must fulfil their own defence ambitions. Europe's own defence aspirations were hollow. Indeed, at times there seemed a perverse correlation existed between the extent to which European forces were being cut and the many new empty acronyms that were created which implied a bright future for an autonomous European defence. The European Security and Defence Identity (ESDI), established first within NATO, which then later became the EU's European Security and Defence Policy (ESDP), exemplified and typified the problem. With the 1991 establishment of Eurocorps, some Americans were wary that European allies sought strategic autonomy from Washington. It is true that Gaullist elements in Paris did harbour grand ambitions for complete and eventual European strategic autonomy, including collective or common defence missions, but Britain and Germany demurred. Britain had concluded as far back as the disastrous 1956 Suez Crisis never again to cross

---

14. The Dayton Accord was signed on 12 November 1995 by the presidents of Bosnia-Herzegovina, Croatia, and Serbia and created a General Framework Agreement for peace in Bosnia, thus bringing one phase of extended war in the Western Balkans to a close. One of the authors, General (Ret.) John R. Allen, was the first US Marine Corps commander on the ground in Sarajevo after the signing of the Dayton Accord.

the Americans. Interestingly, France took the opposite view that France must never again be subject to what Paris saw as American *diktat*. Critically, a newly reunified Germany was content to rely on the Americans and NATO for its defence. Acutely conscious of its Nazi past, the newly restored Germany capital Berlin was also keen to avoid any suggestion that it was seeking to dominate Europe, let alone militarily.

The 1999 Washington Summit was a pivot between the optimism in many quarters in the immediate afterglow of the Cold War sand a more complex future. It took place against the backdrop of a short but violent war between NATO and Serbia over the fate of Kosovo and the Kosovars, the growing threat posed by Salafist Jihadis, and a Russia that had begun to abandon moves towards reinventing itself as a democracy and once again saw itself as an adversary of the Alliance. And then came 9/11. For a brief moment, not least on 12 September 2001, when NATO invoked Article 5, the Alliance seemed to rediscover solidarity in the immediate aftermath of the al-Qaeda attacks on New York and Washington. Indeed, 9/11 was the only time in its history the Alliance has ever invoked Article 5 and even sent NATO airborne early warning and control aircraft to help patrol American skies. However, as the Bush administration embarked on aggressive campaigns in both Afghanistan and Iraq, under the banner of the Global War on Terror, underlying tensions between the US and many of its European allies came to the surface, with France and Germany leading the opposition. The 2010 Lisbon strategic concept simply confirmed those divisions which have, by and large, existed ever since, by offering a post-9/11 Alliance for all seasons—collective defence, crisis management, and collective security—and for none.

Lesson sixteen is that the need to balance the ends, ways, and means of European defence will remain. Since the Lisbon Summit there have been several efforts to adapt the Alliance to face new threats and challenges which are ongoing. At the 2014 Wales Summit a Defence Investment Pledge (DIP) was agreed which sought to balance strategy, capability, and affordability at a time of austerity. It is worth quoting at some length given the implicit strategic ambition therein:

> Taking current commitments into account, we are guided by the following considerations: Allies currently meeting the NATO guideline to spend a minimum of 2% of their Gross Domestic Product (GDP) on defence will aim to continue to do so. Likewise, Allies spending more than 20% of their defence budgets on major equipment, including related Research &

Development, will continue to do so. Allies whose current proportion of GDP spent on defence is below this level will: halt any decline in defence expenditure; aim to increase defence expenditure in real terms as GDP grows; aim to move towards the 2% guideline within a decade with a view to meeting their NATO Capability Targets and filling NATO's capability shortfalls. Allies who currently spend less than 20% of their annual defence spending on major new equipment, including related Research & Development, will aim, within a decade, to increase their annual investments to 20% or more of total defence expenditures. All Allies will: ensure that their land, air and maritime forces meet NATO agreed guidelines for deployability and sustainability and other agreed output metrics; ensure that their armed forces can operate together effectively, including through the implementation of agreed NATO standards and doctrines.

It was also agreed progress would be reviewed annually.[15]

Lesson seventeen is the critical need for the Allies to adapt NATO for future war. Both the 2016 Warsaw Summit and 2018 Brussels Summit were a mix of ambition and contention over whether the commitment to the DIP was hard or soft. The challenge was made more difficult by the pressing need for the Alliance to adapt both its structures and posture to prepare for the hybrid, cyber, and hyperwar challenge of future war. The 2016 election of President Donald Trump introduced a hard and at times capricious edge to American demands for more equitable burden-sharing, even as the Alliance underwent extensive reforms to its command and force structure in an effort to engage around a new 360-degree threat horizon. And yet, mired in debt in the wake of the banking and financial crises, several European allies remained reluctant to meet even the limited obligations they signed up to. With the COVID-19 crisis, it is difficult to see those commitments being realized unless there is a radical change in the way Europeans generate and organize their defence. Future war NATO?

Integration or isolation?

Lesson eighteen is that political union comes before defence union and not as a consequence of it. As Europeans pushed for ever closer political union in the wake of the 1991 Treaty of Maastricht and as the European Community

---

15. See 'The Wales Summit Declaration', https://www.nato.int/cps/en/natohq/official_texts_112964.htm.

became the European Union, European defence became increasingly politicized. A series of initiatives were launched that had more to do with political integration than effective and efficient defence. In 1998, frustrated by the Balkan experience where Europe was utterly dependent on the US to handle a conflict in Europe, the UK and France agreed at St Malo to create a new military capability within the EU by extending the 1992 Petersberg Tasks. Such an EU military capability was designed to focus on effective crisis management whilst leaving what was then seen as residual collective defence to NATO. For the French, St Malo was the first step towards an EU that would one day provide the future centre of gravity for the defence of Europe by Europeans. This ambition was accompanied by political rhetoric that EU military capability was vital to balance US 'hyperpuissance'. Washington was simply concerned that the Europeans would not be up to the military tasks to which their lofty rhetoric referred, and if they were tested they would have to be rescued by the US. In December 1999, the Helsinki Declaration was agreed, according to which the EU would create an operational military capability by 2003 of 50–60,000 deployable person-nel within sixty days, sustainable for up to a year. The European Rapid Reaction Force was designed to meet the full range of the extended Peters-berg Tasks—from peacekeeping to peace-making.[16] In 2000, under the umbrella of the EU's Common Foreign and Security Policy, an EU Military Committee was for the first time also stood up, and in 2007 the Treaty of Lisbon created the Common Security and Defence Policy, which hinted at an eventual NATO-like collective defence role for the EU.

Lesson nineteen is that European defence strategy and European defence investment must be demonstrably linked. The problem was, and indeed remains, that defence investment by EU member-states has never kept pace with political aspirations. Few European states are willing to invest the sums needed to provide military forces for even existing EU and NATO missions. Nor do they want to give up sovereign control over when to send their young people into harm's way that a truly 'common' European defence

---

16. The 1992 Petersberg Tasks were progressively expanded. As the 2004 Venusberg Group report, 'A European Defence Strategy', stated: 'In 2003 the Draft Constitutional Treaty of the EU expanded the Petersberg Tasks to include, "joint disarmament operations, humani-tarian and rescue tasks, military advice and assistance tasks, conflict prevention, peacekeeping, tasks of combat forces in crisis management, including peace-making, and post conflict stabilisation'. See 'A European Defence Strategy', a report by the Venusberg Group (Gutesloh: Bertelsmann), p. 21.

would demand. The result is a form of politico-military stasis in which the defence of Europe has steadily become ever more entangled with the controversial creation of the political edifice called 'Europe'. The divisions within Europe and across the Atlantic have been further exacerbated by post-9/11 divisions over the scope and nature of US-led campaigns in Afghanistan and Iraq.

Then came the 2008 crash and now COVID-19. The banking and Eurozone crises crippled what little investment there was in European defence, and the COVID-19 crisis has simply (and greatly) magnified Europe's struggle to balance strategy, capability, and affordability given the threats it must collectively confront. And even though European leaders continue to agree to new initiatives and acronyms, such as Smart Defence, pooling and sharing, Permanent Structured Cooperation (PESCO), and the European Defence Fund, there are simply not the forces, resources, or political will to realize them. The result is the European defence of Europe today, in which in spite of the ambitions implicit in PESCO, the danger persists that Europeans are moving inexorably towards a lowest-common-denominator European force, an analogue 'European Army' in a digital age which simply bolts together a lot of European legacy forces. COVID-19 is only likely to accelerate this process. If PESCO could be grounded in defence-strategic reality and suffused with sufficient ambition to help forge what no single European state can aspire to by itself, and still be 'owned' by the states that created it, then PESCO could have both place and purpose in the future defence of Europe. If not . . .

A new hinge of history?

Lesson twenty is that Europeans must not dwell on the fading memory of the post-Cold War peace. The August 2019 British decision to reconstitute the 6th Division to fight and win on the cyber and information battlefields of future war matches the American War Cloud initiative to fight to effect in a digital, information age.[17] Such forces will be a critical element in the

17. As Professor Paul Cornish notes in a piece for The Alphen Group, 'The Joint Enterprise Defense Infrastructure (JEDI—informally known as "War Cloud") is the US Department of Defense's programme to enable US armed forces to operate and to prevail in the information age'. He also notes the future of the programme is now in doubt. See Paul Cornish, 'War

deterrence of future war across the span of 5D warfare. Europeans will need to embrace the information-led digital 5D future defence they will need that can counter disinformation, destabilization, disruption, deception, and destruction. Such a twenty-first-century European defence would necessarily be built on a European future military force that could also master the multiple domains of air, sea, land, cyber, space, information, and knowledge, powered by the revolution in military technology, which will increasingly see the application to the battlespace of artificial intelligence, big data, machine-learning, super- and quantum-computing, et al.[18] Irrespective of COVID-19, only with such a force can European defence, and thus European deterrence, be maintained credibly, from which European strategic autonomy might one day emerge.

Throughout the Cold War, and in spite of the many tensions and contentions therein, the Atlantic Alliance never ceased adapting. The driving impetus for such adaptation was the dilemma that has dogged NATO since its foundation in April 1949: how to maintain sufficient conventional forces of the right type and scope at a sufficient level of capability, capacity, readiness, and affordability to make the resort to nuclear weapons a last resort. That challenge, far from disappearing, will only intensify.

The contemporary history of European defence suggests that future war will impose the same level of challenge on Europeans as they faced in the early days of the Cold War. What matters is that Europeans collectively generate the required defence outcomes that are proportionate to the dangers that threaten it, as Robert Schuman suggested. Critically, any such effort will also need to be consistent with the effective maintenance of a credible transatlantic security relationship via the equitable sharing of twenty-first-century burdens that a deep and enduring relationship will demand and entail. The mistake many in Europe now make is to believe that 'strategic autonomy' is the natural heir-apparent to the 1950 Schuman Declaration, and thus the consequence of a political process, rather than of defence investment. Worse, with COVID-19, not a few might give up completely on their own defence. However, the history of the transatlantic

Clouds on the Horizon', The Alphen Group, September 2019, https://thealphengroup.home. blog.

18. Some caution is needed with regard to quantum-computing and its likely application. At the 2020 Davos World Economic Forum Google Chief Executive Officer, Sundar Pinchai, announced a 'breakthrough' in Google's quantum-computing unit which will lead to its full utility being exploited, but only after another decade of development.

relationship is clear: it can only be credible if it is underpinned by a level of European military capability and capacity that is both fair to the American taxpayer and proportionate to the defence of Europe. Those outcomes will only be achieved by increased European investment in a twenty-first-century European defence. Whether it is achieved via the creation of a European Army, or more likely via an army of Europeans, European states are going to have to generate significantly more on defence than they do now, and create far more advanced, deployable forces, even amidst the economic wreckage of COVID-19.

The final lesson from history is thus: deep European defence integration is unlikely to be realized until there is deeper political integration, and given the nature of the risks, challenges, and threats Europeans are likely to face in the post-COVID-19 world, neither Americans nor Europeans can afford to wait. There is one other lesson: Europeans must learn their own contemporary history critically and impartially, not selectively and in a self-serving manner.

3

Russia and Europe's northern and eastern flanks

Another bloody European war?

What threat does Russia pose to Europe? One the many great unknowns in the post-COVID-19 era will be the impact the pandemic has on Russia's foreign, security, and defence policy and thus what threat Moscow will pose to peace. After an early bout of Russian triumphalism in which the Kremlin claimed to be far better prepared to cope with COVID-19 than its Western counterparts, even sending 'aid' to Italy and the US, a dark realism set in. On 12 April 2020 President Putin admitted, 'We have a lot of problems and don't have much to brag about, nor reason to, and we certainly can't relax'.[1] This admission was given extra poignancy when news emerged that the Russian Prime Minister, Mikhail Mishustin, had contracted COVID-19. However, there is a raft of evidence that counsels caution in dealing with Russia, and whilst a sound defence strategy in Europe must be built around constant efforts to engage with Moscow, sound planning also demands a firm focus on dealing with the possible worst of Russian actions.

After all, as recently as 2018, General Sir Mark Carleton-Smith, Head of the British Army, said that Russia posed a bigger threat than Daesh, and that Moscow would seek to exploit any vulnerability and any weakness.[2] It is also certainly true that Russian concepts of 'defence' are evolving fast as the Kremlin's use of coercion sees an increasingly sophisticated use of soft power and hard power (sharp power) in harness. For contemporary Russia,

---

1. Anton Troinovski, 'Putin's Bleak Covid-19 Admission: We Don't Have Much to Brag About', 13 April 2020, https://www.nytimes.com/2020/04/13/world/europe/coronavirus-russia-putin.html.
2. 'British army chief: Russia "far bigger threat than IS"', BBC News, 24 November 2019, https://www.bbc.com/news/uk-46327046.

'defence' is underpinned by offence, whilst the offence now stretches far beyond the traditional Russian focus on the shock use of huge military force. Indeed, the very utility of contemporary Russian force must also be assured by first creating controlled chaos in adversary states, before such chaos can be imposed on Russia.[3] Russia is equally conscious of the damage a cyber-attack might do to its ability to function. Indeed, many in the West fail to understand the sense of vulnerability which pervades the Kremlin and which drives it to seek ever more control. In March 2019, the *Los Angeles Times* reported Russian plans to effectively 'Balkanize' the internet by 'creating a "sovereign" network that the Kremlin could shut off from the Greater World Wide Web'.[4] This would be something similar to the so-called Great Firewall of China, which is not only designed to control media content, but also to limit the extent to which foreign actors can damage China with sustained cyber-attacks. It is also reported that the first tests of such a shut-off took place prior to 1 April 2020. However, it took China some ten years to construct the Great Firewall and it is questionable if Russia has the technology to completely isolate itself from cyber space.

Complex strategic coercion and the nature of future war

For all the undoubted importance of new technologies, relative military strength will remain central to Europe's future war defence and deterrence, and the willingness to use it. Recent deployments by Russia of new weapons systems and the nature of those systems reveals something of Moscow's

3. In a fascinating critique of a 2016 Russian work by Igor Popov and Musa Khamzatov entitled *The War of the Future: A Conceptual Framework and Practical Considerations. Essays on Strategic Thought*, Gudrun Persson of the Swedish Defence Research Agency cites General Valery Gerasimov: 'in the era of globalisation, the weakening of state borders and development of means of communication are the most important factors changing the form of interstate conflicts. In today's conflicts, the focus of the methods used to combat them is shifting towards the integrated application of political, economic, informational, and other non-military measures, implemented with the support of the military force. The so-called hybrid methods'. See Gudrun Persson (2017) *The War of the Future: A Conceptual Framework and Practical Conclusions—Essays on Strategic Thought* (Rome: NDC), p. 10.

4. Sabra Ayres, 'Russia Wants to Unplug Its Internet from the Rest of the World. Is That Even Possible?', 4 March 2019, https://www.latimes.com/world/europe/la-fg-russia-internet-20190304-story.html.

strategic mind-set. To understand such a mind-set, it is important to consider Russian strategy from a Russian perspective.

In April 2019, a 'new' Russian submarine, Belgorod, moved slowly but silkily from the Severodvinsk dry dock in which she had been built. Weighing in at 14,700 tons, the nuclear-powered Belgorod was adapted using the unfinished hull of an Oscar-class submarine and is roughly 40 per cent bigger than an American Virginia-class nuclear attack submarine, and twice as big as a British Astute-class nuclear attack submarine.[5] Believed to be a one-off, but pointing to the future of Russian submarine design, Belgorod is a 'special missions and research boat' designed primarily to support what are called 'special missions' and will carry manned and unmanned underwater vehicles for which she will act as the mother ship. On the surface, Russia's newest submarine, and the world's longest, looks little different from the enormous Soviet nuclear ballistic missile submarines of the past, such as the Typhoon-class. Dive deeper and she represents an entirely new threat as she is armed with the Poseidon or Status-6 Oceanic Multipurpose system (NATO codename Kanyon), and a nuclear-powered, nuclear-tipped autonomous attack system specifically designed to evade US defences.

The drones she will carry are also designed to avoid all current US and NATO defences, and could render coastal cities, naval bases, and deployed Allied task groups and submarines far more vulnerable than hitherto, as her drones make the sea less opaque. Belgorod is also fitted with an underwater dock that will enable it to launch miniature submarines, swarms of drones, and intelligence-gathering capabilities. One aim is to threaten transatlantic underwater communications, as well as cable, oil, and gas infrastructures. Belgorod will also spend much of its active life operating from so-called 'bastions', protected sea-spaces from which in a war Russian submarines would launch ballistic nuclear missiles.

However, Belgorod is also capable of carrying a family of unmanned, nuclear-powered, nuclear-tipped long-range drones that could either devastate a NATO task group or even much of the eastern seaboard of the United States. Designed by the Rubin Design Bureau, the Poseidon system (previously known as the Status-9 oceanic multipurpose, underwater system), together with Skif, a weapon designed to 'sleep' on the sea-bed until

---

5. The Oscar-class of SSGN submarine were designed in the Soviet era to act as a nuclear-powered cruise missile platform. The first was deployed as far back as 1975.

activated, can both be used as so-called third-strike, 'doomsday' weapons capable of carrying a COBALT-60 nuclear warhead of up to 100 mega-tons of TNT.[6] Capable of accelerating during the final phase of its approach to up to 120 mph/190 kph using 'super-cavitation' technology, both systems have a range of over 5,000 nautical miles/8,000 kilometres. Whilst their roots date back to the Soviet era, there is evidence the Skif was deployed as recently as April 2020. Paul Schulte, a former arms control specialist at the UK Ministry of Defence, stated, 'The *Skif* appears to be a last resort doomsday weapon, intended to symbolise that Russia can never be defeated. It poses an outlandish strategic challenge to the West'.[7]

On 24 March 2018, at the Russian Academy of Military Sciences, the Chief of the Russian General Staff, General Valeriy Gerasimov, offered the Russian view of future war. Gerasimov said the conduct of operations would be 'a transition from sequential and concentrated actions to continuous and distributed ones, conducted simultaneously in all spheres of confrontation, and also in distant theatres of military operations'.[8] In the speech, Gerasimov not only envisioned the drastically changing character of war, but also sought to drive it forward. The Gerasimov Doctrine, as some have called it, is designed to weaken adversaries from within by inciting a 'war of all against all'.[9] This approach is particularly tailored for use against democratic adversaries with open societies and multiple communities with a myriad of identities.

He could succeed. In many European states the relationship between the state and the citizen appears to be fast changing, driven by the many influences to which the individual citizen is subject, not least through social media.[10] It is the increasingly contested polis within European states, in

---

6. The Rubin Design Bureau for Marine Engineering is based in St Petersburg and is one of three centres for the design of Russian submarines and underwater drones, and the most advanced.

7. See Chris Hughes, 'Russia Designs World's Biggest "Doomsday" Bomb That Can Be Activated Remotely', 30 April 2020, https://www.mirror.co.uk/news/world-news/russia-designs-worlds-biggest-doomsday-21955137.

8. See '(More) Gerasimov on Future War', *Russian Defence Policy*, 30 March 2018, https://russiandefpolicy.blog/2018/03/30.

9. Thomas Hobbes in *Leviathan*, when elaborating on what he saw as the 'state of nature', famously adapted the Roman idea of 'war of all against all' in *De Cive*. Hobbes wrote, 'Hereby, it is manifest, that during the time men live without a common Power to keep them all in awe, they are in that condition which is called Warre; and such a warre, as is of every man, against every man'. It would be interesting to hear what Hobbes thinks about the societal impact of COVID-19. Richard Tuck (ed.) (1991) *Hobbes' Leviathan* (Cambridge: Cambridge University Press), p. 88.

10. *The Road to Somewhere* by liberal philosopher David Goodhart addressed one of the major divides in contemporary Western society as between those who came from 'somewhere',

which social and political allegiances are so fluid, that the Russians believe opportunity exists for action across the 5Ds of disinformation, deception, destabilization, disruption, and implied and actual destruction in pursuit of Moscow's narrowly defined interests. Russia's use of 5D warfare applies complex coercion from the low end of the conflict spectrum (hybrid warfare) to the very high end (hyperwar). Fake news via social media, interference in elections, and a host of other actions would redefine the relationship and indeed the boundaries between peace and war, as Moscow employed the West's freedoms and openness against it, and exploited that most potent of political weapons—denial.

Russian complex strategic coercion is reinforced and underpinned by the threat of overwhelming conventional military power, particularly at the margins of both NATO and the EU by threatening weaker states, such as those in the Baltic Sea and Black Sea regions, as well as Finland, Norway, and Sweden, at a time and place of Russia's choosing. Such coercion is underpinned by the constant and implicit threat of nuclear and other means of mass destruction and mass disruption (COVID-29?) to intimidate European governments and their respective peoples. In the worst case, the threat of mass destruction would be used to deter the US and NATO from making any attempt to restore seized areas to their legitimate governments. President Putin calls this 'changing the facts on the ground'.[11]

Russian ambitions are strengthened by their grasp of the growing relationship in future war between (dis)information, strategy, capability, and technology. Indeed, it is precisely the fusion of these four elements of warfare into an 'affordable' warfighting strategy that Gerasimov has been pioneering for at least a decade. However, Russia's use of complex strategic

---

rooted in one place and socially conservative, and those that came from 'anywhere', who moved from country to country and were often more liberal in their views. The book fails to address those who move from country to country of origin. At least two of the authors of this book fall into the latter category. See David Goodhart (2017) *The Road to Somewhere: The Populist Revolt and the Future of Politics* (London: Hurst).

11. In a February 2015 speech, President Putin accused the West of 'creating facts on the ground'. 'We have presented our arguments more than once, and I will not repeat them in detail here. But unfortunately our Western partners ignore and dismiss them. We are concerned because, even though it is not yet clear how our "new" relationship with NATO will work, they are creating facts on the ground. This definitely does not promote trust. Furthermore, this kind of conduct has a negative effect on global issues, as it prevents us from developing a positive agenda in international relations and stalls the process of readjusting them in a constructive vein'. See 'Vladimir Putin: Russia and the Changing World', GlobalResearch.com, 15 February 2015, https://www.globalresearch.ca/vladimir-putin-russia-and-the-changing-world/5477500.

coercion is not simply limited to a Russian tendency towards strategic intimidation, as such coercion could also be used to mask Russian force concentrations prior to any major attack on NATO and EU states. Over time adversaries become de-sensitized to low-level coercion and see it as 'white' noise, part of the new 'normal' in an engineered unstable relationship between Russia and its neighbours, affording Moscow the ability to apply pressure where and when it wishes across a whole swath of Europe. By using the implicit threat of force to keep the Western allies off-balance, Moscow effectively offsets any innate advantages afforded the US and its European allies by either their nominally stronger forces, or greater economic and financial resources.

Why complex strategic coercion?

Moscow's complex coercive strategy is driven by a world-view that combines a very particular view of Russian history with the political culture of the Kremlin that is little different from that of Russia prior to the October 1917 Bolshevik Revolution, or indeed thereafter. For Russia, the end of the Cold War was a humiliating defeat, which saw power in Europe move decisively away from Moscow to Berlin and Brussels. For Moscow, the loss of all-important prestige was compounded by NATO and EU enlargement as 'proof' of the designs of an insidious West to destroy what Russians see as the 'legitimate' legacy of the Great Patriotic War, and with it Russian influence in Europe and beyond.

The Russian seizure of Crimea in February 2014 was a case study in complex strategic coercion and a cynical application of Moscow's worldview. During an all-night meeting from 22–23 February that was overseen by President Putin, well-established plans for the seizure of Crimea were finalized, and the order to act given. On 27 February, pro-Russian gunmen seized the parliament building in Simferopol, the capital of Crimea, along with other government buildings. A day later Russian-speaking armed combat soldiers wearing no insignia seized two key airports. On 1 March, the Russian parliament, the Duma, approved President Putin's 'request' for force to be used in Crimea and across much of Ukraine. In a plebiscite on 16 March, some 97 per cent of voters balloted voted for Crimea to be absorbed into the Russian Federation. Two days later President Putin signed a decree confirming the annexation of Crimea. The coercion did not stop there. On

7 April, pro-Russian protesters occupied Ukrainian government buildings in Donetsk, Luhansk, and Kharkov and demanded independence from Kiev. Finally, in May 2015 Donetsk and Luhansk declared 'independence' from Ukraine and also carried out plebiscites. During the entire campaign Western states routinely accused Moscow of orchestrating unrest, not least through the use of fake news and social media, and by supplying forces and resources to aid the rebels, but did little to counter Russia.

Should the West have been surprised? Shortly after the 25 December 2015 publication of the new Russian National Security Strategy, Olga Oliker of the Center for Strategic and International Studies wrote,

> Whatever your personal preference on this point, it's hard not to come away from the strategy with Tom Petty's 'I Won't Back Down' playing in the back of your head. It presents a Russia focused on increasing its influence and prestige and cementing its national unity; a Russia that believes that it is accomplishing its aims, but which simultaneously feels threatened by the United States and its allies. Russia is also concerned about its economy, which Moscow knows is in deep trouble (and not just because of Western sanctions, convenient as they are to blame). In short, this is the strategy document of an ambitious Russia that sees constraints on its ambitions as threats to be overcome, whether they come from within or without.[12]

Since 2009, Russia has been on a course to re-establish what Moscow sees as Russia's rightful Great Power status after almost twenty years of what the Kremlin believes is Western-imposed humiliation. The lofty ideas of partnership with the West of the 1990s have been replaced by a shifting mix of conditional cooperation and confrontation. This duality in Russian strategy is reflected in Article 8 of the December 2015 Russian National Security Strategy which states, 'Russia has demonstrated the ability to safeguard sovereignty, independence, and state and territorial integrity and to protect the rights of compatriots abroad. There has been an increase in the Russian Federation's role in resolving the most important international problems, settling military conflicts, and ensuring strategic stability and the supremacy of international law in interstate relations'.[13]

---

12. See Olga Oliker, 'Unpacking Russia's New National Security Strategy', 7 January 2016 (Washington, DC: CSIS), https://www.csis.org/analysis/unpacking-russias-new-national-security-strategy.
13. 'The Russian National Security Strategy', 31 December 2015, http://www.ieee.es/Galerias/fichero/OtrasPublicaciones/Internacional/2016/Russian-National-Security-Strategy-31Dec2015.pdf.

That Russia felt able to undertake such a military campaign is indicative of the changes President Putin has made to the Russian military. As early as 2007, Russia announced it would professionalize and modernize its armed forces. The relatively poor performance of Russian forces in 2008 during Moscow's seizure of parts of Georgia simply reinforced the Kremlin's determination to rebuild a force seen as central to state power. As Julian Cooper of the University of Birmingham notes in his study of the 2010 State Armaments Programme,

> The aim of the programme was to increase the share of modern armaments held by the armed forces from 15 per cent in 2010 to 30 per cent in 2015 and 70 per cent in 2020. The programme has been implemented through the budget-funded annual state defence order supplemented by state guaranteed credits. By 2014, the military output of the defence industry was growing at an annual rate of over 20 per cent, compared with 6 per cent three years earlier. The volume of new weapons procured steadily increased, the rate of renewal being particularly strong in the strategic missile forces and the air force, but not as impressive in the navy and ground forces. In 2014 the work of the defence industry began to be affected by the Ukraine crisis, with a breakdown of military-related deliveries from Ukraine and the imposition of sanctions by NATO and European Union member countries. The perform-ance of the economy began to deteriorate, putting pressure on state finances. It was decided to postpone for three years the approval of the successor state armament programme, 2016–25. Nevertheless, the implementation of the programme to date has secured a meaningful modernisation of the hardware of the Russian armed forces for the first time since the final years of the USSR.[14]

The bulk of those new forces are now well established in the Central and Western Military Districts which abut the Ukrainian border, and much of the eastern border of the EU and NATO. The equipment used by the deployed force in Crimea also revealed Russia's evolving military method, specifically the crucial role for both Special Forces (Spetsnaz) and specialized forces. This reflects the efforts Moscow has made to improve the deploy-ability and jointness of its elite professional forces. Critically, Ukrainian forces had benefited from no such modernization and the upper echelons of the Ukrainian political and military's command chain were also deeply

---

14. See Julian Cooper (2016) *Russia's State Armament Programme to 2020: A Quantitative Assessment of Implementation 2011–2015* (Stockholm: FOI), Summary.

split, as many senior Ukrainian officers owed their appointment to Putin's ally, former President Yanukovich.[15]

The Russian national interest under Putin

Putin came to power in 2000 in the wake of the chaotic years of the Yeltsin regime, with much of that chaos blamed by Russians on the West. The Putin regime has subsequently sought to consolidate its domestic power by appealing to nostalgic Russian notions of power and fear. The regime has also endeavoured to recreate the image of a Russia powerful enough to re-capture the influence Moscow enjoyed in the 1950s and 1960s at the height of Soviet superpower. In 2013, US Secretary of State John Kerry gave equal billing to Russia in the handling of the Syria crisis, which only served to enhance the reputation of the regime at home and its influence abroad.

Putin is essentially a strategic opportunist. The 2014 withdrawal of two US Brigade Combat Teams from Europe may have seemed a small event, in and of itself, but taken together with President Obama's 'pivot' to Asia, Putin and his team began to question the depth of the American commit-ment to Europe's defence. President Putin also has little truck with ideas of 'international community' and is contemptuous of the idea of 'civil power', so fashionable in European elite circles. Critically, Russia's military renais-sance has taken place in parallel with the Western checks in both Afghanistan and Iraq, and the loss of collective strategic nerve particularly in Europe. The Kremlin is also acutely conscious of Europe's economic travails post-2008 and the *de facto* disarmament many Europeans countries undertook that saw defence investment fall precipitously, even whilst many of them were engaged in extended campaigns in both Afghanistan and Iraq.[16] The refusal

15. In March 2016, one of the authors, Julian Lindley-French, paid a visit to Kiev to give a speech about how to craft national strategy to the Committee of National Security and Defence of the Ukrainian Parliament. The occasion was the very first time the Head of the Committee and the Chief of the Ukrainian Defence Staff had met.

16. To be fair, Lucie Beraud-Sudreau of the International Institute for Strategic Studies (IISS) in a February 2018 article made the following observation. 'Following years of defence cuts, after the end of the Cold War and the 2008 financial crisis, Europe began to reinvest in defence in 2014–15. Two key factors explain this turn of events. Firstly, the economic situation has improved across the continent. Although unemployment remains high in some countries, such as France, Italy and Spain, most states experienced stronger GDP growth rates in 2017, and have more fiscal space to increase defence budgets. Secondly, threat perceptions have significantly changed, with some threats from the south and from the east becoming more

of all but a few NATO European states to meet the 2014 NATO Wales Summit commitment to spend 2 per cent of GDP by 2024 (of which 20 per cent had to be spent per annum on new equipment) also helped Moscow conclude that Europeans lacked the will and capability to block its regional-strategic ambitions, particularly with regard to Ukraine.

However, there are risks, even dangers, for the Putin regime from such an aggressive posture. Whilst the seizure of parts of Ukraine in the short term strengthened the grip of Putin over Russia, Russia faces deep demographic and economic challenges which, unless addressed, will see Russia continue to fade as the West, China, and others eclipse Moscow.[17] Moreover, the east of Ukraine was particularly vulnerable to Russian interference, and even there the performance of Russian forces was unimpressive on occasions. The July 2014 shooting down of Malaysian Airlines flight MH17 by a Russian Army missile battery and the loss of some 300 lives, 198 of whom were Dutch, revealed major failings in Russian command and control.[18] Moscow must now also contend with the impact of the COVID-19 crisis on the Russian economy and the slump in oil and gas exports.

immediate. This is coupled with the general impression among capitals of a more unstable world, and alliance bonds less certain than before'. The flaw in this argument is that defence spending is relative and in overall terms Europe's defence outputs still lag behind those of its main peer competitors and, crucially, the United States. See Lucie Beraud-Sudreau, 'European Defence Spending: The New Consensus', The Military Balance Blog, IISS, 15 February 2018, https://www.iiss.org/blogs/military-balance/2018/02/european-defence-spending.

17. Bobo Lo and Lilia Shevtsova in an authoritative and insightful book write, 'The major problem is the economic model itself, which is based on four pillars—state control, monopoly-building, a commodity-based structure, and militaristic aspects. It is, of course, logical that a monopoly of political power in Russia is accompanied by state monopolism in the economy. True, this phenomenon is not an inevitable feature of all authoritarian regimes. In Russia this type of monopolism is the result of the traditional fusion of power and property, and the attempt of the personalized power to preserve tight control over economic life and not allow independent actors to emerge there'. See Bobo Lo and Lilia Shevtsova (2012) *A 21st Century Myth: Authoritarian Modernization in Russia and China* (Moscow: Carnegie Moscow Center), p. 17, https://carnegieendowment.org/files/BoboLo_Shevtsova_web.pdf.

18. The September 2016 report by the Joint Investigation Team (JIT) states: 'The JIT has been able to identify a large part of the route concerning the arrival and the departure of the BUK-TELAR. This was the result of intercepted telephone conversations, witness statements, photographs and videos that had been posted on social media, and a video never shown before which was obtained from a witness. The system was transported from Russian territory into eastern Ukraine and was later transported on a white Volvo truck with a low-boy trailer. The truck was escorted by several other vehicles and by armed men in uniform'. See JIT, 'Flight MH17 Was Shot Down by a BUK Missile from a Farmland Near Pervomaiskyi', 28 September 2016, Dutch Public prosecutor, https://www.om.nl/@96068/jit-flight-mh17-shot.

Equally, it would be a mistake to believe COVID-19 will make Russia any less aggressive. If the regime's grip on power is weakened, there is the very real danger that Russia could become more, not less aggressive. Moscow's cynical use of power is likely to endure, as it is a central element of Russian strategic culture. The strategic rationale for future action, given the way the Kremlin thinks, is also likely to endure with the long-held belief that a successful intervention in, say, the Baltic States would not only straighten Russia's strategic defence line, create a buffer zone with NATO, and thus consolidate a Russian sphere of influence, but also critically strengthen the regime against growing domestic criticism, especially as President Putin gets older. The Arctic and the High North are also areas of significant strategic interest for Russia, not least because of the natural resources that are believed to lie on and under the sea-bed. The opening up of a so-called north-east sea passage across Russia's north would drastically shorten sea-lines of communication between Europe and Asia, which Moscow would effectively control and is keen to exploit. In other words, if Russia under Putin believes it can succeed through the use of force either because Europe is too weak and divided to stop it, or the Americans too distracted, then in certain circumstances Moscow might be tempted to act.

How could the West respond short of war? The Allies, with Europeans to the fore, would need first to recognize the pending threat and use all non-military and military tools at their disposal to force the Kremlin to reconsider the costs versus benefits of any such action. Europeans would also need to focus diplomatic efforts on building a countervailing coalition, possibly even with post-COVID-19 China if Beijing decides for cooperation rather than confrontation. After all, Beijing has traditionally disliked sovereignty grabs, albeit when committed by other powers. At the same time, an ever resource-hungry China is also very interested in exploiting Russian oil and gas and sees the opening of the north-east passage as a new strategic artery to enable the import of Russian hydrocarbons. Such a convergence of Chinese and Russian interest is likely to undermine Western efforts to force Moscow to change policy through the use of economic sanctions. At most, Europeans could impose heavy sanctions on key officials, suspend Aeroflot flights to Europe and North America and reduce Gazprom's influence over the European energy market. Thus far, existing sanctions, whilst causing some inconvenience, have not deterred Moscow from its settled policy of coercive behaviour. The US, NATO, and the EU did take some action after the invasion of Crimea, and the March 2018 use of nerve toxins by GRU agents in the English town of Salisbury. However, European states remain too divided over how to deal with Russia, not least because of effective Russian statecraft. In September 2019, the French Foreign Minister, Jean-Yves Le Drian, even called for a 'reset' in EU–Russia relations.[19]

The traditional Russian reliance on force as a key component of Russian influence has reinforced the tendency of the Putin regime to imagine (and manufacture) a new threat to Russia from the West. Threat of force has thus again come to be seen by the increasingly 'securitized' Russian state as a key and legitimate component of Russian 'defence', albeit these days more hammer and nail than hammer and sickle. Hard though it is for many European observers to understand, it is not hard to see how Russia, with its particular history, and Putin's Kremlin with its very particular world-view, has come again to this viewpoint. The mistake for European leaders would be to believe that such a world-view is merely a strategic gambit and not a deeply believed 'principle' at the very pinnacle of power in Russia. It is, and COVID-19 could well harden such an adversarial belief system.

Critically, the strategic opportunism implicit in Moscow's complex coer-cive strategy is also afforded by an under-defended Europe, a fractured transatlantic relationship, and an overstretched America faced with the rise of Xi's increasingly aggressive China. Brexit has also reinforced Russian prejudices about the EU. From the Russian perspective the supine British political and bureaucratic elite are an example of what happens to an old Power that tries to accommodate a German-centric European Commission on its historic mission to unite all the peoples of Europe via the aggregation of state power into some form of superpower organized around, and for, Berlin. For the Kremlin there is no such thing as 'community' in inter-national relations; only power, the balance or otherwise thereof, and the zero-sum reality of winners and losers.

How strong are Russia's armed forces?

Just how strong are Russia's armed forces? Russian complex strategic coer-cion is ultimately dependent on a Russian military force sufficiently capable of winning a major war with the advanced expeditionary conventional and

---

19. See Andrew Rittman, 'France Calls for EU-Russia Reset', *EU Observer*, 10 September 2019, https://euobserver.com/foreign/145886.

nuclear capabilities such a war would demand. Given that context, there are three elements to Russian strategy which provide the all-important strategic rationale for Russia's military modernization: intent, opportunity, and capability. Russia's military modernization began with the so-called 'New Look' reforms and the ten-year State Armament Programme from 2011 to 2020.[20] The main elements of the programme were updated Russian Aerospace Forces, enhanced and tightened strategic command and control, new advanced weaponry, and a more professional cadre of officers and non-commissioned officers (NCOs).

The role of force in both policy and strategic communications is central to Moscow's method and any understanding of Russia's use of complex strategic coercion. The Russian Aerospace Forces are particularly important to wider national strategy and a vital component in Moscow's coercive posture because they act as a 'showroom' to Europe (and beyond) of Russian military, and thus strategic capability. It is notable that the biggest tranche of funding in the Strategic Armaments Programme was invested in the development of highly deployable airborne forces, the Russian Air Force and air defence. Whilst most comparable European air forces have seen a marked reduction in combat aircraft since 2014, the Russian Air Force received more than 1,000 new aircraft of both fixed-wing and rotary-wing variants over the same period.[21]

Critically, much investment has been committed to the procurement of new advanced offensive weaponry, such as hypersonic missiles, notably the Avangard, Kinzhal, and Zircon systems. A new intercontinental ballistic missile, the SR28 Sarmat, has been deployed, together with further deployments of mobile systems such as TOPOL M, as well as a raft of short and (controversially) intermediate-range systems, such as the 9M729 Novator (NATO classification SSC-8). According to NATO, it was the Novator system that breached the now defunct Intermediate Nuclear Forces Treaty (INF) and raised the prospect of the US strategic arsenal again being 'decoupled' from the defence of NATO Europe.[22] Novator was the major

20. For an excellent study of Russia's military modernization see Anton Lavrov, 'Russian Military Reform from Georgia to Syria', November 2018 (Washington, DC: CSIS).
21. As above, p. xx.
22. 'Decoupling' was the main aim of Soviet strategy during the latter years of the Cold War. The aim was to neuter the deterrent value of the US nuclear shield to Europe both by threatening the annihilation of the American homeland in the event of a war in Europe, and/or by deploying nuclear systems that in the first instance would limit a war to Europe and thus lead a

factor in Washington's February 2019 decision to withdraw from the INF Treaty and the August 2019 test-firing of an enhanced Mk41 Tomahawk Land Attack Cruise Missile (TLAM) that also breached the treaty, implying the start of a new arms race with profound implications for European defence.[23] Russian nuclear torpedoes have also been tested, as well as new ship-busting systems, including a nuclear-tipped drone earmarked for the Russian nuclear attack submarines, which will also carry the highly advanced nuclear-capable SS-N-18.

Russia's air defence forces have also been markedly upgraded as part of a new multi-layered anti-access/area denial (A2/AD) air defence that current and planned NATO European forces would find hard to penetrate. To that end, the Russian Air Force has created forty-four new missile battalions armed with the advanced S-400 surface-to-air missile and other systems, designed specifically to shoot down US F-16 and, quite possibly, F-35 fighters. Critically, Russia's space-based systems are also being modernized with eighty-five new military satellites, twenty-one of which offer high-resolution imagery and high-speed data transfer, raising the prospect that future war will become progressively space-based as arms control erodes. After all, much of the arms control architecture dates back to the 1960s and early 1970s.[24]

It is Moscow's efforts to seek decisive comparative advantage through technology that should most concern European governments. Russia is investing a significant amount of effort and money to better exploit unmanned and robotic systems, with particular importance placed on the increased use of drones to enable tactical and operational reconnaissance. Whilst the US is also making great strides forward in these areas, the response of most Europeans to what could lead to a sea-change in the character and speed of warfare has been partial and fragmented. Moscow is also

---

US president to conclude that it was too risky to escalate to first use of nuclear weapons, the core policy of NATO's Article 5 collective defence.

23. Paul McLeary, *Defense News*, 19 August 2019, 'US Fires INF-Busting Missile, First Test Since Treaty Signed', https://breakingdefense.com/2019/08/us-fires-inf-busting-missile-first-test-since-treaty-signed.

24. The so-called 'Outer Space Treaty' or, more formally, 'The Treaty on Principles Governing the Activities of States on the Exploration and Use of Outer Space, including the Moon and Other Celestial Bodies', was one of the first true arms control treaties and was opened for signature on 27 January 1967 by the UK, US, and USSR. One hundred and nine states are now party to the Treaty, whilst twenty-three have signed but as yet have not ratified the Treaty. The Treaty does not ban the placing of military weapons in space, but does prohibit the placing of weapons of mass destruction therein.

endeavouring to develop both heavy (long-range) reconnaissance and strike drones, although it will be some time before such systems can be fielded.

Perhaps the most impressive developments in the modernization of Russia's armed forces has been at the highest echelons of strategic command and control. The National Defence Management Centre (NDMC) at Moscow's Znamdenka 19 was established on 1 December 2014, and acts as the brains of a force that is fast becoming steadily more capable across the conflict spectrum. At one level, the NDMC appears to be a twenty-first-century upgrade to the old Stavka, the high command, administrative staff, and general headquarters of the Imperial and Soviet eras. It is also far more than that. The specific remit of the NDMC is to ensure presidential strategy is realized through the efficient and effective application of force and resource, and thus reports directly to President Putin. The NDMC is also the latest Russian attempt to resolve a perpetual balancing act for Moscow between the desire to ensure that strategic command is tight and focused on the President, whilst at the same time promoting some decentralization of operational command across the vast expanse of Russia. To strike this balance, four smaller versions of the NDMC have been created in the four military districts (oblasts)—Western, Central, Eastern, and Southern.

The NDMC has also undertaken a root-and-branch reform of Russia's strategic, operational, and tactical command and control. These reforms are vital for the new joint forces, particularly the quick reaction airborne forces that combine airborne units, naval infantry (marines), and special operations forces (Spetsnaz), as well as the professional, devolved command culture that such forces typically require. The NDMC is also overseeing the deployment of high-tech capabilities that enhance battlefield mobility, as well as improved offensive fires and defensive performance. Important improvements have also been made to the situational awareness of commanders, as well as secure communications between the supreme political authority and operational commanders. In other words, whilst Russian field commanders are encouraged to exploit the tactical battlespace as they see it, they are also never too far from Moscow's long strategic screwdriver, particularly where the lofty ambitions of campaign design meet operational reality. To better promote and enable both the command efficiency and operational flexibility of the force, a new joint battlespace information system has been adopted, complete with live streaming for commanders to improve real-time operational command and decision-making.

For all the impressive strides forward in strategic, operational, and tactical command and control since 2010, it is perhaps the marked change in the personnel of Russia's armed forces that is the most important. The over-arching aim of President Putin in the wake of the 2008 Georgia fiasco (and the failings of the Russian military during the Chechen wars of the 1990s) was to realize a Russian future force that would enhance the strategic and political utility of force, for which professional personnel are essential. Russian forces still rely on a large cadre of conscripts, as they have always done. However, such 'secondary' formations are today part of a large augmentation force which would exploit the 'opportunities' created by a core professional force, rather than the spear-tip force of old. Significant cadres of experienced reserves also mean that Russian forces are far better able to strike a balance between mass and manoeuvre that they have traditionally found challenging. This planned shift in the balance of person-nel between conscripted personnel and professional effectives aims to achieve a 4:5 ratio, with a particular emphasis being placed on ensuring all NCOs are professional. Interestingly, the Russians undertook several detailed studies of Western military campaigns since the end of the Cold War and identified the vital role of tactical leadership at junior levels of the force.

Road-bumps on the way to Russia's future force

Russian military modernization has not all been plain sailing. Effecting change in the balance between a professional and conscript force has faced difficulties, not least because of the decline in the relative attractiveness of military contracts compared with civilian alternatives since 2010. With the COVID-19 economic crisis, the prospect of a military career might again become more attractive. Military modernization and reform have also faced resistance at varying levels, and of varying degrees, across the defence establishment, a phenomenon not entirely unknown in the West.

The Russian Army has proved the most resistant to change. With echoes again of the Tsarist and Soviet past practice of employing massed artillery and armour, much effort has been expended on upgrading artillery and armoured systems, and their supporting formations. These efforts have met with mixed success. For example, Moscow made much of the new T-14A Armata main battle tank, and in particular its enhanced active armour protection. However, final tests of the Armata were delayed until 2020, and it has only been deployed in modest numbers. It is also proving prohibitively expensive. Instead, Russia has opted to improve its existing T-90 series of main battle tanks, with the T-90M including much of the technology intended for the Armata. A sustained effort has also been made to improve the fires and counter-fires capability of the Army as the use of mass artillery still remains central to Russian land doctrine. New multi-launch rocket systems have been deployed, together with heavy-guided artillery munitions. This capability is steadily being reinforced by the increased and increasing use of drones to enhance the battlefield intelligence of artillery regiments. Russia's missile brigades are also increasingly capable of operating at a greater range than hitherto, having been furnished with double the number of launchers compared with 2010. They have also been equipped with new missile systems, such as Iskandr M, with ranges up to 500 km, and Russia is also looking to develop relatively cheap domestically produced drones to enable land-based 'swarm' attacks that could swamp the force protection of forward-deployed enemy forces.

For all the undoubted capability of the Belgorod, the submarine-centric Russian Navy has benefited least of all the main services from the reform programme, even though it is now a very considerably enhanced and more professional force compared to when K-141 Kursk was lost in August 2000.[25] The launch of the Belgorod also reveals a force with a growing capability to project power, albeit with marked limitations. Critically, the ability of the Russian Navy to project power into the Atlantic and Arctic areas of operations has been significantly enhanced with the completion of a massive new missile and drone arsenal on the Kola Peninsula close to the base of the Russian Northern Fleet, Moscow's principal naval force. As a mark of the strategic importance the Kremlin places on the fleet, on 5 June 2020 President Putin issued a decree which ceded the area around the fleet

---

25. In August 2000, the K-141 Kursk was lost whilst on an exercise in the Barents Sea, with 118 of its crew. The loss was attributed to the experimental use of a new bi-propellant for a new generation of torpedoes. Whilst inert on their own, when mixed, the two chemicals become highly explosive. The British experimented with a similar system in the 1950s but abandoned it when a Royal Navy submarine, HMS Sidon, was almost lost. Much that is known about the sequence of events leading to the loss of the Kursk is due to the heroic actions of Lt.-Cdr Rashid Aryapov. He wrote in the pages of a detective novel that the cause of the explosion was due to faults in the torpedo compartment. The subsequent official report was damning in its assessment of crew training and the state of equipment. The loss of the Kursk came to symbolize the nadir of post-Cold War Russian forces.

base at Murmansk from the Western Military District to create the fifth military district. The edict came into force on 1 January 2021. Whilst significant enhancements have also been made to the Russian nuclear ballistic missile submarine force with the (eventual) deployment of four Borei-class boats, three of which are under construction, it is the development and deployment of the eight boats of the advanced hunter-killer Yasen class that are of particular concern to Western navies. Russia also has eleven boats of the effective Akula class and some very 'quiet' conventional submarines of the improved Kilo class, capable of evading detection, as well as new Varshavyanka and Lada classes.[26] Specifically, it is the ability of Russian submarines to fire a range of munitions, including cruise missiles, nuclear-tipped torpedoes, and drones, that makes them a threat to most NATO navies.[27] The Rubin Design Bureau is also rumoured to be working on an advanced Air Independent Propulsion system that would enable Russian conventional submarines to remain submerged for extended periods.

The Russian surface fleet has proven more resistant to modernization, and seems to be in some trouble as contracts for new platforms are either cancelled or scrapped. Part of the problem is that the available shipbuilding yards have been unable to meet the demand of the Navy to replace its ageing cruisers, destroyers, and frigates. In any case, budgets for such large-scale construction have been reduced in recent years, forcing Moscow to make some hard choices. Even the symbol of the Russian Northern Fleet, the thirty-year-old aircraft carrier Admiral Kuznetsov, underwent a very problematic extended refit following its return from operations in the Mediterranean during 2017 and 2018. Equally, Russia is still considering the construction of new aircraft carriers that would be roughly the same size as

---

26. Russia is not the only country to be developing super-quiet submarines. Sweden has the A-19 Gotland class which is equipped with the latest generation of Air Independent Propulsion which enables the submarine to stay below the surface for an extended period and operate very quietly. Sweden is about to deploy the second of the class HMS Uppland. See H.I. Sutton, 'Sweden's Famous Stealthy Submarine Is Now Even Quieter', 17 May 2020, *Forbes Magazine*, forbes.com/sites/hisutton/2020/05/17/swedens-famously-stealthy-submarine-just-got-even-quieter/#48061d902bfb.

27. In December 2017, then UK Chief of the Defence Staff, Air Chief Marshal Sir Stuart Peach, said that Britain was prioritizing the protection of underwater sea cables because if they were disrupted or cut there could be a 'potentially catastrophic' effect on the British economy. He went on to say that the vulnerability of Britain's underwater sea-lines of communication posed 'a new risk to our way of life' as Russia modernizes its navy and perfects unconventional and information warfare. See Arj Singh, 'Russia "Could Cut Undersea Internet Cables", Defence Chief Warns', *The Independent*, 14 December 2017, https://www.independent.co.uk/news/uk/home-news/russia-attack-uk-cables-underwater-sea-protection-a8111536.html.

the UK's Queen Elizabeth-class, of around 70,000 tons and able to carry some forty to fifty fixed- and rotary-wing aircraft.

Russia's enduring military weaknesses say almost as much about Russian intentions as its recently acquired strength. The goal of Moscow's complex strategic coercion at the high end of conflict would be to threaten a lot of damage around Russia's self-declared 'near abroad'. This is because Russia's conventional armed forces could probably only exert limited strategic effect further away without resorting to the use of nuclear weapons, and only for a limited period. This is crucial for the future defence of Europe against Russia. Critically, Russian forces lack the strategic manoeuvre and lift assets which have traditionally given US forces extended reach, punch, and staying power. The blocking by Paris of the sale of two French-built Mistral-class amphibious ships in 2016 was a particular blow to Russia's maritime-amphibious ambitions to create a genuine cadre of elite marines, even if the Russians are now constructing similar ships to replace them.[28]

The Russian Air Force also lacks precision-guided munitions, although strenuous steps are being taken to close that gap with the development of so-called 'smart munitions' deemed a priority. Russia's strategic bomber fleet is very old. However, as the Americans have demonstrated with B52 bombers, even old aircraft can provide a useful platform to extend the range of stand-off missiles and reduce the time to strike, particularly for hypersonic missiles.

---

28. 'Navy Recognition' states: 'Russian Krylov State Research Center has developed the Priboy LHD on its own initiative. It is significantly different from the Mistral landing helicopter dock designed by French DCNS. Priboy is intended for seaborne movement of troops and military equipment and landing on beaches during amphibious operation in conjunction with other naval forces. It can support projection of soldiers and hardware, take part in offensive mining actions and mount sonar beacons of suspended array surveillance systems. Priboy has a normal surface displacement of 23,000 t, a length of 200 m, a width of 34 m, a designed draft of 7.5 m, a full speed of 20 kn, a cruise speed of 14 kn, an endurance of 6,000 nmi or 30 days. The LHD can withstand storms of force 6–7 on the Beaufort scale (strong breeze/near gale). The ship has a crew of 400 sailors and can transport 500–900 soldiers, about 50 infantry fighting vehicles (IFV) and 10 main battle tanks (MBT). Up to 12 military-transport and search-and-rescue (SOR) helicopters can be based on Priboy. The ship incorporates six fast landing craft with 45 t lifting capacity each and six assault boats located on davits. Polyakov pointed out that Priboy is equipped with tactical-level integrated combat management system. The LHD features electronic warfare (EW) and hydroacoustic hardware that includes three-axis detection radar, navigation system, integrated EW and communication suites and underwater sabotage forces detection system. The Priboy's armament suite includes two anti-air gun-missile combat modules, two close-in weapon systems and one 76mm naval gun'. See 'Russian MoD: First LHD Amphibious Assault Ship to Be Built in Russia by 2022', 29 May 2017, https://navyrecognition.com/index.php/news/defence-news/2017/may-2017-navy-naval-forces-defense-industry-technology-maritime-security-global-news/5235-russian-mod-first-lhd-amphibious-assault-ship-to-be-built-in-russia-by-2022.html.

As such, the Tu-22M, the NATO-designated Backfire, and the latest variants of the venerable Tu-95, NATO-designated Bear, are still capable of launching new weapons systems.

In sum, the modernization of the Russian armed forces since 2010 has been impressive. However, the impression of an irresistible force, which is central to Moscow's use of complex strategic coercion, and an image which President Putin undoubtedly seeks to project is still a long way from the truth. The main threat from the force comes in its role within, and relationship to the 'non-linear' forms of warfare Russia could wage, particularly on European democracies close to its borders. Whilst the Russian armed forces of today would certainly be capable of undertaking a lightning thirty-day conventional war at the margins of NATO and the EU, and such a campaign would probably enable them to seize extensive Allied territory before they were stopped, it is hard to see the force being able to sustain a protracted campaign. However, Russia's nuclear forces are being modernized at pace (see the 2019 deployment of the Avangard system), one reason being to deter and prevent the major Western powers from intervening in sufficient force until a fait accompli land grab is completed, or deter them from mounting a rescue campaign thereafter.

What is clear is that Russian grand strategy and military strategy are closely aligned, either through the threat of force or, *in extremis*, the actual use of force. Why Russia would actually use such force is harder to discern, although the Kremlin's failure to reform either Russia's economy or society could create the conditions in which a desperate regime felt compelled to resort to extreme measures. COVID-19? Who knows? Can Russia maintain such an effort? There are some very significant constraints on the Russian defence budget and the slowdown in investment planned in the 2021–30 Strategic Armaments Programme suggests that President Putin's original level of military-strategic ambition might be being reduced. President Putin is already playing military brinkmanship with a Russian economy that will suffer profoundly from the COVID-19 slump. However, much will depend on foreign-generated income from oil and gas sales, much of it from Europe, and the extent to which Russian civil society is willing to accept the onerous burden that is the extended Russian security state (civil and military). Whilst no democrat, President Putin has also shown himself sensitive to the public mood, if not to the public voice, and the COVID-19 crisis clearly made him think, even if Russian information operations against the West have been particularly aggressive. Equally, it would be a mistake to apply Western European standards of life quality to Russia as a reason why Moscow might wish to abandon complex strategic coercion. History abounds with examples of the suffering of the Russian people in the name of Mother Russia.

Russia versus Europe

There are always two sides to threat. Indeed, the very idea of 'threat' presupposes relative strength on one side and relative weakness on another. It is not simply Russia's force modernization and its aggressive posture that is the cause of instability in and around Europe. It is also the uncertain response of Europeans to the threat posed by a Russia that is at best a potent regional military power, albeit armed with a powerful strategic nuclear arsenal. Critically, it seems hard for European political leaders and policy-makers to agree on what constitutes risk, challenge, and threat, even where Russia is concerned. There is little or no consensus between Europeans as to where the main effort, and thus the main security and defence investments, should be made. There is some evidence Europe is finally awakening from what has been a thirty-year strategic slumber, but it is a reawakening that is at best fitful, with little unity of effort or purpose, and even less strategic direction, and COVID-19 may well have brought an abrupt end to even limited defence ambitions. As with all such past moments, the awakening has also been marked by an explosion in arguments and concepts, of which this book is doubtless a part, and they tend to create more heat than light for leaders with little experience in, or understanding of, matters of security and defence. This is particularly so in the wake of the COVID-19 pandemic.

In such circumstances a return to the first principles of defence is advised. European states long ago established the concepts of critical and essential interests, which helped establish red lines that adversaries understood were not to be crossed for fear of war. It was the very fudging of those red lines that helped facilitate the outbreaks of both World War One and World War Two. Since the end of the Cold War, so much of the debate in the European *polis* and *demos* about the future institutional shape of 'Europe' has had little to do with Europe's future defence. The Russian threat reveals that not only have Europeans turned inward, they also routinely confuse interests with values. That confusion has been all too apparent when Europeans have acted beyond Europe's borders, most notably in Iraq,

Afghanistan, and Libya. They have done so only very reluctantly, and often because that was the price the US demanded for continuing to defend Europeans, but they have also been plain incompetent. Europeans have also insisted that any such engagements reflect their values, even if they have refused to invest the forces or resources to realize such ends. Not only are these campaigns reflective of a profound confusion in Europe between interests and values, they also reveal a profound European reluctance to back words with deeds and to recognize that risks can lead to challenge, which can, in turn, lead to war.

It follows that any seasoned and reasoned analysis of the future defence of Europe in the face of the Russian threat must be seen in the context of two main drivers. First, Russia's offensive grand strategy is based on Moscow's systematic identification of the coercive strategic effects the Kremlin seeks to generate in and around Europe, and the role of both implied and actual force in the generation of such effects. Second, Russia is effectively exploiting the evolution in military technology because Europeans choose not to, most dangerously through its concepts of hyperwar and the introduction of radical technologies into the battlespace. Russian developments in artificial intelligence (AI), super-computing, and machine learning, as well as nano-technologies, drones, and other semi or fully autonomous delivery systems, are all designed to intimidate Europeans short of war, in what some rather unhelpfully call the 'grey zone'. They are also effectively exploiting the emergence of new weapons systems for political effect. The result is the kind of imbalance upon which complex strategic coercion feeds. Worryingly, Europe has few hypersonic weapons systems, and has little apparent interest in defending against more exotic systems, such as laser, particle beam, and directed-energy systems. And yet, such systems are starting to appear in an increasingly singular battlespace that now stretches from the depths of the oceans to outer-space, across all landmasses and within and between changing societies and communities. European defence?

The emergence of such technologies also risks deepening divisions in the Alliance between Americans and Europeans upon which Europe's defence depends. The mistake the Americans have traditionally made at such moments of change is to see technology as strategy, whereas the mistake too many Europeans are making is to regard a declaration of intent as proof of strategic influence. It is anything but. The Russians have adopted a very different approach. They have considered the strategic and political objectives that President Putin has set for them and the ends, ways, and means (including technology) available to Russia to realize those goals and set about striking an effective balance. The American approach is markedly different from its Europe allies and Russia. In spite of a well-established tradition of published strategies, the US military-industrial complex has always been a delicate compromise between political, strategic, and industrial interests.[29] Advanced American force concepts, such as technology-led multi-domain warfare, are vital, but they are as much about industrial and technological drivers as sound military planning. For the Russians such considerations are also important but not as ends in themselves. Rather, means are the servants of strategic ambition, i.e. a means to an end. That is why cross-domain warfare is seen by the Russians as much an outcome as a consequence of strategy, both a realizer and an enabler. The problem for many Europeans is that because the strategic ends they seek are so varied and vague, the relationship between ends, ways, and means has little or no defence value or traction. As a consequence, Europeans are in danger of removing themselves from a contest that is essentially about the future dominance of Europe. And, because too many Europeans embrace neither defence strategy nor defence technology in any meaningful and systematic way, seeing defence rather as what can be afforded after the costs of social welfare have been expended, Europeans are fast becoming the prey of power and exaggerating Russian power in the process. The COVID-19 crisis could thus well have been a dangerous tipping point not just for the future of European defence but also for the transatlantic relationship.

Russia's military modernization must thus be seen as not only the foundation instrument for the application of complex strategic coercion across 5D continuous warfare, but also the seizure of an opportunity afforded Moscow by Europe's own innate strategic ambivalence and weakness. In

---

29. In his farewell address on 17 January 1961, President Dwight D. Eisenhower warned: 'In the councils of government, we must guard against the acquisition of unwarranted influence, whether sought or unsought, by the military-industrial complex. The potential for the disastrous rise of misplaced power exists and will persist. We must never let the weight of this combination endanger our liberties or democratic processes. We should take nothing for granted. Only an alert and knowledgeable citizenry can compel the proper meshing of the huge industrial and military machinery of defense with our peaceful methods and goals, so that security and liberty may prosper together'. Ironically, a May 2017 report by *Forbes* pointed out that US defence industries counted for less than 1 per cent of the US economy. See 'The Farewell Address', Dwight D. Eisenhower Presidential Library, https://www.eisenhowerlibrary. gov/sites/default/files/file/farewell_address.pdf. See also Loren Thomson, 'Eisenhower's "Military-Industrial Complex" Shrinks to 1% of Economy', 8 May 2017, *Forbes*, https://www. forbes.com/sites/lorenthompson/2017/05/08/eisenhowers-military-industrial-complex-shrinks-to-1-of-economy/#9d931dbed1f2.

other words, it is Europeans themselves who are affording President Putin his strategic goal—influence over Europe at the least warfighting cost to the Russian Federation. For Moscow, the utility of the Russian future force is primarily seen as a political extortion racket—the ultimate tool of strategic blackmail—aimed at extorting concession from the states around Russia's western and southern borders, with a particular focus on what the Kremlin would call the old Soviet Empire.

The Black Sea region and the virtual Soviet Union

The Black Sea region is central to Russia's complex coercive strategy and thus a case study of its design and application. Moscow's aim is to turn the Black Sea into a Russian lake by either neutering or co-opting the states around it so that Moscow is free to operate therein, and from there securely project its power and influence far into the Middle East and Mediterranean. The Black Sea region is also one of a series of friction points in a wider Euro-strategic struggle between President Putin's Russia and the West, albeit exacerbated in the Black Sea region by regional-specific tensions. The region is made even more complex by the mix of NATO and EU members and partners, making it relatively easy for Moscow to further exploit the benefits and responsibilities each enjoy. Whilst Moscow continues to exert pressure on NATO and EU members such as Bulgaria and Romania, the lack of any firm commitment to extend full membership of either institution to states such as Georgia assists Moscow in its efforts to establish new spheres of influence, both in the region and beyond.

Russia's overall aim is to re-draw the political map of eastern and south-eastern Europe to re-establish a new/old sphere of influence therein, by applying a model of warfare across a mosaic of conflict that incorporates hybrid war, cyber war, and, in the worst case, high-end hyperwar. Central to Russia's strategy is war in many forms, war at the margins of the Alliance and Union, and war at the seams of complex European societies. It is particularly effective in societies which are deeply contested or in which elites are open to undue influence. Russian strategy is made easier by the contentions within the region, most notably between Bulgaria, Romania, and Turkey. All three states have differing threat perceptions and different and changing views about Russia, undermining the very mutual trust central to the credibility of Alliance defence and deterrence. Consequently, there is no permanent security cooperation in the face of Russian coercion and physically defending allies therein because of the poor quality of much of the infrastructure, which would make it hard for NATO to defend Bulgaria and Romania in particular. Bulgaria and Romania are also particularly vulnerable to Russian complex strategic coercion, not least because of the influence of the Russian Orthodox Church.

In spite of the costs of the COVID-19 crisis to the Russian economy, Moscow is likely to continue to exert control and influence over a region vital to its ultimate aim of recreating a buffer zone between Russia and the rest of Europe—a kind of virtual Soviet Union. The Black Sea region is thus the perfect theatre for the sustained application of Russian complex strategic coercion and the applied and systematic use of disinformation, disruption, and destabilization, with the implied threat of destruction, and leveraged by copious doses of deception, often aided and abetted by denial in key Western European capitals.[30] The seizure of Crimea revealed the willingness of Moscow to change borders in Europe by force if it believes the strategic prize worth it, and the risk minimal. Another vital Russian interest now is to extend the ability of the Russian Black Sea Fleet to project influence into southern Europe, the Levant, and beyond into the Gulf and the Middle East and North Africa.

The military-strategic challenge in the Black Sea region is epitomized by the Black Sea Maritime challenge. The Russian Black Sea Fleet could seal off the Black Sea region and use Crimea and Novosibirsk as bases for operations of varying intensity against states therein. Moscow is also seeking a strategic partnership with Turkey (see next section) to enable the Black Seas fleet to gain unfettered access to the Mediterranean, a kind of 1915 Gallipoli campaign in reverse.[31] Critical infrastructure in the region is particularly vulnerable, the loss of which could have profound implications for Europe as a whole. For example, any threat to the Port of Constanta at the mouth of the Danube in Romania would be serious as it has the capacity to handle 100,000,000 tons of goods per year at its 156 berths.[32] It is also where the

---

30. See J. Lindley-French (2015) *NATO: Countering Strategic Maskirovka* (Calgary: CGAI).

31. In 1915, at the behest of the then British First Lord of the Admiralty, Winston Churchill, Britain and France tried to force Turkey out of World War One by forcing the Bosporus passage. It proved a spectacular disaster. Russia understands that and realizes that Turkey must, if possible, be neutralized as a threat to the passage of the Russian Black Seas Fleet, even though Ankara is a NATO ally.

32. See 'Constanta Port', https://www.portofconstantza.com/apmc/portal/static.do?package_id=infgen_port_maritim&x=load.

Danube-Black Sea Canal begins, a vital transit between Romania and Bulgaria, Serbia, Hungary, Austria, Slovakia, and Germany.

How can countries in the region counter Russian 5D warfare? Firstly, by helping to embed the very concept of 5D warfare at the heart of an adapted NATO defence and deterrence posture. Both Bulgaria and Romania must also become far more deeply embedded in the EU's Common Foreign and Security Policy (CFSP) and Common Security and Defence Policy (CSDP). Cross-regional institutional ties also need to be strengthened, such as the Regional Co-operation Council, and strategies, such as South-East Europe 2020, strengthened and taken forward as implementable action plans. Investments in infrastructure that further embed Romania, Bulgaria, and Europe's wider free economy are also vital.

Specific security and defence adaptations would include (*inter alia*) new security concepts for all the states in the region to counter coercion throughout the hybrid-cyber-hyper mosaic with improved indicators to identify when and where a hybrid attack is underway, and where it could lead. Progress would be dependent on strengthened intelligence relationships with strong allies, such as the United States and the Western European allies, both through close bilateral as well as multilateral relationships. However, information security will be critical to the creation of such relationships.

There are also a range of practical political steps states in the region should take to render themselves more resilient in the face of war at the seams of their respective societies. Critical infrastructure, most notably the Port of Constanta, need to be rendered far more resilient to cyber and other forms of disruptive attack. 'Critical' people also need to be made more robust by making it harder for Russia and its agents to use corruption as a strategic weapon. And, of course, security and defence forces must be modernized to ensure they meet the challenge of the coming age, not the past.

Turkey, Russia, and the values–interest dilemma

Turkey is the hinge between Europe's eastern and southern strategic flanks; it is also a critical player in the struggle between Russia and the West. And, like it or not, Europeans no longer make the rules of the road of contemporary geopolitics. Consequently, relations between the West and Turkey, and between Europe and Turkey in particular, reveal the dilemma and tension that exists in contemporary European defence between values and interests; specifically, the extent to which allies and partners must share values as much as interests.

The strategic importance of a friendly Ankara for the successful future defence of Europe cannot be over-stated. Turkey is also as critical to countering Russia as it is to countering al-Qaeda, Daesh, and their ilk. However, the relationship between the West and Turkey is in deep trouble and there remains a real danger that Russia will succeed in its efforts to instrumentalize Ankara in its efforts to stymie and even paralyse NATO. The July 2019 delivery to Turkey of the advanced Russian S-400 air defence missile system led swiftly to Turkey's ousting from the F35 advanced fighter programme by Washington under the Countering American Adversaries Through Sanctions Act (CAATSA).[33]

Dealing with President Erdogan will thus be a test-case for how Americans and Europeans maintain vital partnerships with leaders with whom it shares few values. Moscow seeks to portray Turkey's decision to acquire the S-400, which was designed specifically to shoot down US F-16 fighters, and to jointly develop the new S-500 system, as evidence that President Erdogan now aligns himself with President Putin.[34] Whilst President Erdogan has become increasingly frustrated with his Western allies, it is an exaggeration to suggest Turkey is now Moscow's ally, even if Turkey's frustration with its European allies in particular is understandable. For example, the United Nations estimates that Turkey is host to some 2,900,000 Syrian refugees, although Ankara claims it to be as high as 3,500,000.[35] Turkey has repeatedly threatened to walk away from a 2015 agreement with the EU that was brokered by German Chancellor Angela Merkel under which Ankara would stem the flow of refugees and irregular migrants into Europe. Ankara claims that Brussels has not paid the agreed amount of money to support the

---

33. CAATSA came into force when it was signed into American law by the President on 2 August 2017. It was aimed primarily at Iran, North Korea, and Russia but is now being used in an attempt to leverage Turkey.

34. According to MilitaryToday.com, 'The S-500 is a new long-range anti-aircraft and anti-ballistic missile system that was recently developed in Russia. It can be seen as an advanced version of the S-400. Its development of this air defense system commenced in 2002. It was developed by Almaz-Antey company. This system is also referred as the Prometey (*Prometheus*) and Triumfator-M. Prototype testing was expected to begin in 2015. Production of the S-500 air defense system reportedly commenced in 2017. It is planned to be fielded in 2020. Russia plans to field ten battalions of S-500 missiles'. http://www.military-today.com/missiles/s500. htm.

35. See 'The EU-Turkey Refugee Agreement: A Review', *Deutsche Welt*, 18 March 2003, https:// www.dw.com/en/the-eu-turkey-refugee-agreement-a-review/a-43028295.

refugees in Turkey, and that no-visa travel for Turkish citizens agreed under the agreement has also not been implemented.

The sense of alienation from 'Europe' Turks feel has been compounded by the final realization by Ankara that Turkey would be unlikely to be offered full membership of the EU. The accession process began as early as 1987 with negotiations for full EU membership starting in 2005, albeit painfully slowly. In February 2019, the European Parliament voted to suspend all accession talks with Turkey, partly in response the draconian wave of arrests that followed the failed July 2016 coup. There are additional factors that fuel Turkey's sense of grievance. US support for Kurdish forces in the struggle against Daesh in Syria triggered deep concerns in Ankara that Washington would eventually back the creation of a *de facto* Kurdish state in northern Syria adjacent to Turkey's border. The very idea is inimical to Turks. President Erdogan was also offended by what he saw as tacit European and US support for the failed coup. The all-too-evident distaste of many European leaders is also a factor. They, like several other liberal Western European leaders, view Erdogan as a reactionary determined to reverse the separation of mosque and state by Ataturk in the wake of Turkey's defeat in World War One.

However, the relationship with Ankara must be seen from the perspective of grand strategy and Europe's wider security and defence. Turkey's purchase of the S-400 does not mean Ankara is now a Russian ally, and both Americans and Europeans need to tread carefully. The West's Turkey dilemma is in part caused by the tendency of Western European leaders to view all relationships through a liberal lens, which makes it hard for them to deal with those who do not share their 'European values', even if they are vital to the defence of Europe. Of course, neither Americans nor Europeans must abandon those values for the sake of a strategic relationship with Turkey. However, the dictates of power and interests also demand of them a far greater effort to understand Turkey's strategic perspective and the stakes should Ankara be 'lost'. President Erdogan is a traditional Turkish leader of a country faced with a baffling array of strategic challenges who must now also cope with the consequences of COVID-19. Turkey faces Russia to the north, Iran to the east, and Syria, Lebanon, and Israel to the south, with the Balkans to contend with to the west. Shorn of what Ankara no longer regards as reliable Western allies, Erdogan is behaving like a classical Turkish, Ottoman, or Byzantine leader of old, precisely because he understands all too well his country's strengths and its many weaknesses and vulnerabilities.[36]

Strategically, Turkey sits at the crossroads between Europe and Asia, the West and the Middle East, critically and decisively between Russia, the Black Sea, and the Mediterranean, and between the Muslim and non-Muslim worlds. That is Turkey's strength but it is also Turkey's desperate weakness. President Erdogan is thus simply doing what generations of Turkish/Ottoman leaders have done in the past; focusing exclusively on what he regards as Turkey's vital interests and making states in need of Turkish support work for the 'privilege'. President Erdogan is thus a classical Turkish strategic horse-trader willing to deal with anyone who can offer Turkey a good deal.

Turkey's is also a front-line NATO member nation, and has been since 1952. Indeed, there has been a NATO headquarters in Izmir ever since, longer than any other NATO headquarters in the Alliance, except for Naples. It is the cornerstone of a strategic framework that was created first to contain the Soviet Union and now looks to the Black Sea, the Middle East, and beyond. Turkey also continues to play a critical role in deterring Russian aggression in the Black Sea region in spite of Ankara's decision to buy Russian S-400 anti-aircraft missiles. Critically, a new strategic framework is needed that recognizes the unique Turkish perspective and the role that Ankara plays in the broader Middle East, Eastern European, and Central Asia region, particularly to its south and Syria, but which also re-commits Ankara to the Alliance. Much of that effort will be based on improving military-to-military relationships, but far more will need to be done with a new political accommodation afforded Ankara. At the very least, the EU will need to prove to Turkey that it is an honest partner and honour the agreement to allow Turks access to Europe. Americans and Europeans must also work far more closely together to ensure Turkey and the Kurds find a way to live together in reasonable peace. Central to any such effort will be convincing Kurds that their homeland in modern-day Iraq and Syria is safe from Turkish attack, and that Kurdish ambitions in Eastern Turkey stop well short of armed insurrection therein, or worse, the formation of a hostile Kurdish rump state along the southern border of Turkey should the Kurds

36. The First Crusade of 1095–9 began following appeals from the Byzantine Emperor Alexios I Komnenos for the help of European Christendom for what he saw as the threat to his kingdom from the expansion of Islam. However, when the Crusaders arrived, he made them pay for all his support and pushed them to move on quickly into the Levant. His support was, at best, tacit.

succeed in uniting the three Syrian Kurdish Cantons. Equally, neither Americans nor Europeans should countenance a further slaughter of the Kurdish people who have suffered enough, and Turkey should be under no illusions about that.

In essence, the dilemma Turkey creates for European defence is a test of statecraft. Since the end of the Cold War Europeans have by and large abandoned an interest-led security and defence policy for a values-led approach. Such a posture has contributed significantly to the rapid relative decline of Europeans. The strategic relationship with Turkey still has a vital role to play in the military defence of Europe and there are specific steps that could be taken by both Americans and Europeans to ease tensions. First, the boundary between US European Command (EUCOM) and US Central Command (CENTCOM) runs along the Turkish–Syrian border. Because of the nature of interaction between the two commands, the boundary does not facilitate effective military operations and effective coalition building, nor does it enable diplomatic and economic pressure to be exerted if needs be. Over the last fifteen years CENTCOM has become *primus inter pares* among all the US Combatant Commands because of the priority given to deployments and operations in Iraq and Afghanistan. However, the place and nature of this boundary has also contributed to a tendency to under-estimate the significance of Turkish sensitivities about the US arming of Kurdish factions in the struggle against Daesh.

Second, Europeans need to offer Turkey a 'special relationship' with the EU that goes far beyond any Association Agreement, even if it falls short of EU membership. Put simply, growing Turkish suspicions that it will be pushed out of Europe and accusations that Turkey has a hidden Islamist foreign policy should be ended. Turkey would not be a threat to European civilization if it ever became an EU member, nor is Turkey in Putin's pocket.

Turkey's decision to buy the S-400 missile system from Russia was a mistake that has rightly angered the US. However, NATO is a much stronger alliance with Turkey as a committed and positive member nation than without it because of its geographic location, its strong and professional military forces, and its influence in the Black Sea region, the Middle East and North Africa, and the Mediterranean. Turkey has also been a strong NATO ally for some seventy years.

In an age of renewed Great Power competition, Turkey remains an essential ally and member of NATO. Indeed, how Europeans, in particular, deal with Turkey will demonstrate the extent or otherwise they understand they are part of such a dangerous age. To keep the Alliance strong and cohesive, and an effective deterrent against Russian aggression in the greater Black Sea region and beyond, the future defence of Europe will depend on a reset in the relationship with Turkey and a long-term strategic trajectory built on a renewed commitment to protect and defend the heir to the Byzantine and Ottoman empires, one that demonstrates an understanding and respect for Turkey's own sovereign concerns and geography.

A big strategic question Americans and Europeans should ask themselves is not what Turkey can do for them, but how important Turkey is to their security, and the price they are willing to pay to keep Turkey onside. There is a particular urgency to this challenge of statecraft for a Europe in headlong retreat from power-realism that insists on a rules-based global system in a world where those with real power seemingly prefer *Realpolitik*.

Conclusion: a challenging neighbourhood

If the Euro-Atlantic community are in any doubt about the growing and evolving threat to its ease, and the need for a pragmatic approach to the fostering of critical strategic partnerships, they need look no further than recent events. In August 2019, the SU-70 Okhotnik or Hunter-B drone took to the air for the first time. This long-range unmanned Russian strike drone represents another step on the road to a transformed Russian future force. In September 2019, the Chinese Dongfeng 41 ballistic/drone intercontinental ballistic missile was revealed at the seventieth anniversary parade of the Chinese Communist State in Beijing. This system, which combines a ballistic launcher with a hypersonic, nuclear-tipped glide vehicle, is believed to reduce the time to target between China and the US to a matter of minutes. In October 2019, the Polish site for the AEGIS Ashore Missile Defense System was completed. Part of the European Phased Adaptive Approach, the site is a vital component in Alliance efforts to protect populations from missiles launched from beyond the Euro-Atlantic area. Given the pace of the new arms race that is clearly underway between the US, China, and Russia, it may be too little too late.

The essential point is that the threat posed by Russia to NATO's eastern flank is not simply a stand-alone and cannot be seen in strategic isolation. It is the harbinger of the future of warfare with which European defence must contend throughout the hybrid war, cyber war, and hyperwar mosaic. In recent years Russia has held two massive military exercises to test its force modernization, Zapad 17 and Vostok 18. There were two specific aspects of Vostok 18 that should worry Europe's leaders. First, the Vostok series of exercises were originally designed by Russia to test war *against* China, but was adapted to test large, mass-mobile Russian forces going to big war allied *with* China. Vostok 18 was also a sign of the hardening of geopolitical blocs as the two great illiberal powers seek common cause against America and the democratic, global West, something the contentions over COVID-19 have done little to reduce. Second, the Russians and Chinese are developing extended-reach all-arms warfare built on effective coordination between disparate but powerful forces over great distances which are able to mask their concentration prior to any attack, and thereafter operate autonomously or in concert as part of an 'organically' intelligent force.[37] To illustrate the point, Vostok 18 saw large-scale deployments of mainly Russian forces in Russia's Southern and Central Military Districts (Oblast), whilst in the eastern Mediterranean the Russian Navy simultaneously conducted a large-scale exercise.

The challenge to NATO was clear. Vostok 18 also tested reconnaissance-strike contouring, large-scale combat arms, training between different types of companies, communications between disparate forces, and new technologies, such as SPECTRUM, a Russian electronics warfare capability that was declared operational just prior to the exercise. Drone and counter-drone tactics and technologies were also tested, along with large-scale integration between ground formations and air power with conventional and nuclear systems—in other words, a kind of 'deep jointness'. The Chinese contribution to Vostok 18 was relatively modest, but its political and military symbolism was enormous. Indeed, fewer than 3,200 Chinese troops, some

---

37. In a March 2017 statement before the US Senate Armed Forces Sub-Committee on AirLand, Lieutenant-General (Ret.) David A. Deptula USAF, Dean of the Mitchell Institute for Aerospace Studies, effectively defined the challenge of all-arms warfare in the twenty-first century by stating, 'Change with respect to the military involves four principal factors—advanced technologies, new concepts of operation, organizational change, and the human dimension. Advanced technologies and the new capabilities they yield, enable new concepts of operation that produce order-of-magnitude increases in our ability to achieve desired military effects. Organizational change codifies changes and enhances our ability to execute our national security strategy. The final and essential element to progress is the human dimension. People are fundamental to everything we do, especially when it comes to leadership'. See 'The Future of All Arms Warfare in the Twenty-First Century', Homeland Security Digital Library, https://www.armed-services.senate.gov/imo/media/doc/Deptula_03-15-17.pdf.

thirty aircraft, and an indeterminate number of main battle tanks were believed to have taken part. And whilst talk of a formal Russo-Chinese alliance is probably exaggerated, some form of strategic 'accommodation of convenience' is clearly underway and it is unclear whether the COVID-19 crisis and its aftermath will deepen or challenge such a partnership.

Equally, history has shown that such accommodations between like-minded powers can lead to pacts and axes which shift the balance of power decisively. Were such a partnership to lead to a new Russo-Chinese force built on combined arms and with it a new joint expeditionary capability, it would enable Beijing and Moscow to exert pressure anywhere around the Russo-Chinese land mass, and the implications for Europe's future defence would be profound.

Are the Russians and Chinese actively preparing for a major war? No, or at least not directly. Moreover, notwithstanding Vostok 18, it remains open to question to what extent they are preparing for such a future war together, but they are exploring synergies of design, command, and the capability to act. They are both engaged in a major arms race—China with America, Russia with the rest of Europe—even if many non-Russian Europeans refuse to recognize such a challenge. Moreover, the design and shape of Vostok 18 also implied the Russians and Chinese are both seeking to create a trans-formative framework for future military action that, unless countered, could give them decisive advantage at a time and place of their choosing. Ironic-ally, both Moscow and Beijing seem to understand the first principle of war that Europeans invented, but which many Europeans seem now to have abandoned: success in high-end warfare depends on the successful inter-action of and balance between strategic concept, force concept, technology concept, and an intelligence and information concept with the architecture of war held together with a robust and effective decision-making and communications structure.[38] Of all the Western powers, only the Americans are systematically thinking about future war in this way, and actually doing something about it.

Europe's history proves how dangerous arms races can be and must thus be avoided if at all possible. History also shows the danger when one side

---

38. There is nothing particularly new in such thinking. The nineteenth-century military theorist Count Antoine-Henri von Jomini wrote in his 1830 book, *The Art of War*, 'Strategy decides where to act; logistics brings the troops to this point; grand tactics decides the manner of execution and the employment of the troops'. See Lawrence Freedman (2013) *Strategy: A History* (Oxford: Oxford University Press), p. 84.

arms for war and the other side fails to respond. Whether Europeans like it or not, COVID-19 or no, preventing future war will thus require a new type and level of European defence and another burden-sharing dilemma for an already sorely pressed transatlantic relationship. The Americans will seek to maintain their edge in the new future war arms race and insist Europeans 'do their bit'. After all, whilst the American defence-technological base may be under challenge from the Chinese, the US is still the world's most advanced military power. Equally, given the pace of Chinese military-technological development, as well as Chinese strategic ambitions, American supremacy over time or distance can no longer either be guaranteed or assumed. The transatlantic relationship would be strengthened immeasurably, and thus help to convince both China and Russia that such ambitions are dangerously misplaced, if Europe became far more serious about future war, its nature, its consequences, and the technologies that are driving the strategies behind it, if for no other reason than ensuring the defence of Europeans. If Europeans do not respond, or use COVID-19 as an excuse to justify more defence pretence, then it is hard to see how the transatlantic relationship can survive in any meaningful way. Simply suggesting that arms races are nasty, danger-ous things, which tends to be the standard European response, and that Europe is not going to engage, borders on latter-day appeasement. Indeed, there may come a point when the relationship between the military strength of the illiberal Great Powers becomes so preponderant over the self-chosen weakness of Europe's decidedly less-than-great 'powers' that war and defeat again become real possibilities. Burden-sharing? Anthony H. Cordesmann puts the challenge succinctly: 'The days of relying on peace dividends and meaningless goals for levels of spending are over. There is a real Russian threat, as well as a real threat of violent extremism. NATO needs to return to the kind of serious force planning and focus on military strategy that shaped the NATO force planning exercise in the 1960s . . . It needs to set real military requirements and really meet them'.[39]

Perhaps the most damning indictment of the failure of Europe's leaders to face up to strategic responsibility and reality came from Sir Richard Dear-love, the former head of Britain's Secret Intelligence Service (MI6). In an article for *Prospect Magazine* Dearlove said that the EU 'leaked like a

---

39. See Anthony H. Cordesmann (2018) *The U.S., NATO and the Defense of Europe: Underlying Trends* (Washington, DC: CSIS), https://www.csis.org/analysis/us-nato-and-defense-europe-underlying-trends.

colander' and that 'though the UK participates in various European and Brussels-based security bodies they are of little consequence'. Dearlove continued: 'With the exception of Europol, these bodies have no operational capacity and with 28 members of vastly varying levels of professionalism in intelligence and security, the convoy must accommodate the slowest and leakiest of the ships of state'.[40] Taken together, these strategic failures show all too clearly that Europe's endemic strategic weakness goes to the very top of power, and borders on a form of strategic illiteracy. Critically, European leaders lack either a shared European strategic culture or strategic rigour and there is little or no transmission between words and deeds. For too long 'solidarity' has placed the appearance of being united before unity of action, with the result that a strategic disconnect has emerged between strategy, politics, security, and defence that Europe's adversaries are exploiting.

Is Russia a threat to Europe? Yes, but only because Europeans permit it to be so. Will it be more or less of a threat after COVID-19? Who knows. Should Europeans hope for the best but prepare for the worst? No question. However, should the Russians launch a determined military attack on Europe's eastern flank so long as their objectives were limited to their own vicinity, it is hard to believe they would not succeed.

40. See Agnes Chambre, 'Former MI6 Boss: Brexit Would Make Britain More Secure', 24 March 2016, *Politics Home*, https://www.politicshome.com/news/europe/eu-policy-agenda/brexit/news/73111/former-mi6-boss-brexit-would-make-uk-more-secure.

4

Demons and dragons
Europe's southern flank

360-degree Europe?

What threats does Europe's southern flank pose to European defence? This is a book about European defence, not the Middle East and North Africa (MENA). However, some understanding of the impact of events to Europe's south is essential. Rather than offer a broad sweep of events across MENA, this chapter uses a series of vignettes to demonstrate the scope of the challenge the region for both Americans and Europeans, and how it shines a light on the current state of European security and defence. The six vignettes are: the state versus the anti-state; Syria and the humbling of the West; the prospects of regional-strategic war; Iran and the West's nuclear dilemma; Libya, Europe, and failed transition; and COVID-19 and fragile states. The Israeli-Palestinian conflict is excluded from that list because Europeans have so little influence over it and tacitly accept that any such role is subject to US leadership, and in spite of being the source of much grievance across the Arab world, it poses little direct threat to Europe . . . as yet. All six vignettes are profoundly challenging and will be made more so by the COVID-19 crisis as already fragile states across the region must also confront a demographic, economic, societal, and even confessional crisis. As such, all six vignettes say a lot about European strategic ambition for their own security and defence.

The October 2018 murder of Saudi journalist Jamal Khashoggi at the Saudi Consulate in Istanbul revealed an essential dilemma for Europeans and their defence: the need to rely on Saudi Arabia and ultra-conservative regimes across the Gulf not only to provide much of the oil which sustains the European economy, but also to provide the main bulwark of Western policy in the Gulf and beyond. Indeed, Saudi Arabia remains by far the world's largest oil exporter, whilst the biggest importers of crude oil are the EU, followed by China, the US, and India.[1] This simple set of facts reveals the paradoxical relationship Europeans have between their values and interests. Moreover, shale-rich America is far less reliant on the region for oil and gas, and yet it is Washington that guarantees the continued flow of oil to Europe.

Any assessment of threat is intensely political, particularly the scope and extent of the terrorist threat Europe today faces, much of which is in some way linked to events to Europe's south and south-east. The multicultural nature of contemporary Western European society in particular, in spite of the many strengths it affords Europeans, means governments (and analysts) must tread a justly narrow path if they are not to imply any group and/or groups are implicitly responsible for or implacably associated with any security threat. Critically, the relationship between the massive majority of mainstream European Muslims and Salafist Jihadism is no more intimate than that between the majority of mainstream non-Muslim Europeans and white supremacists. Whilst that may seem an obvious statement, it is still important to repeat it, and often. That said, the political sensitivities within the communities that comprise contemporary European society, and which terrorists seek to exploit, also raise a legitimate question for European establishments: are Europeans able to recognize the threats they face or only recognize as much threat as the European social model permits?

Before any recasting of defence can be realized, Europeans need to agree about the nature and scope of threats beyond Russia, and thereafter agree clear priorities for both policy and force planning to cope with threat around the 360 degrees of Europe's contemporary threat horizon. Such a shared threat assessment has not proven at all easy to either fathom or fashion hitherto, and there seems little prospect of it being any easier in the future. One reason for this is the marked division between how Eastern and some Southern European states see the threat posed by Moscow. Some Southern European states see Russia, if not as an ally, at least as a potential partner.[2]

---

1. CIA World Factbook 2018, https://www.cia.gov/library/publications/the-world-factbook/geos/xx.html.
2. In a July 2016 piece entitled 'A Marriage of Convenience? The Future of Italy-Russia Relations', Angelantonio Rosato wrote, 'Rome and Moscow have a relatively strong and deep-rooted partnership that is likely to stand the test of time, barring the worst-case scenario of a "hot war" between NATO and Russia. This peculiar partnership between a regional power and

This distinction is reversed when it comes to the threat posed by Salafist Jihadism. Southern European states see the chaos to their south across the Mediterranean as the main threat to their security; those in the East of the Alliance and Union less so. The so-called 'Southerners' are particularly exercised by the danger that mass, poorly regulated flows of irregular migrants could be exploited by the likes of al-Qaeda and Daesh to strengthen their presence across a region stretching from Spain to Greece. Conversely, Central and Eastern European states do not regard the terrorist threat as their main concern, beyond seeking to prevent their EU partners from forcing them to accept migrants in any great numbers.

The result is that both NATO and the EU are profoundly divided and incapable of agreeing where best to invest the greatest effort for maximum security and/or defence effect. Given the economic impact of the COVID-19 crisis, this divide could be further exacerbated by an inability to close an extended ends, ways, and means gap in European defence. This is important because security and defence is always a balance that has to be struck between the ends to be sought, the ways to achieve them, and the means available. President Putin clearly understands the dilemma in which Europeans find themselves and is actively seeking to accentuate that dilemma by undermining the rules-based system central to the democratic concept of European security by implying and, in the case of Ukraine, actually using force. Russian ambitions are not merely confined to the High North, the Baltics, and Eastern Europe. Putin is also seeking to undermine the European body politic, a strategy he shares with al-Qaeda and Daesh, both of which also seek to weaken the bonds between leaders and led in the European democracies, as well as between the people themselves. In their varying ways, both Russia and the Salafists are engaged in a systematic campaign to weaken democracy and its institutions across Europe, mainly through the exploitation and merging of hybrid and cyber warfare.

a former superpower works on the basis that neither Russia nor Italy interferes in the domestic affairs of the other, and they recognise their respective spheres of influence. This means that Italy's Russia policy does not fit well with the EU's overall approach. It also helps to explain Rome's reluctant support for EU sanctions against Russia. When it comes down to it, Italy's only real interest in the eastern neighbourhood is to avoid the most dangerous scenario of NATO involvement in the Ukraine crisis – something that could have a disastrous impact on its relations with Russia'. Angelantonio Rosato, 'A Marriage of Convenience: The Future of Italy-Russia Relations', European Council on Foreign Relations, 16 July 2016, https://www.ecfr.eu/article/commentary_a_marriage_of_convenience_the_future_of_italyrussia_relations.

Russia's modus operandi is the use and application of disinformation to generate illicit influence through cyber means, the internet, and other message multipliers. The 'MO' of al-Qaeda and Daesh is also to use the internet to sow discontent in immigrant communities across Europe and, at the same time, use such technologies as a recruiting sergeant. The difference between Russia and the Salafists is that whilst Moscow is committed to building a force that can operate throughout the hybrid-cyber-hyper mosaic, al-Qaeda and Daesh focus more on generating a sustained strategic insurgency as an end in and of itself. Given the ambitions of the latter, such potential mass disruption could also include the development and use of radiological, chemical, and even biological weapons. Such groupings will have certainly studied the impact of COVID-19 on Europeans.

The state versus the anti-state

In January 2020, in a new twist to the debate over NATO's Open Door enlargement policy, President Trump proposed expanding NATO membership to states across MENA. Trump called on Europeans to replace US forces in the region and contribute more to the stability therein, play a more significant role in containing Iran, and become more engaged in the fight against Daesh. On 27 January 2020, with Israel's Prime Minister Benjamin Netanyahu at his side, President Trump also announced a new 'Deal of the Century' peace plan for the Middle East, which was immediately condemned by Palestinians, even though it proposed the eventual creation of a Palestinian state with a capital in a part of East Jerusalem. To underline the complexity of the environment with which President Trump was seeking to engage, as he spoke the UN Security Council was also considering a new peace plan for Libya, with both Russian and Turkish influence growing therein. In effect, President Trump highlighted three dilemmas with which Europeans must contend across MENA, all of which have profound implications for European defence: first, US demands for a much greater European effort in and around its own neighbourhood as part of an expanding US definition of transatlantic burden-sharing; second, the growing importance of MENA to Europe's own security and stability; and third, the intensifying confluence of geopolitics and terrorism to the south of Europe.

The leaders of many Arab states believe they are facing two potentially existential threats: anti-state, Sunni fundamentalism in the form of Daesh and al-Qaeda, and Iran's Shia-inspired regional-strategic ambitions. Sadly, in contemporary history such threats are nothing new, as war and conflict have been tragically an ever-present reality in the Middle East at least since the collapse of the Ottoman Empire and the May 1916 Sykes-Picot Accord which carved up much of the region between Imperial Britain and France. The recent past has offered no respite. For example, between September 1980 and August 1988 Iran and Iraq fought out a bloody stalemate that cost at least 600,000 lives, and possibly as many as a million. In 1991, a US-led coalition retook Kuwait from Saddam Hussein after his August 1990 invasion of the sheikdom. In March 2003, the US led another coalition that defeated and occupied Iraq, ostensibly to prevent Saddam acquiring weapons of mass destruction. The 2003 invasion proved so misguided that it led in time to a profound loss of Western self-confidence, a crisis in US leadership, and the effective end of Europeans as serious powers in the region.[3] Today, the strands of ambition and irresolution are in danger of coming together to create the conditions for a new general Middle East war focused on the Gulf, but with consequences far beyond.

There are many conflicts in MENA, some of which Alexander the Great would still recognize, fuelled and intensified by mistrust between elites and peoples, although not the far later struggles between Shia and Sunni, between Persian Iran and many Arab states, as well as between Israel and an Iranian-inspired, proxy-led coalitions. Over the past century Europeans have also been engaged in several wars in the region, several of which Europeans imposed on the region in some form or another because it was deemed to be a zone of vital Western/European interest, mainly because of the abundance of hydrocarbons. A major war in the region would have profound consequences for Europe. It would also further destabilize societies and render them more vulnerable to Salafist Jihadism.[4] Critically, key

---

3. A major study of the effort to stabilize Iraq concluded, 'The United States went into Iraq with a maximalist agenda – standing up a model democracy that would serve as a beacon for the entire region – and a minimalist application of money and manpower . . . The difficulties it encountered owe much to this distinction between the scope of America's ambitions and the scale of its commitment'. James Dobbins, Seth G. Jones, Benjamin Runkle, and Siddarth Mohandas (2009) *Occupying Iraq: A History of the Coalition Provisional Authority* (Santa Monica, CA: RAND), p. 327.

4. Salafist Jihadism is defined as 'an approach to jihadism that is coupled with an adherence to Salafism. Salafi-jihadists tend to emphasize the military exploits of the Salaf (the early generations of Muslims) to give their violence an even more immediate divine imperative. Most jihadist groups today can be classified as Salafi-jihadists, including al-Qaida and ISIS. Given their exclusivist view that their approach to Islam is the only authentic one, Salafi-jihadists often

Arab allies of the West, such as Egypt, Jordan, and Lebanon, are becoming increasingly vulnerable to such challenges, something Russia's presence in the region only exacerbates.

Europeans must also bear significant responsibility for conflicts and thus tread carefully because history is eloquent in MENA. In May 1916, as the Ottoman Empire collapsed, the Anglo-French Sykes-Picot Accord was struck. Under the terms of this agreement the Middle East was carved up to serve British and French interests with a series of 'protectorates' established, none of which was strong enough to dominate the region, but all of which inherited ancient disputes and grievances. In time, these protectorates became states. During the period of decolonization in the 1950s and early 1960s it appeared that Arab nationalism would be transformed as the expression of an emergent 'Arab nation'. However, defeats by Israel in 1948, 1967, and 1973 established the perception on the 'Arab Street' reinforced by the Muslim Brotherhood that Arab governments were either incompetent, in the pocket of a West that was inimical to Arab interests, or both. This perception, allied to a rapidly growing population and social and economic deprivation, has been critical in enabling the steady rise of violent extremism and Salafist Jihadism. Slowly, the creed of the Caliphate as an alternative to the 'failed' state grew, with Europeans painted as but the latest iteration of violent Crusaders justifying their oppression by some latter-day interpretation of 'just war'.[5] Saudi Arabia and its oil wealth was central to the rise of violent extremism, and allegations persist that powerful forces within Saudi Arabia bought off al-Qaeda and its affiliates, although no link has ever been established to the Saudi state itself. The collapse of Syria, Saddam Hussein,

---

justify violence against other Muslims, including non-combatants, by recourse to takfir, or the excommunication of fellow Muslims. For these groups, if Muslims have been deemed to be apostates, then violence against them is licit'. Shadi Hamid and Rashid Dev, 'Islamism, Salafism, and Jihadism: A Primer', 15 July 2016, https://www.brookings.edu/blog/markaz/2016/07/15/islamism-salafism-and-jihadism-a-primer.

5. It is hard for modern Europeans to properly understand the violence their forebears visited on the peoples of what today is called the Middle East. The First Crusade began in 1095 and led to over two centuries of brutal European efforts to seize much of the Levant in the name of just war, which echoes across the ages. Christopher Tyerman wrote, 'A just war was not necessarily a holy war, although holy wars were, to their adherents, just. While holy war depended on God's will, constituted a religious act, was directed by clergy or divinely sanctioned lay rulers, and offered spiritual rewards, just war formed a legal category justified by secular necessity, conduct and aim, attracting temporal benefits. The fusion of the two became characteristic of later Christian formulations'. See Christopher Tyerman (2006) *God's War: A New History of the Crusades* (London: Penguin), p. 35.

and the wars in Iraq have proved fertile soil for the further rise of Salafist extremism and its mutation into Daesh.

The threat from Daesh has not dissipated in spite of the November 2017 loss of its last city, Raqqa, near the Iraqi-Syrian border. To many the vision of Daesh remains compelling. In June 2014, Daesh declared the creation of a 'Caliphate', a form of state that would be governed by God's law, or Sharia, by a caliph, God's deputy-on-Earth. A fundamentalist Salafist group, Daesh demands complete allegiance in its mission to defend the 'Umma' (community of devout Muslims) against infidels and apostates. Daesh both competes with al-Qaeda and, through its extended network, at times cooperates with it. Born from tensions within societies across MENA, Daesh also exploits those tensions.

Any new political settlement critical to a wider peace in the region must come first and foremost from within the region itself, but there is little sign of that happening. What influence Americans and Europeans could bring to bear would require leadership, patience, and cohesion between both the Allies and their partners in the region, of which there is also little evidence. Neither the US nor its European allies have or share a grand strategic political vision for the region, and there is little or no strategic unity of effort or purpose between them. The January 2020 White House Peace Plan also revealed that there is little or no political ownership of any such strategy at the highest levels in the region, Brussels, or any European chancellery. Attacks in Europe, such as the November 2015 attack on the Bataclan Club in Paris, have brought a focus on the threat that al-Qaeda and Daesh continue to pose. However, the response has been overwhelmingly on the tactical, intelligence-led prevention of further attacks, rather than any European vision to deal with the underlying causes of conflict. Indeed, there is little or no political desire in Europe to consider the bigger strategic picture and there is little willingness in Europe to engage political capital or action in a stable MENA. What European 'strategy' there is represents essentially one of reactive containment.

The situation is further complicated by the new geopolitics of the region, and the growing tensions between the West on one side, and China and Russia on the other. This tension effectively prevents the drafting of any political strategy that might reduce tensions and ease the poverty and helplessness that fuels the Salafist cause. Even with the apparent 'defeat' of Daesh in Syria, Europe will continue to face a form of hybrid, virtual Caliphate that stretches across MENA, and a protracted struggle along

Europe's southern border. Through its skilful exploitation of the internet, al-Qaeda and Daesh will also continue to gain recruits to their cause from within Europe.

In spite of the January 2020 White House Plan, and irrespective of the enhanced NATO role in the region envisaged under it, any meaningful effort to better support partner states in the region would need close US–European cooperation, not least over easing the Israeli-Palestinian struggle. There is little such cooperation, creating a vacuum for others such as Iran and Russia to exploit.

Syria and the humbling of the West

The US and its European allies are divided over how to engage the Middle East. The war in Syria and the 2013 disagreement over whether to take military action against the Assad regime for Damascus's repeated contravention of the Chemical Weapons Convention (CWC) revealed a profound divergence between the Allies over their concept of security for the Middle East.[6] The August 2013 decision by the British House of Commons to refuse to authorize any use of force by the Cameron government of the time revealed just how divided the West had become over Syria, even before the Trump administration. The British decision also had profound consequences for the Obama strategy and encouraged Russian opportunism.

In 2013, the UK and France had significant air and sea assets in the Eastern Mediterranean. The US had also despatched a carrier strike group, centred on the 104,000-ton nuclear-powered aircraft carrier USS Harry S. Truman, significantly increasing the capability and capacity of coalition forces. In principle, at least, coalition leaders could have mounted a robust response to Syria's clear breach of the CWC. And yet, both Washington and its Allies dissembled, encouraging both the Assad regime and the Russians to become bolder.

---

6. The Organisation for the Prohibition of Chemical Weapons, or OPCW, states the purpose of the CWC: 'The Convention aims to eliminate an entire category of weapons of mass destruction by prohibiting the development, production, acquisition, stockpiling, retention, transfer or use of chemical weapons by States Parties. States Parties, in turn, must take the steps necessary to enforce that prohibition in respect of persons (natural or legal) within their jurisdiction'. https://www.opcw.org/chemical-weapons-convention.

Russia's decisive September 2015 military intervention in Syrian not only tipped the power balance in favour of the regime against an array of Western-backed rebel groupings, it also turned the conflict into a regional-strategic struggle with geopolitical implications. The justification for Russia's intervention, the struggle against terrorism, as defined by Moscow, also conveniently confused Europeans as to Russia's real aims, coming soon after Moscow's 2014 attack on Ukraine. And it revealed how far most Europeans have retreated from any meaningful engagement in MENA, a region vital to their own security.

In 2016, an advanced, integrated Russian air defence system was established in Syria, centred on long-range S-300 and S-400 surface-to-air missiles at Moscow's recently acquired air base at Latakia and its naval facility at Tartus, enabling Russia to extend its military influence far into the Mediterranean. In effect, Moscow 'trumped' the Western coalition and laid the groundwork for Assad's Pyrrhic victory. The West's divisions also did incalculable damage to the reputation of Western powers, whilst reinforcing Russian influence across MENA.

The ambivalence of Europeans over Syria demonstrates the profound limitation on the willingness and ability of Europe to act anywhere across MENA. This reluctance places additional pressure on the US and, given the domestic salience of Israel in the American body politic, raises deep issues about whether Americans and Europeans can ever agree a shared policy for the region. There is also a marked difference of approach. Many Europeans emphasize international law as the basis for any coercive action because for them the window between legitimate punitive action and dangerous escalation is narrow, even though several European states have played an important military role in the Global Coalition to Counter ISIL. There have also been limitations on the capability of European forces, which have been reinforced by a lack of 'domestic' European political support for any US-led campaigns in the wake of the wars in Afghanistan and Iraq. Consequently, several European governments find themselves in the invidious position of wanting to support US leadership for wider strategic reasons, such as the centrality of the US to their own defence, whilst also wishing to avoid the ire of their own populations tired of such engagements.

Furthermore, however limited, any European action in support of the US in the region will remain dependent on sound American leadership. Whilst the Obama administration worked hard to include allies in its thinking, the Trump administration became increasingly assertive and unilateral in its decision-making, undermining the cohesion of the coalition.

The administration also repeatedly sent mixed messages about its strategic aims, confusing allies and informing adversaries as to its intentions, and further undermining faith in US leadership. For example, preparations for the 2019 US strikes on Syrian chemical facilities supposedly included eight targets under consideration, which included air bases, chemical weapons storage, and research facilities. Unsure about the impact of such a strike on his domestic US political support, and lacking the leadership skills the maintenance of a coalition demands, President Trump effectively tele-graphed US intentions to both Damascus and Moscow. Consequently, Damascus dispersed its air and other forces, sending essential units and assets to the Russian air base of Latakia, thus undermining the effectiveness of coalition action, and the confidence of American allies in US strategy.

The consequences of the West's failure in Syria are profound. First, the refusal of the US and its European allies to act against the Assad regime for using chemical weapons against its own people risked not only the CWC, but also the very basis of international law which is central to the European security concept. Second, Russia in effect 'won' the war in Syria and removed any meaningful Western influence therein, helped in part by the capricious nature of US policy under President Trump. Third, the defeat also undermined any rationale for US–European cooperation in a region deemed vital to both American and European interests, with potentially profound strategic implications for the future of European defence. The implicit tension between Americans and Europeans over how to deal with threats beyond an invasion of NATO members by Russia in Europe also raises a profound set of questions about the political and strategic utility of the Atlantic Alliance in the twenty-first century, particularly the continued utility over the medium to longer term of any such relationship with Europeans, especially for the more isolationist wings of both the Democratic and Republican parties in the US.

Given the importance of the region to European security and defence, the absence of a European political strategy for the Middle East worthy of the name is telling. The essential paradox of the West's failure against Assad is that Europeans are now more vulnerable to a range of threats. For example, Libya warned in 2015 that not only was Daesh using the migration crisis to smuggle its fighters into Europe, they were profiting from the trade.[7] The rise of Daesh (it has by no means fallen) is a symptom of several, complex,

7. See 'Islamic State Militants "Smuggled into Europe"', BBC News, 17 May 2015, https://www.bbc.com/news/world-africa-32770390.

and interlocking conflicts and factors that Europeans need to urgently address. Central to any meaningful Western strategy would be joint American and European action to help re-establish strong, legitimate states across the region. Naturally, any such outcome would take many years to realize, possibly generations, and would require strategic patience and levels of political and actual investment that neither contemporary Americans nor Europeans seem willing to countenance.

The lack of any such strategy has again profoundly hindered the West's ability to confront Daesh. The first phase of the mission of the sixty-five-nation Global Coalition to Defeat ISIS was to 'blunt ISIS's strategic, tactical and operational momentum in Iraq'.[8] Whilst that effort met with some significant successes in 2016 and 2017, the Coalition lacked a shared political objective that could begin to remove the underlying causes of Salafist Jihadism and help move the region towards a more stable future. Consequently, the strategy has stalled. If there is to be any chance of future strategic success, Americans and Europeans must together demonstrate a far greater degree of strategic judgement and policy coherence allied to a willingness to invest far more time and money in the region. Any such joint approach was difficult even prior to the COVID-19 crisis, and it is hard to believe that many Europeans will have the energy or the money to deal with the complexities of the Middle East, and the undoubted threats that are posed to Europe.

Critically, the struggle against a Hydra-headed Daesh, and its many affiliates, cannot be separated from the wider regional-strategic conflict between states that is, in turn, mired in the confessional divide between Shia and Sunni Islam. In spite of its apparent 'defeat', Daesh is mutating. Along with al-Qaeda, Daesh will seek to cause mayhem in states across MENA, and seek every opportunity to attack Europe. Moreover, the current struggle between Middle Eastern (and increasingly European) states and anti-state elements, such as al-Qaeda, Daesh, and their many affiliates,

---

8. The Global Coalition to Defeat ISIS was formed in September 2014. It states: 'The Coalition's 80 members are committed to tackling Daesh on all fronts, to dismantling its networks and countering its global ambitions. Beyond the military campaign in Iraq and Syria, the Coalition is committed to: tackling Daesh's financing and economic infrastructure; preventing the flow of foreign terrorist fighters across borders; supporting stabilisation and the restoration of essential public services to areas liberated from Daesh; and countering the group's propaganda'. https://theglobalcoalition.org/en/mission.

could be but the curtain-raiser to a wider Middle East war between states, with profound implications for the future defence of Europe.

The prospects of regional-strategic war

The war in Yemen may, on the face of it, appear to be a 'small war in a faraway country about which we know little', but it could be the place where the fourth Gulf War starts that would have profound implications for the security and defence of Europe.[9] The war in Yemen reflects the complexity of the wider region where the fundamentalist threat and the struggle for regional supremacy merge.

At its core, the struggle in Yemen, like so many across the region, is a proxy for regional-strategic supremacy between Saudi Arabia and the Gulf Cooperation Council (GCC), on one side, and Iran, with implicit backing from Russia, on the other. Yemen's strategic position, like that of Ukraine in Europe, also makes it vulnerable to interference. Sitting at the mouth of the Red Sea, whoever controls Yemen controls access to the Suez Canal through which much of the world's trade flows, and it is also adjacent to the Persian Gulf over which China and Iran are seeking to extend their respective influence. For example, any Iranian threat to both the Straits of Hormuz and the Gulf of Aden would threaten to strangle the free flow of oil from Saudi Arabia and the Gulf States, with profound implications for the world beyond, most notably China and Europe.

There are also tensions within Europe. Whilst much of European debate on the war has been on the humanitarian tragedy in Yemen, leading to calls for limits on the sale of European weapons to the Saudis and their Gulf allies,

---

9. The 1938 quote about Czechoslovakia at the time of the failed Munich Accord with Hitler by then British Prime Minister Neville Chamberlain is well known. However, the speech Chamberlain gave in an address to the British people on 27 September 1938 puts his thinking on appeasement in a wider strategic context: 'However much we may sympathize with a small nation confronted by a big and powerful neighbor, we cannot in all circumstances undertake to involve the whole British Empire in war simply on her account. If we have to fight it must be on larger issues than that. I am myself a man of peace to the depths of my soul. Armed conflict between nations is a nightmare to me; but if I were convinced that any nation had made up its mind to dominate the world by fear of its force, I should feel that it must be resisted. Under such a domination life for people who believe in liberty would not be worth living; but war is a fearful thing, and we must be very clear, before we embark upon it, that it is really the great issues that are at stake, and that the call to risk everything in their defense, when all the consequences are weighed, is irresistible'. http://www.historyguide.org/europe/munich.html.

France and Germany have also been at loggerheads over arms exports. The Germans threatened to block French arms exports to the Saudi-led coalition because the weapons included German-made components, whilst France countered by suggesting German companies were getting around Berlin's export ban by using South African shell companies and accused Germany of hypocrisy. In August 2019 there was a tentative agreement between Paris and Berlin to enable French exports to continue, but friction persists.

There are wider implications for European defence. Irrespective of the rights and wrongs of European arms exports to the region, if they are ultimately blocked, the ability of European states to equip their own armed forces would be damaged, given the importance of such markets for the European aerospace and defence industry, particularly those of the UK, France, and Germany.[10] For Europeans one essential challenge concerns their willingness to support regimes they do not particularly like because their interests trump their values. The US and some European governments have long seen the Saudis and their GCC allies as a potential bulwark against expanding Iranian, Russian, and Chinese influence in a region still vital for the flow of oil to the West. The GCC also provides military bases for extending Western influence across the Middle East region and into the Indian Ocean. In the wake of the Syrian War many states in the region are hedging their bets with the Russians to see if the US scales back its commitment. There is also little support for any US stand against China as Beijing is now one of the biggest providers of foreign direct investment, with Chinese influence in the region growing fast. For example, in 2016 China and Djibouti agreed to establish a military base in the Horn of Africa with the clear intention of projecting Chinese power into the region. In May 2020 a long pier was seen being constructed, suggesting the base was being prepared for use by China's growing blue-water fleet, particularly Beijing's new aircraft carriers.[11]

---

10. See 'Germany Quintuples Arms Sales to Saudi Arabia and Europe', *Deutsche Welt*, 14 November 2017, https://www.dw.com/en/germany-quintuples-arms-sales-to-saudi-arabia-and-egypt/a-41370500.

11. James McClaren wrote, 'The *Shandong* [the newest of China's aircraft carriers] sends a message not only to those regional powers attempting to check China's plans to exercise hegemony inside the nine-dash line disputed area of the South China Sea, but also to the bigger global powers. In particular, it's a warning bell for the United States, which is increasingly concerned that the pace of Chinese ship building and military technology development will diminish its military dominance and allow growing Chinese assertiveness to expand into the wider Indian-Pacific region unconstrained'. See James McClaren, 'With Its New Aircraft Carrier, Is China

The Middle East may well be moving from proxy wars to an all-out regional-strategic war between states that would have profound implications for European defence. The September 2019 drone attack on the Aramco oil refinery in Saudi Arabia was allegedly carried out by Yemeni Houthi rebels. However, the attack, which reduced the world oil supply temporarily by 5 per cent, clearly suggested deep Iranian involvement, specifically the Iranian Revolutionary Guard Corps, as the attack came in the wake of the failure of the Joint Comprehensive Plan of Action (JCPOA). It is Iran and its ambitions which could in time offer the greatest threat to European defence.

Iran and the West's nuclear dilemma

The reason Iran poses the most obvious albeit as yet indistinct threat to European defence is a complex mix of ambition, technology, and proximity. Iran also poses another dilemma for Europeans. There are circumstances when being close to the US makes Europe more vulnerable. And yet, the sorry tale of JCPOA also reveals the extent to which even America's closest Europeans differ over the conduct of statecraft in the Middle East.

For all its flaws, the JCPOA was the only agreement signed up to by the US, Europe's three major powers – the UK, France, and Germany – China, Russia, and, of course, Iran. The Accord had been agreed on 14 July 2015 in Vienna between the Islamic Republic of Iran and the so-called 'E3/EU+3'. The specific purpose of the JCPOA was to limit Iranian ambitions to build nuclear weapons, but the Plan was as much about the contemporary geo-politics and regional-strategic security and stability of the Middle East. For Europeans the JCPOA was also vital to reaffirm an institutional approach to arms control by buttressing the 1968 Nuclear Non-Proliferation Treaty as the essential benchmark for preventing the spread of nuclear weapons. Under the Plan, Iran was to be transformed from a so-called 'threshold state' into a non-nuclear weapons state, and was thus required to end all 'possible military dimensions' of its nuclear programme, and submit to strengthened safeguards and an intrusive verification and inspection regime by the International Atomic Energy Authority (IAEA). However, because IAEA was unable to carry out snap inspections, the Trump administration

Now a Blue Water Navy?', *The Diplomat*, 25 January 2020, https://thediplomat.com/2020/01/with-its-new-aircraft-carrier-is-china-now-a-blue-water-navy.

became profoundly suspicious that Iran was cheating, suspicions the European allies did not share, at least not publicly, even though on 6 June 2018 the IAEA reported that Iran was in compliance. The Trump administration's concerns were echoed in Israel, most notably by Israeli Premier Benjamin Netanyahu.

Under the JCPOA, the EU and the US, as well as the United Nations Security Council (UNSC), agreed to lift a range of trade sanctions and unfreeze some $150 billion of Iranian oil assets held in foreign banks. However, sanctions relief was also linked to Iran's compliance over time and would only take place in stages. Critically, there was to be no complete relief from sanctions until the JCPOA had been implemented in full and the Arak reactor destroyed, which was at the centre of Iran's weapon's programme. At US insistence, a strong 'snap-back' regime was also put in place which allowed for sanctions to be reimposed quickly if the Plan was breached, and without recourse to a further UNSC Resolution.

On 8 May 2018, the United States withdrew from the JCPOA on the grounds that it was insufficiently robust and that Iran was cheating, and quickly reimposed sanctions. The regional-strategic situation deteriorated rapidly thereafter, as did relations between the Trump administration and its European allies, many of which suspected that the administration's justifications had more to do with the JCPOA having been crafted by the Obama administration than any systemic failure of diplomacy. On 17 May 2018, in a sign of the depth of transatlantic tensions, the European Commission even declared new US sanctions on Iran to be 'illegal' if they were applied to Europeans doing business with Iran, and instructed the European Central Bank to facilitate investment to Iran.

In July 2019 the UK, France, and Germany together warned both Tehran and Washington about the deteriorating situation in the Gulf. In the wake of the September 2019 attacks on the Aramco refinery, the US despatched the aircraft carrier USS Abraham Lincoln and its strike group to the Gulf, together with a missile defence battery and a bomber group. Washington's aim was to ratchet up pressure on Tehran a year after the Trump administration had withdrawn from the JCPOA. On 29 December 2019, in the wake of several attacks on Western-flagged oil tankers in the Gulf, the US launched a series of missile strikes against Iranian-backed militias in both Iraq and Syria, whilst on 4 January 2020, the US killed Iran's top general and commander of the Quds Brigade, Qasem Soleimani, with a missile strike shortly after he had arrived at Baghdad International Airport. On 8 January

Iran retaliated by launching a salvo of ballistic missiles at two bases in Iraq where US forces were stationed. In spite of some European naval support in the Gulf to help prevent attacks on shipping, US–European relations had become stretched over how to deal with a potentially significant threat with important implications for the future defence of Europe.

US and European differences over the conduct of statecraft in a crisis are not just semantic, but substantive. A key phrase in the JCPOA reads, 'They [the Parties to the Plan] anticipate that full implementation of this JCPOA will contribute to regional and international peace and security'. The Trump administration believed Tehran (and President Obama) made no real attempt to implement that provision and decided to exert what it calls 'maximum pressure' on Tehran to change its wider foreign policy. Brian Hook, the US Special Representative on Iran, highlighted the relationship between the JCPOA and Iran's overall behaviour, something Europeans were far less concerned about. Calling the US actions a 'response to Iranian aggression', Hook said, 'Everything we are doing is defensive'. He went on: 'Iran is still the leading sponsor of terrorism in the world. If they're behaving this way without a nuclear weapon, imagine how they'll behave with one'.[12] Europeans believed such language was simply unhelpful, removing any room for further negotiations with Iran and forcing them to choose sides in a dangerous dichotomy which only helped the hardliners in Tehran. Indeed, they felt trapped between hardliners in both Tehran and Washington and unable to move either.

Such divisions between the US and its major European allies over Iran could also portend a profound split in the transatlantic relationship. For a long time, the US and its major European allies have disagreed over how to handle the Middle East, in general, and Iran, in particular. In the past these disagreements have been massaged. However, an activist Trump administration may well lead to a widening gulf between the US and its major allies over how to deal with all crises, again with profound implications for European defence. Europeans feel particularly uncomfortable with the administration attempting to link all Iranian foreign policy to the JCPOA, having preferred instead to have slowly built a relationship via the Plan before engaging Iran on a broad spectrum of issues. Unfortunately, for the

---

12. See Josh Glancy, 'We Want a Better Deal, Not War with Iran, Says Envoy Turning the Screw for Donald Trump', 12 May 2019, https://www.thetimes.co.uk/article/we-want-a-better-deal-not-war-with-iran-says-envoy-turning-the-screw-for-donald-trump-7rbjllgsm.

Trump administration the JCPOA was a weak 'deal' which Iran 'won' from a weak Obama administration. Brian Hook went on: 'We have two goals that overlap . . . One is that we'd like to get a new and better deal that succeeds the Iran nuclear deal. It will be comprehensive: nukes, missiles, regional aggression [by Iran] and human rights', making 'Iran's foreign policy unsustainable', referring to Iran's support for Hamas, Hezbollah, and Islamic Jihad, as well as Houthi militias in Yemen.[13] Critically, Americans and Europeans remain divided over Iran. Whilst there is some evidence Iran had been cheating on some of the Plan's provisions and Washington (and Tel Aviv) had been right to be concerned about that, a leaked July 2019 diplomatic telegram from Sir Kim Darroch, the UK's former ambassador to Washington, also accused the Trump administration of exaggerating the claim for political ends.[14] European critics noted the timing of the US withdrawal from the Plan and its proximity to a 2018 visit to the US by Israeli Premier Netanyahu.

There should be no illusions as to the extent of Iran's regional-strategic ambitions. Iran is a Persian, Shia country in an Arab, predominantly Sunni region and there is every reason to believe that, unless contained, Iran will continue to use proxy militias and terrorist groups to destabilize the Arab states to its west and south. Nor has Iran given up its ambitions to become a nuclear power, even if (or partially because) Tehran is also fully aware that Saudi money paid for much of Pakistan's nuclear programme, and that Riyadh is quite capable of rapidly becoming a nuclear power.[15]

---

13. Ibid.
14. In April 2018 Israeli Prime Minister Benjamin Netanyahu went public with his claims that Iran was cheating on the JCPOA. Specifically, Netanyahu accused Tehran of moving details of its nuclear programme, Project Amad, to an archive to be reactivated later. He claimed Israel had penetrated the archive and obtained 55,000 pages: 55,000 files on 183 CDs. See Khrishnadev Calamur, 'Netanyahu's Bizarre PowerPoint Presentation on Iran: Israel's Leader Says Iran Cheated on the Nuclear Deal, Adding Doubts about the Agreement's Survival. But He Mostly Described Past Programs', *The Atlantic*, 30 April 2018, https://www.theatlantic.com/international/archive/2018/04/netanyahu-iran-nuclear-deal/559250.
15. In November 2013, the BBC's Mark Urban reported that, 'Amos Yadlin, a former head of Israeli military intelligence, told a conference in Sweden that if Iran got the bomb, the Saudis will not wait one month. They already paid for the bomb, they will go to Pakistan and bring what they need to bring'. See Mark Urban, 'Saudi Nuclear Weapons on Order from Pakistan', BBC News, 6 November 2013, https://www.bbc.com/news/world-middle-east-24823846. Moreover, in a February 2019 piece for Durham University's *Global Policy* magazine, Scott Montgomery wrote, 'For over a decade, that is, intelligence people have reported that the Saudis paid for most of Pakistan's arsenal and that an agreement exists between the two nations to the effect that the first in a crisis has access to what it already paid for. Such an arrangement, not surprisingly, has been routinely denied when mentioned in public fora. Yet we might note

The transatlantic relationship? The tragedy for Europeans is that if the JCPOA seemed to represent the brashness of US foreign policy under President Trump, it has also become the embodiment of Europe's abandonment of hard power as an instrument of policy. If there is a conflict, Europeans will be forced to take sides. If they are not clearly on the American side, or insufficiently so, the implications for the future defence of Europe would be incalculable. The best that might thus be said of the West's approach to Iran is that the US plays 'bad cop', whilst the Europeans cast themselves as 'good cops'. Iran will certainly seek to gain from any profound division between the Americans and their European allies.

Libya, Europe, and failed transition

If there is one state that embodies the risks and threats to Southern Europe from instability across MENA, it is Libya. A decade on from the Anglo-French-led military campaign which toppled Colonel Muammar Qadhafi, Libya remains a broken state that is not only stalled on the transitional road to a stable, functioning, representative state, but has also become a major point of departure for millions of desperate people making a march of misery towards Europe. Moreover, as the influence of Russia, Turkey, and Daesh grows, Americans, but in particular Europeans, are unclear and unwilling what action to take. The embodiment of a profound Alliance split is also in Libya as NATO's southern states reject the idea that Russia poses the greatest threat to European defence.

It had been so different back in 2011. A just legal framework for the whole of Libya would take time, but by backing the forces in Tripoli, a functioning state could be rebuilt. And yet, such hopes have been dashed. There is no clear seat of government with Libya still deeply divided between Benghazi and Tripoli, and Daesh-backed Islamist groups continue to insist on a strict interpretation of Sharia law, which has alienated the Berber population and

the uniquely close relationship between the two nations, which recently made news by Prince Salman's visit with Prime Minister Khan. Moreover, were the Pakistanis to site nuclear weapons in Saudi Arabia, it would simply be following the precedent set by NATO, with around 150 U.S. warheads present in five countries, Belgium, Germany, Italy, Netherlands, and Turkey. The practice, in fact, has a kinder, gentler title: "nuclear sharing"'. See Scott L. Montgomery, 'Why Saudis Want Nuclear – And Will Get It', 27 February 2019, https://www.globalpolicyjournal.com/blog/27/02/2019/why-saudis-want-nuclear-and-will-get-it.

stalled transitional arrangements. Public order remains fragmented and uncertain, enabling warlords and criminal gangs to trade in human trafficking and the slavery of huge numbers of migrants.

Libya seems locked in transition with little progress having been made in mitigating conflict across security, economic, and political spheres. Libya's rich natural resources should have been at the centre of the country's rebuilding, and yet they have become a kind of hostage in a society in which guns rather than politicians still determine Libya's future. A lack of good governance has seen political moderation and accountability evaporate with hoped-for democratic institutions by and large stillborn. What has emerged instead is a failed state in which secular, tribal, and Islamist elements perpetually vie for power and wealth.

Libya's failure has been a European failure. Some 220 miles/350 kilometres from Malta, the EU could have played a vital role in stabilizing Libya. And yet, Europe's efforts have been lamentable, with Italy effectively left alone to fashion what passes for policy in a region vital to European security and defence. In August 2011, the EU appointed a Special Representative for the Southern Mediterranean, but little progress has been made in what became known as the second Libyan Civil War, which continues. Perhaps the greatest humiliation was in January 2020 when Turkey began deploying troops to Libya ostensibly to help stabilize the country, although President Erdogan is believed to have a keen eye on Libya's resources. The Libyan fiasco begs another question of Europeans. If Europe cannot play a meaningful and constructive role in a country vital to the security and defence of Europe, then what hope do Europeans have of playing any role across the wider region, and what does such a failure say about the ability and willingness of Europeans to secure and defend themselves in the wake of the COVID-19 crisis?

COVID-19 and fragile states

On 21 April 2020 David Beasley, Executive Director of the World Food Programme, wrote:

> with COVID-19, I want to stress that we are not only facing a global health pandemic but also a global humanitarian catastrophe. Millions of civilians living in conflict-scarred nations, including many women and children, face being pushed to the brink of starvation, with the spectre of famine a very real

and dangerous possibility. This sounds truly shocking but let me give you the numbers: 821 million people go to bed hungry every night all over the world, chronically hungry, and as the new Global Report on Food Crisis published today shows, there are a further 135 million people facing crisis levels of hunger or worse. That means 135 million people on earth are marching towards the brink of starvation. But now the World Food Programme analysis shows that, due to the Coronavirus, an additional 130 million people could be pushed to the brink of starvation by the end of 2020. That's a total of 265 million people.[16]

In May 2020, a report by Sky News following a warning issued by the United Nations Refugee Agency stated:

> The impact of coronavirus on Yemen will be devastating after years of civil war, the head of the United Nations Refugee Agency in the country has told Sky News. Speaking from the Yemeni capital, Sana'a, Jean-Nicolas Beuze said the number of suspected COVID-19 cases in the country appears to be multiplying fast and, at the same time, international aid agencies are being forced to abandon critical programmes. The report continued, 'Half of the health facilities have been destroyed by five years of conflict. People die from many other causes too such as dengue fever, malaria, cholera . . . more than 24 million Yemenis – 80% of the population – are in need of humanitarian assistance. Half of the country's health facilities are dysfunctional and nearly a quarter of the country's districts have no doctors. We know that the immunity among the population is very low. We are speaking here about people who maybe eat once a day. We are speaking about children who have not been vaccinated.
>
> We are speaking about people who have fled their homes because their homes were shelled or bombed and therefore do not have any livelihood . . . All the humanitarian partners here . . . are missing critical funding. The UNHCR will be closing, in a few days, a number of lifeline programmes. So we will be leaving 3.6 million internally displaced and 280,000 refugees without any form of assistance. It's a life and death situation for them'.[17]

A number of authoritative sources, such the *Scientific American* and *ReliefWeb. int*, have put the likely numbers of climate migrants by the year 2050 at some

---

16. See 'WFP Chief Warns of Hunger Pandemic as COVID-19 Spreads (Statement to UN Security Council)', WFP News, 21 April 2020, https://www.wfp.org/news/wfp-chief-warns-hunger-pandemic-covid-19-spreads-statement-un-security-council.
17. See Mark Stone, 'Coronavirus Will "Delete Yemen from Maps All Over the World"', Sky News, 18 May 2020, https://news.sky.com/story/coronavirus-will-delete-yemen-from-maps-all-over-the-world-11989917.

200 million.[18] If just 10 per cent of these desperate people attempt to make their way to Europe, the arrival of 20 million non-Europeans would have a very significant impact on the fabric of European society. Defending Europe from, say, Russian or Chinese aggression might thus be relatively easy compared to the potential impact of climate migration. COVID-19 could well accelerate such a trend for it would combine the pressures of climate stress and pandemic which afflict most states across MENA. In April 2020, the International Office of Migration estimated some 650,000 migrants are waiting in Libya alone to cross to Europe.[19]

COVID-19 swept across the region in early 2020. Some of the richer states in the Gulf were able to take relatively effective action to control the pandemic. However, fragile and war-torn states were not. Iraq, Syria, Libya, and Yemen rapidly become epicentres of the pandemic, adding further misery to the desperation faced by millions. Migrant populations are particularly vulnerable as most have already left fragile and failing states where there was little or no organized healthcare by Western standards.

Fragile states also tend to share certain characteristics which facilitate the spread of a pathogen. They all tend to have a growing population, many of which for cultural and economic reasons live in large family groups, and many of whom also live in squalid conditions in rapidly growing but poorly serviced and densely populated mega-cities. Basic health provision is further exacerbated by poverty and poorly protected health professionals who are amongst the most vulnerable during an emergency such as COVID-19.

Poor governance is likely to collapse during any such emergency as trust in authority is low even during relatively stable periods. Existing social and political pressures intensify during such emergencies, leading to an increase in the numbers of both internally displaced peoples and refugees, which can also lead to international tensions, such as those that exist between Turkey and EU states. Such circumstances are fertile breeding grounds for violent extremism, most notably Salafist Jihadism, and worsen existing conflicts, such as that in the Sahel.

18. See Andrea Thompson (2018) "Wave of Climate Migration Looms, but It "Doesn't Have to Be a Crisis"", https://www.scientificamerican.com/article/wave-of-climate-migration-looms-but-it-doesnt-have-to-be-a-crisis and Kamel Baher (2017) 'Climate Migrants Might Reach One Billion by 2050', https://reliefweb.int/report/world/climate-migrants-might-reach-one-billion-2050.

19. See Faras Chani, 'Nearly 1000 Migrants "Returned to Libya This Year"', Al Jazeera, 14 January 2020, https://www.aljazeera.com/news/2020/01/1000-migrants-returned-libya-year-200114132748736.html.

MENA and the bonfire of European illusions

In conclusion, MENA is the place where European illusions could well burn if not attended to. Given the scale of the crisis across MENA, and the threat posed to Europe, both Americans and Europeans together need to better support each other in fashioning a worst-case strategy for the region. Western strategy, such as it exists, is partial and uncoordinated, focused essentially on trying to reinforce fragile states in North Africa, most notably Libya, whilst buttressing the Gulf States as a bulwark against Iran in the wider Middle East. Further political, economic, and even security and military support is likely to remain vital, but on a scale otherwise unappreciated in either the US or Europe. However politically challenging, and as a bulwark against a general regional collapse, any such support would need to take place in parallel with the discrete promotion of political reforms and the strengthening of pan-regional institutions, such as the Arab League, to include the creation of a Rapid Reaction Force that could intervene early in a crisis in support of its member-states.

All such efforts presuppose some form of European grand strategy for the region, but history does not bode well for such an effort, even if Europeans were capable of it. In the past Europeans have been guilty of too much grand ambition in the Middle East, albeit for narrow, national purposes. Today, there is a lack of any meaningful strategic ambition of any sort. It is precisely such strategic ambition any US–European joint strategy for the region would need if the Middle East and much of North Africa is not to become an even greater threat to itself and Europe. Neither American nor European efforts thus far have in any way met the challenge.

Regional-strategic frictions will have geopolitical implications. Tensions between the West and Iran are likely to intensify, due mainly to efforts by hardliners around Ayatollah Khamenei and the Iranian Revolutionary Guard to foment regional instability. The US policy of 'maximum pressure' and its hard-hitting sanctions is driving the Iranian economy into a deep recession at a time when the population is also suffering from the effects of the COVID-19 crisis. However, there are also profound tensions between the US and its European allies over how to deal with the regime in Tehran. With Iran soon to be successfully freed from its destabilization of Syria, and depending on how Tehran reacts to the COVID-19 crisis, there is little reason to believe that the regime will not seek to extend its proxy war against Saudi Arabia and the Gulf States. The economic disruption caused by renewed US sanctions and COVID-19 could well lead to further adventurism by the Tehran regime, as it seeks to shore up its faltering domestic position. With the Assad regime in Syria little more than a client state, and Iraq split down a Sunni-Shia divide that has enabled Iran to keep Baghdad politically off-balance, the Iranians clearly feel emboldened to further complicate the situation in Yemen for the Saudis and their allies. If successful, Iran would force Riyadh to face instability and uncertainty on three of its four sides. Thus, whilst Persian Shia Iran is unlikely ever to exert direct control over Sunni Arab Arabia, it is well positioned to further destabilize the Kingdom, the sheikdoms, and the emirates of the GCC. Such an outcome would not be in the Western or European interest.

In the wake of the COVID-19 crisis, and faced with the threat of growing Iranian, Russian, and possibly Chinese influence, as well as the threat posed by Daesh and al-Qaeda across the region, allied to the continuing dependence of Europe in particular on Saudi and Gulf oil, it would seem that both Americans and Europeans have little option but to support Saudi Arabia and its Gulf allies. What that 'support' consists of will depend, to a large extent, on whether Americans and Europeans can agree on what to do. One of the many paradoxes of the West's engagement with the contemporary wars of the Middle East is that whilst Europeans are far less engaged than the US, they are far more vulnerable to the consequences, especially should oil exports be disrupted. The Trump administration's decision to abandon the JCPOA, and reimpose sanctions on Tehran, has shown how hard it is for Americans and Europeans to agree on any joint course of action in the Middle East. However, Americans and Europeans must also collectively find ways to exert pressure, albeit discreetly, on the Saudis and their allies, to improve their conduct in Yemen in the short term and end the conflict as soon as possible. Yemen has become a humanitarian catastrophe.

MENA is at a strategic tipping point, and not just for the region but also for the strategic partnership between the US and its European allies upon which the future defence of Europe rests. If Europeans simply emphasize values, they will lose influence over partners that remain vital to their interests. If Americans focus simply on their interests, other than guaranteeing the security of Israel, it is increasingly hard to see why Washington should engage in conflicts that are more about European values. Should the divide deepen in Europe's strategic backyard, there can be no question that other powers, most notably China, will move rapidly to fill the influence vacuum caused by Europe's disastrous retreat from the region.

Europeans could well have to contend with some form of grand strategic super-insurgency in its strategic backyard. Daesh has genuinely grand strategic ambitions with a leadership that believes that fate and the Almighty will assure their mission to change the world and, in time, create a global Caliphate. The first step is destruction of the state in the Middle East, and then the world over, even as it uses the means of the state against the state, funding its campaigns from the sale of captured resources, such as oil and gas and enslaved captives, and using force, disinformation, and brutality in much the same way as many modern states. Moreover, Daesh is secretly backed by several state and factional supporters who mistakenly believe it can be manipulated to back their narrower ends, not unlike those that financed the rise of Hitler and the Nazi Party in Germany in the early 1930s.

Salafist attacks on Europe only confirm the scope and intensity of the terrorist threat with which Europeans must contend. Many of the terrorists hail from poorly integrated Muslim communities within Europe, both long-established and recent arrivals, with younger people particularly prone to radicalization. Almost by way of response there is a growing threat of reactionary, nativist movements transmuting into terrorist networks. All such groups, be they Salafist or nativist, are prone to manipulation by external powers, which in turn threatens to thwart the search for a reasoned balance between internal security and external defence. COVID-19 has made this situation even more complicated as poorer communities seem to suffer proportionately more than their more affluent counterparts. Worse, significant evidence exists of growing synergies between terrorist networks and organized crime – organized criminal networks that also have close relations with illiberal regimes the world over and, regrettably, would appear to have significant relations with some regimes within Europe as well.

It is unlikely that Europe could resist a determined Russian attack on its eastern flank. Imagine if such an attack took place in parallel with mass disruption in Southern Europe due to the collapse of states across North Africa.

5

China

The irresistible rise of China?

What are the implications of China's rise for European defence? China's meteoric rise is fast resetting the strategic context of all the main themes herein of contemporary power: the ability and capacity of the US to lead, the need for far greater European strategic responsibility, the nature of globalization as a mechanism for changing the global balance of power, the role of COVID-19 as an accelerant of change, and how power changes both behaviour and allegiance. China will thus be the priority strategic challenger to the US for the coming decade and probably far longer, with the most profound implications for the future defence of Europe. Therefore, it is the rise of China more than any other factor that is challenging and changing all the political and strategic assumptions upon which European defence stands. Europeans need to understand that and quickly. Indeed, two factors above all others are helping to define the twenty-first-century security environment and the changing military balance of power that for Washington is fast coming to define the American security dilemma: the rise of China's military capability and European military weakness.

In May 2020, three events suggested the flavour of China's challenge. On 6 May the UK's National Cyber Security Centre and the US Cybersecurity and Infrastructure Security Agency issued a Joint Advisory Statement that said, 'state actors are actively targeting organisations involved in both national and international COVID-19 responses'. The statement went on, 'The global reach and international supply chains of those organisations increase exposure to malicious actors. Actors view supply chains as a weak link that they can exploit to obtain access to better protected targets'.[1] The

---

1. 'States Trying to Steal Vaccine Secrets, Security Agencies Say', *The Times*, 6 May 2020.

Americans and British believe China is not only at the forefront of such efforts, but also engaged daily in industrial levels of espionage and digital aggression. On 15 May it emerged that Taiwan was growing increasingly concerned about Chinese military activity near the strategically important Pratas Islands (what the Chinese call Dongsha) in the South China Sea. Such activity appeared to pave the way for a massive August 2020 Chinese amphibious exercise which was designed to test the ability of the People's Liberation Navy to seize contested islands. Song Zhongping, a Chinese military expert, said that such exercises were designed to deter Taiwanese 'separatists'. 'Exercises such as this are aimed at islands like the Dongsha . . . and the larger island, namely Taiwan. If Taiwan secessionists insist on secession, military exercises can turn into action any time'.[2]

However, perhaps the most worrying development were reports that the Pentagon had war-gamed a major conflict with China and lost. Specifically, in a war game simulated for 2030, the Americans concluded the US Navy would simply be overwhelmed by the new attack submarines, aircraft carriers, and destroyers allied to the new medium-range missile systems and long-range anti-ship missiles that are already in the Chinese arsenal. Bonnie Glaser of the Center for Strategic and International Studies (CSIS) stated, 'Every simulation that has been conducted looking at the threat from China by 2030 have all ended up with the defeat of the US'.[3]

China's impact on European defence is different to Russia's, but over time it will be potentially just as dangerous, if not more so. Beijing's influence is more insidious, with growing economic and political influence within Europe being used to steadily undermine the transatlantic relationship and steadily shift the global balance of power in its favour. Moreover, the growing might and reach of the Chinese armed forces is forcing the increasingly overstretched armed forces of the US to make risky choices about where to position the bulk of its forces. In Europe, those pressures also magnify the threat posed by Russian forces. China's intelligence services are engaged in a major campaign to steal both military and civilian secrets which extends to the wholesale theft of intellectual property. Washington's worst nightmare is that one day it might have to confront three simultaneous, engineered crises in the Indo-Pacific, the Middle East and North Africa, and

2. See Didi Tang, 'Beijing Island War Games Rattle Taiwan', *The Times*, 15 May 2020.
3. See Michael Evans, 'US "Would Lose Any War" Fought in the Pacific with China', *The Times*, 16 May 2020.

Europe faced by Chinese and Russian forces of sufficient capability and capacity that the Americans are simply unable to be in all three theatres in strength, without the support of capable European forces.

China does not lack strategic ambition. President Xi Jinping has set the goal of China being the dominant global power by 2050. China's behaviour during the COVID-19 crisis certainly conforms to that ambition and can thus be explained in two ways. First, control, secrecy, and the masking of failure comes naturally to the leadership of the Chinese Communist Party (CCP). Second, China is becoming sufficiently powerful that it need not care too much about what others think of it. In spite of the crisis, there is every likelihood that China's power and influence will continue to grow, as will the CCP's obsession with secrecy. Indeed, China is Europe's coming power. This poses a profound dilemma for Europeans because their respective economies are increasingly dependent on a state that shares few of Europe's values, and in many ways is contemptuous of them.

Equally, COVID-19 has done profound damage to European trust in China. It has also deepened tensions with the US, the guarantor of European defence. China also sought to exploit the crisis for military-strategic gain at the expense of the US, which does little to suggest the post-COVID-19 world will be one of harmony between Washington and Beijing. As *The Times* wrote in May 2020, 'Whilst world attention has been focused on the coronavirus, China has engaged in naval exercises in the South China Sea and sunk a Vietnamese fishing vessel in those waters. The vast expanse of ocean is the site of several maritime and island territorial claims by neighbouring states; by projecting naval power. Beijing seeks to supplant diplomacy with a show of military hardware and newly-built facilities. It also brazenly confronts the US . . . These tensions are not due to some unfortunate diplomatic misunderstanding. They are increasing because of Chinese provocation'.[4] In other words, as European governments consider to what extent the COVID-19 crisis will afford them an extended military-strategic vacation, Beijing is using the crisis to extend its military power and influence.

Equally, COVID-19 has done damage to China and its reputation for reliability and trustworthiness. For example, whilst the British government continues to state publicly that it believes COVID-19 was born in an appalling 'wet' Wuhan market where it leapt the inter-species barrier

---

4. 'China's Challenge', *The Times*, 4 May 2020.

between bats and humans, it is also considering the possibility that the pathogen may have escaped from a government laboratory in the Chinese city, the Wuhan Institute of Virology. In May 2020, the Five Eyes Intelligence Group (the US, the UK, Australia, Canada, and New Zealand) allegedly accused the Chinese of endangering foreign countries by suppressing information about the early days of the outbreak. It also suggested that China refused to share live samples of the virus and destroyed evidence at the Wuhan Institute of Virology.

China's behaviour during the crisis confirmed that Beijing saw COVID-19 as part of a geopolitical power struggle and employed propaganda and disinformation to that end. For China, geopolitics is the permanent power struggle between balance and imbalance, and who controls power and its pivot: the strategic yin and yang. That pivot is increasingly the Indo-Pacific and it is increasingly contested. Many already believe that China 'won' the COVID-19 crisis and that the Middle Kingdom will become even more 'Middle' to world affairs. China is certainly doing all it can to foster such a belief.

COVID-19 has revealed some fundamental truths about the Beijing regime, but it also begs a question Europeans should ask themselves: why is China so aggressive? Historically, autocracies have often resorted to external adventurism. It is partly the nature of such beasts, but it is also because of the political settlements that enables an autocratic elite to retain power. Over the past century, Wilhelmine Germany, Nazi Germany, Imperial Japan, and the Soviet Union have all embarked on expansionist adventures given the chance. After decades consolidating its power at home, neo-Communist Beijing seems to have embarked on a similar if somewhat more sophisticated variant of autocratic adventurism. One reason is the domestic imperative which drives China to expand its economy, and which rather belies the lazy Western idea that China always takes a long view, often followed by the 1972 Zhou Enlai aphorism that it is too early to assess the impact of the 1789 French Revolution.[5]

In his 2013 'China Dream' speech, President Xi Jinping revealed both the strength and weakness of Beijing.[6] Put simply, the unfettered control of the

---

5. In fact, it may have been that Zhou was referring to the impact of the 1968 French student riots also known as the Paris Spring. As one of Mao Tse Tung's deputies, Zhou Enlai was renowned for the cryptic nature of many of his comments.
6. In a 2013 piece published shortly after Xi's speech, Robert Lawrence Kuhn wrote in *The New York Times*: 'Modernization' means China regaining its position as a world leader in science and

CCP is built on an implicit contract with the Chinese people. In the wake of the 1989 Tiananmen massacre of pro-democracy protesters, the Chinese state effectively offered the Chinese people a deal which endures to this day: unquestioned power in return for rising individual prosperity. Beijing has managed to fulfil that pledge through the astronomic growth of the Chinese economy, with growth rates routinely at or above 10 per cent per annum. Since the 'liberalization' of the Chinese economy on the death of Mao Tse Tung, and his succession by Deng Xiaoping, much of that growth came from the internal modernization of China itself. However, and even though the dependence on foreign exports is declining, Beijing is constantly nervous about the political implications of a major economic slowdown. That is why Beijing is so determined to maintain growth by any means, including through externally driven extractive (an Arctic Belt and Road Initiative (BRI)?) and exploitative policies abroad, hence the BRI. It also explains why the post-COVID-19 crisis is so dangerous for China as well. In the event of a major economic shock, the fall-back policy for the regime is to unleash Chinese nationalism and its burgeoning military power projection is part of that strategy. It is for these reasons China's national strategy might best be described as the ruthless and unrelenting search for comparative strategic advantage. It is a strategy reinforced by cherry-picking the best the West has to offer whilst limiting foreign access to the enormous Chinese market and maintaining the Yuan at an artificially low exchange rate, a source of much tension with the Americans. If Europeans remain oblivious to such ambitions, they will do so at their ultimate cost.

Jekyll and Hyde China

The COVID-19 crisis has also revealed China to be a Jekyll and Hyde power. To the outside world, China is a Dr Jekyll that used 'mask diplomacy': the sending of protective equipment to other countries, much of which was sub-standard, to present itself as a kind of saviour, even if it omitted to mention that several European states, the UK and the

---

technology as well as in economics and business; the resurgence of Chinese civilization, culture and military might; and China participating actively in all areas of human endeavour'. See Robert Lawrence Kuhn, 'Xi Jinping's Chinese Dream', 4 June 2013, https://www.nytimes.com/2013/06/05/opinion/global/xi-jinpings-chinese-dream.html.

Netherlands to the fore, had actually sent so-called personal protective equipment (PPE) to China early in the crisis in a vain attempt to assist Beijing in managing the spread of the disease. At home China is ever more Mr Hyde, as the Xi regime becomes even more repressive, and the shift towards autocracy and away from oligarchy evident since President Xi came to power accelerates. For Europeans, an essential question must be: when will China also become Mr Hyde towards them?

There is a wider, almost ideological aspect to China's post-COVID-19 propaganda. 'Autocracy is better' is the essential domestic message of the regime to its people, with 'proof' of a China that returned to some form of 'normalcy' far earlier than less 'efficient' Western democracies. 'Trust the Party and it will take care of all your needs' has been the mantra. What the regime has also failed to admit is that not only was its lockdown draconian to the point of repression, but the real death toll in China will probably never be known. Worse, Beijing may never learn the lessons it needs to about pandemic control and management. Rather, Beijing has wrapped itself ever tighter in a Chinese nationalist flag, making it hard for other powers to deal with it.

If COVID-19 was essentially a failure of China's food hygiene, the crisis led to a profound failure of US statecraft. A crisis comparison between Beijing and Washington is thus revealing. Only a few years ago it seemed the sun would never set on American power, but how like London in the 1890s contemporary Washington now seems with the appearance of might masking a far weaker reality. The Americans certainly appear to have been the big losers of the COVID-19 crisis, a view both Beijing and Moscow are only too keen to encourage. During the crisis the Trump administration shifted daily from bluster to incompetence back to bluster, whilst profound tensions rapidly came to the fore between Washington, US states, and several mega-cities, such as New York, which left some wondering if the United States of America was any more integrated than the United States of Europe. The carefully calculated image of Chinese and Russian 'aid' being sent to the US only reinforced a growing sense of an America in decline, as it was clearly designed to do.

China has also undermined Washington's leadership of the free world by using the crisis to offer loans and debt relief to a raft of countries, not least in Europe, to 'help' them emerge from the economic crisis. Washington has also walked willingly into carefully laid PR traps. President Trump was right about the many failings of the World Health Organization (WHO). The refusal of the WHO leadership, particularly Director-General Tedros Adhanom Ghebreyesus, to heed Taiwan's early warnings about the crisis suggested China was exerting undue political pressure upon it. Still, the image of America flouncing out of the WHO by threatening to withdraw funding at the height of a pandemic simply enabled China to appear statesmanlike.

Chinaization

COVID-19 has revealed much of globalization to be 'Chinaization', and Europeans need to be clear-eyed about the implications of supporting a process that is in fact designed to undermine the very power upon which they depend for their defence. Indeed, Presidents Xi Jinping and Putin made their disdain clear for the West's idea of a rules-based international system at the G20 in Osaka in June 2019, although Xi differs slightly from Putin because he does not reject completely such a system but thinks the US manages it badly and he would do a far better job. COVID-19 has also revealed China to be a very nineteenth-century 'European' power, in some respects a classically expansionist, revisionist state playing a geopolitical power 'game' in an increasingly fragile international system.[7] Those Europeans who now believe peace to be perpetual should thus look to their own past. Prior to the collapse of the pre-World War One European system, the balance of power system was deemed by many leaders and commentators of the time to be stable and effective. Viewed through that classical power prism, Beijing's determination to exert strategic influence at America's zero-sum expense will more likely destabilize an already tottering international system, and not solely in the military domain. China is also seeking to undermine the primacy of the dollar by establishing the Yuan as an alternative system of transfers and payments, whilst holding a significant level of American foreign debt, although how China would leverage such

---

7. Henry Kissinger wrote, 'In the West, the only examples of functioning balance-of-power systems were among the city-states of ancient Greece and Renaissance Italy, and the European state system which arose out of the peace of Westphalia in 1648. The distinguishing feature of these systems was to elevate a fact of life—the existence of a number of states of substantially equal strength—into a guiding principle of world order'. Henry A. Kissinger (1994) *Diplomacy* (New York: Touchstone), p. 21.

debt for strategic gain is not easy to see.[8] Still, if successful, China could over time critically undermine the ability of Washington to act. Whilst the challenge of Russia is regional, strategically parochial, and primarily military, the challenge posed by China to the US and the wider West stretches across the wide panoply of superpower.

COVID-19 has also revealed the difference between Chinaization and globalization. Beijing's strategic method is to use the West's openness against it by using the remnants of a US-assured peace to further strengthen Beijing's influence by not directly challenging a waning world order until the 'correlation of forces' is overwhelmingly in its favour. At the same time, Beijing is also seeking to complicate the strategic choices of the US by exploiting the overstretch of American forces and resources that results from China's rise.

In such a grand strategic context there was a certain symmetry in the coincidence of the launch of the *EU Global Strategy* in June 2016, and the rejection by the UN's Permanent Court of Arbitration in The Hague of China's claim to sovereignty over some 3 million square kilometres of the South China Sea, through which some $5 trillion of world trade passes every year, and under which huge oil and gas resources are believed to rest. Whereas the EU document hinted at possible wider grand strategic European ambitions firmly established on the principle of a world of law, China's quick denunciation of The Hague judgement, and thus with it the *de facto* rejection of the United Nations Convention on the Law of the Sea (UNCLOS), suggested instead a twenty-first century that could be every bit as cold as the waters Beijing claims as its own. For Europeans, the South China Sea might seem far distant but events therein are potentially momentous for world security and beg a series of geopolitical questions Europeans must sooner or later confront. Are European words ever going to be

---

8. According to Investopedia, China held 5.1 per cent of US foreign debt or $1,123 trillion at the end of 2018. That is slightly higher than Japan which holds 4.7 per cent of US foreign debt or $1.042 trillion. Investopedia's assessment is thus: 'While around 5% of the national debt isn't exactly insignificant, the Treasury Department has had no problems finding buyers for its products even after a rating downgrade. If the Chinese suddenly decided to call in all of the federal government's obligations (which isn't possible, given the maturities of debt securities), it is very likely that others would step in to service the market. This includes the Federal Reserve, which already owns more than three times as much debt as China'. See 'China Owns US Debt, but How Much?', https://www.investopedia.com/articles/investing/080615/china-owns-us-debt-how-much.asp.

matched by real European power? Can the European vision of a world of law (*Lexpolitik?*) ever be realized without major investment in *Machtpolitik*? What could Europe do to exert influence in a region that is fast becoming the crucible of Great Power competition, and which does not take too kindly to post-imperial European interventions?

For all of Beijing's sophisticated COVID-19 information operations, Europeans need to understand that China is no democracy. Moreover, it is a power with a growing penchant, capacity, and military capability for the most cynical *Machtpolitik*. Indeed, it is Beijing that is increasingly the driver of change in geopolitics, far more than Washington, Brussels, Berlin, London, Paris, or even Moscow, which is very much a junior partner to China. Consequently, the language of the EU *Global Strategy* too often reads as wistful, wishful thinking because for the first time in some 400 years Europe is not shaping geopolitics, but rather is subject to it. This profound shift in geopolitics has been implicit in China's behaviour during the COVID-19 crisis, just as it was explicit in the manner and tone of Beijing's rejection of The Hague judgement. Taken together, the two crises suggest a world that is fast approaching a decisive geopolitical tipping point, the beginning of an era of intense grand strategic competition, and with it the threat of a major war at some time in the future.

Beijing has not ruled out a negotiated political settlement with the many states around the East Asian strategic region, such as Brunei, the Philippines, Malaysia, Taiwan, and Vietnam, all of which contest the many Chinese maritime and territorial claims. However, any such settlement would be on China's terms, part of a China-centric regional-strategic system that would turn regional states into little more than satellites, albeit sweetened by the offering of bilateral agreements and settlements. This new phase of Chinese statecraft should be studied very carefully by those Europeans attracted by Chinese money.

China is also increasingly a player in Europe. On the face of it, China's BRI is constructive and involves some sixty-eight countries stretching along some 6,000 kilometres of sea lines between Southeast Asia, the Pacific (Oceania), and North Africa. The 'Belt' demands immense Chinese investment in roads and railways across Central and Western Asia, the Middle East, and, critically, Europe. It invokes memories of the ancient Silk Road, a complex network of trade routes that linked China to Europe for 2,000 years from the second century BC to the eighteenth century. Even in China some question the cost of the BRI.

The nature of Chinese investment should be cause for some concern for Europeans because it is clearly linked to extending Chinese state power and influence. For example, the extent of Huawei's involvement in the development of critical Europe's digital infrastructure was demonstrated by the January 2020 decision of the British government to permit the company to provide up to 35 per cent of 'non-sensitive' parts of Britain's developing 5G network. This was a decision that in May 2020 was reviewed as its critics became more assertive given China's role in the COVID-19 crisis and the US decision to block the supply of semiconductors to the company. Whilst much of Europe's focus is on countering Russia's use of complex strategic coercion, 5D warfare, and the sustained and systematic application of deception, disinformation, destabilization, disruption, and implied destruction, there should perhaps be a sixth 'D'—Chinese debt.

The Chinese-Italian 'all-round' strategic partnership should perhaps be of most concern to the Alliance. Established in 2016, Europe's fourth biggest economy, and NATO's sixth largest military force, the strategic partnership led in 2019 to Italy joining the BRI. Mired in debt and desperate for foreign direct investment, both China and Russia have been willing to accommodate Italy, to the point where a former Italian prime minister, Paolo Gentiloni, in 2019 described the decision as 'geopolitically unwise'.[9] His point was well made because any such investment comes with the assumption on the part of both Beijing and Moscow that Italy will be sympathetic to both, thus potentially undermining Alliance solidarity in a US-led crisis.

Belt and chains?

Europeans should be under no illusions as to the level of strategic ambition driving the BRI. This $1 trillion project is central to Beijing's efforts to influence the future strategic choices of European states, and is thus pivotal to Beijing's efforts to construct a China-centric international system that ties countries to Beijing both economically and strategically. As such, the BRI is a critical part of Beijing's broader strategic competition with the US. Given the centrality of the US to the defence of Europe both now and into the future, Europeans may well be faced with an uncomfortable choice,

9. https://www.cnbc.com/2019/03/25/italy-joining-chinas-belt-and-road-project-is-unwise-former-pm.html.

although the experience of COVID-19 should have made any such choice easier to make.

It is not hard to see why so many hard-pressed Europeans are attracted by Chinese investment. China's entry into Europe came in the aftermath of the 2008–10 banking, Eurozone, and sovereign debt crises, which had been triggered in part by greedy American banks, insufficiently regulated European banks, and the debt splurge many Eurozone states had indulged in following the 1999 creation of the Euro. In some respects, the crisis had a similar effect to a major war given the acceleration in the re-distribution of power and wealth from West to East it triggered, and the bankrupting of Europe.

In the wake of the crisis, many Eurozone members were forced into extended periods of austerity with profound social and political consequences and state budgets slashed, most notably defence. In such circumstances, hard-pressed political elites cast around for any source of foreign direct and indirect investment that could ease domestic pressures. China exploited that need to great strategic effect with investment programmes that tied countries to Beijing via debt trap diplomacy. One example in Europe is the so-called '17 + 1' initiative, a Chinese investment alternative to the EU and US.

However, Chinese investment is not aid and development. Rather, China uses its money, and the state corporations that serve Beijing, as a tool of strategic influence, and if needs be coercion. First, Beijing offers cheap loans for the development of infrastructure in poorer countries. This promotes reliance and dependency upon China by driving up the debt–GDP ratios of the countries involved. Second, when a country defaults on its debt, Beijing aggressively demands recompense, often in the form of strategic infrastructure being transferred to Chinese control. One lesson for Europe is Sri Lanka. China recently (and effectively) seized the Sri Lankan port of Hambantota when Sri Lanka defaulted on its massive Chinese debt. Ironically, the Hambantota case has parallels with the 1842 ceding by China's Qing dynasty of Hong Kong Island to the British during the First Opium War.[10]

10. 'The First Opium War was fought from March 18, 1839, to August 29, 1842, and was also known as the First Anglo-Chinese War. 69 British troops and approximately 18,000 Chinese soldiers perished. As a result of the war, Britain won trade rights, access to five treaty ports, and Hong Kong. The Second Opium War was fought from October 23, 1856, to October 18, 1860, and was also known as the Arrow War or the Second Anglo-Chinese War (although France joined in). Approximately 2,900 Western troops were killed or wounded, while China

Britain had engineered the acquisition of Hong Kong Island, in line with its strategic aim of the time; to expand its mercantilist and imperial ambitions in South and East Asia. For China, the Sri Lankan port is no less strategic to Beijing than Hong Kong was to the British.

Interestingly, it is not the only parallel between China's BRI and Britain's imperial past. In May 2019, Jonathan Hillman published a CSIS commentary entitled 'War and Peace on China's Digital Silk Road',[11] in which he highlights efforts by the British to control strategic communications.[12] In the wake of victory over Napoleon, what had been primarily a commercially driven, mercantilist empire increasingly became an exercise in *Machtpolitik*, as British corporate and state interests merged, much like China today. The British strategy involved the construction of All Red Lines, an exclusive network of telegraph lines which helped facilitate London's command and control of the Empire, and gave Britain a critical strategic communications advantage over rivals. The British also used naval power to control the choke points of the world's sea lanes: Gibraltar, Suez, Aden, Singapore, etc. For a time, Britannia really did rule the waves. With the BRI China is endeavouring to do a similar thing in this digital age by seeking critical control over digital networks whilst erecting its own 'Great Firewall of China'.

In another eerily striking historical parallel to the British laying of telegraph cables in the nineteenth century, some 95 per cent of all international communications still take place via cables laid on the sea-bed. One of China's flagship projects is called, not without some irony, PEACE. The Pakistan East Africa Cable Express is designed to enable the fastest internet link between Asia and Africa. China, or rather the state enterprise Huawei, is laying or enhancing some one hundred digital lines under the sea to massively expand the rate of data transfer. The PEACE cable begins in the

had 12,000 to 30,000 killed or wounded. Britain won southern Kowloon and Western powers got extra-territorial rights and trade privileges. China's Summer Palaces were looted and burned'. See Kallie Szczepanski, 'What Is Extraterritoriality?', 29 January 2019, https://www.thoughtco.com/what-is-extraterritoriality-194996.

11. Jonathan Hillman, 'War and Peace on China's Digital Silk Road', 16 May 2019 (Washington, DC: CSIS).

12. There were, in effect, two British Empires. The first grew up after the first English landings on continental North America with the first settlement at Jamestown in 1607 and ended with the outbreak of the Napoleonic Wars in 1793 and the loss of the American colonies. Mercantilist in nature, the British state took a relatively low profile in its formation. The second British Empire developed in the wake of the 1815 victory over Napoleon and was much more about grand strategy and state power than the first British Empire.

Pakistani port of Gwadar in Pakistan, which is also part of the China–Pakistan Economic Corridor, where China is also seeking to establish a naval base. The strategic aim is clear and thus a clear lesson for Europeans: to increase Beijing's capacity to coerce those it does not control, whilst enhancing its influence over those it effectively does.

What are the specific implications of the BRI for the future defence of Europe? The dilemma that many Central and Eastern European countries (CEEC) face, but seemingly refuse to countenance, concerns the nature, length, and political implications of the many political strings attached to Chinese money. They also refuse to consider the wider strategic implications of such dependence, most notably the likely impact of Chinese money on their strategic relationships with the US. In November 2015, formal China–CEEC cooperation was established at a major conference in China's Suzhou city. The Accord was (and is) effectively the entry point for the BRI into Europe. The sheer scale and ambition of the Accord's many projects again reflects China's strategic ambition, ranging from development programmes to industrial capacity-building, innovative financing agreements, trade enhancement, and beyond. The flipside is the leverage the Accord affords China to coerce EU and NATO members, and implications for the political and strategic cohesion of both institutions. It is a concern to both Brussels and Washington. The danger is that in a crisis certain EU and NATO members would be 'persuaded' by Beijing to withhold their support for the Americans and thus, in effect, paralyse the Alliance.

The BRI should be treated by Europeans with much caution because of the expansionist grand strategy of which it is an essential part, and given the internal Chinese political imperatives that drive it. Those in Europe who say American power is little different are profoundly wrong. The US may have a worldwide presence, but it has no aspirations to exert the kind of control over other states that Beijing seeks through the BRI. Interestingly, there are signs that the lustre of the BRI is beginning to wear off for both debtor states and China itself. Beijing may well discover that the returns on such strategic investment are not as advantageous as it had hoped.

China, the US, and European defence

China's military-strategic method is to impose strategic complexity on the US by investing in the seven multi-domains of future war—air, sea, land, space, cyber, information/espionage, and knowledge—whilst extending the very concept of conflict itself into strategic investment as part of a complex concept of strategic coercion. For Beijing, the power to influence others is thus an essential strategic commodity and, in many ways, the real strategic purpose of Beijing's wealth-creation. It would be naïve in the very least for Europeans to believe China is either going to stop seeking more power at the expense of the US, or indeed become less adversarial with the Americans and the wider West. Would a bipolar US–Chinese strategic relationship make the world, and by extension Europe, more secure? History would suggest not. Rather, it would place Europe on a new global frontline, and certainly make the world much more dangerously competitive as both sought allies, and partners of the US became embroiled in new bipolar stand-off.

Chinese military ambitions are fuelled by the structural transfer of wealth and power underway from West to East which has enabled the Chinese defence budget to grow by 60 per cent since 2012.[13] In 2019, a CSIS report stated, 'how much China actually spends on its military is widely debated. The Stockholm International Peace Research Institute (SIPRI) estimates the overall 2018 figure at $250 billion and the International Institute for Strategic Studies (IISS) puts the number at $209 billion in 2017. The US Department of Defense (DoD) concludes that China's 2018 defense budget likely exceeded $200 billion'.[14] Whilst Chinese defence expenditure would appear to be far below US defence expenditure in 2019, the gap is not as wide as it appears, with profound implications for the assumptions upon which European defence rests. First, the US must spread its forces and resources across the globe, whilst China can concentrate its military power, mainly in and around East Asia. Second, declared Chinese defence expenditure is believed to be far below the actual amount Beijing spends, particularly in crucial areas such as defence research and development. Third, China would also appear to get more bang for each buck than the Americans. Pork-barrel politics in Washington increases overhead costs and imposes inefficiencies on the US defence effort with which the Chinese do not have to contend, and undermines the ability of any administration to spend money effectively.

13. See 'China's Defense Budget', 6 March 2019, GlobalSecurity.org, https://www.globalsecurity. org/military/world/china/budget.htm.
14. See 'What Does China Really Spend on Its Military?', 2019 (Washington, DC: CSIS), https:// chinapower.csis.org/military-spending.

Beijing's aggressive military-strategic ambitions are also clear for those willing to look at the evidence. China continues to arm the series of reefs and atolls it has illegally seized, fast turning them into advanced military bases, as part of the so-called 'string of pearls'. Beijing also claims that all movements by the air and sea forces of other states across the South China Sea now breach China's sovereignty unless authorized by Beijing which, it warns, it reserves the right to forcefully defend. If Beijing continues to assert 'rights' that are seen by many states the world over as illegal, then China is on a collision course with other powers, most notably the US. In the worst case, and this book is about the worst case, such a conflict would have profound implications for European defence, most notably the ability of the US to assure the security and defence of Europe faced with the challenge of a burgeoning global-reach military superpower in the East in what could rapidly become a simultaneous multi-front war in several theatres of China's choosing.

To that end, China is making massive strides forward in its efforts to become a global-reach military power. The modernizing Chinese People's Liberation Army (PLA) is some 2,000,000 strong in 2021 with 500,000 reserves. Much of its doctrine emphasizes mass in concert with manoeuvre. The People's Liberation Army Air Force (PLAAF) can boast over 5,000 aircraft, many of which are of the latest variants. The Chinese People's Liberation Navy (PLN) has a total strength of some 600 ships in 2021. By 2023, China aims to have three different classes of heavy aircraft carrier at sea. The Type 003 carrier class will be nuclear-powered and will represent a step-change in Beijing's ability to project Chinese power. There are still some significant limitations on China's ability to conduct sustained 'blue water' operations, partly because of a lack of experience of such, and partly because of difficulties developing the required supply trains. China is also developing its maritime-amphibious capabilities through a significant upgrading of its 20,000-strong Marine Corps. China is also investing in new hunter-killer submarines, a 'carrier-killer' ballistic missile, as well as hypersonic missile technology and stealth aircraft. The military-strategic intent is clear: Beijing aims to match the US, at least in East Asia, and probably far beyond. In May 2020, *The Times* quoted a senior US defence source about the developing Chinese fleet base in Djibouti: 'After 9/11 we thought that China was largely defensive militarily . . . There was no blue water navy and no long-range missiles or any basing strategy outside their region . . . all that has changed. In the 20 years since, China has a blue-water navy and an offensive missile capability, they have man-made islands in the East and South China Seas for military purposes and they have a base overseas [Djibouti] and, we believe, plans for one in Pakistan [Gwadar]'.[15]

It is China's People's Liberation Army Rocket Force (PLARF) which perhaps best reveals the step-change in Beijing's military-strategic ambitions over the past decade. On 29 September 2011 a Long March 2F rocket powered into the sky carrying Tiangong-1, Beijing's first space laboratory. Shortly afterwards, China's Shenzhou 8 lifter was launched and linked up with the orbiting laboratory some 350 kilometres above the Earth. Both launches marked the emergence of China as a space power. In June 2019, Beijing launched the latest Long March 11 rocket which is capable of putting a 50-ton payload into low Earth orbit, and which can be launched at short notice. China is increasing the number of warheads that could strike the US, to over 100 by 2022. In 2021, China has the largest land-based missile force in the world, with some 1,900 ballistic and 350 advanced cruise missiles.

China is a sovereign power and is breaking no law or convention in using its wealth to make such strategic choices. Chinese defence investment conforms to a pattern of extending regional and extra-regional coercive influence. Beijing is also signalling to the non-aligned world that China will contest what it regards as the old Western-imposed world order. China will continue to invest in advanced, high-end expeditionary military capability, even as much of Europe effectively and unilaterally divests itself of such capabilities. Europeans should be under no illusion that the post-COVID-19 geopolitical and military-strategic shift could be profound. Moreover, as the gap between US and Chinese capability narrows and as the lag between the US military and European allies grows, the defence of Europe will steadily erode. In any consequent security vacuum many Europeans would find themselves increasingly at the mercy of another strategic predator—Russia.

Can Europeans reasonably expect to rely on the US for their security and defence, and China for much of their infrastructure investment? Within certain very defined limits such a balancing act might be maintained, especially if China observes the kind of rules enshrined in the World Trade Organization. The problem is China has a history of breaching such rules, most notably when it concerns intellectual property rights, forced technology transfer, and industrial and technological espionage. China, it

15. Michael Evans, 'Beijing's African Port Ready for Aircraft Carriers', *The Times*, 19 May 2020.

seems, will place few limits on the strategic ambition implicit in the BRI, which is precisely why it is so seductive and so dangerous given the level of indebtedness to Beijing it can generate. Whilst China has occasionally offered debt forgiveness, it is rare, and only when a bigger strategic prize is in the offing.

For the sake of Europe's future defence, which will remain overwhelmingly US-centric for the foreseeable future, and unless there is a profound change by Europeans in their ability to defend themselves, Europeans must understand the implications for the fierce strategic competition underway between the US and China. Post-COVID-19 tensions, and the 'tech' Cold War that is being fought out between the US and China, are merely symptoms of a structural competition that will shape geopolitics in the twenty-first century. Sooner rather than later those Europeans seduced by Chinese money may well be forced to choose sides.

Given the strategic implications for the defence of Europe, it is vital that Europeans understand the differences and consequences of choosing between democratic America and autocratic China. Yes, the US can drive hard bargains with its European allies at times, and yes, US corporations often play hard ball. However, the Americans have been and continue to be extraordinarily generous to Europeans in affording them a defence that is far beyond that which Europeans themselves seem willing to afford. In 2018 alone the US European Deterrence Initiative designed to bolster the US force posture in Europe and strengthen deterrence against Russian aggression saw some $4.8 billion dispensed above and beyond that already committed to maintain some 30,000 US personnel in Europe. General Curtis Scaparotti, NATO's former Supreme Allied Commander Europe, stated: 'This year's budget builds on previous EDI investments that enhance our deterrence posture and improve the readiness of forces in Europe. As we continue to address the dynamic security environment in Europe, EDI funding increases our capabilities to deter and defend against Russian aggression. Additionally, these significant investments will further galvanize U.S. support to the collective defense of our NATO allies, as well as bolster the capacity of our U.S. partners'.[16] Do Europeans really want to put such commitment at risk?

---

16. See 2018 European Deterrence Initiative (EDI) Factsheet, U.S. European Command Public Affairs Office, https://nl.search.yahoo.com/search?fr=mcafee&type=E211NLoGo&p=European+Defense+Initiative.

Moreover, the relationship between the US government and US business is not as intertwined as it is between other governments and their national champions, such as can be found, say, in France or Sweden. In China, it is the opposite. Indeed, Chinese companies are legally required to act as agents of the Chinese state. It is precisely this ability to use corporate entities for strategic leverage which is making so many British lawmakers uneasy about Huawei's possible role in the development of Britain's future 5G digital telecommunications network, particularly so in the wake of COVID-19.

Europeans should be under no illusions about the nature of Chinese power, or the scope of Beijing's ambitions. As China moves towards peer power parity with the US, there is every reason to believe Beijing will resort to *Machtpolitik* to achieve what it deems are its critical interests. What will Europeans do if China seeks to end the independence of Taiwan and 'unify' the country, much as it has successfully done with Hong Kong and Macau?[17] Whilst the two territories were returned through diplomacy with fading European powers, Taipei is heavily armed, mainly with US military equipment, and shows little inclination to be 'unified' peacefully with mainland China. And, whilst the US is nominally committed to a 'One China' policy, it has also committed to preventing Taiwan's forced reunification with the mainland. What view do Europeans have over China's aggression in its own region? Beijing is also likely to intensify its various territorial disputes with Japan, Malaysia, the Philippines, and Vietnam in the South and East China Seas, as it asserts its control over a large swathe of East Asia. What if China were to seek to extend its influence, including its military reach, far into the Indian Ocean and South Pacific, increasing friction with that other emergent Asian Great Power, India? Beyond the somewhat symbolic, some would say desultory, despatch of a few European warships to the region, what role for Europe therein? What will Europe do if in concert with Russia China also seeks to extend its military influence into the Atlantic, Europe, and the Arctic?

17. The Basic Law with which Hong Kong enjoys limited autonomy from Beijing was agreed as part of Britain's departure in 1997. It is due to last some fifty years and since the Accord was agreed Beijing has for the most part observed the treaty. However, those in Hong Kong protesting for more basic rights face a hard reality: China will not permit much unrest before it moves into Hong Kong in force to re-establish what it will claim is 'order'.

COVID-19, China, and geopolitics

The world is not as yet back in a new Cold War. For all the contention between the US and China, any understanding of that dangerous era means any such comparison with today is at best partial and at worst lazy. There is still time for Beijing and Washington to find a balance and reach an enduring, mutually beneficial, new and more balanced relationship. For such a balance to be struck China would need to profoundly alter the behaviours the COVID-19 crisis has revealed. Equally, a new kind of Cold War could also quickly erupt. COVID-19 has accelerated geopolitics precisely because China was in the eye of the storm and precisely because US–Chinese strategic competition defines twenty-first-century competition. Indeed, from the perspective of global peace and prosperity, as well as European defence, COVID-19 could not have emerged in a worse country. However, has China 'won' the COVID-19 crisis?

In November 1956, at a reception at the Polish Embassy in Moscow, Soviet leader Nikita Khrushchev was blunt in an address to Western envoys: 'About the capitalist states it does not depend on you whether or not we exist. If you don't like us, don't accept our invitations, and don't invite us to come to see you. Whether you like it or not, history is on our side. We will bury you!'[18] There are those in the Xi regime who would like to create a similar sense of historic fatalism in the minds of today's Western 'bloc'. And yet Khrushchev was wrong, and the rest, as they say, is history. Over time the profound contradictions at the heart of the Soviet state caught up with Moscow and in 1991 the USSR collapsed.

Much of China's meteoric growth since 1989 came under the leadership of a pragmatic oligarchy. In 2012, the CCP abandoned the oligarchy for something much more akin to Stalin's cult of the personality; a military-backed, one-strong-man rule. Since then the regime has become progressively more rigid, a rigidity the current crisis seems to have reinforced. Party officials who have not kow-towed to the Party line have been purged, whilst huge numbers of the Uighur, Kazakh, and Muslim minorities have been sent to 're-education' camps. The Chinese economy has become progressively more centralized with ever more state-owned 'enterprises' doing the bidding of what is today a control state. In other words, China

18. 'We Will Bury You!', *Time Magazine*, 26 November 1956, vol. 26.

may appear to be strong and unified, but like the Soviet Union before it, much of that unity is probably an illusion.

Consequently, if properly galvanized, there is every reason to believe the economic dynamism and freer spirit of the US and its allies will again prevail, but only if the West makes it harder for the likes of China to exploit its riches of knowledge and technology. The profound mistake of the Trump administration has been to believe America's leadership of the free world is a burden on the US, driven by an even more historically mistaken belief that international relations are simplistically transactional. Since the late 1940s, when President Harry S. Truman first stepped up to provide such post-war American leadership to the free world, key advisers, such as Paul Nitze and George Kennan, knew only too well that such leadership was in the American interest. What was true then is true today, albeit with a large caveat; now more than ever Americans needs Europeans to finally take some strategic responsibility.

Historically, power has rarely been ethical and almost always amoral. By contemporary European standards China's behaviour during the COVID-19 crisis was unacceptable, and yet it is Europe that has made itself uniquely vulnerable to Chinaization in the guise of globalization. Indeed, there is a certain tragic charm in the way many European leaders have embraced a kind of naïve, China-empowering globalism given it was Europe that invented *Realpolitik*, although Sun Tzu might beg to differ. Therefore, if anything has to change now as a consequence of this crisis, it is that Europe's rush towards vulnerability must end. Like pandemics before it, COVID-19 will accelerate existing strategic, political, economic, and even social change, but it can also act as a wake-up call for Europeans to finally summon up the political courage to face such hard realities.

Europeans will also need to consider a more comprehensive concept of security. Indeed, as the popular and political clamour grows in Europe's democracies for more to be spent on 'human security', it could well be that in the short to medium term state security and national defence suffer. Russia and China would be happy to help encourage such an outcome. Clearly, the next political cycle in Europe will be devoted to dealing and then coping with the consequences of COVID-19. Europe's all-too-reactive politicians will need to be careful that they strike a working balance between human security and national defence.

If China is to be denied the strategic fruits of its strategy, America must learn to lead the free world again. Given the challenge of China, that begs a further question: lead where? First, a shared understanding is needed that China is the main external strategic challenge to the world's democracies. Second, a shared Allied recognition is also required that the relationship with China has become dangerously unbalanced, with too many Western supply chains now dependent on a country that is as much predator as partner. Third, the future transatlantic relationship and European cohesion need to be seen against the backdrop of such challenges. Fourth, and perhaps most important of all, Europe's intergovernmental institutions need to become far more robust in the face of shock.

Where to start? Given the scale and scope of China's strategic challenge to the US, it is hard to see how a determined Russian attack on Europe could be halted before it had seized a significant area to the east of the Alliance and the EU. If such an attack took place simultaneously with a collapse of much of North Africa, and by extension Southern Europe, any defence against such an attack would be even less likely. If such an attack took place when US forces were involved in a major confrontation with China, the defence of Europe would be wholly dependent on Europeans. Such a series of complex but plausible scenarios begs two further questions: can America still defend Europe and, in the worst case, could Europe defend Europe?

6

Could NATO (still) defend Europe?

America, Europe, and multi-domain warfare

COVID-19 or no, could NATO still defend Europe? Implicit in that question is whether the US will always be able and willing to defend Europe. After all, the Americans are still the hard-power backbone of the Alliance. However, NATO is also the litmus test of the profound change European defence is undergoing, which is reflected herein. As such, US and European contentions over the future of multi-domain warfare, the impact of US military overstretch and European defence under-stretch, the changing relationship between defence and deterrence, and the very nature of deterrence in the face of 5D warfare all beg a fundamental question: to what should NATO be adapted?

In 2021, the US has some 1,400,000 personnel in its armed forces, the third largest after China and India. The US Army is 475,000 strong with much of the force of a high quality, whilst the US Air Force can deploy over 5,000 advanced aircraft with 406 intercontinental ballistic missile (ICBMs) plus an assorted array of advanced missile systems. The United States Navy remains the world's pre-eminent naval force with a fleet of some 480 vessels, many of them the most technically sophisticated anywhere, plus almost 4,000 aircraft, much of them part of the United States Marine Corps.

After years focused on counter-insurgency operations, the US armed forces are once again looking at how to fight and win a future war, with the Pentagon now intensively engaged in the generation of new military capabilities to fight and win 'multi-domain' warfare. However, in April 2018 then Secretary of Defense Jim Mattis told the Senate Armed Services Committee that, 'The negative impact on military readiness resulting from the longest continuous period of combat in our nation's history [has] created an over-stretched and under-resourced military'. He went on to suggest that over the same period China and Russia had sought to exploit US military overstretch by investing in advanced defence technologies. 'China', said Mattis, is 'modernising its conventional military forces to a degree that will challenge US military superiority', and that as a result, 'long-term strategic competition—not terrorism—is now the primary focus of US national security'.[1] This marked shift in US strategy was reflected in the March 2019 US National Defense Strategy which set the ambition for the US future force: 'The operations and capabilities supported by the [defence] budget will strongly position the US military for great power competition for decades to come'.[2]

The American vision of multi-domain warfare spans across air, sea, land, cyber, and space, and looks to exploit new technologies in the battlespace, such as artificial intelligence (AI), robotics, and digital. The 2020 defence budget also included $58 billion for advanced aircraft and $35 billion for new warships, the biggest allocation for over twenty years (although that has since been scaled back), whilst $14 billion was set aside for space systems, $10 billion for cyber war, and in a sign of the times $4.6 billion for AI and other autonomous systems and hypersonic weaponry.

The plans for the future US Army are also ambitious. In March 2019, the US Army's Futures and Concepts Center Director, Lt.-Gen. Eric Wesley, said, 'There is going to be a fundamental change in the organizational structure . . . with a new focus on large-scale ground combat operations anticipated in the future operating environment that will require echelons above brigade, all of which will solve unique and distinct problems that a given BCT (Brigade Combat Team) cannot solve by itself'.[3] Multi-domain operations (MDO) allied to the organization and application of high technology are thus driving the new Army Doctrine as it considers how to fight war from the hybrid ('grey zone') to the hyperwar. To better prepare the US Army, a new Four-Star command has been stood up in Austin, Texas entitled Army Futures Command. The aim is for the US to field an MDO-capable force by 2028, with long-range precision fires,

---

1. See Michael T. Klare, 'The US Military Is Preparing for a New War', *The Nation*, 5 June 2019, thenation.com/article/us-military-is-preparing for new-wars-china-russia.
2. Ibid.
3. Jen Judson, 'The US Army Is Preparing for Major Changes to Force Structure', *Defense News*, 5 March 2019, defensenews.com/land/2019/03/06/major-army-force-structure-changes-afoot.

appropriate deployed air and missile defence, and the force and command structure to match.

Much is being made of the advanced weapons systems being developed by the Chinese and Russians, but the US still remains at the cutting edge of future war technology. For example, the B-21 stealth bomber is due to enter service in 2025 with the US Air Force and marks a transition as it could be either manned or unmanned. Washington is also considering developing an advanced reusable space plane, the Phantom Express. First tested in 2020, it could be launched and re-launched ten days in a row with a range of military applications. The SR-72 drone will be a long-range hypersonic intelligence-gathering and strike weapon capable of reaching speeds of up to Mach 6. The US is also developing railgun technologies that will launch a projectile at hypersonic speed up to 150 km, with the so-called Hi-Fire system close to completion. The US Navy is also looking to the future. Construction will soon start on a new class of Columbia-class nuclear submarine that will combine stealth with virtually unlimited range which is due to enter service in 2031. The Future Surface Combatant will be armed with lasers and railguns powered by its own 58-megawatt electrical motors.

How does the US effort compare with its European counterparts? There are some next-generation capabilities being worked up by Europeans, such as the British Sea-Ceptor hypersonic air defence system which has just entered service with the Royal Navy. However, most Europeans are only beginning to talk about such systems, and they are few and far between. For example, the proposed Franco-German Future Combat Air System, and the alternative British-led 6G 'Tempest' fighter, are both only at the conceptual stage. Moreover, the bulk of European armed forces are already anachronistic, with many simply obsolete. At the very least, interoperability between the US future force and the lack of readiness and responsiveness of European forces could become deeply problematic.[4] In such circumstances, NATO

4. NATO Secretary-General Jens Stoltenberg has made much of the NATO Readiness Initiative and the so-called '4x30s': the deployment of thirty land battalions, thirty combat ships and thirty squadrons within thirty days. And, whilst improvements to Allied readiness are being made, it is unclear whether the scale of force or the time it would take to deploy matches the threat it is designed to deter. A 30 October 2019 report by the Heritage Foundation stated that 'Four 30s' derives from the plan's objective that NATO should be able to respond to any aggression with thirty battalions, thirty squadrons of aircraft, and thirty warships within thirty days. The plan was endorsed at the July 2018 NATO summit in Brussels, Belgium, but the declaration 'did not include Four Thirties initiative specifics, including which nations would contribute which types of forces and a timeframe for implementation'. See 'Assessing the Global Operating Environment:

might stumble on as a political talk-shop, but any future war of any magnitude would need to be fought by the US with a few chosen allies, but not as an Alliance.

Whilst in 2021 the United States is *the* defence of Europe, by the end of the decade the US may no longer be able to defend Europe, unless Europeans begin to rapidly modernize both their thinking and their forces to meet the future war challenge, regardless of the impact of the COVID-19 crisis on their respective economies. In short, the transatlantic relationship will face profound change that could well fundamentally shift the nature of the American military commitment to Europe. The US has no choice. As an increasingly challenged Washington knows, whilst the US is the only global power, it is under growing pressure the world over as the ends, ways, and means of America's global strategy are challenged simultaneously by China, Russia, al-Qaeda, and Daesh. In such circumstances, it should be strikingly clear to the Europeans allies that for the United States to continue to ensure and assure Europe's defence, it will need far better support from Europe. Specifically and critically, Europeans will need to become far more effective first responders in the event of a major crisis in and around Europe. However, even before the COVID-19 crisis there was little enthusiasm in Europe to recognize America's changing strategic reality, or the implications of such change for the future defence of Europe.

Overstretch and under-stretch

Since 1949, Europe's defence has been established on the principle that the US is Europe's pivotal Power. And, in spite of tensions that have dogged the life of the Alliance, Europeans have been only too happy to organize their respective national security and defence efforts around the US. However, in the wake of deep tensions over the US-led invasion of Iraq and the Afghanistan campaign, and in light of President Trump's particular brand of assertiveness towards his European allies, tensions have deepened.

Many commentators dismiss those tensions as simply another round of the sometimes prickly relationship between Washington and its continental European allies. However, there are deeper structural reasons that are

Europe',   https://www.heritage.org/military-strength/assessing-the-global-operating-environment/europe.

accelerating strategic drift in the transatlantic relationship, which could reinforce growing American disenchantment with its European allies. The range of pressures developing on the US and its armed forces caused by the military-strategic rise of China, the changing nature/revolution in military technology, and the need to plan for different types and level of threat in multiple theatres simultaneously across a wide spectrum of conflicts all contribute to US military overstretch. All of the above will demand the intelligent and enduring application of still immense American force and resource over both time and distance. Equally, even as US forces become increasingly dispersed and overstretched, Europeans still demand that the US maintain its security and defence guarantee to Europe, whilst Europeans make at best modest efforts to ease America's ability to do so. If this drift continues, it is hard to see how the transatlantic relationship can survive in its current form—or, indeed, its primary institution, NATO. Put simply, the American commitment to Europe is taken too much for granted by too many Europeans, even if they regularly complain about US policy and strategy on issues that they themselves lack the power to influence. Consequently, the transatlantic status quo is unlikely to be sustainable for the Americans, with huge strategic implications for European defence if Washington at some point concludes it is unable to maintain the security and defence guarantee. With the rise of Asia, and the shift of the world power away from Europe, necessary changes are underway to US foreign, security, and defence policy that, sooner or later, will force Europeans to radically reconsider their defence effort. Given the extent of the shock caused by the COVID-19 crisis, such a reconsideration of Europe and its defence might come far quicker than many Europeans assume, and might need to be made in the midst of a deep economic slump. The question then arises: how and in what format should such a consideration take place? Would it simply be a reflection of more defence budget cuts to assist in economic recovery or could there be a more fundamental rethink of European security and defence that the crisis triggers? It should be the latter, but experience would suggest the former. However, given existing pressures on the US, COVID-19 will make Washington's support for Europe's future defence inevitably more conditional, with the primary 'condition' being the need for Europeans to do far more in pursuit of their own defence. At the very least, the US will demand of their European allies that they develop twenty-first-century civilian and military capabilities far better able to cope with a range of crises, from COVID-19 to full-scale future war.

And yet, Europeans seem all too willing, too often, to wilfully ignore the changing nature of US foreign and security policy. They also seem to collectively fail to realize the implications of that change for their own defence. The enforced focus of much the American strategic effort will increasingly be on the Indo-Pacific. The growing role of Russia and China in the Middle East will further complicate American grand strategic calculations as both Beijing and Moscow intend.

There are also other profound implications for Europe from US military overstretch. In the event of a major military emergency in Europe it is hard to envisage that the United States would wish to use NATO in the first instance. By its very nature, NATO may be simply and fatally too slow to respond and react in a fast-moving, high-end emergency. And, possibly faced with multiple crises in multiple theatres, the US would be forced to use its forces as decisively and as efficiently as it possibly could, where it could. In any such emergency too many of the NATO European allies would take too long to act, or are so militarily weak that they would actively impede decisive US action. Such failings reinforce a growing US penchant for coalitions of the willing and able, rather than the 'entangling alliances' that George Washington warned against in his Farewell Address.[5]

Furthermore, for Americans the very idea of the West is changing and Europeans can no longer afford to assume they are the indispensable allies in the absence of their own defence action. For the Americans, the West is fast becoming an American-led global space, a global community of democracies that includes increasingly consequential actors such as Australia, Japan, South Korea, Taiwan, Indonesia, the Philippines, and maybe even India. For global America, shared values and interests extend well beyond the traditional West, and the aggregate GDP of such states adds enormous heft to the concept of a global community of democracies acting in concert, not least because they all have a more robust of defence, and their respective

---

5. In his 1796 Farewell Address President George Washington said, 'The great rule of conduct for us in regard to foreign nations is in extending our commercial relations, to have with them as little political connection as possible. So far as we have already formed engagements, let them be fulfilled with perfect good faith. Here let us stop. Europe has a set of primary interests which to us have none; or a very remote relation. Hence she must be engaged in frequent controversies, the causes of which are essentially foreign to our concerns. Hence, therefore, it must be unwise in us to implicate ourselves by artificial ties in the ordinary vicissitudes of her politics, or the ordinary combinations and collisions of her friendships or enmities'. How times change. See 'Washington's Farewell Address', USHistory.org, http://www.ushistory.org/documents/far ewelladdress.htm.

roles in it—even Japan. Coalitions of such states are also increasingly more attractive to the US as policy instruments than formal alliances. Informal groupings, such as the Five Eyes intelligence-sharing mechanism, are also more flexible than formal alliances like NATO.[6] In other words, Europeans have a diminished place in the American strategic body politic, and unless they act, their importance is likely to diminish further.

Against the backdrop of the COVID-19 crisis, and implicit in the changing nature and scope of America's security and defence commitment to Europe, there is another big question Europeans need to ask themselves: what price are they willing to pay to ensure the maintenance of America's defence guarantee to Europe? Long used to free-riding on the US taxpayer, it is a question that is only now beginning to dawn on many Europeans and their leaders. If not addressed, burden-sharing and the tensions it has created within the Alliance, which has been made worse by the costs of COVID-19, are only likely to increase and threaten in time to cripple the strategic cohesion upon which NATO stands.

Whilst both the US Senate and House of Representatives have in recent years re-affirmed their support for NATO in the face of President Trump's often explicit threats to withdraw from it, the changing nature of America itself will soon weaken the transatlantic bond. For much of the Cold War most of America's elite saw its historical and philosophical roots deeply intertwined with Europe. Moreover, American realist internationalism was also deeply invested in an essentially 'European' idea of international relations, reinforced by Europe itself being the epicentre of world affairs. No longer. Indeed, in some respects for many American legislators Europe is fast becoming a strategic backwater. Critically, in time Americans who draw their heritage from Europe will become a minority and, as the British found during an often testy relationship with President Obama, the changing face of America's leadership will not automatically afford Europeans a 'special relationship' unless they earn it.[7] If the transatlantic relationship is to endure, it will not only become far more transactional and established on shared

---

6. Five Eyes, or FVEY, emerged with the March 1946 'UKUSA Agreement' which formed the basis for today's intelligence-sharing arrangements between the UK, the US, Australia, Canada, and New Zealand, with significant levels of intelligence for the 'eyes only' of officials from those five states. It is unusual in the level of trust it demonstrates between five sovereign states.

7. *National Geographic* states, 'The U.S. Census Bureau has projected that non-Hispanic whites will make up less than 50 percent of the population by 2044, a change that almost certainly will recast American race relations and the role and status of white Americans, who have long been a comfortable majority'. See Michele Norris, 'As America Changes, Some Anxious Whites Feel

strategic interest, but the level and extent of the American commitment will depend on what Europeans can do for Americans.

There are still benefits to the US from having a close strategic relationship with the European allies. Washington clearly benefits from having forces stationed permanently in Europe, not least because it enables advantageous pre-positioning for possible US operations beyond Europe's borders. However, what would happen if Europeans were to profoundly disagree with a US operation that was launched from European soil, or even attempted to block it? Past US administrations would have listened respectfully to the Allies and then gone ahead anyway, but avoided making any link between the disagreement and the wider security relationship. Such pragmatism can no longer be assumed. For example, if there was to be a further schism of the intensity that afflicted the relationship in 2003 on the eve of the US-led invasion of Iraq, the damage to the transatlantic relationship and the Alliance would be incalculable, even if it survived.

Such tensions are never far from the surface of the transatlantic relationship. In July 2019 the UK endeavoured to create a European maritime security task force to protect shipping passing through the Gulf in the wake of the seizure of a British-flagged ship by the Iranian Revolutionary Guards Corps. The initiative failed because France and Germany objected to any action that would be seen to support the Trump administration's decision to abandon the Iranian nuclear deal. The UK's now small Royal Navy then joined the United States Navy in protecting shipments of oil of far more strategic significance to the economies of Europe (and China) than energy-self-sufficient America.[8] At some point the Americans will

---

Left Behind', April 2018, https://www.nationalgeographic.com/magazine/2018/04/race-rising-anxiety-white-america.

8. *US News* writes: 'The United States expects domestic oil production to reach new heights this year [2019] and next, and that prices—for both crude and gasoline—will be lower than they were in 2018. Government forecasters are sticking to their forecast that the United States—already the world's biggest oil producer—will become a net exporter of crude and petroleum products in 2020. The U.S. Energy Information Administration said Tuesday that it expects the United States to pump 12.4 million barrels of crude a day in 2019 and 13.2 million barrels a day in 2020. The January average was 12 million barrels a day, up 90,000 from December. Most of the increase is expected to come from the Permian Basin in Texas and New Mexico, where production has been booming for several years as operators use hydraulic fracturing and other techniques to squeeze more oil and gas from shale formations'. See David Koenig, 'US Expects Record Domestic Oil Production in 2019, 2020', 12 February 2019, https://www.usnews.com/news/best-states/new-mexico/articles/2019-02-12/us-expects-record-domestic-oil-production-in-2019–2020.

demand Europeans take sides, and will make Europeans pay a price when they do not.

The US, NATO, and the future defence of Europe . . .

What are the implications of such change for NATO? On 22 May 2019, the Chairman of NATO's Military Committee, Air Chief Marshal Sir Stuart Peach, announced a new Military Strategy for the Alliance which stated: 'The [NATO military] strategy will guide Allied military decision-making and provide NATO's Military Authorities with a definitive policy reference, enabling us to deliver our core mission—defending almost 1 billion people'.[9]

If the Alliance is serious about fulfilling that challenging mission, then it will need both the US and Europe to be fully engaged. At the core of NATO's many challenges, and a major reason why Washington might opt not to place the Alliance front and centre during any major emergency, is a refusal on the part of many of the European Allies to properly consider worst-case scenarios such as a Russian military attack somewhere along NATO's eastern flank that meeting the implicit challenge of the Military Strategy demands. However, Europe's relative military weakness has already enabled the Russian war plan to effectively trump NATO's defence planning. NATO has a standing defence plan because the Allies cannot agree on one, which is all too indicative of the malaise at the core of European defence. By the time NATO would move in the face of Russian aggression they could well have achieved their 'limited' war aims in the Baltic States, and simply stop, by which time the bulk of NATO forces would just be beginning to move, if they were moving at all. NATO would then quickly rediscover von Moltke the Elder's famous dictum that no battle plan survives first contact with the enemy as there would be little or no time to rotate forces and resources through some neatly conceived campaign plan.[10] They would be faced, instead, with a Russian fait accompli in perhaps the Baltic

---

9. See 'NATO Chiefs of Defence Discuss Future Alliance Adaptation', 22 May 2019, https://www.nato.int/cps/en/natohq/news_166244.htm?selectedLocale=en.
10. In fact, von Moltke's much-quoted truism actually paraphrases what he really wrote: 'The tactical result of an engagement forms the base for new strategic decisions because victory or defeat in a battle changes the situation to such a degree that no human acumen is able to see beyond the first battle' (Hughes and Bell 1993).

States or the Black Sea region. In such circumstances would NATO Europe be willing to go to war with nuclear-tipped Russia to rescue their allies? If they did, they would do so knowing all too well the risk of nuclear war. If they did not, NATO would be dead, the EU weakened, and the transatlantic relationship broken, Russia's grand prize.

The hard truth is that NATO Europeans, or, indeed, all Europeans, are woefully ill-prepared and ill-equipped to face a major Russian attack. And, without some major changes to the defence policies of European states, the situation is likely to become increasingly perilous unless US forces remain present in strength in Europe and are able to reinforce at speed and move those reinforcements quickly into position. However, that essential NATO equation was increasingly hard to maintain even before the COVID-19 crisis, and given the economic cost, it is likely to be even harder now. Critically, there is little chance that European forces could even act as first responders during any crisis, except the most permissive. The 'correlation of forces' between Russian forces in Moscow's Western Military District and those on NATO's eastern flank is dangerously out of balance, and the forces supporting NATO's Enhanced Forward Presence lack the weight, the mass, and the manoeuvre to properly contain any attack, which would be violent, fast, and brutal. NATO's imbalance is exacerbated by a lack of cooperation between Allied governments, a lack of cohesion between NATO's various headquarters, insufficiently robust command structure, and a critical lack of forces and resources available to NATO commanders in an emergency. Such 'disconnectivity' undermines the trip-wire approach to Allied deterrence which implies a strategic and force continuity that simply does not exist. For example, Professor Paul Cornish in a presentation given in Tel Aviv in June 2018 highlighted the challenge:

> Given defence cuts, we currently have low-level, tactical troop formations exposed to very high levels of strategic risk. The UK troops in Estonia are a good example—using language coined during the Cold War, some have described these deployments as a 'trip-wire'. But a trip-wire only functions as such if it is being watched closely and if something decisive (and usually explosive) happens when it is tripped. In the absence of very significant reinforcements— equipped, trained and poised to react when needed—these battalion-based deployments could not qualify as a *military* trip-wire; the most that could be said of them is that they might serve as a 'political trip-wire' of some sort. But a political bluff can always be called—so it's not a trip-wire at all.[11]

---

11. Furnished by the author.

That dilemma implies a further question: is the connectivity between NATO's conventional and nuclear deterrents any longer sufficient to prevent a Russian attack at the margins of the Alliance?

. . . and deterring means defending

If NATO cannot defend against an attack, it cannot deter any such attack, and NATO's primary deterrent are its conventional forces. That is the implicit message in NATO's 2019 military strategy.[12] To re-emphasize this dilemma again reveals perhaps the core paradox for the defence of Europe, both now and into the future; the growing worldwide pressures on US forces, which are critically exacerbated by severe limitations on, and shortfalls in, the capabilities and capacities of NATO's European Allies. This innate tension at the heart of the Alliance's defence and deterrence posture means the strategy is simply unable to balance, let alone ease, the profound and growing tensions that exist between the ends, ways, and means of NATO's Strategic Concept, which was last revised at the 2010 Lisbon Summit and the continued relevance of which is open to question. The NATO Military Strategy also falls far short of the implicit strategic ambition that is needed to provide a credible deterrent and defence posture around 360 degrees of threat, the stated Alliance mission. NATO forces lack the weight of arms, surety of structure, and speed of response upon which any credible deterrence stands. The strategy also fails to adequately close NATO's two critical and dangerous deterrence gaps: the gap between NATO's conventional and nuclear deterrents and the gap between NATO's forward-deployed forces and the bulk of the national forces the Alliance would need to call upon in an emergency.

Since the end of the Cold War, quality, heavy, rapidly deployable European forces have drained away, undermining NATO defence and deterrence. Those that do exist are simply too slow, too few in number, subject to too many national caveats, or far too distant from the area of operations to meet a major attack by Russian forces. It is a crisis that would

---

12. In May 2019, General Joseph Dunsford, Chairman of the US Joint Chiefs, said, 'It is the first NATO military strategy in decades. It clearly articulates the challenges that confront NATO and it provides the framework for the various plans that will be in place if deterrence fails'. Paul McCleary, 'Dunsford: Leaders Mull First NATO Military Strategy in Decades', *Breaking Defense*, 30 May 2019, https://breakingdefense.com/2019/05/dunford-first-nato-strategy-okd-in-decades.

be made far worse if the Allies faced simultaneous crises on multiple fronts, and in several global theatres, as could well be the case.

NATO's much-touted Enhanced and Tailored Forward Presence in Eastern and South-Eastern Europe is thus a bluff. In the Baltic States there are four brigades with no tanks, combat aircraft, and little artillery and air defence, reinforced by one multinational NATO battlegroup in each of the Baltic States designed to act as a 'trip-wire' force in the event of a Russian attack, but trip-wire to what? On the other side of the Estonian–Russian border, the Russian Order of Battle includes the 1st Guards Tank Army, 6th and 20th Combined Arms Armies, 11th Army Corps in Kaliningrad, three airborne divisions, three Spetsnaz Special Forces Brigades, ten rocket and artillery brigades, and thirty tank/motor rifle brigades/regiments plus one naval infantry brigade. There are also significant Russian air and naval assets in the region, all of which are reinforced by Russia's short-range theatre and strategic nuclear forces. Indeed, if conflict broke out, and given the capability of Russia's increasingly sophisticated and integrated air defence, NATO aircraft would find it hard to even get off the ground from most airfields in Eastern Europe. Moreover, the S-400 and in time S-500 air defence systems Russia is fielding will make it very hard to put NATO air forces in the same battlespace as Russian forces.

In other words, Russian forces enjoy dangerous local and possibly regional-strategic superiority. New military strategy or no, at their current level of readiness the bulk of NATO forces would take months to assemble. Moreover, in a war, vital US reinforcements would need to cross an again contested Atlantic and land at one vulnerable port, Bremerhaven. Thereafter, the military mobility of such reinforcements across Europe would be severely constrained and, in spite of recent NATO and EU efforts to remove physical and legal impediments, such mobility is likely to remain compromised for the foreseeable future. NATO is making significant efforts to improve military mobility, what the Alliance calls 'Flexible Logistics', with the US European Deterrence Initiative (EDI) (known as the European Reassurance Initiative prior to 2017) making an important contribution.

The main focus of the Alliance effort vital to the readiness of NATO forces is on four fronts: authorities and legislation to facilitate border crossing; command and control to direct the logistic moves; adequate lift capabilities that can transport troops and their equipment; and an infrastructure that can cope with large quantities of heavy military transport. Enhanced military mobility is part of an overarching aim to establish a 'readiness culture' in Europe that would markedly improve the capacity of Alliance forces to respond to emergencies. However, after making military mobility a flagship Permanent Structured Cooperation (PESCO) project in 2019, the EU cut the funding to nothing. It is hard to see how such mobility could be achieved without close EU–NATO cooperation.

NATO: adapting to what?

If NATO is to mount a credible twenty-first-century defence and deterrence, there is a further question: just how should the Alliance adapt? If the credibility of NATO deterrence is to be reinforced, and quickly, existing forces and command resources would need to be used far more effectively and efficiently around the entire 360 degrees of complex strategic coercion. That imperative places particular importance on NATO's force hubs in Germany and Poland, around which NATO pivots. This space is vital both for the defence of the eastern flank and the Baltic Sea region, as well as for reinforcing Allies in south-east and southern Europe in an emergency.

At the 2018 Brussels Summit, NATO took further steps to 'adapt' the Alliance to meet the challenge posed by evolving and dynamic threats, and thus ease the defence and deterrence dilemma with which NATO forces must contend. Article 5 on collective defence was to be modernized to ensure an adapted Allied defence and deterrence posture, with specific focus on the NATO Command Structure. Conscious of the growing pressures they faced, Washington pushed the NATO allies to agree to a NATO Readiness Initiative built around the so-called '4x30s' (thirty land battalions, thirty combat ships, and thirty air squadrons deployable within thirty days) to reinforce the credibility of Alliance deterrence in an emergency, particularly on NATO's eastern flank by enabling rapid reinforcement of forward-deployed forces. The proposed force is a kind of beefed-up version of the old Allied Command Europe Mobile Force which was disbanded in 2002 (because of British defence cuts) which could act as a strategic reserve and move quickly to any NATO hot-spot. Critically, the new force would plug a dangerous gap that exists between NATO's spearhead forces, so-called follow-on forces (the enhanced NATO Response Force or eNRF), and the bulk of the NATO force structure, some of which would take up to 120 days to mobilize in an emergency. If, that is, all the NATO nations keep their word and actively fulfil their commitments to the Alliance.

The adaptation of the NATO Command Structure is thus a vital step towards an Alliance that will be able to respond quickly to crises across both the conflict spectrum and the Euro-Atlantic theatre, vital for credible deterrence. To assist, it is envisioned a new Joint Force Command in Norfolk, Virginia will act as a vital partner for Allied Command Transformation, to reinforce effective interoperability between the main fighting forces of the Alliance and their American counterparts. It will also undertake some of the duties of the old Supreme Allied Command Atlantic, specifically the secure transit of US forces across the Atlantic in the face of the Russian maritime threat. The 2017 creation of a NATO Strategic Direction South Hub shows efforts are underway to create a thinking Alliance that can better harness the expertise needed to address complex environments from which threat can be generated through the hybrid–cyber–hyper war mosaic. These are only the first steps after years of European neglect of their own armed forces, the Alliance, and the changing nature of the dynamic threat they must together face. However, as the Americans move towards an advanced twenty-first-century deployable multi-domain force, it is hard to see how such synergy could be maintained with legacy European forces. For the Alliance the implications are profound, for failure would add further impetus to Washington's increasing reliance upon coalitions of the strategically able and capable. Critically, these reforms were agreed prior to the COVID-19 crisis. And yet, it is hard to believe the credibility of NATO as a defensive alliance could be maintained if the force goals implicit therein are not realized.

General Omar Bradley once said, 'Amateurs talk strategy, professionals talk logistics'.[13] The critical twenty-first-century need of the Alliance and the defence of Europe must be the proven and demonstrable ability to generate and command high-end military force quickly, move the right force to the right place rapidly, and then sustain such a force for the entirety of an emergency. If not, the very foundation of military power

---

13. There are limits to truisms. At the height of the Afghanistan and Iraq campaign Max Boot wrote, in a 2006 piece for the *Los Angeles Times*, '"Amateurs talk strategy. Professionals talk logistics." That well-worn saying, sometimes attributed to Gen. Omar Bradley, contains an obvious element of wisdom. Modern militaries cannot fight without a lengthy supply chain, and the success or failure of major operations can turn on the work of anonymous logisticians. Yet there is a danger of professional soldiers becoming so focused on supply lines that they lose sight of larger strategic imperatives'. See Max Boot, 'Our Enemies Aren't Drinking Lattes', *Los Angeles Times*, 5 July 2006, https://www.latimes.com/archives/la-xpm-2006-jul-05-oe-boot5-story.html.

projection (there is no such thing as a static defence these days), and with it twenty-first-century Article 5 NATO defence and deterrence, will be critically undermined. Indeed, force readiness and force rotation throughout the entirety of an emergency are the twin components upon which the Alliance conventional deterrent depends. The danger is that if European forces are too weak or too slow, or US forces are simply busy elsewhere, the threshold to NATO's possible use of nuclear weapons in a European war would be lowered. For all the shortfalls and weaknesses in the front-line forces of the NATO European allies, it is logistics, or rather the lack of them, which is perhaps most telling of NATO Europe's withering capabilities. There are some efforts underway to address this critical Alliance weakness. Under German command a new Joint Support and Enabling Command has been established in Ulm, Germany to make more efficient use of existing resources in support of NATO's forward-deployed forces, as well as to enable critical communications, rear-area security, and rapid reinforcement. This is a belated but important step.

However, there remain simply too many serious impediments to NATO command effectiveness in a crisis, such as the location of key commands, as well as the cohesion between them. This is reinforced by too many false European assumptions underpinning NATO policy and planning about the nature of future conflict, and how it could impact upon Alliance forces. What NATO needs is a reinforced heavy European command hub in the pivotal German–Polish space that could respond to emergencies in strength across the full bandwidth of Alliance contingencies. Such a hub would entail a cluster of mutually reinforcing, hardened, deployable headquarters able to shift their respective centres of gravity in support of each other to meet all and any emergency. The Poles are acutely aware that they sit not only in the midst of NATO's pivotal space, but also in the middle of several of NATO's European-generated deterrence gaps, which is why there have been calls from Warsaw for American forces to be stationed in Poland. These have been caused by a lack of deployable European conventional combat forces and the 'gap' with the strategic nuclear deterrent and the lack of anything in between. Should conventional deterrence fail, Western leaders would be faced with the prospect of the early resort to nuclear weapons or surrender. The prospect of deterrence being dangerously weakened was made worse in June 2020 when President Trump threatened to withdraw 9,800 American troops from Europe—28 per cent of the US contribution to Alliance deterrence. The Americans have rightly agreed to stand up a divisional headquarters in Poznan, supported by 1,000 personnel, and designated as 1st ID (Fwd) to build on the existing Mission Command Element. And yet, a major shift in the European posture of US forces would be a mistake because the Americans need their German command and logistics hub, as well as their vital strategic relationship with the *Bundeswehr*, to provide the hard-core foundation of any reinforced defence should the need arise. It would thus be better to leave US forces permanently stationed in Germany. How to strike such a force balance?

NATO's Multinational Corps Northeast (MNCNE) is an example of both the Alliance's strength and its inherent weakness, as well as the challenge such weakness poses for the US. MNCNE would be pivotal to any organized NATO response to a Russian attack on the Baltic States. Indeed, former NATO Supreme Allied Commander Europe (SACEUR) General Phil Breedlove called the headquarters NATO's 'unblinking eye' on the Baltic Sea region, and thus central to Alliance defence and deterrence. MNCNE is certainly doing all in its power to meet threats to the Alliance across NATO's eastern front, and its burden was considerably eased in autumn 2020 with the deployment to Europe of elements of the reactivated US V Corps. However, MNCNE has never been properly tested in a major crash-test exercise, nor have the other high-readiness force corps headquarters. The result is that MNCNE is not really sure about its place or its role in the conflict cycle.

The constraints on MNCNE typify the problems faced by NATO Europe as a whole, and the difficulty of adapting the Alliance to even current concepts of warfare, let alone the future war concepts with which Europe must contend. Critically, MNCNE has no authority to coordinate between the separate forces of the three Baltic States in the event of a Russian attack, even though it would provide command and control for Baltic ground forces in such an event, acting in effect as a Baltic Corps HQ with NATO-trained Baltic commanders and staff officers. MNCNE would also be pivotal for organizing the reception, staging, and onward movement of reinforcing US and other Allied forces into Poland, whilst acting as a corps-level HQ to command Polish forces. And yet, Szczecin, the home of MNCNE, is some 900 km from the Lithuanian border.

NATO, the UK, and COVID-19

For all the tactical pressures faced by the Alliance, it will only be able to maintain a credible defence and deterrence posture if Europe's three major powers lead NATO Europe's defence-strategic efforts and afford the Alliance new command hubs. The preface to the 2015 UK National Security Strategy and Strategic Security and Defence Review states: 'Our [the UK's] Armed Forces and security and intelligence agencies (the Secret Intelligence Service, the Security Service, and the Government Communications Headquarters) are respected around the world for their capability, agility, reach and ability to fight and work alongside our close allies. We took tough decisions to balance the defence budget in 2010, and are now in a position to invest in the highly deployable Armed Forces that we need to guarantee our security'.[14] The plight of the UK's armed forces, traditionally one of Europe's most capable, was reflective of the enduring crisis in the European defence effort even before the COVID-19 crisis.[15] For many years the British have been playing smoke and mirrors with their defence budget. The 2015 review was a conscious attempt by London to balance the growing pre-COVID-19 demands for enhanced security and defence with London's then determination to reduce radically the national debt and deficit that had ballooned during the financial crash, with the ultimate aim of achieving a budget surplus by the financial year 2020–1. Whilst that goal was subsequently abandoned, defence was starved of much-needed resources, and increasingly hollowed out. Even before COVID-19, the 2015 Strategic Defence and Security Review (SDSR) revealed a UK trying to execute a politically perilous defence-strategic balancing act. Like most of its European allies, the slightest shock or unexpected commitment to its defence planning assumptions threatened to cripple the entire British defence edifice. The effect was to implicitly shift more of the burden for the defence of the UK and wider Europe onto the Americans. And then came COVID-19.

All European democracies struggle to balance security, strategy, defence capability and capacity, and affordability at the best of times. In a crisis, such as COVID-19, such an effort becomes infinitely harder and more complex. Critically for the Alliance, when NATO's three major European powers,

---

14. 'National Security Strategy and Strategic Defence and Security Review 2015', https://www.gov.uk/government/publications/national-security-strategy-and-strategic-defence-and-security-review-2015.

15. In an October 2019 conversation between one of the authors and a very senior British politician, the latter recounted a conversation he had had with then Chancellor of the Exchequer, Philip Hammond. The politician asked why so many cuts were being made to Britain's armed forces. Hammond allegedly replied, 'Because there are no votes in defence'. The politician then said, 'So that means the end to the first duty of the state being to defend its citizens'. A lot of votes will be decided by how effectively London responds to the COVID-19 crisis. Defence?

the UK, France, and Germany, fail to strike such a balance, the rest of Europe tends to follow. Rather than confront the defence dilemma caused by a worsening strategic environment and decreasing defence budgets, successive British governments have chosen instead to resort to political spin, often at the expense of sound strategy or defence policy. Like so many of their European counterparts, it is not only the Americas that are victims of such defence pretence. London has also shifted the burden of policy onto Britain's hard-pressed armed forces, expanding the range and number of critical tasks they must undertake while reducing the forces and resources available to them at one and the same time. The 2015 SDSR made much about the UK maintaining defence expenditure at the NATO guide-line of 2 per cent GDP until the financial year 2020–1, reinforced by a real-terms increase in defence spending of 1 per cent per annum in real terms each year over that period. There was also a commitment to find an additional £12 billion to realize a defence investment budget up to £178 billion over the 2016–25 period. However, in the wake of COVID-19, it is hard to see the British maintaining even that modest (by strategic standards) commitment. Worse, close analysis reveals that much of this 'new' money was simply existing resources re-tagged, with much of the money earmarked for non-defence counter-terror spend. Understandably, such financial game-playing does not play well in Washington, particularly now as the Americans also come under intense pressure.

The UK is but one example but all NATO Europeans use creative defence accounting to some extent or another to give the impression they are meeting their obligations to the Alliance. Moreover, the level at which such obligations are set has too often been about what NATO Europeans are willing to afford for their own defence, not what they should. COVID-19 has now become the focus of almost all national security policy in Europe—indeed, it is cast in those terms—but far from evaporating, the military threats to Europe that existed prior to the crisis could well intensify, with profound implications for the US and its armed forces. Moreover, like many Europeans, the British quite deliberately blur the lines between security and defence to present defence cuts as security efficiencies. Indeed, hiding cuts was one of the main reasons for merging the 2015 UK National Security Strategy and SDSR 2015, and to blur the lines between the strategic counter-terrorist strategy and what Professor Mike Clarke has suggested would be a 'strategic raider' role of the British future force. The UK's latest Integrated Foreign, Security, and Defence Review has simply been hijacked by COVID-19. The strategic consequence is that the UK's armed forces will change from being a warfighting force into a deterrence force postured to only conduct strategic deterrence, high-end counter-terror operations, and strike some limited level of both power and force projection. The essential fallacy of such a posture is that deterrence can only be assured by a credible ability to fight and win a war against an adversary or range of adversaries. As such, like so many Europeans, the British have broken the essential link between force and threat, and the impact of COVID-19 on the national exchequer is only likely to make the consequent gap wider.

Consequently, the British have effectively abandoned a continental defence, the *raison d'être* of the Alliance. Even Britain's apparent maritime-amphibious renaissance is not what it might appear at first glance. Since the time of Sir Francis Drake in the sixteenth century, the UK's Royal Navy has endeavoured to undertake both sea control and sea presence.[16] In 1920, in the immediate aftermath of World War One, the Royal Navy was still the pre-eminent naval force on the planet and could boast thirty-three super-Dreadnought and Dreadnought battleships and nine battlecruisers.[17] By 2020, the once mighty Royal Navy was reduced to a fleet of two heavy aircraft carriers (one of which will be maintained at a lower level of readiness), two amphibious assault ships, eight frigates, five destroyers, four completed nuclear attack submarines, and four ageing nuclear ballistic missile submarines. Even supporting such a modest force will prove difficult, as evident from the efforts to 'crew' the two new Queen Elizabeth-class heavy carriers, and the rest of a now small navy.

In the wake of COVID-19 the fleet could well now shrink further, if the number of planned Type 26 Global Combat Ships and Type 31e frigates is further reduced. Worse, operating and maintenance budgets have been cut. The effective 'mothballing' of one of the relatively new and highly advanced Type 45 destroyers, as well as problems with the 'life-extensions' of the long-serving Type 23 frigates, mean the actual capability the British can put

16. Briton Sir Julian Stafford Corbett and American Alfred Thayer Mahan disagreed about the use of sea power, partly because they both wrote at a time when Britain was a status quo power with an Empire, and the US an emerging world power. Corbett saw command of the sea as part of grand strategy and essentially concerning the control of maritime communications, whether for commercial or military purposes. For Mahan the primary purpose of the sea was as an arena for decisive battle in which a nation's fleet would seek out and destroy the enemy fleet in a decisive naval battle.

17. See Statement of the First Lord of the Admiralty, Explanatory of the Naval Estimates 1919–1920, https://www.naval-history.net/WW1NavyBritishAdmiraltyEstimates1919.htm.

to sea is significantly below the stated strength of the fleet. There is even a suggestion that one of the two new 70,000 Queen Elizabeth-class aircraft carriers will also be mothballed, with one reason cited being the cost of the COVID-19 crisis. It is a failure the Royal Navy shares with many European navies and again places undue pressure on the United States Navy. The United States Navy also faces pressures but it is working to increase not just the size of its surface fleet but also its all-important deployability and the increased use of advanced technologies such as hypersonic systems, as well as 'intelligent' unmanned surface and sub-surface craft.

The British Army faces similar challenges in the wake of COVID-19. Under SDSR 2015, the Army 2025 concept saw plans for a rapid Reaction and Adaptable Force abandoned in favour of two 5,000-strong Strike Brigades, organized around the Parachute Regiment (plus the Royal Marines Commandos), with much of the rest of the force configured to sustain those two brigades. There is some limited capacity to 'surge' via the so-called Reserve Force, but the only significant new platform the Army will receive is a new Armoured Infantry Fighting Vehicle to enhance battlefield manoeuvre. Paradoxically, whilst London makes much of the £2 billion of 'additional' resources to be invested in UK Special Operating Forces, it is hard to see how such a quality force could be recruited from such a small force base of some 82,500 soldiers and maintain its fighting edge. The Royal Air Force, which is in desperate need of modernization, has received two additional Typhoon air defence/fast attack squadrons of some twelve aircraft, with aircraft brought out of store, whilst the delivery of forty-two F-35s has been accelerated for use by both the Fleet Air Arm and RAF by 2023, twenty-four of which will be on the new aircraft carriers. Moreover, whilst a commitment was made to eventually procure 138 F-35s by 2035, even before COVID-19 the specific year-on-year build-up of the force was unclear. Some eight C-17 Globemasters, plus some twenty-two A400M transport aircraft, have also been retained, together with a force of fourteen C-130Js. However, the number of such aircraft a US Stryker Brigade needs in support is markedly larger than is likely to be available to the British Army's Strike Brigades. The impact the COVID-19 crisis will have on such modest strategic effort is as yet unclear, but the best that can be hoped for is that British forces will be on hold for the foreseeable future. China? Russia? Worse, with the cost of the 'Successor' programme to replace the four Trident-armed Vanguard-class nuclear ballistic missiles submarines with four Dreadnought-class boats now increased from £25 billion to some £41 billion over a decade, and with the likelihood of new funds being injected into the British defence budget unlikely given COVID-19, the cost of the new nuclear deterrent will 'warp' the UK's armed forces even more towards nuclear deterrence at the expense of warfighting defence and deterrence.

In effect, the UK is trying to create both a strategic nuclear deterrent and a global-reach conventional strike force on a defence budget which could only probably afford one or the other, but not both, even before COVID-19. Put simply, the UK, like so many European countries, must make a choice: it cannot be a Tier One power if such a status comes at the expense of the US taxpayer *and* maintain the vital strategic relationship with the US upon which almost the entirety of the UK's defence planning assumptions are founded. Indeed, the British are a microcosm of European defence pretence and the pressures such pretence places on an overstretched US, the enduring central pillar of Europe's defence.

The British example is also a stark reminder that the defence-strategic choices made by the European allies have a profound effect on the Americans and their armed forces, and by extension, the credibility of NATO as a defensive alliance. And, whilst it is certainly the case that US public support for the Alliance, and by extension the defence of Europe, remains remarkably high, it is hard to see such support being sustained if the overstretch to which US forces are subject is made worse by extended deployments to the European theatre to offset self-imposed European military weakness. This is particularly so in the wake of the COVID-19 crisis. At the very least, the US would probably look to the British to deploy a corps headquarters and two divisional headquarters in an emergency. Now, that is unlikely.

Future war NATO?

Winston Churchill reputedly once said: 'However beautiful the strategy, one must occasionally look at the results'.[18] The real Alliance question is essentially simple: what must Europeans do to enable the US to continue to ensure the defence of Europe through NATO? There are some signs that NATO is beginning to adapt to future war across the hybrid, cyber, and

---

18. Like quite a few Churchill quotes, it is disputed that he ever said this. See 'Churchill', winstonchurchill.org, https://winstonchurchill.org/publications/finest-hour/finest-hour-141/history-detectives-red-herrings-famous-words-churchill-never-said.

hyper war mosaic. NATO Secretary-General Jens Stoltenberg pointed out in 2018 that there had been 'four consecutive years of real increases in defence spending' and that 'All allies are increasing defence spending. More allies are spending 2% GDP on defence and the majority of Allies now have plans to do so by 2024'.[19] He paid particular attention to the $87 billion more that Canada and the European allies have spent on defence since 2014. And that, 'When it comes to capabilities, Allies have committed to investing 20% of their defence spending on major equipment'.

However, that was before the COVID-19 crisis and even then, in terms of maintaining a relative balance of military power, it was simply not enough given events elsewhere. Indeed, one does not have to read deeply between the lines to see that Stoltenberg's political aim was to forestall more Alliance-bashing from President Trump over more equitable burden-sharing. For NATO to have any future, the European allies must understand that burden-sharing will be the elephant at NATO summits long after President Trump has left the White House, and deep into the COVID-19 crisis. Indeed, if the European allies and Canada want the Alliance to survive, as it must, they will need not only to fulfil their collective commitments to the Alliance, but go significantly beyond. Critically, and to assist such an aim, a more sophisticated concept of burden-sharing might include spending on all activities that would enhance defence and deterrence, such as cyber-architectures and critical transportation infrastructures.

Furthermore, for all of America's understandable frustration with its European allies, the US needs its allies, as much as it ever did during the Cold War. This is precisely because the overstretch of US armed forces is caused primarily by the emergence of China which is fast eroding the relative military superiority of the US. Above all, America's European allies must finally come to realize that America will only be able to defend them if they do far more to defend themselves. The 4x30 NATO Readiness Initiative was not a huge commitment in the wider European defence scheme of things, and was only a start, but even that force goal caused contention in Europe. Still, 'thirty mechanised battalions, thirty air squadrons, thirty combat vessels, ready to use within thirty days or less' was an important signal for the European allies to send to Washington at a difficult

---

19. Press conference by NATO Secretary General Jens Stoltenberg following the meeting of the North Atlantic Council (NAC) in Defence Ministers' session, 7 June 2018, https://www.nato.int/cps/en/natohq/opinions_155264.htm?selectedLocale=en.

moment.[20] For the sake of the Alliance it is vital NATO Europeans maintain such commitments even when faced by the financial and economic consequences of COVID-19. If not, the European allies will lose what little military momentum there is in adapting the Alliance, and with it the enhanced and improved military mobility vital to both NATO defence and deterrence.

COVID-19 or no, the NATO Command Structure and Force Structure must continue to be steadily reinforced and modernized, and Alliance efforts to strengthen its defences against irregular threats confirmed with the Cyberspace Operations Centre, Counter Hybrid Support, and Counter-Terrorism Teams vital to that end. If not, NATO's collective defence structures could well be out-flanked by a determined enemy, much like the Maginot Line in June 1940, especially so if US forces are over-engaged in a major crisis in the Indo-Pacific.

Europeans must wake up and smell the American coffee

European leaders are in denial about the changing nature of America's grand strategic challenge and its implications for NATO and European defence. The refusal of many NATO leaders to update an increasingly anachronistic Strategic Concept is proof of that denial. The critical NATO need now is for Europeans to generate sufficiency of strategic ambition to in turn generate a force/forces able to act as a credible first responder in the event of a high-end emergency with Russia. That means Europeans willing to consider and prepare for the military worst case in spite of the COVID-19 crisis.

NATO's adapted post-COVID-19 Strategic Concept must also envision a future Alliance that enables US forces to act as the global West's grand strategic heavy mobile force able to support front-line allies, be they in the Indo-Pacific or Europe. To that end, the work the Alliance has done on establishing NATO Standards from force generation to coalition command and control (C2) and beyond should be shared, and further developed, with the likes of Australia, Japan, and South Korea. Thankfully, a start on such collaboration, and a precedent for its further development, has already been

20. 'Defence Ministers to Agree NATO Readiness Initiative', 7 June 2018, https://www.nato.int/cps/en/natohq/news_155348.htm.

established. In the aftermath of the NATO International Security Assistance Force campaign in Afghanistan and the Counter-ISIL Coalition, several partner countries have embraced NATO Standards in anticipation of the need to participate in future coalitions of the willing and able. The wider use of NATO Standards for coalition force generation and command and control would enable the world's democracies (the US-led Global Community of Democracies), centred upon the US, to form not only a new strategic and political grouping based on Western values (the Global West), but also a matrix of capable first responders to which the US could add critical weight, when and where necessary.

However, if NATO's defence and deterrence posture is to remain credible, it must not only envision the Alliance in a global context but also prepare NATO for the new technology challenge the West is facing from China and Russia *and* the threat posed by those intolerant of all and any who do not share their strict interpretation of faith. These threats will not only survive the COVID-19 crisis—it could well exacerbate them. In other words, the future for NATO must, and can only be, as part of a US-centric, partnership-rich Global 'West' that is more idea than place. Such 'deterrence' will not be established or assured by diluting the cross-domain fighting power of US forces or by forcing them to offset Allied weaknesses in Europe. All such an impoverishment of US forces would achieve is to afford adversaries the timing and opportunity to do their worst in any way they would wish, and wherever they might choose. Rather, any and all adversaries must be fully aware that the future US strategic heavy mobile force could, and would, act swiftly and decisively across the seven domains of contemporary and future warfare, supported effectively and by powerful allies able to defend their own regions.

NATO must be central to such strategic adaptation. If not, formal alliances will become less formal and the command centre of gravity of Western deterrence/defence will move inexorably towards Five Eyes-type structures that are organized around global-reach US forces. Fleet of mind, eye, and foot, NATO forces must be capable of striking anywhere and anytime across many domains. This is because if Europeans can begin to better enable US forces, it would also enable the Americans to reverse the current adverse strategic trend in which it is all too easy for adversaries to keep the Alliance and its members off-balance—politically, socially, and militarily. This new transatlantic relationship, for that is what it would need, would force adversaries into uncertainty over where, how, when, and with what the US would strike in support of their allies the world over, all of whom would, in effect, become trip-wires, albeit powerful ones.

The simple, hard, and immutable big truth is that Europe's future defence is and will remain dependent on the US for the foreseeable future. However, the global overstretch of US forces will intensify, particularly if the current European policy trajectory is adhered to, because military power, like all power, is relative. China and Russia, not to mention the Americans, are fast far outstripping European military power with profound implications for the future defence of Europe. Given the changing character of war, the future defence of Europe will continue to be established on a simple premise that, in turn, should be an integral part of a much-needed new transatlantic strategic 'contract' between Americans and Europeans: how best can Europeans help maintain the power of the US, and the value of its conventional and nuclear deterrent in and around Europe?

Can NATO (still) defend Europe? In fact, NATO is not really in the defence business; it is in the deterrence business. If deterrence failed, the answer is probably no. COVID-19 has simply made the NATO challenge starker.

7

Could Europe defend Europe?

The European defence of Europe

The counterpart to the question of whether NATO could defend Europe is, in extremis, could Europe defend Europe? To answer that question, aspiration must de dispassionately detached from capability. For any such defence to be at all credible, all of the issues discussed herein would need in their sum to form an extremely tight and cohesive European defence effort. European strategic autonomy would need to be matched by shared European strategic responsibility, the Franco-German defence axis would need to be far more than lofty political rhetoric, European national defence establishments would need to be combined to the point of integration, and a European strategic public–private partnership would be needed that fully enabled Permanent Structured Cooperation (PESCO). Critically, such a defence edifice would need to be capable of changing and adapting fast.

For Europeans, the hard reality yet to be faced by so many of them is that defence power is relative, and never absolute. There have been efforts to end the malaise. The Franco-British Defence and Security Co-operation Treaty of 2 November 2010 was an attempt to kick-start an ambitious collective effort. Like so many such European defence initiatives, it has stalled. The Treaty states that the two countries will pool 'their capacities through coordinating development, acquisition, deployment and maintenance of a range of capabilities, facilities, equipment, materials and services, to perform the full spectrum of missions, including the most demanding missions'.[1] Almost a decade on, and in spite of some successes, such ambition remains by

---

1. See 'Treaty between the United Kingdom of Great Britain and Northern Ireland and the French Republic for Defence and Security Co-operation', London, 2 November 2010 (the Treaty entered into force on 1 July 2011) (London: Cabinet Office), p. 4.

and large unrealized, especially and particularly when compared with the evolution of US, Russian, and Chinese forces over the same period.

In a sense, the Treaty is a microcosm of the essential challenge facing a European defence of Europe—not enough money to do the job on their own, not enough trust to do it together. Logically, in the wake of the COVID-19 crisis the pressure on Europeans to do more together will grow if they are to afford both human security and national defence, which might lead to the German vision of a European Defence Union. With the UK outside the EU, such a vision might be easier to realize, and paradoxically, cooperation might also be easier with a UK that no longer sees European defence as some 'backdoor' device to sucker them into some kind of European super-state by duplicating the role and function of NATO.

The critical weakness of European defence remains military. Whilst the Americans can deploy over 12 per cent of their force at any one time, many Europeans can at best deploy only 3 per cent at any one time. And, whilst the Americans spend less than 40 per cent of the US defence budget on personnel, some Europeans are spending well over 70 per cent.[2] Shortfalls remain across the European force inventories of key enablers, such as transport aircraft and helicopters, deployed force protection, and the ability to gather quickly actionable intelligence, including by satellite. There has been some modest progress made in the development of advanced expeditionary forces (SOF, specialized forces and enhanced logistics), which are vital for all forms of operations across the defence and security spectrum. The most significant progress has taken place within the NATO framework, usually at the behest of increasingly concerned and frustrated Americans. COVID-19 has also revealed a host of missing capabilities, particularly a lack of troops and limited combat support and combat support services. The COVID-19 crisis also revealed that critical civilian agencies had little or no idea how to run crisis logistics, which in an emergency demanding the use of all national means could prove decisive. The result is that the deployability and mobility of European forces, together with their sustainability and logistics, survivability, effective engagement, and C4ISR (Command, Control, Communications, Computers, Intelligence, Surveillance, and Reconnaissance), remain severely constrained.

---

2. Authors' own research.

Strategic autonomy?

At the heart of the European defence debate is French-inspired 'strategic autonomy'. The *Oxford English Dictionary* defines 'autonomy' as the right of self-government, personal freedom, and freedom of the will.[3] Those who do, indeed, aspire to European strategic autonomy in the realm of defence need to properly imagine the defence of Europe without the Americans, for only then will they understand the true cost of defending Europe. Beyond the markedly increased cost, they must also realize that mounting such a defence will require a very different approach and that Europeans will need to go a very long way from where European 'defence' is today.

For France, strategic autonomy reinforces the need for autonomous, high-end, very expensive European military capabilities, most of which Paris would hope are French. Paris is not lacking in ambition, even if its ambition far exceeds its money. Strategic autonomy would demand of Europeans the ability to undertake 'autonomous' assessment and analysis of the strategic environment (satellites), 'autonomy' of decision-making (stand-alone strategic European military headquarters), and autonomy of action across both the military and defence-industrial landscape. Critically, this would also require greatly enhanced European strategic lift, strategic intelligence, transportation, and military mobility, so-called 'enablers', many of which continue to be provided by the US. Paris is also keen for the development of a European 'strategic culture' to underpin autonomy, with a particular focus on bespoke intelligence-sharing and contingency planning exclusively by Europeans. Paris points to Article 42:7 of the Lisbon Treaty, the so-called Mutual Defence Clause, as the treaty-legal basis for strategic autonomy, although the language was tempered by both the British and Germans to ensure that if Europeans found themselves unable to cope with a crisis, they could appeal to the US through NATO. It states,

> If a Member State is the victim of armed aggression on its territory, the other Member States shall have towards it an obligation of aid and assistance by all the means in their power, in accordance with Article 51 of the United Nations Charter. This shall not prejudice the specific character of the security and defence policy of certain Member States. Commitments and cooperation in this area shall be consistent with commitments under the North Atlantic

---

3. *The Concise Oxford Dictionary* (1982) (Oxford: Oxford University Press).

Treaty Organization, which, for those States which are members of it, remains the foundation of their collective defence and the forum for its implementation.[4]

The Franco–German defence axis

The Franco-German relationship is central to any aspirations for European strategic autonomy. It is not an easy relationship. The post-war de-Nazification of Germany was so thorough that even today, Germans sceptical about the value of US-enabled European defence would still only consider a larger defence role for Germany if it was firmly embedded in multilateral institutions. For many of them, the institutional framework would need to be so tight that it would be a latter-day European Defence Community (EDC).[5] Many German universities even face legal or policy firewalls that prevent them from engaging in defence-related research, with the only way to overcome such firewalls being a focus on dual-use technologies, such as artificial intelligence (AI), cyber, lightweight materials, medical treatment for traumatic wounds, and a host of other military-applicable areas. However, the cultural antipathy to such efforts must not be underestimated. Former German defence minister and now President of the European Commission, Ursula von der Leyen, admitted as much in a 2019 interview, in which she called for the creation of an 'army of Europeans' that might one day lead to the creation of a European Army as a way to solve the German defence dilemma.[6]

4. https://researchbriefings.parliament.uk/ResearchBriefing/Summary/CBP-7390.
5. The 'de-Nazification' of Germany began immediately on its 8 May 1945 surrender. It was an Allied initiative to rid German society, culture, press, judiciary, and what was left of the armed forces of any trace of National Socialist ideology. At its heart was the determination to impose on Germans collective guilt and responsibility for World War Two, which remains deeply embedded in the German political psyche.
6. To be precise, in March 2019 von der Leyen said, 'A European army is a vision that might become a reality in generations to come. What we see today and what we already achieved is the first concrete steps on this way. By giving birth to the European Defence Union, we have started to build what I like to call the "Army of the Europeans." We maintain national armies, under the authority of sovereign states, but better coordinated and mutually reinforcing. One goal is to overcome the fragmentation of military systems by developing and procuring more common solutions. This will improve efficiency and effectiveness. The European Defense Fund provides much incentive for that. And the overall aim is a safe and secure Europe!' See Michalis Tsikalas, 'Ursula von der Leyen: "We Are Building a European Defense Union"', eksther-imerin.com, http://www.ekathimerini.com/238679/article/ekathimerini/news/ursula-von-der-leyen-we-are-building-a-european-defense-union.

Given its Gaullist heritage, France takes a very different view, preferring instead the creation of a permanent army of Europeans, i.e. of nation-states, with France at its core. Indeed, France's contemporary position might best be described as 'Macron-Gaullism'. The French and Germans also take a different view on the role of institutionalized European defence. For the French the EU's Common Security and Defence Policy, which remains important to Germans as a legitimizer of force, is effectively dead, killed in the sands of the Sahel by what Paris saw as limited European solidarity with France for a counter-terrorism mission that Paris believes to be of importance to the whole of Europe. This divide again highlights the profound split that has been apparent in Europe in much of the debate about European defence since the Cold War between those wedded to the idea of a common European defence, and those who believe collective defence is the only credible strategy, mainly because it affords continued close links with the Americans, and because the British would never countenance being part of a common defence. As Winston Churchill famously said in May 1953 when Paris was pressing hard for Britain to join the EDC, 'We are with them, but not of them'.[7]

Paris has also wavered between the common and collective approaches to European defence, talking 'common' defence when it appeared such a defence would mean more France and less Germany, but retreating to US-led collective defence when French aspirations and ambitions were rebuffed. Today, Paris is putting much of its effort into what President Macron dubbed the European Intervention Initiative or E2I, a collective security and defence framework outside of the EU that could accommodate post-Brexit Britain, still Europe's most capable military actor. The 2019 Franco-German Aachen Treaty appeared to offer a compromise between the collective and common approaches to European defence with the French idea that 'strategic autonomy' will only be built by having the EU less, not more, involved in defence, with the focus rather on the creation of a state-led army of Europeans. And yet for the Germans, 'strategic autonomy' could only result from ever more EU defence, even if for Berlin NATO

---

7. Churchill famously made this comment to the House of Commons on 11 May 1953. It was part of a speech in which he accused the French of being 'anti-British' over the EDC and said that Britain had done more than any other power to support the Treaty. Still, his comment definitively killed off any chance Britain would join the EDC. See Julian Lindley-French (2007) *A Chronology of European Security and Defence 1945–2007* (Oxford: Oxford University Press), p. 43.

remains the main focus of any real defence of Europe, and any such strategic 'autonomy' would not be too autonomous from either NATO or the Americans.

Germany is essentially the primary dilemma for the future defence of Europe. There can be no credible defence of continental Europe without a militarily powerful Germany, and yet Germany remains deeply reluctant to play such a role. Paradoxically, during the Cold War the Federal Republic often fielded the largest army in European NATO, even when the Americans had over 300,000 troops stationed in Europe (as opposed to the 30,000 or so today).[8] However, the very presence of US forces reassured Germans and more importantly other Europeans that Germany was a threat to no-one and had no ambitions to rebuild the *Wehrmacht*. Even today, some seventy years on from the beginning of the Cold War, with concerns about how German power is perceived, allied to a 'healthy' level of free-riding on the US taxpayer, as well as a German foreign policy that can at best be described as mercantilist, Berlin would probably only countenance providing significantly more military weight to the defence of Europe if it was legitimized by the creation of some form of hybrid European Army, i.e. a part intergovernmental, part supranational force that would be eventually, and implausibly, run by Brussels.

In other words, whilst the French and Germans can agree for now on a future European force that is 'inter-service', the Germans insist it must have the explicit ambition to one day become 'common', whilst the French will do all they can to prevent that, whatever the European rhetoric that routinely emerges from Paris. In any case, the French have a point, because the history of EU defence aspirations suggests that the moment one attaches the word 'common' to any European defence policy or initiative, it is far more likely to stand up legions of lawyers than warriors.

Whilst it would be easy to dismiss such ambitions as fanciful, it would be a mistake, even if one leading European diplomat with much experience of defence said in a late 2019 conversation with one of the authors that the EU is dysfunctional and can play no role in collective defence. However, the very idea of collective defence is changing, with a new balance needed between power projection and people protection. For such a defence to be credible, the 'hardening' of European society and its critical infrastructures,

---

8. Figures supplied by one of this book's authors, F. Ben Hodges, when he was General commanding US Army Europe.

and critically the ability for effective consequence management and post-attack recovery, will require large-scale synergies. This is not least because of very high levels of European civilian resources across Europe that will be needed, and the rapid movement of civilian first responders, for which the EU will be vital.

For all the talk of a Franco-German axis, the most important defence-strategic relationship for France within Europe remains with non-PESCO, non-EU, and Europe's only other nuclear and power projection power—the UK.[9] For France, the paradox of the European strategic autonomy it champions is that the rest of Europe lacks the strategic tradition and/or strategic culture to form the basis of a truly autonomous and strategic European defence capability. Only those on the front lines of European defence, such as the Baltic States and Poland, really understand or believe that a credible European military force would be important, but they lack the requisite political, economic, and military weight.

Strategic autonomy is a consequence

Strategic autonomy is a consequence. Indeed, only if Europeans build more effective armed forces with many more capabilities and capacities, allied to a structure of multi-domain enablers, could 'strategic autonomy' from the Americans be realized. It was hard to envisage such ambitions even prior to COVID-19. In post-crisis Europe the only way to realize such a force would be via such a deep level of cohesion that, to all intents and purposes, it would mean that a long step had already been taken down the road to a European Army. Beyond Euro-federalist hard-liners (most of whom seem to live in Belgium), few European states are willing to surrender the kind of sovereignty that would see supranational institutions deciding whether their young men and women should be sent into harm's way. Even before COVID-19 Europeans repeatedly balked at the kind of investments that would be needed to even realize Robert Schuman's 1950 vision of a European defence effort 'proportionate to the dangers which threaten it' (see, "Declaration of 9th May 1950 delivered by Robert Schuman"

---

9. See Julian Lindley-French (2010) *Britain and France: A Dialogue of Decline?* (London: Chatham House).

Foundation Robert Schuman Robert-schuman.eu/en/European-issues/
0204-declaration-of-9th-may-1950-delivered-by-robert.schuman).

There are other factors underpinning Europe's defence drift which make
it unlikely Europeans will ever be able to defend themselves against all
contingencies. Over the past twenty years, two fundamental shifts have
taken place which are now accelerating. First, Europe is no longer the
cockpit of systemic struggle, which has now moved to the Indo-Pacific.
Second, the military domain is being revolutionized by new civilian technologies that stretch from AI to new forms of biological warfare in which
Europeans play little or no role. Given the impact such change is having on
the character of warfare and Europe's absence from it, strategic autonomy is
becoming an ever more distant prospect for Europeans. Indeed, far from
being better able to play a full role across the new landscape of conflict, the
greater danger is that Europeans will further dilute and undermine the cross-
domain fighting power of US forces by forcing them to offset Europeans'
weaknesses, thus affording America's adversaries the chance to choose the
time and place to do their worst in any way they would wish.

Even before COVID-19, most Europeans were either unwilling or
unable to spend the money that would be needed to realize any form of
strategic autonomy beyond the declaratory. COVID-19 probably killed
such aspirations, even for those Europeans uncomfortable with their continuing dependence on the US. The result is a gulf between the stated
ambition of European defence and the reality that has dogged Europe since
1949. Today, Europe's enduring reality is that Europe can neither defend
itself adequately in the face of the threats it faces, nor is it capable of easing
the growing pressure on US forces that would enable the Americans to
better defend Europe.

One reason for the failure of such ambitions has been the disingenuous
nature of many of them. Since the failure of the EDC in 1954, many of those
same Europeans who have promoted 'strategic autonomy' have done so not
because they want to enhance the security of Europe, but rather because
they see defence as the first duty of the state and, relieved of such a duty by
deepening European defence integration, the road would then be clear for
the creation of a European super-state. From Jean Monnet on, European
federalists have, in effect, wanted the Americans to underwrite said 'autonomy' by acting as Europe's defence guarantor, but for political rather than
defence ends. The result is that European defence has been trapped between
political aspiration and defence realism, and subject to inadequate policies

that bear little or no relation to the defence effort needed. In other words, the strategic autonomy many Europeans call for would lead to a Europe incapable of being autonomous.

An integrated European defence?

The essential dilemma of European defence is how a group of medium and small powers in a relatively small geographic space combine their security and defence to such an extent that they can effectively deter, defend, and respond to big threat across the spectrum of human security and national defence. Indeed, beyond the aspirational, could Europeans mount a credible defence if Americans forces were overwhelmingly engaged elsewhere in the world, or a fundamental shift in US policy suddenly took place? In such circumstances would Europe defend itself against a Russian incursion whilst, at the same time, endeavouring to deal with the complex threats that emerge from instability to its south and to its east? What role for the EU? After all, with the UK having left the EU, some 80 per cent of all the military capabilities committed to the defence of Europe are now outside the EU.[10] From its very inception the EU's Common Security and Defence Policy (CSDP) has implied a much deeper level of European defence integration and the search for a new balance between defence efficiency and effectiveness, and yet it has stalled on the political altar of state sovereignty. The European response to the pandemic was atomized and would likely have been far more efficient if a more integrated planning and application of human security had been adopted. Ideally, yes, but until the triple challenges of democracy, identity, and the effective accountability of power to the people are met, common prescriptions for European defence are likely to remain both partial and aspirational.

Furthermore, the future defence of Europe must also survive Europe's political turmoil. Brexit rendered any aspiration for meaningfully autonomous European defence even more distant, for it is only the EU that can

---

10. In February 2018, NATO Secretary-General Jens Stoltenberg said that with the UK's departure from the EU, 80 per cent of all European defence spending will come from outside the EU. He also said that the effective defence of Europe will require the merging of EU and NATO assets. See George Allison, 'After the UK Leaves the EU, 80 per cent of NATO Spending Will Come from Outside the EU', 22 February 2018, https://ukdefencejournal.org. uk/uk-leaves-eu-80-percent-nato-spending-will-come-outside-eu-says-alliance-head.

drive the necessary defence integration upon which such a defence would necessarily be mounted. Indeed, for autonomy to be at all possible, an integrated common defence would need to combine and aggregate the limited defence and fighting power of the smaller European powers with those outside such a framework, most notably the UK. There would be others that would resist such integration, but above all France, in spite of enduring calls from Paris for more European integration.

Could NATO also adopt plans for a more integrated European defence? Such an approach would require a radical departure for the Alliance, built around a European pillar that was far more singular and integrated, possibly reducing the size of the North Atlantic Council to five ambassadors—the UK, Canada, the EU, Turkey, and the US. Given the struggle to make even modest adjustments to NATO's Strategic Concept, it is hard to see the circumstances in which any such shift would take place either prior to a catastrophe or the UK, Norway, and Turkey leaving the Alliance. If anything, with the rise of nativist forces in Europe, and the polarization of politics in many European states, the political unity of Europe upon which an integrated European defence would necessarily rely is an ever more distant dream. A process of disintegration has been 'ably' assisted by Russian strategic influence campaigns and the disinformation, deception, and destabilization central to Moscow's applications of complex strategic coercion and 5D warfare.

A European strategic public–private defence partnership?

The European defence dilemma does not simply concern how to afford, control, and organize a European force, but how also to integrate the rapidly advancing technology that would be needed to empower such a European force. For example, the Pentagon has established an outpost of some 500 people in Silicon Valley in California, the sole purpose of which is to survey the tech-scape for new battlespace-applicable technologies. Europe has nothing comparable and is thus daily falling further behind in the twenty-first-century arms race. The contemporary and, by and large, state-led European approach to defence seems increasingly anachronistic given the central role technology and big-tech firms will play in defence. Worse, in the wake of COVID-19, unless there is a massive increase in taxation at a time of recession, even depression, it is again hard to see how Europeans can generate the critical mass of research and productive capacity to exploit such technologies. And yet, the influence tech and other commercial enterprises will necessarily have on Europe's future defence will be vital if Europeans are to mount a serious defence as some of the major tech companies have GDPs that far exceed many European countries, which remain, for the most part, outside of any real conversations about future defence. Critically, Europe will need to pull the private sector, and not just the European private sector, fully and squarely into such conversation if the European defence dilemma is to be resolved, because much of the requisite technology resides outside of Europe. There is a major caveat; many of these companies rely on China for crucial parts of their supply chain, and in the wake of COVID-19, some of them will be ripe for Chinese takeover bids, in some cases masked by shell companies. Would Europeans be willing to block any Chinese attempts to quietly control the flow of technology to European defence when so many European countries, with Italy to the fore, are increasingly dependent on Chinese money?

At the very least, European defence reality demands a much stronger and much earlier role for big-tech in Europe's defence-strategic planning. Unfortunately, the very idea of such openness goes against the traditional European view of how defence is procured and raises the danger of excessive Chinese influence in the wake of COVID-19. Such an approach would also need to overcome the super-statist, Euro-protectionist instincts of the EU and increasingly irrelevant but influential European national defence-industrial 'champions', too many of which remain metal-bashers in an age of digital superpower because of little more than parochial politics. There is an old saying to justify the continuance of the transatlantic relationship: 'We'd better hang together or we'll certainly hang separately'. The same now goes for any future strategic public–private partnership European states and the EU would need to forge with big-tech and the entirety of the tech supply chain to realize a credible digital-based European defence in the twenty-first century.

Can Europeans defence innovate?

The refusal/inability of Europeans to think big about big-tech in future defence is making European defence look increasingly like a twenty-first-century Maginot Line, the French defensive line of the 1930s. Whilst the Line looked impressive on paper, it collapsed within days in June 1940 because it was ill-conceived and obsolete, vulnerable to being outflanked, and reflective of a static concept of warfare in an age of manoeuvre, much like European defence today. In essence, the Maginot Line was an attempt by the French to fight World War One more effectively. The imperative now is for Europeans to forge a new relationship between strategy, policy, and technology precisely because technology is ever more driving policy and strategy and likely to force upon Europeans a profound reconsideration of just what collective action means. Whether it is maintaining interoperability with the US future force or deterring the future forces of others, Europeans will need to apply a host of new technologies to their defence. Such technologies could very quickly destroy at a stroke the increasingly obsolete and vulnerable systems and societal architecture upon which European defence depends. This will not be easy in a Europe that is as diverse, as open, and as enduringly jealous as the Europe of today.

The British scientist and wartime technologist Sir Barnes Wallis once said, 'There is a natural opposition among men to anything they have not thought of themselves'.[11] If Europeans are to have any chance of mounting a credible European defence that is sufficiently autonomous when and where it needs to be, then innovation, or rather the capacity to innovate, must be the driver of future European defence. The problem is that such innovation rarely happens in Europe outside of war. Wallis was one of those fathers of wartime innovation that were a crucial component of the Allied strategy in World War Two. Indeed, it was the fusion of innovation, science, technology, and capability that Wallis helped forge, most notably the brilliant military execution by RAF 617 (Dambusters) Squadron in the destruction of two of the Mohne and Eder dams in May 1943. To succeed, Operation Chastise needed six separate strands of development to come together: a new strategy (attacks on infrastructure vital to German industry), a new technological idea (Barnes Wallis's vision of a bouncing bomb), a new bomb (the Upkeep mine), a new way of casting steel, a new explosive (RDX), and a new aircraft (the Mark III Avro Lancaster bomber). That all six elements came together was only possible because Britain was at war, enabling Churchill to drive over traditional political and bureaucratic barriers. Thankfully, Europe is not at war, but nor is it at peace, particularly so in

11. https://www.azquotes.com/quote/661218.

the wake of the COVID-19 crisis, and changing the peacetime mind-set of Europeans will be the first vital step on the road to defence-strategic innovation. Indeed, if Europeans are ever to defend Europe, they will need to summon up a kind of 'wartime' spirit of cohesion and innovation. Is that plausible?

Prior to COVID-19, there were signs Europe was just slowly beginning to emerge from the great European defence depression that followed the banking and Eurozone crises of 2008–10. Europe was also just again beginning to consider its place in the world of the twenty-first century, after decades of introverted obsession with the institutional shape of 'Europe'. Now? The tragedy for Europe's defence of Europe given COVID-19, whether the centre of gravity is the EU or NATO, is that the already deep gulf between stated ambition and actual capability could well deepen further still.

Furthermore, a brief survey of recent and ongoing EU missions in Africa, Asia, and Europe reveal that for all the talk of European strategic autonomy, most such operations remain more firmly rooted in the peacekeeping past. There are also a range of issues over which Europeans simply disagree, such as how best to organize Europe's coercive power, and whether 'Europe' should even aspire to high-end military capabilities. There are also profound differences over how to deal with China and Russia, and the balance to strike between power and partnership, with the Italians firm in their belief that Russia poses no threat and should even be seen as a partner.[12] However, the ultimate block on a twenty-first-century European defence concerns the development of a digital-based capability that reaches across the hybrid-cyber-hyperwar mosaic. Some tentative steps have been taken. The 2014 EU Cyber Defence Policy Framework is a case in point, as is the EU Maritime Security Strategy. The EU has also sought to promote greater synergy between security, defence, and justice in an attempt to mitigate the threat posed by complex strategic coercion, including efforts to mitigate the

---

12. GlobalSecurity.org wrote, 'Italy's relationship with Russia is complex, encompassing historical ideological sympathies, geostrategic calculations, commercial pressure, energy dependence, and personal relationships between top leaders. The combination of these factors creates a strong tendency for Italy's foreign policy to be highly receptive to Russian efforts to gain greater political influence in the EU and to support Russia's efforts to dilute American security interests in Europe. In its relationship with Russia, energy is the most important bilateral issue and the quest for stable energy supplies from Russia frequently forces Italy to compromise on security and political issues'. https://www.globalsecurity.org/military/world/europe/it-forrel-ru.htm.

vulnerability of Europe's energy security. However, the reality is that without the Americans, Europe's security and defence does look like the Maginot Line and would collapse equally quickly if tested.

PESCO

In December 2014, in an effort to boost European defence innovation, the EU launched PESCO, or Permanent Structured Cooperation, amidst the usual political fanfare. The aim was to inject energy into the European defence process by creating Pioneer Groups of member-states to ease capability shortfalls by fulfilling 'higher criteria for military capabilities' through binding commitments to each other that would enable Europeans 'to undertake the most challenging missions'.[13] With its 'voluntary' projects across the operational and defence-industrial landscape, PESCO was meant to pave the way to an eventual European Defence Union (EDU). A European Defence Fund was also set up to provide seed-corn money for PESCO projects. However, the €5.5 billion ($6.5 billion) on offer was also spread over five years and was paltry compared to defence investments elsewhere. And, even though it is planned to rise to €22.5 billion, it has to be spread across an array of countries and projects.

Furthermore, the two main players, Germany and France, want different things from PESCO. Berlin is still sensitive about defence leadership for fear of history and the EU beginning to look ever more like a putative German Empire, and seeks to embed its defence efforts in both NATO and the Union. Germany is also acutely aware that if Berlin honours the NATO Defence Investment Pledge to spend 2 per cent on defence, it would realize a *Bundeswehr* with a budget of some $70 billion per annum, dwarfing the respective budgets of the British and French. This would mean a defence-strategic prominence for modern Germany that would be difficult to sell domestically, as well as externally in some quarters. PESCO acts as a defence

13. The 'Notification on Permanent Structured Cooperation (PESCO) to the Council and to the High Representative of the Union for Foreign Affairs and Security Policy' of June 2017 states, ' "Permanent Structured Cooperation" is provided for in Articles 42 and 46 of the Treaty on European Union and Protocol No 10 to the Treaty. It can only be activated once and is established by a Council decision to be adopted by qualified majority, in order to bring together all willing Member States in the area of defence, "whose military capabilities fulfil higher criteria" and which have made "more binding commitments with a view to the most demanding missions" and operations'. https://www.consilium.europa.eu/media/31511/171113-pesco-notification.pdf.

alibi for the Germans to help avoid Germany's hard reality: there can be no meaningful European defence of Europe in the twenty-first century without a modern, democratic Germany that is not only willing to share burdens, but also lead.

France, on the other hand, sees PESCO very differently. With echoes of its Gaullist traditions, Paris still harbours the ambition to create an autonomous European military core group that would support France and its expeditionary missions, even though the Sahel campaign in Mali has profoundly shaken French faith in the CSDP as a European means to French strategic ends. PESCO also implies a further level of defence-industrial protectionism to ensure European capabilities are built with French defence equipment. To be fair, mercantilist Germany also harbours such ambitions.

Therefore, PESCO must be seen against the backdrop of an enduring struggle which afflicts European defence. PESCO could be a first meaningful step towards an integrated defence that will one day also lead to integrated supreme political authority to oversee it; in other words, an important step on the road towards a real EDU, and by extension some form of European government. Alternatively, PESCO could be a pragmatic mechanism to assist Europeans to close the yawning gap between what they need to spend on their own defence and what they are willing or able to spend. For either vision to be realized, Europeans, both individually and collectively, will need to properly recognize the dangers they collectively face and invest proportionately and efficiently across the security and defence spectrum. That Europe is facing a growing threat is clear. However, that threat is as much a function of European weakness as, say, Russian 'strength' or the chaos to Europe's south. European military weakness is helping to destabilize both. There is a third alternative. PESCO will continue to suffer from the same malaise that has bedevilled so many EU defence projects. Indeed, in the wake of the COVID-19 crisis, the more likely outcome is that PESCO becomes yet another of those unfunded EU defence aspirations, such as the Headline Goal, or the European Rapid Reaction Force. Take, for example, the once much-heralded but now largely forgotten EU battlegroups, or what one senior French military officer called 'EU lunch groups';[14] in other words, European politics again dressed up as European defence.

14. In conversation with one of the authors of this book.

PESCO should remain focused on the pragmatic. COVID-19 has revealed the enduring European need to strengthen Europe's emergency civilian capabilities, particularly to ensure strengthened consequence management. There is also an equally urgent need to improve civil-military operational effectiveness, as well as civilian and military rapid reaction when a broad set of European instruments need to be mobilized simultaneously. In many ways, the true litmus test of EU defence ambitions, of which PESCO is a part, will be if a balance can be struck between force synergy and force integration. If PESCO leads to an enhanced and more autonomous European pillar of a revamped post-Brexit NATO, and thus helps make European defence industries more agile, efficient, and future technology-oriented, then the EU would have made an important contribution to the transformation of Europe's defence. However, if PESCO is an attempt to compete with NATO and an EU that seeks to duplicate the Alliance, or more specifically Supreme Headquarters Allied Powers Europe (SHAPE), it will fail.

Could Europe defend Europe?

Given the changing character of war, a European defence of Europe was problematic even prior to the COVID-19 crisis. A common defence of Europe seems even more unlikely. The future role of Europeans in their own defence must be focused on collective effort with institutional partnerships to the fore.

The 2010 NATO Strategic Concept affirmed three 'essential core tasks' for the Alliance: collective defence, crisis management, and cooperative security.[15] As part of that mission the Strategic Partnership NATO enjoys with the EU is vital to the realization of the Alliance's own mission because of the interactive and interlocking nature of the threats Europeans face. As the COVID-19 crisis has revealed, sound European security and defence places as much importance on resiliency and effective and rapid recovery from shock (consequence management) as military-based defence and deterrence. That is why the NATO–EU Strategic Partnership is central to

---

15. See 'Active Engagement, Modern Defence: Strategic Concept for the Defence and Security of Members of the North Atlantic Treaty Organization', Lisbon, November 2010 (Brussels: NATO), https://www.nato.int/strategic-concept/pdf/Strat_Concept_web_en.pdf.

effective political consultations, coordinated planning, the efficient and effective application of resources, minimization of duplication, and the maximization of defence cost-effectiveness.

A pragmatic approach to the future defence of Europe must also lay to rest the political ghost that is a European Army, precisely because it hampers the EU–NATO Strategic Partnership by allowing some to harbour the mistaken belief that there is an alternative to the Americans and NATO. The high-end threats that are again endangering Europe, and the further constraints COVID-19 will impose on Europe's ability to afford its own future war defence, will reinforce the roles of both, but only if Europeans themselves are able to do far more for their defence. In theory, a common EU defence would afford Europeans the very thing that has been missing since the inception of NATO in 1949, and the European Coal and Steel Community in 1950: an affordable European strategic force that is credible as both a deterrent and a defence. And yes, such a force could also go a long way to offset the defence burdens imposed on the US by its responsibilities to the Alliance. However, it would simply not work in practice.

That is not to suggest the EU has no role to play in Europe's security and defence. The very idea of defence is evolving and there are places and operations where it would make more sense for European forces to operate under an EU flag. However, it is in the building of the vital civilian aspects of defence and deterrence and the creation of a more resilient and robust Europe where the EU can add real value. In the event of a major 5D attack on Europe, the capacity of Europeans post-attack to generate vital recovery would need to stretch across a high-end spectrum of stabilization efforts from an intensive civilian-led first response, through governance and support for the rule of law. It is in these vital areas that the EU's role cannot be contested, including the removal of legal impediments to rapid response and recovery, a civilian rapid response force able to act in extremis, and the more effective application of moneys in pursuit of effect. The lessons from the COVID-19 crisis must be rigorously applied and quickly to realize such a capability.

There is a further issue that Europeans must confront if European defence and deterrence is to be credible in the face of emerging threats. Any effective defence presupposes a cohesive home base from which to mount such an effort. With war at the seams of European society already a reality, it is questionable if European society is sufficiently cohesive to withstand the shock of future war, even if COVID-19 has revealed impressive levels of social discipline. The polarization of politics within Europe could well continue in the face of mass irregular migration which is also unlikely to ease. Russia will use its not inconsiderable bag of dirty tricks to exacerbate any consequent tensions. Russia will continue to develop new strategies and capabilities to exploit the many gaps in European societies and defence by employing continuous warfare across 5Ds—disinformation, deception, destabilization, disruption, as well as implied and actual destruction—which is central to a disabling concept of complex strategic coercion across the hybrid war, cyber war, hyper war continuum. In Russia, such a strategy is at the heart of the thinking of the Chief of the Russian General Staff General Valery Gerasimov, who uses the threat of war, allied to the means of war, to force compliance through coercion short of war.[16] Such entropy will undermine the political unity of societies and, indeed, the very idea of defence. It also begs a further question: how can such threats be countered without destroying the very liberties and freedoms to be defended?

The military challenge for European defence is not the creation of imaginary European armies, but how to meet the test of future war. Gerasimov also places particular emphasis on exploiting Europe's many defence and deterrence gaps, and the gulf between relatively weak conventional forces and its last-resort strategic nuclear deterrent. Europeans need collectively to realize the scale of the challenge they face and the nature of the kaleidoscopic threat before they can together fashion a meaningful European defence strategy. That means a collective capacity for robust analysis.

For Europe to mount a credible future war defence, there can be no quick fixes. However, to paraphrase Churchill, action is needed 'this day', and such action will need to come first from the UK, France, and Germany.[17] Indeed, to counter Russia, and its many proxies, European defence will need a very much enhanced collective European effort to demonstrate to their

---

16. There is some debate about whether there is any such thing as the Gerasimov Doctrine. Mark Galeotti wrote, 'Everywhere, you'll find scholars, pundits, and policymakers talking about the threat the "Gerasimov doctrine"—named after Russia's chief of the general staff—poses to the West. It's a new way of war, "an expanded theory of modern warfare," or even "a vision of total warfare." There's one small problem. It doesn't exist. And the longer we pretend it does, the longer we misunderstand the—real, but different—challenge Russia poses'. Mark Galeotti, 'I'm Sorry for Creating the "Gerasimov Doctrine"', *Foreign Affairs*, 5 March 2018, https://foreignpolicy.com/2018/03/05/im-sorry-for-creating-the-gerasimov-doctrine.

17. When Churchill wanted immediate action, he was wont to write at the head of memos, 'Action this Day!'

adversaries the means and the will to defend themselves, both within the Alliance and without, and that will demand leadership from Europe's three still weighty regional-strategic powers. However, to do so, Berlin, Paris, and London must lead Europeans towards a new concept of deterrence via a range of integrated civilian and military options, tools, governments, and institutions, reinforced by diplomacy and constant engagement. Indeed, Europeans would do well to heed the wise guidance of Belgium's one-time foreign minister Pierre Harmel, who foresaw European defence as the dual-track engagement of dialogue and firm defence maintained in constant harness.[18]

As for future war deterrence, NATO remains the only serious vehicle for such a future across the hybrid, cyber, hyper war mosaic. After all, NATO is first and foremost a European institution, albeit guaranteed by the Americans. Equally, for the impressive efforts to adapt, NATO must change far more quickly and must do so by Europeans increasing their defence weight within the Alliance, COVID-19 or no. Seen in that light, the 2010 NATO Strategic Concept is now hopelessly out of date and the only reason a new one is not being actively drafted is dangerously indicative: the Allies cannot agree on the NATO they want, and are waiting to see the future direction of US policy and strategy. The alternative is that the Allies forge the collective defence and collective security explicit in the current Strategic Concept into a much deeper joint operating model and imbue NATO with much greater strategic ambition.

The Alliance also needs a new, pan-European concept of conflict escalation that could demonstrably exert pressure across policy, diplomacy, and economy, as well as across the twenty-first-century military domains of land, sea, air, space, cyber, information, and knowledge. Nuclear force must and will remain the credible last-resort bastion of Allied defence and deterrence. That would mean a much more considered and joined-up Alliance, including the use of offensive cyber operations with strengthened and more mobile conventional forces, streamlined command structures, and other forms of

18. The November 2017 GLOBSEC NATO Adaptation Initiative 'One Alliance: The Future Tasks of the Adapted Alliance' states, 'Perhaps most famously fifty years ago Pierre Harmel of Belgium led the landmark "Report of the Council on the Future Tasks of the Alliance", which re-established the need for NATO and properly established at the core of the Alliance the twin strategic purposes of deterrence and dialogue: purposes which remain pertinent today'. John R. Allen, Julian Lindley-French, Giampaolo Di Paola, Wolf Langheld, Tomas Valasek, and Alexander Vershbow (2017) *The GLOBSEC NATO Adaptation Initiative: One Alliance—The Future Tasks of the Adapted Alliance* (Bratislava: GLOBSEC), p. 36.

'traditional' but updated defence and deterrence postures. It will also demand of Europeans that they agree to more devolved command authority within the Alliance, as well as collectively preparing seriously for coming sentient machine warfare. In other words, what is needed is a twenty-first-century NATO Strategic Concept with a Harmelian dual-track approach at its heart that not only better unifies the Alliance, but also builds real strategic weight into an EU–NATO Strategic Partnership.

George Kennan famously suggested that the US should not jump around like an elephant frightened by a mouse. COVID-19 for Europeans has been just such an elephant. The worst-case scenario for Europeans and their future defence is a sudden and violent series of interconnected crises, any one of which would present a major challenge to European political leaders and policy-makers. Such a storm is in the making, but for too long European political leaders and policy-makers have refused to acknowledge it. Through a toxic combination of wishful thinking, inadequate and/or misplaced investments, and endemic short-termism, Europeans have steadily placed Europe at ever more risk, and quite possibly danger. It is simply too easy for adversaries to destabilize Europe at the outset of any crisis, and keep Europeans politically, strategically, and militarily off-balance.

What if America was unable to be 'there' in strength? What would Europe do then? What if the Americans are not always able to ride over the strategic horizon like the US Seventh Cavalry in one of those western movies of old? Indeed, even if the US were to ride over the horizon with a heavy force to save Europe's lightly armed 'homesteaders' from Russian aggression, Moscow's forces would need first to be held in place by NATO's initial response. As for the EU, it has demonstrated no meaningful capacity or capability to deal with such a crisis, or crises, of any serious magnitude, and shows little sign of ever being able to do so.

Therefore, it is vital that NATO Europeans, as well as EU member-states (it is the same strategic family), understand the nature of the new twenty-first-century transatlantic security contract future war will demand, and the dangers that must result from a Europe that by and large lacks any strategic culture *sui generis*. The Americans will continue to guarantee Europe's defence, but only if Europeans help ease the worldwide pressure on the US and its forces. That means Europeans able and willing to join the Americans in future 'broad coalitions', not just against the likes of Daesh, but in wider state-on-state conflicts. It also means Europeans being willing to bear far more of the burden of defending and securing Europe in the face of twenty-first-century future war. Indeed, in the twenty-first century NATO will only make sense from an American strategic perspective if it is part of a US-led worldwide web of democracies that can work together politically, strategically, and militarily. That is why countries such as Australia, Japan, and South Korea are such an important part of America's 'broad coalition', and why by extension they are also strategic partners of Europe. Canberra has already established the precedent for using NATO Standards as a model for the generation of globally capable coalitions. It is also why in 2014 Japan changed Article 9 of its constitution to allow for reinterpretation of collective self-defence and the possibility of offensive military operations, and why South Korea is also keen for close involvement with the Alliance.

Taken together, Moscow's aggression in Ukraine and pressure on the Baltic States, Beijing's ambitions in the South China Sea and well beyond, as well as the quasi state-like ambitions of the Caliphate in a broken Middle East and North Africa mark the start of a new age of global challenge to the once Western-led world order. Europeans would like to think that good old-fashioned *Machtpolitik* is a thing of the past; they must think again.

Lessons from the COVID-19 crisis? The past defence of Europe was not simply about forces, but the capable infrastructures that enabled forces to move quickly across the area of operations in an emergency. The simple truth is that far from preparing to defend themselves, Europeans and their defences are becoming progressively weaker, and objectively are not geared to the evolving nature of twenty-first-century crises and reinforce the need for urgent remedial action.

Critically, the only logical assumption relevant to future European defence planning is that Europe's reliance on the Americans, both through NATO and bilaterally, will endure and probably intensify for the foreseeable future. Logically, therefore, the centre of gravity of the main effort to modernize European defence should be a modernized Alliance. However, does the Alliance have sufficient ambition to meet the future war challenge? The test will be the willingness of the Allies to change NATO practice, in many cases legal practice. For example, the relationship between Article 4 consultations and Article 5 actions will need to be made demonstrably closer, as the nature of what would constitute an attack is changing and widening.

Devils are always in the details. To that end, there needs to be a much better grip by NATO on the specifics of high-end crisis management, in particular the escalation of resource and force in any given crisis. There also needs to be a far better grip of the transition from contested peace to all-out war. When should the Very High-Readiness Joint Task Force (VJTF) move forward to the Baltic States in the conflict cycle, and when to start generating and moving the rest of the NATO Command Structure, such as NATO planners, to prepare for the rapid movement of the rest of the NATO Response Force? How quickly can Air Policing become Air Defence so that Allied air power could be forward-deployed rapidly in an emergency? How can Rapid Air Movement be made rapid across borders? The 2018 NATO Enablement Plan is impressive, but there are still many legal, political, and even physical barriers that need to be overcome.

The minimum down-payment Europeans must make on their own future defence is a European future force worthy of the name. Such a force would need to be physically and intellectually equipped with appropriate enablers to operate to effect across the seven domains of air, sea, land, cyber, space, information, and knowledge. It would be supported by a European defence and technological industrial base that embraces the revolution in military technology and the application to the battlespace of AI, big data, machine-learning, super-computing et al. This is because technology will play an ever more important role in the yawning gap between strategy, capability, and affordability on the edge of which European defence constantly teeters.

Could Europeans defend Europe? No, and not for a long time to come.

8

Hyperwar
Europe's digital and nuclear flanks

The digital Dreadnought

What role should technology play in Europe's future defence? On 10 February 1906, with Union flags flying, the brand-new HMS Dreadnought was launched. She was the first all-big-gun, fully armoured, high-speed, turbine-driven battleship which not only gave a name to an entire class of mighty warships, but made everything that had sailed before her immediately obsolete. She also triggered an arms race with Wilhelmine Germany which would only really end with the Royal Navy's strategic victory at the 1916 Battle of Jutland.[1]

HMS Dreadnought was not simply a step forward in military technology. The advance she represented drove strategy, and thus changed the very character of naval warfare. At a stroke she increased the distance between target and enemy, as well as the speed (rate) of fire and the depth of protection for platforms and systems that has continued pretty much unabated to this day. Through her gun director system she also introduced a degree of automation hitherto unknown, and revealed a profound dilemma in warfare that also exists today. As the range of gunfire increased, the need for enhanced intelligence (forewarning) and signalling (command and control) also became far more important. Britain overcame the

---

1. On 31 May 1916 the Grand Fleet of the Royal Navy and Germany's High Seas Fleet finally met in a full fleet action. The Battle of Jutland was the second biggest naval battle in history in terms of ships committed after the October 1944 Battle of Leyte Gulf. Whilst the Royal Navy lost more ships and men than the High Seas Fleet, the result was a decisive strategic victory for the British who were able to main the blockade of Imperial Germany and thus hasten its defeat.

challenge of the former in World War One with Room 40 (the British naval signals intelligence unit that was the forerunner to the contemporary GCHQ), but failed profoundly the challenge of the latter which led to almost catastrophic consequences at Jutland.[2]

Imagine a new HMS Dreadnought. A fully autonomous, artificially intelligent, machine-learning, robotic military platform that arms and defends itself independently of any direct human command. A ship, submarine, tank, aircraft, or missile (or a multiple-platform 'entity') capable of launching intelligent swarms of robotic drones, each armed with the 'intelligence' to independently seek out enemy vulnerabilities across systems, platforms, communications, and command chains, as well as critical infrastructures—civilian and military—and learn from each other how to penetrate enemy defences.

Technology will drive defence strategy in the twenty-first century, at least as much as policy, affordability, or strategic environment. A credible future defence of Europe will thus need to be an artificial intelligence (AI)-enabled defence, mounted across the full conflict spectrum of future mosaic war. The Americans are certainly moving in that direction. The 2018 US National Defense Strategy, and the June 2018 US Joint Artificial Intelligence System (JAIC), both assert that AI will change the character of war.

Ten years hence, another major war in Europe would be a hyperwar. This would be ultra-fast warfare that combines a myriad of systems to wreak havoc in an instant. AI would not be a stand-alone technology, but act in concert with machine-learning, human enhancement, genetic manipulation, data analytics, simulation, behavioural science, drone technologies, quantum-based sensors that can reveal the ocean depths and whatever is sailing within it, cyber warfare, synthetic technologies and nanotechnologies linked to 3D printing, hypersonic weapons, smart weapons, unmanned combat aerial vehicles that form part of attack swarms, and the use of big data to create synthetic reality to better inform often automated decision-making. Such a war, and its full array of technologies, could not

---

2. Andrew Gordon, in his seminal work on the Battle of Jutland, and in considering recent British attempts to solve the signalling problem in battle, wrote, 'So great (although unquantifiable) are the potential frailties of long-range signalling, that the "Northwood" system of centralized control may prove, under test of the next major crisis, to be a command and control "Maginot Line" which a resourceful enemy could outmanoeuvre and defeat, leaving our forces in disarray'. See Andrew Gordon (2005) *The Rules of the Game: Jutland and British Naval Command* (London: John Murray), p. 591.

happen tomorrow, but elements of it will progressively enter the battlespace with which Europeans will need to contend and for which Europeans will need to prepare and plan, and probably sooner than many Europeans think. This is not least because unlike HMS Dreadnought, hyperwar is being driven by technological change underway in the US civilian sector, as well as the strategic ambitions of China and to a lesser extent Russia.

The prospect of such warfare raises a whole raft of policy dilemmas for America's European allies as much of the developments taking place in offensive military capabilities are in the domains of cyber, space, and information, with the role of traditional conventional force reduced. For Europeans with limited resources, that implies some very hard choices, particularly in the wake of the COVID-19 crisis. Should they first address lacunae in warfighting materiel and command and control, with the priority the maintenance of effective interoperability with US forces for high-end combat missions? Or should they focus instead on hardening critical infrastructure and making existing capabilities more resilient? Almost certainly, the US will push for the former, whilst domestic politics in post-COVID-19 Europe will almost certainly lean towards the latter as Europeans emphasize human security at the expense of national defence.

Hyperwar law

In 1970 Gordon Moore established Moore's Law. This simplistic but nevertheless compelling paradigm states that computer-processing power will double every two years.[3] Whilst not universally popular amongst technologists, the explanatory power of Moore's Law has proven to be remarkably robust. Today, Europeans must confront a kind of hyperwar law in which computer-led warfare doubles its own 'processing' power via systems, sensors, platforms, architectures, mass, precision, agility, adaptability, and range to potentially devastating effect, and then doubles again the destructive and adaptive capacity. Credible defence will thus rest on constantly updating ever-accelerating defence planning cycles within which constantly changing

---

3. The website 'Moore's Law' states, 'Moore's Law is a computing term which originated around 1970; the simplified version of this law states that processor speeds, or overall processing power for computers will double every two years'. http://www.mooreslaw.org.

defence planning assumptions match the pace of development of machine warfare. The assumption today across much of Europe is that defence technology has an operational life of some twenty to thirty years, with ten to fifteen years to cover the entire procurement cycle, including research and technology development, Main Gate procurement go-ahead, construction, testing, and fielding. Hyperwar law, and future war technology, will make such assumptions little more than a form of appeasement.

Even in today's battlespace, far-reaching applications of AI, machine-learning, super-computing, big data and nano-technologies suggest a whole host of new ways to use violent means to political ends; Clausewitz's ghastly purpose of war. Hyperwar will exponentially accelerate the speed of war across multi-domain warfare conducted via air, at sea, on land, in space, in cyber space, and increasingly via information and deep, destructive human and machine-generated 'knowledge'. Defence? Defence will need to be mounted at the hyper speed of war—hyper-defence—whilst deterrence will rely on the demonstrable reality of European hyper-defence. Only with a Europe defended by AI-empowered intelligence analysis, decision support, and an AI-enabled European force will Europeans mount a credible defence against such a threat. As architecture is increasingly constructed and shaped by computer technology, Europeans will also need to do something they have traditionally found very hard: learn to trust each other and think and act holistically. Therefore, and irrespective of COVID-19, Europeans need to collectively undertake an assessment for future war of the systems, structures, weapons, and people they will need to fight it. Without any such study it will be impossible for Europeans to understand the capacities and capabilities they will need to generate and how best to procure and afford them. Above all, they will have no sense of the urgency with which they need to act.

NATO and hyper-deterrence

If NATO has one future purpose (and NATO today has far too many purposes), it would be as both champion and guardian of hyper-deterrence with such new thinking central to the real and radical adaptation of the Alliance.

Global Strategic Trends states, 'Applications of artificial intelligence will enable machines to develop perception, reasoning, solve problems, learn and plan'.[4] The twenty-first century will thus be the first tech-cognitive age of warfare in which technology could well surpass the capacity of humans to 'think' and act across all domains of conflict. As one of the authors wrote in a book co-written with technologist Amir Hussein, 'Whilst the implications of AI are very broad, as we head deeper into this new era, we will find that artificial intelligence combined with myriad exponential technologies will carry us forward inexorably toward a different form of warfare that will unfold at speed we cannot fully anticipate. A form of warfare we call Hyperwar'.[5] For Europeans, there is both 'good' news and very bad news. AI will not simply be the preserve of the enormously big and powerful; superpower technology for a superpower strategy. Indeed, such will be its relative affordability that AI could also enable smaller, weaker powers to withstand attacks from traditionally stronger powers with more able and larger forces. The very bad news is that Europe is lagging far behind in an accelerating AI-enabled future war arms race.

Europeans face a dangerous deterrence gap between weak European conventional forces and last-resort strategic nuclear deterrents, which threaten to lower the threshold of nuclear first use should contemporary deterrence fail. Warfare will become steadily more technology-cognitive and this will force Europeans to completely rethink 'deterrence'. Indeed, for too long deterrence has been locked into a mono-nuclear realm, with even the deterrent value of proportionately strong conventional forces little understood by many Europeans. Even without AI, new thinking on deterrence is desperately needed to enable new and emerging non-nuclear technologies to be 'bundled' and applied via new strategy and new thinking to exert deterrent effect across the conflict spectrum.

For such hyper-deterrence to be established, a critical change of mind-set would also be needed in Europe. For example, several European states, with Italy to the fore, refuse to even admit that Europe is in an arms race with the Russians. The Russians certainly seem to think so. General Gerasimov's 2018 speech to the Russian Academy of Military Sciences not only reflected Moscow's siege mentality but also a Russia permanently engaged in conflict with the West. As Christoph Bilan states,

4. *Global Strategic Trends: The Future Starts Here*, Sixth Edition (2018) (London: Cabinet Office), p. 16.
5. John R. Allen and Amir Husein (2018) 'Hyperwar and Shifts in Global Power in the AI Century', in John R. Allen and Amir Husein (eds.) *Hyperwar: Conflict and Competition in the AI Century* (Austin, TX: SparkCognition Press), p. 11.

In Russian eyes, the prevalence of local conflicts like the one in Syria underlines the importance of armed forces' ability to wage war with present-day characteristics. Modern conflict, from Russia's top brass point of view, is determined by nigh-borderless battle spaces, transcending territorial boundaries as well as those of domain. Likewise, it is no longer sequential with alternating phases of combat and recovery but conducted without pause. Being able to employ highly mobile forces and precision ammunition in concert with extended electronic warfare capabilities is regarded as vital by the Russian MoD. Furthermore, and in tune with a number of speeches since 2013, Gerasimov once more points out that the improvement of command and control (C2) technologies and procedures deserves particular attention.[6]

Russia is particularly interested in the militarization of AI. In 2018, the Russian Ministry of Defence released a ten-point plan to place AI at the core of Russian military modernization, driven by AI consortia across government, industry, and academia. Moscow is bolstering automation by creating a Fund for Analytical Algorithms, together with a state system for training and educating AI specialists. The plan also includes an AI lab at the Era Technopolis, and a National Center for Artificial Intelligence to 'monitor' closely global AI activities, and actively wargame AI military applications.[7]

Europe's choice is thus stark. Europeans can continue to try and convince the Russians to stop their arms development across the future war-scape, which is not likely to succeed given the current attitude of President Putin and the *Siloviki* who run the Russian government, not to mention the centrality the regime places on the security state and the Russian arms industry as a driver of technology.[8] Or, Europeans could counter Russia by engaging sufficiently in the development of the capabilities and capacities needed to re-establish a credible hyper-deterrence posture built on AI systems. If Europeans continue to pretend no such race is underway, even as Russia develops ingenious systems to one day attack Europe, should it so

---

6. Christoph Bilan, 'Science, Science, and Science: Gerasimov's 2018 Speech', April 2018, http://sipol.at/en/2018/04/10/gerasimov2018.
7. See Samuel Bendett, 'Here's How the Russian Military Is Organizing to Develop AI', 20 July 2018, Defense One, https://www.defenseone.com/ideas/2018/07/russian-militarys-ai-development-roadmap/149900.
8. A *Silovik* is a politician who enters political life from the Russian security or military services. The *Siloviki* are also known as 'securocrats' and tend to be right-wing and nationalistic, strongly supporting the Kremlin's line.

decide, then the only possible outcome in which Europeans are investing is future shock!

To be credible, hyper-deterrence would need to demonstrably deter across the hybrid, AI, cyber war, electronic warfare, and hyperwar mosaic, as well as across the air, sea, land, cyber, space, nuclear, information, and knowledge force domains, and match the speed with which comprehensive, interoperable, deterrent effects can range up an escalatory ladder. It would need also to combine and enhance resiliency, strengthen critical protection, and enhance military power projection. Strategic messaging and public diplomacy would be central to such a radically new deterrence model, raising the threshold and cost of 'success' for any adversary, forcing them onto the defensive.

Europe and hyperwar

Hyperwar is all about the merger of concept and technology. In a future European hyperwar, speed of attack (and defence) will become the determining factor for victory or defeat as autonomous military systems enter the arsenals of powers, large and small. Indeed, it has always been thus, with speed determining the outcome, although never at speeds like this. The arrival of such systems will also change the very nature of warfare.

In Clausewitzian terms the 'Schwerpunkt' in warfare, and the decisive 'terrain' upon which future war will be fought, will become the speed of action and effect itself, which could accelerate exponentially to the point where human fiat may not only become a constraint, but a fatal weakness.[9] In such circumstances technology may well become the new centre of gravity in warfare; neither people nor territory. In other words, if a critical system is defeated, the centre of gravity of a state, an alliance and/or a coalition, would crumble and fast.

Such warfare will also change the very utility of essentially analogue forces as small, relatively lightly manned but highly networked forces wreak great

---

9. There has been much academic debate about the precise meaning of 'schwerpunkt' in Clausewitz's thinking. For the purposes of this book it is taken to mean the centre of gravity of an action to produce the most immediate and grave effect on an enemy. Clausewitz suggested three 'centres of gravity': destruction of an enemy army if it is germane to the strategic aim; seizure or complete breakdown in functioning of an enemy capital; and/or delivery of a crippling blow to an ally that is central to an enemy's war aims.

damage over ostensibly larger and more 'powerful' military formations as AI renders their use and application greatly more efficient at the decisive point of engagement. As the range grows between attacker and target, and the speed of decision and action accelerate, ageing, 'throw-away' platforms will be given a new lease of life. Aircraft, ships, submarines, and tanks will 'host' intelligent drone swarms and hypersonic stand-off munitions able to launch far from targets and evade any defence. In such warfare, the critical advantage will fall to those states and/or alliances that can attract the best brains, and access intellectual property irrespective of whomsoever generates it, both legally and illegally, if they have the productive capacity ('dark factories') to establish an AI-enabled or future war AI force.

The applications of such technologies on the radically transformed future battlespace will see the digital invade and eclipse the analogue rapidly, and will not be confined to states alone. Indeed, future war will tend to favour proxy warriors and attacks by ostensibly weaker powers and groups in which asymmetry has possibly grand strategic effects. The focus of any attack will thus be on European society, and will, in effect, be little short of a new form of total war. Sophisticated insurgent and terrorist groups, sustained by state and other rich backers, are already deploying 'smart' improvised explosive devices (IEDs) that, as they become more AI-'rich', will also infuse tactics, and become far more flexible and deadly.

The pace of technology is such that it could well soon be possible for hostile actors to 'print' robotic air and sea assets on advanced 3D printers, controlled at distance by complex, dual-use control systems freely available on the commercial market. Indeed, the black market in arms is already acting as a transfer mechanism for the sale of such capabilities to those with the resources to procure them. Experience suggests that as the applications of both commercial and military technology merge, the price of both will drop, even if the price of the all-important semi-conductors that drive them actually increases in line with their capability and sophistication.

Relatively smaller but nevertheless richer powers seeking to influence both regional balances of power and wider geopolitics will become increasingly influential. Non-state actors, such as organized criminals and global-reach terrorists, will be better able to undertake complex strategic coercion and 5D warfare more normally associated with Great Powers. Regional powers could quickly close the deterrence gap between conventional and nuclear forces, and through AI create entirely new means of coercion short of nuclear war. Even peer competitors, with Europe perhaps to the fore, and with arsenals replete with obsolete or obsolescent military platforms and systems, could leverage such capabilities by retro-fitting them with AI-enabling technologies. The merger of sophisticated systems with robust but basic platforms will also inform future war. For example, an insurgent attack on the Russian-held Hmeymin airbase in Syria used drones which were only defeated after the Russians employed advanced defensive technologies. Any such capability would place a forward-deployed European force at great risk if it lacked the necessary adaptive force protection.

At sea, such attacks could use small, remotely controlled boats packed with explosives. Iran has proven itself to be particularly adept at the use of such systems, as the June 2019 attack on two oil-bearing super tankers demonstrated. In a sense, history has again gone full circle as such platforms are latter-day variants of the Elizabethan Royal Navy's use of 'fire-ships' to attack the Duke of Medina Sidonia's Spanish Armada whilst at anchor in Calais in 1588.[10] Critically, drones are increasingly used to disrupt missions by the most advanced Western forces, US and Allied Special Operations Forces, who find it hard to evade surveillance by even relatively cheap, off-the-shelf systems, and to surprise them. Iran's use of drones to provide terminal guidance to the cruise missile attack of the Abqaiq oil and gas separation facility was a capability 'surprise' to the US. That the Saudis could not defend against the attack was to be expected, but that the US did not see it coming was a marked new development. In the era of hyperwar the capacity of 'weaker' powers to wield technologies will be as surprising as the technologies themselves.

The Chinese have for many years also converted older aircraft to use as autonomous drones in a first-wave force to saturate an adversary's air defences.[11] Europeans could, and should, as a matter of urgency, consider

10. The English use of fire-ships at Calais in 1588 to break up the formation of the Spanish Armada was an early use of drones, although it was not as successful as legend would have it. Arthur Herman wrote, 'One by one they [small English ships packed with tar and hemp] came alight. Spanish lookouts spotted them, and shouted the alarm. Rushing up on deck, Medina Sidonia ordered all ships to cut their cables and drift clear of the danger. All except one, the galleas San Lorenzo, did so without incident, the fireships slid past without harming a single ship and without so much as an explosion. But for the first time, the Armada had lost its formation. As dawn came up on Monday, August 6, Howard and the English fleet moved in on the scattered Spanish ships'. Arthur Herman (2004) *To Rule the Waves: How the British Navy Shaped the Modern World* (London: Hodder & Stoughton), pp. 126–7.

11. John R. Allen and Amir Husein wrote, 'For years, the Chinese PLAAF (People's Liberation Army Air Force) has been converting older fifties and sixties' era jets such as the J-6 . . . and J-7 into autonomous drones. It is not quite clear how the Chinese intend to employ these systems, and hypotheses range from using these as a "first wave" intended to saturate opposing

how the use of AI-based control algorithms with sensors on obsolescent platforms might prove a cost-effective avenue to enhancing the deterrent and defence value of their existing forces. There is a precedent. Back in the 1990s Boeing retro-fitted guidance kits to 'dumb' bombs to create the Joint Direct Attack Munition or JDAM. The Turks have also successfully applied a similar system and such developments could also be applied to legacy systems and structures to render them far more fleet of foot, quickly and cheaply.[12] In such an environment, Boydian notions of OODA (Observe, Orient, Decide, and Act) that date back to the 1950s will be replaced by a kind of super-charged Boyd in which decision-making will be both accelerated and potentially critically undermined as the decision-action cycle between peace and war and within warfare itself accelerates.[13] Pearl Harbor 2? After a certain point the OODA loop could simply collapse through the sheer speed of events, unless any defence can match such command hyper-speed.

5G, digital decapitation, and disruptive technologies

If a kind of Pearl Harbor 2 were to befall Europe, it would probably take the form of digital decapitation. Source code is the software 'brain' at the heart of any computer, its directing command. If one controls source code, one controls the command machine and all the systems and platforms that support 'command'. As the human and the machine become ever more intertwined, it might even become possible to assert that control of the machine is the control of humanity. What aids us can also kill us. The Internet of Things is central to future war: a super-network of connected

air defences, to more fanciful hypotheses involving higher degrees of autonomy that may even enable air-to-air combat'. John R. Allen and Amir Husein (eds.) *Hyperwar: Conflict and Competition in the AI Century* (Austin, TX: SparkCognition Press), pp. 18–19.

12. Ibid., p. 19.
13. Frans Osinga makes an important point about Boyd's thinking about the evolving OODA loop: 'The rapid OODA loop idea is a very important one, but in itself often misunderstood. Whereas, rapid OODA loop is often equated with superior speed in decision-making, Boyd employs the OODA loop model to show how organisms evolve and adapt . . . While rapid OODA looping—as in rapid decision-making—is quite relevant for success at the tactical level, and to some extent also at the operational level, Boyd regards the OODA loop schematic in general as a model for organizational learning, or even more general, the way organisms adapt and thus evolve'. Machine-swarm learning? See Frans Osinga (2005) *Science, Strategy and War: The Strategic Theory of John Boyd* (Amsterdam: Eburon), p. 315.

machines, systems, appliances, and people which talk to each other, interact with each other, and increasingly learn from each other and at increasingly high speeds. It is that threat which is behind US concerns about China and its ambitions to create a digital Silk Road that reaches deep into Europe's digital space.

Fantasy? Imagine if all road and rail signals, power networks, air traffic control, food distribution, and communications beyond word of mouth or flags suddenly collapsed—a catastrophic collapse of critical infrastructure. Is such a cataclysm possible? '5G' represents a step-change in the speed and load-bearing bandwidth of wireless networks that support such infrastructure, and hyperwar law suggests it will not stop there. By 2030 the applications that use 6G will afford states and peoples a whole raft of information-rich advantages. However, like all Western states, European states are becoming increasingly dependent on the digital infrastructure that such capability both informs and demands. The US is concerned that China's willingness to fund European 5G digital networks is part of wider Chinese strategic ambitions to enforce European compliance with Chinese state interests. These concerns were intensified by the January 2020 decision by the British government to permit the Chinese state enterprise Huawei to provide equipment for the UK's 5G roll-out, a decision that has since been reviewed since the COVID-19 crisis.

Technology changes power; breakthrough technology can magnify power to the point at which it momentarily appears irresistible. It can also be disruptive even for its own architects. That was the strategic essence of HMS Dreadnought in 1906. Indeed, she was the military 5G of the developing analogue age of power and as such was as disruptive for Britain as she was for Britain's adversaries, and without the productive capacity to exploit it could prove suicidal.

'Disruptive' technology has the power to transform societies in ways that are only starting to be understood. For example, at its most benign 5G is simply the means to enable a super-fast, super-network of distributed, stand-alone computers to undertake a myriad of functions critical to the daily lives of European citizens. Such a network offers life-transforming super-efficiency, thus reducing the cost of actions, and greatly increasing the value of output. At worst, control of such a network offers critical command over those same actions and, by concentrating the power of distributed networks for malicious ends, could also destroy states, institutions, and people. Imagine both the benefits and risks of digital control over all the roads, railways, and airports in a European state. It is such a vision which Huawei, and China, is offering Europeans. As part of its 5G 'package', a European state would effectively be handing over access and control of its digital roads, railways, and airports to China. This is why the Huawei 'deal' is lucrative, seductive, and potentially dangerous, even though GCHQ has argued differently. 5G also has a host of military applications, not least as the beating heart of artificially intelligent drone swarms—the digital 'queen', if one will—of a future attack hive. During any European future war such swarms would probe, fail, learn, adapt to, then finally overcome defences, intelligently exploiting weakness to maximum devastating effect. Digital decapitation.

Former NATO Supreme Commander General Jim Jones is clear about 5G and the strategic ambitions implicit in the role of Huawei. 'Huawei is a tool of state power and a critical asset in China's global economic and geopolitical competitions and ambitions'.[14] Even the most cursory glance at Chinese national strategy confirms Beijing's strategic intent to use whatever tech-cognitive means are at its disposal, both financial and economic (fintech) and military (miltech), to gain strategic advantage. The threat allegedly posed by Huawei is because as an agent of the Chinese state it can offer its deep digital infrastructure products significantly more cheaply to hard-pressed European governments than many of its Western commercial competitors. Moreover, Huawei is already deeply embedded in European networks and removing it would be highly complex and very expensive. This is not least because Huawei offers not simply a new 5G 'product', but an entire digital infrastructure, and much of its technology is better than anything in the West, which has fallen behind in the development of such capabilities.

In 2010, the UK set up the Huawei Cyber Security Evaluation Cell (HCSEC) near Banbury in Oxfordshire, as part of its National Cyber Security Centre, part funded by the Chinese tech company, which has also offered to work closely with British authorities to overcome any concerns. The Cell was given a specific remit to quantify the nature and scope of the threat posed by Huawei. In late 2018, HCSEC allegedly stripped back networking gear, together with millions of lines of source

---

14. All General Jones quotes in this section from 'Recommendations on 5G and National Security', Atlantic Council, Scowcroft Center for Strategic and Security, Strategic Insights Memo No. 3, 11 February 2019.

code, to assess the extent to which Huawei afforded Beijing a 'Trojan horse' to conduct industrial and military espionage, as well as other command capabilities. Allegedly, HCSEC discovered that Huawei had tried to mask the real source codes. Consequently, the head of MI6 warned against any 4G and 5G network that relied on Huawei.[15] In January 2020, in spite of all those concerns, the British government still gave the go-ahead for Huawei to be permitted to bid for 'non-core' aspects of Britain's future 5G network. This revealed a tension that exists in many European states as they seek to balance the need for modernization of their respective critical infrastructures with the security implications of allowing Chinese companies to participate in a costly process made cheaper by Beijing through state subsidies.

Elements of 5D warfare, particularly the planned and systematic application of disinformation, deception, destabilization, and disruption against open European societies by China and Russia, are already fact. And yet, many Europeans refuse to consider the worst-case implications of such deals, and the dangerous interaction that a fusion of strategy, capability, and technology could afford adversaries. Worse, the determined European focus on the cheap and the short term is fast creating the conditions for a digital decapitation and/or the critical undermining of European defence cohesion as countries desperate for Chinese investment effectively sell their strategic soul in some form of latter-day Faustian pact.[16] France's President Macron even accused the Italians of being naive in their dealings with China, even as President Xi was about to visit France in March 2019.

If the West, in general, or more specifically Europe, is to avoid waking up one day to find itself facing digital decapitation, Europeans must return to digital realism by better understanding interactions between the digital domain, power, and coercion. General Jones recommended a series of actions to prevent Chinese digital dominance. Even before COVID-19, Jones called on the US and its allies to halt work with Huawei, whilst 'technical standards [could be] designed to withstand cyberattacks'. He also called on the US to establish a 'long-term national spectrum strategy' that would confirm federal control over all aspects of 5G and its application, as

---

15. See Bob Seely MP, Dr Peter Varnish OBE, and Dr John Hemmings, 'Defending Our Data: Huawei, 5G and the Five Eyes' (2019) (London: Henry Jackson Society).
16. In Christopher Marlowe's *circa* 1592 play *The Tragic History of the Life and Death of Doctor Faustus*, even Satan's agent on Earth, Mephistopheles, warns Faustus against taking Satan's offer of short-term knowledge in return for eternal damnation: 'Oh Faustus, turn away from these frivolous demands which strike a terror to my fading soul' (see Marlowe 2001).

well as the streamlining of US federal procurement practices that build cost into bids for 5G development work that Huawei simply does not have to consider. The EU and its member-states would be well advised to consider similar steps, even as the EU and its member-states develop a settled plan to deal with Huawei. Critically, General Jones has also highlighted a fundamental flaw in the West's privatization of much of its security technology and China's one-way exploitation of it.

There is, of course, one easy way for China to demonstrate at a stroke that the fears of General Jones and others are ill-founded. It could open up its own domestic market to Huawei's competitors, and show a willingness to purchase significant parts of its own burgeoning 5G network from American and European contractors. It could also cede control of Huawei's *source* codes to its European customers, thus making it impossible for Beijing to manipulate to advantage. Such steps are unlikely.

Europe's nuclear flank

Samuel Huntington once wrote, 'The West won the world not by the superiority of its ideas or values or religion [. . .] but rather by its superiority in applying organized violence. Westerners often forget this fact; non-Westerners never do'.[17] In April 2020 it was rumoured that Moscow had deployed a new nuclear weapon codenamed Skif. With a range of almost 10,000 kms/6,250 miles and capable of a speed of some 96 km/h or 70 mph, the weapon is designed to sit on the ocean floor and await activation. In effect, a long-range nuclear torpedo is believed to be capable of devastating a NATO fleet or polluting large parts of the eastern seaboard of the US with COBALT-60.

On observing the first successful test of an atomic bomb at the Trinity site on 16 July 1945, lead scientist Robert Oppenheimer quoted the *Bhagavad Gita*.[18] 'Now', he said, 'I am become Death, the destroyer of worlds'. A new and dangerous shift is taking place in the nuclear balance driven by the *New Realpolitik* that is shaping Europe's world and the technology of future war,

17. Samuel P. Huntington (1996) *The Clash of Civilizations and the Remaking of World Order* (New York: Touchstone).
18. The *Bhagavad Gita* is an epic Hindu morality tale, possibly as old as 4,000 years, which translated means 'The Song of God'. Its main theme is the moral dilemma leaders face when they consider waging war.

which is again tipping the balance between the nuclear offensive and the defensive. Consequently, the global arms control architecture is in urgent need of renovation. Yet many Europeans (and not a few Americans) seem in denial of a fast-changing reality and lack any real interest in arms control. In 2014, Belgium, Germany, Luxembourg, the Netherlands, and Norway moved to have the remaining 200 or so European-based US nuclear warheads removed from their soil. One role of nuclear weapons is to offset weaknesses in conventional forces, but the very same countries wanted to rid NATO of a cornerstone nuclear defence. As such, the decision epitomizes the nuclear dilemma of European defence.

In his 2019 State of the Russian Federation speech, President Putin hailed a new family of Russian nuclear-tipped missiles designed to evade European and American defences, heralding the dawn of a new age of nuclear coercion. Russia is not alone. China has recently deployed a new hypersonic cruise missile (HGW), the DF-17 HGV (Pentagon codename WU-17), which has a range of over 1,500 miles and will fly at speeds designed to frustrate all Allied air defence systems. This new strategic nuclear arms race is unlike any previous arms race, and if it goes unchecked, it could well mark the end of all the arms control frameworks in which Europeans have invested so much political capital over the years. What makes this new arms race particularly dangerous is the combination of technology with an ambition to render obsolete institutionalized mutual restraint.

In a famous 1981 paper, *The Spread of Nuclear Weapons: More May Be Better*, Kenneth Waltz wrote: 'What will a world populated by a larger number of nuclear states look like? . . . Those who dread a world with more nuclear states do little more than assert that more is worse and claim without substantiation that new nuclear states will be less responsible and less capable of self-control than the old ones have been. They express fears that many felt when they imagined how a nuclear China would behave. Such fears have proved unfounded as nuclear weapons have slowly spread. I have found many reasons for believing that with more nuclear states the world will have a promising future'.[19] Waltz's relative optimism could well be tested in an unstable but highly advanced world as conventional force and AI-enabled future force combine with newly intelligent nuclear weapons,

---

19. Kenneth Waltz (1981) *The Spread of Nuclear Weapons: More May Be Better*, Adelphi Papers, Number 171 (London: International Institute for Strategic Studies).

and their associated hypersonic delivery systems. In other words, a new future war age of cognitive mutually assured destruction (c-MAD?) beckons.

Perhaps another dangerous truism of future war is that as the number of nuclear arsenals increases, so will the freedom of small and medium states to undertake conventional action. The Great Equalizer? For smaller states the fusion of affordable future war tech and nuclear weapons technology that is more than eighty years old also offers the ultimate 'offset strategy', possibly enabling them to act punitively against Europe, whilst preventing direct Western 'punishment' as a consequence of their actions. One of the many paradoxes of tech-cognitive warfare will be that whilst radical new technologies are re-drawing the battlespace, it is 'old' nuclear weapons that will remain the ultimate arbiter of peace and war. Technology is driving policy and strategy. Consequently, the entire arms control edifice of the second half of the twentieth century will need to be rethought because it was predicated on the fact that nuclear technology was only available to the most powerful few, even if there remains a very high level of interest in non-proliferation agreements and even certain disarmament initiatives.

The 2018 US Nuclear Posture Review (NPR) and US National Military Strategy (NMS) reveal the extent and pace of this new nuclear arms race, as well as its implications for European defence. The combination of nuclear weapons with new systems and platforms represents a marked step-change in danger from previous ages and further exacerbates Europe's growing deterrence gap between its conventional and nuclear forces. Equally, such technologies could also close the gap as digital attack and new AI-enabled technologies offer an alternative to the 'traditional' conventional nuclear balance.

Moscow is purposively seeking to exploit Europe's 'deterrence gap'. Moscow envisions Russian strategic, tactical, and short-range nuclear and nuclear-capable systems being used as essentially 'political' weapons in a crisis, i.e. to use the threat of nuclear weapons to consolidate any gains Russia's conventional forces may make in a future European war. It is a policy made possible by new technology, which is why Russia is expending so much effort to upgrade its missile arsenal. Russian intercontinental missiles (ICBMs) (any missile with a range in excess of 5,500 km), intermediate-range ballistic missiles (IRBMs) (3,000–5,000 km), medium-range ballistic missiles (MBRMs) (1,000–3,000 km), and short-range ballistic missiles (SRMs) (up to 1,000 km) are all being upgraded.

Moscow is also trying once again to divide the US from its European allies and the changing nature of its capabilities is helping it. Most Europeans agreed with the US that Russian breaches of the Intermediate Nuclear Forces Treaty (INF) were the main cause of its demise. However, neither the UK, France, Germany, nor any NATO European showed any desire to exert pressure on Moscow for such behaviour. The specific reason for the American withdrawal from the INF was the Russian 9M279 Novator system. Whilst it was not obvious Novator broke INF rules, the nature of its motor meant it could. Whilst the Americans wanted to call Russia out, many Europeans would have been content to have preserved the Treaty even though Russia was in breach of it. This reveals again a dangerous mismatch between US and European strategy, reminiscent of the Euromissiles crisis of the 1970s and 1980s.

Moreover, much of the arms control is essentially Euro-centric, and yet much of the weapons proliferation is now global. The Americans would have liked to have renegotiated the INF to include Chinese systems, but Beijing has flatly refused. Consequently, it is not just the INF that is broken, but much of the erstwhile arms control regime in which Europeans place so much faith.

New Russian systems are also being deployed, such as the RS-28 Sarmat (NATO codename Satan 2). A successor to the Soviet-era heavy SS-18 missiles, Sarmat was deployed in 2020 and can carry up to ten heavy thermonuclear warheads or fifteen 'lighter' yield warheads. The RSM-56 Bulava submarine-launched ballistic missile (SLBM) has a range of some 10,000 km and can carry 10 x 150 kiloton warheads, and is designed for deployment on the new Borei-class heavy ballistic missile submarines.[20] Moscow is also developing an updated SS-27 Topol missile, named the SS-29 (or RS-24 Yars), which is reported to be able to carry three 'heavy' multiple independently targetable re-entry vehicles (MIRV) warheads, fast, and over a range of up to 11,000 km. The Russians have also deployed the nuclear-capable Iskandr missile with a range of some 400–500 km, and are also believed to be developing a nuclear torpedo, known as the Status-6 system, with a nuclear warhead of 100 megatons (Pentagon codename: Kanyon), with a possible range of up to 10,000 km, with a speed of up to 100 km/hr, and able to dive to 1,000 metres. The key factor with all such

20. On 29 October 2019 the Russian Ministry of Defence announced the successful test launch of the Bulava ICBM in the White Sea from the Knyaz Vladimir, a new Borei-class SSBN. See Nicole Darrah, 'Russian Nuclear Sub Successfully Test-Launches Intercontinental Ballistic Missile, Government Claims', Fox News, 30 October 2019, https://www.foxnews.com/world/russia-submarine-icbm-nuclear-test-missile.

systems is that they all have the capability to evade and avoid early detection, much of NATO's emerging ballistic missile defence (which was deliberately not designed to counter them), and so (again) destabilize the Euro-strategic balance.

The Russians also fully understand the political utility of nuclear weapons. Back in 1977 the Soviet Union deployed the mobile, triple-warhead SS-20 theatre ballistic missile. The SS-20 profoundly destabilized the Euro-strategic balance. Not unlike the 2018 NPR, the then Carter Administration responded with a call for new US systems to counter the SS-20 which led to the ill-considered European deployment of the so-called Enhanced Radiation Weapon or Neutron Bomb (ERW), a system designed to kill people but with 'limited' blast-effect which lessened 'collateral' physical damage. The ERW was a propaganda coup for the Soviets, who quickly dubbed it the 'Capitalist Bomb'. It also led to a political furore in Europe and threatened the cohesion of the Alliance, and even the stability of some European states, most notably the Federal Republic of (West) Germany, the designated nuclear killing zone in the event of a Third World War.

The Americans then further moved to counter the SS-20 with their own theatre missile systems, Pershing 2 and Cruise. Through a combination of 'fake news' 1970s-style, and very genuine concerns amongst large segments of the European population, Moscow helped foment a huge popular revolt against the US deployment of these systems. Moscow's aim then, as it is today, was to effectively decouple the defence of Europe from the US strategic deterrent, which is precisely why the UK and France had insisted on acquiring their own 'independent' nuclear systems in the 1960s (allied to a strong dose of post-imperial hubris). Today, Moscow is deploying a new generation of nuclear weapons as part of its future war strategy with the specific aim of re-exerting influence over what it regards as Russia's trad-itional spheres of influence across much of Central, Eastern, and Northern Europe. Mass destabilization, mass disruption, and the threat of mass destruc-tion seem, sadly, to have returned as the terrifying triplets of European insecurity.

Whilst both the UK and France are in the process of modernizing their own nuclear deterrent systems, a danger exists that if Washington moves to reintroduce shorter-range nuclear weapons to Europe, beyond the B-61, it would afford Moscow all the political leverage it would need to re-ignite a new wave of anti-nuclear, anti-US protests across much of Europe. One idea mooted in the NPR is the placing of 'low-yield' nuclear warheads atop existing, long-range Trident SLBM systems that would somehow contribute to deterrence via a 'sub-strategic role' for such weapons. This is dangerous thinking. For example, if any of the fourteen American Ohio-class or the four British Vanguard-class, or forthcoming Dreadnought-class 'boomers' (SSBN), were ever to launch a Trident II D5 missile, Moscow would probably assume it heralded a full thermonuclear strategic salvo.

The key to successful mutual deterrence is balance, and that balance is fast eroding in the crucible of hyperwar technology because the defence is not matching the speed of development of the offence. The specific role nuclear weapons have played in deterrence is to threaten a 'counter-force' strike capable of destroying the silos of enemy missiles or large-scale military formations or a 'counter-value' strike that destroys cities and people. As such, deterrence, coercion, and destruction have always formed a triangle of implied mutually assured destruction.[21] First, as technology advances, 'deterrence' will need to cover the world and become decidedly multilateral. Second, deterrence will also need to become more 'smart'. For example, the targets of submarine-launched missiles are hard to discern, especially if they are MIRV-ed (can deploy multiple independently targetable re-entry vehicles (warheads)), or even more so if they are MaRV-ed (manoeuvrable re-entry vehicles) and are increasingly capable of evading missile defences. This danger is further multiplied if ballistic missiles are fired on a so-called 'flat trajectory' and so reach their target more quickly, or increasingly sophisticated cruise missiles are used. Third, the increasing and comparative mass disruptive effect of a range of new weapons suggests any given level of destruction will become more tailored to desired strategic effect.

The new technologies that are entering the battlespace could be harnessed to provide such new concepts and methods of deterrence. AI-enabled systems, allied to offensive cyber capabilities, could be designed to so damage an adversary irrespective of whether it survives a nuclear first or second strike that such a strike, first or second, would be politically pointless in all

---

21. Peter Roberts and Andrew Hardie have considered the role and utility of deterrence in the twenty-first century. They conclude that, 'Strategies of deterrence encompass a vast array of activities and national philosophies. The concept has persisted since ancient times and remains useful today whether in its conventional or nuclear form. The practice of deterrence has adapted to new technologies, changing distributions of power and new kinds of threats by being sufficiently malleable. It is therefore naïve to assume that the modern world—whether due to societal shifts or technological development—somehow makes deterrence irrelevant'. See Peter Roberts and Andrew Hardie, 'The Validity of Deterrence in the Twenty-First Century', RUSI Occasional Paper, August 2015 (London: RUSI), p. 34.

conceivable scenarios. Indeed, even emerging 'conventional' systems are potentially so devastating that if applied to (and with) new robotics, cyber, swarm, and other technologies, entering the battlespace could be precise enough, tailored enough, and utterly devastating enough to serve a deterrent function. Critically, any new concept of European defence in future war must also include a concept of deterrence that moves beyond mutually assured nuclear destruction and combines new thinking with new strategy and new technology.

NATO must be at the centre of a transformative European defence and deterrence. Indeed, defence and deterrence are NATO's only real tasks. However, NATO adaptation is nothing like transformative enough, and far too slow to properly confront the scale of threat-bearing change underway. At the very least, the Alliance concept of nuclear deterrence needs to be fundamentally rethought far beyond the current thinking in the 2019 Military Strategy. Such an aim will, in turn, require Europe's political leaders to all agree the strategic direction of travel of the Alliance. And, whilst NATO's Military Strategy identifies the main components of a future warfighting force, they are insufficiently coherent and cohesive, with the pace of development best described as strategically leisurely. For example, NATO's ageing dual-capable aircraft (DCA), and France's 'sub-strategic' air-launched nuclear systems, would be unlikely even today to penetrate increasingly sophisticated Russian anti-access, area-denial (A2/AD) capabilities. They are thus of little deterrent value.

Ideally, NATO should transform adaptation to set a much more ambitious future war/future defence agenda designed to foster a new Alliance deterrence posture. A transformed Alliance deterrent posture would include and incorporate new, non-nuclear deterrence across the sweep of twenty-first-century conventional, 'unconventional', and nuclear forces as part of a broad-based deterrence that would further combine the projection of power with the protection of people. That said, credible Allied conventional military forces, allied to future war technologies, remain the best way to plug Europe's (and by extension NATO's) deterrence gap. For that reason, the very idea of what constitutes a 'conventional' force in the twenty-first century must also include in the mix capabilities and capacities capable of deterring 'unconventional' new technologies. Difficult though it would be, such an effort would need to include AI, machine-learning, super and quantum computing, big data, nano-technology, offensive cyber capabilities, and militarized biotechnologies.

There is a wider nuclear challenge which has profound implications for the future of European defence, particularly for Europe's two nuclear powers, the UK and France. When President Obama proposed moving the world towards what he called a Global Zero, there was little reasonable chance he would succeed.[22] Rather, he awakened a long dormant political debate in Europe about the role of nuclear weapons in its defence without offering a realistic alternative. He also opened up an opportunity for Russia and others to exacerbate the divisions in Europe. Clearly, the multilateral reduction of nuclear weapons is a good thing, and with some 23,000 warheads the world over, there is clearly work to do. However, focusing purely on an outdated bilateral track with Russia not only beefs up an untrustworthy and aggressive Moscow, but more importantly (and inadvertently) actually increases the incentives for the likes of China and India to build up to US and Russian warhead levels, precisely so they could be seen as equals—the essence of both countries' national strategies. That is why obsolescent arms control looks ever more like a series of past legal tracts that is observed in the breach by the powerful. And a desperate last delusional resort for the weak.

Public policy, private technology

Paul Cornish writes, 'an internationally distributed, information-enabled, agile war of attrition seems highly likely to challenge the values and interests of western states and their allies. The significance is clear; the information domain is not merely another feature on the strategic landscape, it is an environment for which the West needs to act strategically—or it will fail'.[23] Information will play a vital role in hyperwar and hyper-deterrence. Europe needs to grasp the concept that if Europeans are to prevail in high-end future

---

22. *DW* state, 'In a landmark speech in Prague in April 2009, US President Barack Obama unveiled his vision of a world freed from the nuclear threat. "I state clearly and with conviction America's commitment to seek the peace and security of a world without nuclear weapons," Obama said, balancing his vision—which he admitted may take the efforts of generations— with the immediate need of securing the world from the danger of nuclear terrorism'. See 'Global Zero: Obama's Utopian Pathway to a Nuclear-Free World', 6 May 2010, https://www.dw.com/en/global-zero-obamas-utopian-pathway-to-a-nuclear-free-world/a-5538827-0.
23. Paul Cornish, 'War Clouds on the Horizon', The Alphen Group, September 2019, https://thealphengroup.home.blog.

digital operations, they will also need to fully engage in this critical domain of future war.

Given that challenge, critical to Europe's future defence will be not just the speed and scope of such a defence but also its ability to 'smartly' understand when an attack is an attack. Effective defence will thus place particular importance on machine-learning and the 'synthetization' of data that apply algorithms generated by a whole raft of sensors across the conflict spectrum of 5D warfare. It is equally vital Europeans are better able to understand and apply such new technologies in support of defence and deterrence. That would demand, in turn, a major makeover of European procurement and the European Defence and Technological Industrial Base (EDTIB).

Paul Cornish's work on the Joint Enterprise Defense Infrastructure, or JEDI ('may the force be with you'), also known as the 'War Cloud', has highlighted some of the challenges of adapting procurement to meet fast-evolving threats. JEDI is the Pentagon programme designed to ensure the US and its forces can win digital wars.[24] However, in a sign of the cost, some $100 billion over ten years, and, indeed, the complexity of such strategies, the programme has faced a raft of challenges. Hard lessons are also being learnt about the problems of critical joint ventures with commercial enterprises that are equally critical to the future success of national security projects, both in the US and Europe. Europe also lacks the capability and coherence to establish an integrated strategic information network, which is probably a critical failing as the future defence of Europe will not only demand a much more extensive strategic public–private partnership than 'statist' Europeans are used to, but what is seen as the 'defence' supply chain will also need to be radically reconsidered. Worse, COVID-19 is likely to increase, not decrease, the European penchant for leaden-footed statist responses.

Such innovation is proving challenging even for the Americans. The US strategy was only stood up in December 2018 as a commercial general-purpose cloud solution designed to ensure information superiority through data aggregation and analysis by merging centralized computing with tactical 'edge'-enabling technologies, such as AI. JEDI was designed to act as the cloud service provider and be responsible for handling mission-critical,

24. Ibid.

operational, and intelligence material very rapidly across information classifications, and then disseminate it to US forces the world over.

The problem lay in forging the detail of the vital strategic public partnership. By August 2019, the Pentagon was ready to award the JEDI contract, and in October awarded it to Microsoft. Amazon Web Services and Microsoft Azure were the main contenders, whilst Oracle and IBM had been ruled out earlier in the competition. However, Oracle questioned the right of the Pentagon to use a single vendor, suggesting that they had been unfairly barred from bidding by a flawed process that tipped the contract in favour of Microsoft. Finally, on 12 July 2019, a US court found in favour of the Pentagon and Oracle's claim was dismissed. However, the contract was again delayed when President Trump expressed concerns about cost, although Trump's fraught relationship with Amazon CEO Jeff Bezos might also have been a factor. This salutary lesson highlights the dangers when strategic state and commercial interests conflict. However, the critical importance of strategic public–private partnerships to future war defence against peer competitors cannot be denied, even if most Europeans are in denial about that.

NATO? NATO's Cyberspace Operations Centre (CyOC), which will be fully operational in 2023, is a start, but the depth and speed of the relationship between the Allies and the Alliance in the cyber domain needs to become far more assured. In principle, CyOC will provide mission-critical Alliance-wide cyber-space situational awareness, as well as the centralized planning needed for effective cyber-space operations and missions. This is vital. Of all the seven domains of future war, information will be the glue that binds the hybrid war, cyber war, hyperwar mosaic of future war.

The critical challenge will be to maintain unity of purpose across some thirty countries with very different strategic and corporate cultures, as well as profoundly differing attitudes to the role of the private sector in state defence. Cornish again: 'Information can be a strategic asset if it is networked among like-minded governments and organizations, but a gaping strategic vulnerability if it is not. JEDI is vital, not only in the national security interest of the US but also to ensure that the West's strategic information network is as coherent and decisive as it can be. For both reasons, the JEDI contracting process should be concluded as a matter of urgency'.[25]

---

25. Ibid.

AI, machine-learning et al. will be the great force multipliers in twenty-first-century future war, and any future war defence of Europe will need such capability that will also engender new defence system architectures. Equally, such architecture must be affordable. To that end, there are a range of relatively low-cost 'starter-kit' AI capabilities being developed that could act as an effects-multiplier for Europe's future war defence. These include image recognition, autonomous flight control, active intelligent counter-measures, and path planning and ultra-efficient algorithms. However, the same technologies will also further enable enemies and insurgents to fuse their 'intel', often open source and from a range of cheap sensors, to enable them to create a big-picture understanding of Europe's critical vulnerabilities and how to exploit them instantly. Such systems will also enable adversaries to better understand and counter any threat they may face through the development of intelligent, agile systems that can self-adapt to emerging threats. Like it or not, Europe is engaged in a future war technology arms race, even if many of Europe's analogue leaders are incapable of recognizing that.

The revolution in (applied) military technology

There are some in Europe beginning to take tentative steps on the road to an AI-enhanced twenty-first-century European defence. The French are investing some $1.85 billion over five years on AI-related research and development, including the setting up of a French version of the US Defense Advanced Research Projects Agency (DARPA). The British have set up a major public–private partnership to develop an AI industry with defence applications. However, the emphasis, as with most Europeans, is the application of AI only as a means of reducing operating and maintenance costs in armed forces, a particularly chronic issue in Germany. The hard truth is that Europe lacks the necessary defence vision to see the vital applications AI will have to its future defence, and there are questions as to whether such ambitions will even survive the COVID-19 crisis.

Innovation will be vital to the future defence of Europe. There are two types of innovation: pure thinking that leads to new technologies and applications, and new thinking that corrals existing thinking and technologies into new capabilities. John McCarthy of Stanford University puts AI into context: 'Intelligence is the computational part of the ability to achieve goals in the world', and AI is 'the science and engineering of making intelligent machines, especially intelligent computer programs. It is related to the similar task of using computers to understand human intelligence, but AI does not have to confine itself to methods that are biologically observable'.[26] A lot has happened over the decade since McCarthy wrote that paper. Crucially, the pace of development has accelerated to the extent that a future war in Europe is again plausible. What has changed over the last ten years in particular is the advent of super-computing (speed of computing and sheer capacity to compute) and access to big data, lots of it. And, as both continue to grow, so too will the power of algorithms and their ability to 'think'.

The problem for Europeans is that, in spite of the sterling efforts of Allied Command Transformation (ACT), and the more modest considerations of the European Defence Agency, the words 'Europe', 'defence', and 'innovation' are not natural bedfellows. The challenge AI and associated technologies and strategies pose to Europe's future defence is daunting, but equally significant are the opportunities. Worryingly, the Europeans are not alone in the struggle to exploit defence innovation. The former US Deputy Secretary of Defense, Robert O. Work, wrote, 'The United States is not used to competing with strategic rivals on equal technological footing, but it is going to have to start learning or risk being left behind entirely as we enter the AI-era'.[27] Work went on to suggest that the fundamental premise upon which the so-called Third Offset Strategy was based—the need to exploit to advantage AI, robotics, and a range of technologies to afford Washington strategic advantage—is being threatened precisely by the exploitation of such technologies by China and other strategic and near-peer competitors.[28]

Implicit in Work's well-placed comment is also a threat to the transatlantic relationship and NATO. The US is determined to prepare its armed forces for AI-dominated future war. If Europe does not follow suit, it is hard to see how its obsolescent civil and military security and defence structures can maintain any real ability or capacity to work efficiently and effectively with its American ally. Whither NATO? Whither interoperability?

---

26. http://jmc.stanford.edu/artificial-intelligence/what-is-ai/index.html.
27. Robert O. Work (2018) 'So This Is What It Feels Like to Be Offset: The US Can No Longer Assume Technological and Military Superiority in the AI Era', in John R. Allen and Amir Husein (eds.) *Hyperwar: Conflict and Competition in the AI Century* (Austin, TX: SparkCognition Press), p. 25.
28. Ibid.

A relatively rudimentary analysis of Chinese ambitions in the field reinforces the perception that a new form of AI bipolarity could well come to dominate future war. President Xi Jinping has overseen a $150 billion Chinese investment in its domestic AI industry. Beijing is also leveraging commercial advantages in critical machine-learning technologies and systems, such as synthetic vision, data analysis, and 'hyper-speed' software generation, much of it driven by extensive espionage campaigns. The specific aim is clear: to generate the technology to effectively destroy the US battle command network by disrupting intelligence, command, control, and communications at critical nodes. The implications for Europe are self-evident. If America cannot defend itself, how can it defend Europe? There is a further problem with China in that it operates from a position of grand strategic singularity in that there is no clear separation between the strategic vision and resource allocations of the Party, State Owned Enterprise, and the so-called Chinese private sector. This is a unity of effort that neither the US nor Europe can possibly duplicate.

There is also every likelihood that Russia will benefit from Chinese technological prowess throughout the hybrid-cyber-hyperwar mosaic. Central to both Chinese and Russian strategies is a firm grip of complex strategic coercion and its application, and the complex and targeted use of cyber, electronic, and physical attacks across the full 5D spectrum of disinformation, deception, destabilization, disruption, and destruction, much of it driven by AI-enabled machine-learning, and, if called upon, a ruthless application of power in pursuit of national goals; in other words, the pursuit of a capacity to inflict a new yet more devastating digital Pearl Harbor from which the West might never recover. Again, both Russia and China enjoy an advantage over Western democracies, natural to any authoritarian state, in that they have a unity of effort and focus that any liberal democracy finds very hard to create. Could it prove decisive?

There are two other dangers about which Europeans seem to be in denial: the possibility of major war in Europe, and the role disruptive technologies would play in any such war. Holger Mey has written,

> We are on the threshold of a new epoch, presumably, even a new evolutionary stage. The digitalization of the economy and society is in full swing and with this comes the need to critically re-assess all of society's institutions and to re-design many of them. The intelligence of machines ensures that they take on more and more activities and skills that were previously the privilege of people. At the same time, we should not forget that the intelligence of brutal

power politicians and functionaries has done their societies no good. Present day humanity is caught up in the tension between a bestial past in the wilderness and a capacity for critical reason integrated into one's respective culture or civilization.

Mey continued, 'Time and again it is said that the computer must be controlled by humans. However, this statement falls short of answering the question who is in control. Should it be Adolf Hitler, Josef Stalin, Mao Zedong or Pol Pot? The real challenge is to make sure the computer is controlled by the *right* humans, the "good humans"'.[29]

Much of this book has been about the drifting apart of the transatlantic allies, and much of that is due to the causes and consequence of European military weakness. However, whilst transatlantic strategic drift has also been driven by politics on both sides of the Atlantic, it could well also become subject to technological divergence. Indeed, divergent views about the place of technology in future war, particularly the role of AI in such a war, could break the transatlantic relationship. One thing is clear: the nature of any future war in Europe would be radically different from past major wars, if no less destructive. The future of European defence needs to be just as radical.

There have been many attempts to overcome these problems, but all have failed, the European Defence Agency being the most obvious. As a consequence, there are still too many outdated, metal-bashing defence industries in Europe, bashing too many outdated bits of metal to produce far too few over-priced and under-performing outdated bits of defence equipment. Production runs are simply neither long enough nor big enough to produce the necessary economies of scale. Even further, the inflated cost of such platforms is made worse by a 'Christmas tree' effect—the hanging of too many systems on too few platforms, rendering both the platform and the system sub-optimal weapons with systems integration rendered virtually impossible by governments' constantly changing requirements.

In the post-COVID-19 world a new European Defence Innovation Partnership is needed, which would necessarily include post-Brexit UK, with the whole idea of false competition abandoned. To make such a partnership reality, Europe's defence-industrial prime contractors would need to form a standing partnership with government. And yes, companies such as Airbus, EADS, Thales, and BAE Systems would need to be brought

---

29. Holger Mey (2019) 'Foreword', in Denise Feldner (ed.) *Re-designing Institutions: Concepts for the Digitally Connected Society* (Berlin: Springer).

into discussions about defence requirements far earlier in the planning/ political cycle than is the case today, but only as part of an effort to exponentially expand the European defence supply chain.

Indeed, the entire European industrial/service supply chain needs to be far better exploited, not just the bespoke defence supply chain. And, where possible, as much hardware and software as possible should be bought off the shelf, even from the Americans (if they permit it!). Bringing government and the private sector into closer orbit and alignment on requirements development, R&D, and procurement is the only way European democracies can credibly compete with authoritarian regimes where there's virtually no distinction between a government and a 'commercial' entity. In hyperwar, inter-institutional friction would be a massive strategic vulnerability that would hinder any response with which adversaries would probably not have to contend.

Take the new British heavy aircraft carriers, HMS Queen Elizabeth and HMS Prince of Wales. The construction of the two carriers by the Aircraft Carrier Alliance is a story of innovation which points to the future of European defence procurement. The ships were built in sections across the UK, with each section then floated on barges to Rosyth where they were assembled. To realize the project, prime contractors BAE Systems and Thales UK had to make use of much existing expertise from the declining North Sea oil industry and exploit a much wider supply chain than has traditionally been the case for such projects. This helped lead to the Defence Growth Partnership and attempts by the British to generate much more defence capability for each pound spent.[30] However, if a real Defence Innovation Partnership is ever to be realized, European politicians must begin to answer a question they have been dodging since the end of the Cold War: what does the defence of Europe require (not how much defence of Europe can it afford)?

---

30. The Defence Growth Partnership states, 'The Defence Growth Partnership (DGP) is a partnership between Government and the Defence Industry. It is jointly led by the Department of Business, Energy, and Industrial Strategy (BEIS) and the Defence Industry, with the support of the Ministry of Defence (MOD) as the UK customer. The DGP also works closely with the UK's Department of International Trade—Defence and Security Organisation (UKTI DSO) as well as academia and R&D . . . The DGP is working to secure a truly competitive, sustainable and globally successful UK Defence sector that provides affordable leading-edge capability and through-life support for our Armed Forces and international customers, as well as bringing wider economic benefits to the UK'. https://www. defencegrowthpartnership.co.uk/about/what-is-the-dgp.

The gathering (tech-)storm

The new revolution in military technology is fact, and Europeans could well be approaching a digital Dreadnought moment. And yet, its implications are also uncertain, which begs a series of further fundamental question for Europeans. In the wake of COVID-19 European states will also need to make some big choices about the capabilities the European future force will need, but can they make the right choices? In spite of NATO efforts to coordinate European procurement and acquisition policy and practice, and the advent of the European Defence Agency, no framework exists to properly facilitate the defence outcomes the Europeans would need to be able to deter a future war and fight one.

The essential problem for Europeans is that European defence cannot be transformed without spending lots of money. Any such increase is unlikely in the wake of the COVID-19 crisis. However, such investments would also need to be matched by an efficient and effective application of money to ensure agreed equipment goals based on shared ideas of military requirement also leading to the fielding of military capability, and rapidly. To realize such an end, Europeans would also need to buy the military equipment they need and not, as is too often the case, what they want. It might be argued that the UK's two new aircraft carriers are a case in point. HMS Queen Elizabeth and HMS Prince of Wales are impressive-looking ships, and did a lot to support employment in Scotland at a time of economic austerity and the threat of separatism. However, with a revolution in military technology underway, there is the real danger they could rapidly go the same way as the immediately pre-Dreadnought King Edward VII-class and sail at great expense into obsolescence.

A European future defence strategy worthy of the name would thus mean an entirely different way of thinking about how Europeans defend themselves, and how they assure their still vital relationship with the US. Where could such new thinking be generated? The NATO Defence Planning Process, the EU's Permanent Structured Cooperation, or some future adaptation of European strategic autonomy through a Common Security and Defence Policy that welds together collective approaches and common structures? Or would it need to come from the three residual power states of Europe—the UK, France, and Germany, supported by Poland and other more activist European states? Would an increasingly harmonized NATO and EU requirements development process be a prerequisite for a future defence strategy, and could those advocating such thinking ensure political impetus overcomes bureaucratic resistance? At present, no such strategy could be envisaged without the complete restructuring of Europe's defence industries into something approaching a truly European Defence and Technological Development Base.

Technology and future defence

The central contention of this chapter is that technology will drive European defence strategy in the twenty-first century, at least as much as policy or environment. Any credible future defence of Europe will be an AI-enabled defence, mounted across the full mosaic of hybrid war, cyber war, and hyperwar: ultra-fast warfare that involves and combines a myriad of systems able to wreak havoc in an instant. AI would sit at the core of such war and its conduct, but not as a stand-alone technology. Rather, it would provide the 'thinking brain' that reinforces and enables human command. There is also the likely danger that AI will be embedded in a whole host of dark services, from fully autonomous machine-learning to human enhancement and genetic manipulation. Data analytics, simulation, behavioural science, drone technologies, and quantum-based sensors that can reveal the ocean depths, and whatever is sailing within it, would also all rely upon AI. All of the above would critically inform cyber warfare, synthetic technologies, and nano-technologies and in turn underpin 3D printing, hypersonic weapons, smart weapons, unmanned combat aerial vehicles, attack swarms, and the use of big data to create synthetic reality to better inform often automated decision-making.

Hyperwar is coming to Europe, driven not by Europeans but by techno-logical change underway in the US, China, and Russia. There can be no credible future European defence without the necessary investments in future tech, for without it Europeans will be unable to address the unique requirements of future war. If Europeans do not act, then they face at best a Dreadnought moment, or at worst a new Pearl Harbor.

Cry havoc, and loose the dogs of digital war?

9

Defending Europe

A return to European statecraft

Statecraft is the art of governance and the science of action in international affairs. It concerns big power, its application, and how to resist such power when others seek to impose. It is thus about peace and war. The purpose of this book is to consider the manner in which peace might be preserved in twenty-first-century Europe and how a mix of statecraft, policy, and strategy could best maintain it. The purpose of this chapter is to establish the essential change agents vital to such an end: managing Russia and a new dual-track approach, the re-establishing of context-relevant European strategic realism and responsibility, the building of a new strategic public–private partnership, the crafting of the vital future NATO–EU strategic partnership, and sharpening the spear-tip of NATO.

However, before Europe's return to statecraft can be explored, consideration must be given to the impact of COVID-19 on European defence. COVID-19 will impose on Europeans dark choices. Indeed, COVID-19 cannot be seen in isolation from other systemic trends that are impacting upon Europeans. COVID-19, the expanding bandwidth of war, the state of European public finances, and the changing nature of European society effectively mean that no European state can any longer afford to both secure its people domestically and, at the same time, credibly defend them from external threats. In spite of the costs COVID-19 will impose on Europeans and their respective economies, for the transatlantic relationship to credibly endure, the Americans will also need militarily capable Europeans.

COVID-19 has finally revealed the extent of the fundamental change of mind-set that is needed on the part of both leaders and led in Europe about the nature of the world in which they live. Europe's world is changing fast and all the past assumptions that for over seventy years have underpinned Europe's defence are fast evaporating. Falsely reassuring though such assumptions may be for European leaders schooled during the comforting afterglow of the Cold War when seemingly eternal debates took place over the future shape of Europe's soft superpower and the institutions that underpinned them, such assumptions were false then and dangerously so now. In spite of the terrible tragedy in the Western Balkans, the 1990s was a time when the only 'power' in Europe it was polite to consider was 'soft', not hard, nasty, metallic, digital, and destructive.[1] Indeed, any residual 'hard'-power legitimacy seemed wholly value-dependent on the European pursuit of 'soft', humanitarian ends.[2] That world has come and gone in what, by any standard of history, is a blink of the systemic eye. Indeed, some thirty years after 'perpetual' peace was declared by Europeans, soft power seems anachronistically optimistic in a world which is fast moving into a new age of geopolitical tension and in which systemic war can no longer be ruled out.

COVID-19 has thus redefined the debate over the future of European security and defence. However, it is still the changing character of war, not peace, that is and will be *the* vital and ultimate determinant in Europe's future defence. In a future war the impact of new technologies on the battlespace cannot be overstated, with artificial intelligence (AI), cyber, machine-learning, and a host of new technologies accelerating the speed and scope of deception, disinformation, disruption, destabilization, and politically decapitating destruction. The fusion of COVID-19 and future

1. Joseph S. Nye writes, 'Governments use military power to issue threats, fight, and with a combination of skill and luck, achieve desired outcomes within a reasonable time. Economic power is often a similarly straightforward matter. Governments freeze foreign bank accounts overnight, and can distribute bribes or aid promptly (although economic sanctions often take a long time, if ever, to produce desired outcomes). Soft power is more difficult, because many of its crucial resources are outside the control of governments, and their effects depend heavily on acceptance by the receiving audiences. Moreover, soft power resources often work indirectly by shaping the environment for policy, and sometimes take years to produce the desired outcomes'. See Joseph S. Nye (2005) *Soft Power: The Means to Success in World Politics* (New York: Public Affairs), p. 99.
2. In a famous April 1999 speech in Chicago against the backdrop of the Kosovo war, then British Prime Minister Tony Blair laid out the principles for what he called humanitarian interventionism. 'No longer is our existence as states under threat. Now our actions are guided by a more subtle blend of mutual self-interest and moral purpose in defending the values we cherish. In the end values and interests merge. If we can establish and spread the values of liberty, the rule of law, human rights and an open society then that is in our national interests too. The spread of our values makes us safer. As John Kennedy put it, "Freedom is indivisible and when one man is enslaved who is free?"' See Blair's Chicago Speech, 24 April 1999, https://keeptonyblairforpm. wordpress.com/blair-speech-transcripts-from-1997–2007/#chicago.

war will thus demand that both Europeans and their North American allies go back to some basic first principles, such as effective civil defence and suitably hardened physical and information infrastructures, if forces are to act, fight, and move around Europe quickly in an emergency. During the Cold War the physical and legal infrastructures necessary for such military mobility were taken as a matter of defensive course. Not so today. Therefore, COVID-19 already provides specific lessons about the utility of force and the rapid movement of mass resources in a crisis and should be ruthlessly examined.

Specific lessons from COVID-19

What are those lessons? First, COVID-19 should have been predicted or at least better prepared for. Failure to do so and the relatively slow first response and panicky political response has led to the pandemic dominating the strategic agenda on both sides of the Atlantic, and it will do so for the foreseeable future. Any such focus on COVID-19 could well come at the expense of Europe's future defence preparedness. Second, competition with China will likely increase and accelerate. For too long, European leaders have had a naïve view of globalism and connived in making Europe more vulnerable than it should be to Chinese influence. Europeans must now seek a more balanced relationship with China, and that will and must include the use and utility of force against China if needs be. Third, Europeans must become far more sensitive to the growing pressure China's rise places on the US and its armed forces. For too long Europeans have believed the US armed forces are designed primarily to act in the European, not the American, interest. Imagine Europe without them. Fourth, globalization will not end with COVID-19 but it is likely to slow down, with a process of re-regionalization also likely to ensue. Europeans need to better understand the strategic implications of such change. Fifth, Europeans must undertake a full and dispassionate assessment of crisis management during COVID-19, looking at what worked and what did not, and considering all the implications for Europe's future defence.

The defence implications of COVID-19 are also profound because the cost of combating the pandemic could have severe implications for the ability of Europeans to act in a high-end military emergency. Striking a new, affordable, and credible comprehensive security balance between human security and national defence will prove difficult. Specifically, human security will demand much more state investment in pandemic resiliency, with higher taxation to that end as many European citizens now place the importance of such human security and the resiliency and redundancy of health systems far above national defence. It would be a profound mistake to bow to such political pressures because far tighter synergies will also be needed between security and defence if such demands are not to lead to a profound weakening of both. At the very least, much greater consideration will need to be given to bio-defences.

Debt to GDP ratios spiralled in most European states during the crisis as a consequence of social lockdowns. This followed after years of relative austerity that had already hollowed out the state structures of many European states. As such, COVID-19 could well mark the end of the 'just-in-time' hand-to-mouth European state. However, it also means Europeans must face another profound challenge if they are to afford critical public services given such high levels of public debt. It will be the single most pressing policy challenge for European leaders for much of the 2020s and the 'engine' of European vulnerability. The temptation for some Europeans will be to take up China's offer of cheap money, even if such 'largesse' would have the most profound strategic consequences for Europe and its defence. Globalization has become 'Chinaization' over the past decade and made Europeans ever more vulnerable to Chinese coercion. Chinaization has also been a Faustian pact as China has for too long been allowed pretty much open access to the West's intellectual and technological property, particularly ICT, with far too many of Europe's critical supply chains now China-dependent.

COVID-19 has also created the impression of a US in retreat, even decline. It is an impression that has been reinforced by Washington accepting aid from China and Russia and threatening to withdraw from the World Health Organization. Critically, the US appeared little more coherent in its response to COVID-19 than Europe where intergovernmental institutions, such as the EU, were by and large absent from the effort.

COVID-19 has also shone a light on the nature and extent of systemic change and reinforced the need for Europeans to be able to act in their own defence within the framework of a reformed and revitalized transatlantic relationship. Any such transformation must involve the creation of a much stronger and more cohesive European pillar across the comprehensive security spectrum, with European defence brought out of the analogue age in which much of it is trapped. Allied worst-case analyses and capacity-planning must also be restored (including civil defence) as North Americans and Europeans consider shared best practice, not least because one day an engineered pandemic could be the prelude to future war.

Where to begin? At the heart of the future Alliance, a new Digitization Concept is needed as the first step towards the far greater exploitation of technology in pursuit of both better people protection and enhanced power projection, with AI and robotics to the fore. During the Cold War a range of strategic metals were identified that the West deemed vital to its security. Europeans and their North American allies should identify a list of strategic technologies, the development, production, and application of which must always be under their control. Given the nature of future war, such technologies will need to be both civilian and military-relevant. 5G would be a good place to start.

Managing Russia: the new dual-track

In November 2020, General Sir Nick Carter, the Chief of the UK Defence Staff, warned of a risk of a third world war (Forbes 2020). And, given tensions around Europe and much of the world beyond, European armed forces could find themselves fighting a major war, and far more quickly than many European leaders or peoples today realize. Given the threat, European leaders must together enact a series of steps to reinforce deterrence if they are to protect their respective peoples, built on a new defence agenda.

A new dual-track approach is thus needed with Russia engaged through both strength and dialogue. Russia is a desperate state, short of time, short of people, and as it declines it will also become short of resources and capabilities. Consequently, the threat Russia poses is not a reflection of its residual strengths. Indeed, if governed properly and effectively, such strengths could still be put to good use for its long-suffering people. Rather, the Russian threat is a function of its relative decline and growing weakness, allied to Kremlin paranoia that seems to condemn Russia to never escape its past. There is also a very real danger that at some point the regime will face collapse as a consequence of its own innate contradictions. Such a moment could come swiftly and brutally and would pose a moment of maximum danger for Europe.

In effect, Russia is an 'in-between' power: in between power and weakness, in between the regional and the global, and in between democracy and autocracy. The result is (as ever) a Russian paradox: a great nation desperately in need of reform, but a society and an elite scared of change and unable to face the challenge of it, and constantly looking for others to blame for its own inadequacies. Consequently, Russia is a nuclear-edged crisis waiting to happen on Europe's doorstep and an over-securitized state built by an economy no bigger than that of Spain that sees everything in terms only an over-securitized state can—all threat, no opportunity. Managing the Russian crisis is thus a priority for the Euro-Atlantic community writ large and anyone who believes in European peace. Of course, it is vital the Alliance, the EU, and all the states therein seek every opportunity to talk with Russia. However, given the nature of the Putin Kremlin, any such dialogue must always be informed by strength. Peace through strength? Ultimately, strong European defences are the only way Europeans can be assured against extreme, unpredictable violent action by the Russian state.

Establishing the new dual-track will not be easy. The aim of contemporary Russian policy is to make the Atlantic wider and Europe weaker. It is no artifice. President Putin, and the people around him, believe deeply in the paradigm of an aggrieved Russia, even if history tells a different story. Indeed, President Putin has suggested that the collapse of the Soviet Union was one of the greatest tragedies ever to befall world affairs and that if he could turn the clock back, he would. As such, the Kremlin is nostalgic for a past that never was. There is also a messianic quality to Putin's leadership that is ever more apparent as he gets older. He is convinced he is on a mission to 'save' Russia from a perfidious West. Promoting chaos in Europe is his strategic metier, and creating windows of opportunity for chaos his constant aim, especially in those states along Russia's western and southern borders.

Are there opportunities for dialogue? For all Putin's apparent success in Crimea, the regime is vulnerable. Whilst the seizure of Eastern Ukraine strengthened Putin's grip over Russia in the short term, a grip which was reflected in the gerrymandered 2018 presidential elections, there is growing popular dissatisfaction at home to which the Kremlin is sensitive. Russia also faces deep demographic, social, and economic challenges which, unless addressed, will see Russia continue to fade as a power, as the US, China, India, and even some European powers steadily eclipse Moscow. Russia might make strategic overtures to Beijing, but Russia still depends on a strong economic relationship with European states to its west, most notably Germany, to sustain its economy and its society. And yet, Russia will also remain prone to aggressive, often unpredictable action and sustained low-boil hostility. The 2018 killing of a British citizen in Salisbury by the Russian nerve agent Novichok during a bungled GRU operation to assassinate a former Russian agent simply confirmed the nature of the regime and the reckless lengths to which it is willing to go to impose its fiat.[3]

The tendency of many European powers is to constantly seek to accommodate Russia, whatever its actions. This is a profound mistake. 'Resetting' relations with Moscow before it has agreed to moderate its actions, which is President Macron's declared aim, simply looks like weakness to the Kremlin. European policy towards Ukraine is a case in point. The so-called Steinmeyer Formula (named after the former German foreign minister and now German President, Frank-Walter Steinmeyer) was a well-meaning attempt to establish peace in Ukraine by building on the so-called Minsk Process which President Putin has by and large treated with contempt. The Formula implies that the Donbass might eventually be returned to Ukrainian control, but only after elections have been held under Russian auspices and an interim administration established whilst Moscow is still effectively in control. In essence, the Formula only confirms Moscow in its belief that Europeans are weak and more can be wrested from them by being firm and threatening force. Worse, the opening of the Nord Stream 2 gas pipeline has reinforced Moscow's prejudice that whatever its behaviour, mercantilist Berlin will sooner or later accommodate Russia. Russian aggression in Syria, Russian meddling in Libya, and Moscow's sustained use of mercenaries through the Russian private security company, The Wagner Group, are further examples of Russian 'excursions' beyond the normal conventions of international affairs, even though the Group performed abysmally in Libya in 2020.

Moscow's aim is to restore a sphere of influence over the countries to the west and south and Russia. Its method is complex strategic coercion. Seizing the east of Ukraine was thus a test of how Russia might act elsewhere, and a reminder to President Lukashenka in Belarus that Minsk is closer to Moscow than Brussels. The Donbass was always vulnerable to Russian incursion, partly because of the hold the idea of *Russki Mir* (Russian World) has on the Russian strategic mind, but also because of the large number of Russian

---

3. GRU or GU (Glavnoye razvedyvatel'noye upravleniye) is the Main Intelligence Directorate of the General Staff of the Armed Forces of the Russian Federation. It is independent of the other intelligence agencies such as SVR, FSB, and FSO.

speakers in the region. There are similar blocks of ethnic Russians in EU and NATO states who could also be manipulated if *Russki Mir* becomes even more bombastic. The West partly understands that, which is why the forces of many NATO allies have been deployed to the Baltic States as part of the Alliance's Enhanced Forward Presence, and the Tailored Forward Presence in the Black Sea region. As a consequence, any attempt by Russia to seize part or all of a NATO member-state would be met by the forces of several Allies, most notably the US.

Moscow would thus need to be mired in the deepest of crises to even consider taking such a step. The problem is that just such a self-inflicted crisis is by no means implausible. Moreover, Russia's propensity to employ brutal force should never be underestimated given Moscow's profoundly cynical view of power and its use. Ask the people of Chechnya, Georgia, Syria, and, of course, Ukraine. The nature of internal power politics in Moscow often leaves Russian leaders facing a dark choice between their own physical demise and that of their families, or some desperate foreign adventure. History suggests that in such circumstances most Russian leaders would almost certainly choose the latter, especially if faced with an over-deployed America and an under-defended and divided Europe. To the Kremlin, Russian military might is thus the very essence of personal presidential power, personal security, and making Russia indispensable to the rest of Europe. Indeed, indispensable is exactly what Russia has now become in the Levant because of its 'successful' use of force in the Syrian tragedy; a tragedy enabled by Western weakness which has also enabled Russia to become the region's strategic referee.

Ultimately, the challenge posed by Russia to the rest of Europe is one of political culture. The Russian political mind tends to regard the worst case as the default, whilst many leaders across the rest of Europe regard the worst case as something to be denied. The gap between the two views is where danger lurks, particularly as Moscow is always able to deploy a whole host of spurious historical and humanitarian *casus belli*. That is the essence of its strategic method and paranoia. The aggressive expansionism of NATO, the 'mistreatment' of ethnic Russians, and the need to create a buffer between Russia and a 'Fascist' West all inform Moscow's self-serving strategic narrative. Therefore, Americans and Europeans need to understand how easy it would be for the Kremlin to convince itself of the 'vital' need to 'act decisively' at the moment of greatest opportunity. One only has to look at a map to see what such desperate action might be: straighten Russia's strategic borders by restoring a buffer zone between Russia and the West, link Kaliningrad directly to Russia in much the same way as the Kerch Strait Bridge now links Russia to Crimea, and create a new Russian sphere of influence further to the west . . . and it would all be NATO's fault. Given the strength of Russian forces facing the Baltic States and NATO's relative weakness therein, no quick rescue would be possible in the event of a desperate Russian land grab. Therefore, the Western allies must use all the military and non-military tools at their disposal to convince the Kremlin that the costs of any such adventurism would far outweigh the benefits, even if the regime was mired in crisis. Convincing Moscow and managing Russia is thus central to Europe's future defence. Perhaps COVID-19 will moderate Moscow's behaviour, perhaps not, but no such effort is likely to be at all successful unless Europeans become far more strategically realist and responsible.

Re-establishing European strategic realism and responsibility

The re-establishment of European strategic realism and responsibility is central to the thesis herein. It will require a new concept of comprehensive European security in the post-COVID-19 world that restores strategic ambition with human security and national defence. COVID-19 has shown once and for all that Europe cannot isolate itself from twenty-first-century geopolitics, even if strategic ambition for much of the European political class stretches little beyond Brussels and the EU. China's increasing assertiveness in South and East Asia (and far beyond) highlights a global shift towards a new seismic, systemic epicentre of power with profound implications for Europe. China's ambition is well stated: to become the world's leading power by 2050 with the most profound implications for the US, and by extension for Europe itself. The US–China struggle is now well under-way and could well intensify in the wake of the COVID-19 crisis as Beijing moves to impose its writ on Hong Kong and intimidate Taiwan. Moreover, China and Russia are already engaged in industrial levels of cyber warfare against Europeans, using the ether as a domain for systemic warfare, again revealing both the nature and future of geopolitics in the twenty-first century. Their aim is not so much the permanent destruction of a European state's centre of political gravity through the destruction of its armed forces, à la Clausewitz.[4] Rather, it is to keep European societies socially and politically off balance and change the balance of resources liberal states commit to people protection at the expense of national defence through a form of permanent 5D warfare: the complex weaving of digital and information attacks, the threat of attack, and, if needs be, actual attacks on critical national infrastructures, systems, and people. It would therefore be a profound mistake to believe Europeans, à la Plato, have seen the end of war, partly because 'war' in the hybrid-cyber-hyper age will come in many forms.

Against such a backdrop the French idea of European strategic autonomy is essentially correct, even if it is in part a French reaction to Paris's misplaced perception of an over-mighty America. However, France would make more progress with its plans if Paris focused on re-establishing European strategic responsibility. This is because autonomy can only flow as a consequence of responsibility. It is certainly time. The re-establishment of strategic responsibility would at the very least require Europeans to undertake a common analysis of threat and collectively invest in sufficient military and appropriate capabilities to enable them to share high-end risk with the Americans pursuant to their own defence. Indeed, such responsibility is the only way the US taxpayer is likely to agree that Washington should continue to act as Europe's defence guarantor at the highest level of conflict. Indeed, European strategic responsibility, strategic autonomy, and equitable transatlantic burden-sharing are intrinsically linked.

In practice, European strategic responsibility would require Europe's collective armed forces to be capable of effective, fast, high-end first response in and around Europe in an emergency. For such a vision to be realized, European force generation would also need to be sufficiently robust to enable Europeans to move rapidly and effectively command and sustain such a force. It would also need to be led by Europe's three most powerful military actors, the UK, France, and Germany, with smaller European states organized into compatible groupings under the auspices of both the EU and NATO, and able to undertake far more robust military operations than at

---

4. In *On War*, Clausewitz wrote, 'Our discussion has shown that while in war many different roads can lead to the goal, to the attainment of the political object, fighting is the only possible means. Everything is governed by the supreme law, the decision by force of arms. . . . To sum up: of all the possible aims in war, the destruction of the enemy's armed forces always appears as the highest'. See Mark McNeilly, 'The Battle of the Military Theorists: Clausewitz v Sun Tzu', History News Network, 25 January 2015, https://historynewsnetwork.org/article/158123.

present. The German-led Framework Nation Concept was an early step on the road to the creation of just such a hub-and-spoke European force, but as ever it was too little offered up as very much. Therefore, it is now up to the UK, France, and Germany to put their money where their many words are and collectively go far further.

The outcome should be an affordable, capable European future force built on a dramatically improved procurement, acquisition, and technology development with the time between conception and completion/ delivery of new equipment drastically cut. However, for such a framework to be established, the US itself would need to be far clearer about the future strategic partnership it seeks with its European allies and the minimum it wants and expects from them. Indeed, it is America's coming defence choices that are likely to resonate far more deeply in Europe than European choices. This is because unless Europeans do far more for their own defence, in time the US will simply be unable or unwilling to defend Europe. Moreover, the direction of travel of a technology-led American military strategy over the medium to longer term will force Europeans to choose between maintaining military interoperability with a US future force across the hybrid, cyber, and hyperwar mosaic, or effectively decouple.

How should Europe's future defence be organized? A profound political divide continues to dog European defence between those who still see the Alliance as the natural focus for collective defence, and those who believe the EU should move towards some form of common defence. At the heart of this debate is the continuing centrality of the US to the defence of Europe. Consequently, it boils down to an essential dichotomy: more or less America. Some suggest that Europeans will only be strategically responsible if Europeans are also strategically autonomous. Others continue to believe the necessary strategic ambition to underpin a more strategically assertive Europe also means any such effort must remain NATO-centric. This political divide is also reflected in the debate over the size, capability, political centre of gravity, and above all the military-strategic ambition of a European future force.

It is a pointless debate. Europeans tried a 'common' approach in the past with the European Defence Community. It failed for the same reason it would likely fail today; most of Europe's nation-states, whilst prepared to share significant degrees of national sovereignty, are not, as yet, prepared to cede control over the legitimate use of violence in which their citizens would be led by any supranational institution, however worthy. Therefore, if a European future force of any value and weight is ever to be created, which is proportionate à la Schuman to the many threats and challenges Europeans will likely face, some form of hybrid common-collective structure must evolve over time. This is also because the resiliency and robustness of European civilian and critical infrastructures will likely be as important as the 'projectability' of European military power in any credible European defence and deterrence posture.

It is also unlikely Europeans will together generate the strategic forces needed to ease burdens on the US unless there is at least some level of increased European strategic responsibility demonstrably commensurate with the threat. However, strategic responsibility will only emerge as a direct consequence of the forces and resources Europeans apply to defence, and in the wake of COVID-19 striking such a balance will be hard. Moreover, real European strategic autonomy is likely only ever to develop if political and military structures develop in harmony. Therefore, if EU structures are to be strengthened, most notably the Common Foreign and Security Policy (CFSP), the Common Security and Defence Policy (CSDP), and Permanent Structured Cooperation (PESCO), they will only do so if they purposively take place in parallel with the development of a reformed and adapted NATO. Consequently, before a European future force that is properly strategic in both scope and ambition could ever be realized, much greater efforts will be needed to promote convergence of the security and defence policies of EU and NATO member-states. This can only happen if there is a shared level of strategic ambition.

Finally, responsibility, autonomy, and affordability go hand in hand. All European states struggle to match ends with ways and means and too many retreat into European 'theology' when they cannot. Such delusion will only hinder the practical and pragmatic contemporary development of European strategic responsibility. There is a twist. To realize such strategic responsibility, Europeans will also need real access to US technology, not least to strike a politically acceptable balance between capability and affordability. Such a requirement will, in turn, test the US export control system and, by extension, further test the importance of capable allies to the US. That begs a further question: just how important are capable allies to the US?

Building a strategic public–private partnership

In an authoritative August 2019 piece for *RealClearDefense*, Elsa B. Kania of the Technology and National Security Program at the Center for a New American Security wrote, 'The lessons that are worth learning also harken back to a history of American governmental investments in science and technology that created a foundation for today's commercial developments. Looking forward, U.S. policy should concentrate on recognizing and redoubling our own initiatives to promote public-private partnership in critical technologies, while sustaining and increasing investments in American research and innovation'.[5] Europe?

There are both *integrative* strategies and *innovative* strategies required to better incorporate emerging technologies into Europe's future defence posture. Europeans first need to focus together on how best to integrate emerging technologies with existing legacy platforms, not least because many Europeans are locked into maintaining such legacy equipment for the foreseeable future. And, while some EU efforts are underway to better synchronize the requirements development process with a coherent R&D and procurement strategy, Europeans will also need to systematically integrate those technologies into existing platforms and systems.

History is again a useful signpost. Back in the early 1940s Blitzkrieg was the hyperwar breakthrough of its age. This was not because of any one revolutionary technology or doctrine, but rather because some visionary Germans saw how hyperwar outcomes could be achieved through the symbiotic combination of modern technology; the highly mobile gun platform (tank); highly mobile, flying artillery (the Stuka); and the wireless radio (the networking system of its time), reinforced by a robust and flexible German command structure and fighting culture that could decide and then act with great intellectual coherence and at high speed.[6] The outcome, of

---

5. See Elsa B. Kania, 'In Military-Civil Fusion, China Is Learning Lessons from the United States and Starting to Innovate', 27 August 2019, https://www.realcleardefense.com/articles/2019/08/27/in_military-civil_fusion_china_is_learning_lessons_from_the_united_states_and_starting_to_innovate_114699.html.
6. In fact, one of the architects of Blitzkrieg was Heinz Guderian who admitted that he owed much of his thinking to British strategists such as Colonel J.F.C. Fuller and Basil Liddell Hart. Guderian once famously said that British thinking on manoeuvre warfare was excellent but thankfully the British Army did not read its own doctrine—a charge he also laid against both the American and French armed forces of the 1930s.

course, was rapid defeat of Poland in 1939 and the subsequent and even more rapid collapse of the French command structure and defeat of the British Expeditionary Force in May and June 1940. Both the British and French were knocked off balance and then crippled by the speed of Blitz-krieg and the effectiveness of the integrated technologies that supported it. Ultimately (and thankfully), Hitler's Germany failed in its war aims because, unlike the British, German industry did not go to war with the *Wehrmacht* in an integrated manner. Consequently, the development strategies that would have fielded an invincible mass of military requirements were not realized and much of German logistics remained decidedly anachronistic. When the Germans first came up against a world-class defensive system that also combined technology (the Spitfire, Hurricane, and radar) in the form of the RAF and a world-beating air defence command structure (the Dowding System), they were defeated in the Battle of Britain. When they attempted to drive the hyper-sharp spear-tip of the *Wehrmacht* into the immense heart of the Soviet Union, it was eventually ground to dust by the sheer mass of Russia and the Red Army.

Consequently, while German R&D efforts of the age produced impressive hyperwar-like advanced technologies, they could not be fielded either in the time or the numbers needed to succeed because, given the accelerating pace and scale of the conflict and the power of the adversaries ranged against Germany, it simply took too long from concept to deployment. In other words, as demand rose, resources diminished. Thus, the most advanced combined arms manoeuvre force ever to be developed in Europe, the Panzer Divisions of the *Wehrmacht*, eventually ground to a halt crushed by incompetent grand strategy and an inability to match the ends, ways, and means imposed upon it, although not before they had inflicted huge suffering on the people of Europe and done immense damage. The bottom line of history would suggest that the future war defence of Europe will only be afforded, given the likely nature of future high-end war, if Europeans pursue simultaneous integrative and innovative strategies to create a new concept of warfighting that ensures deterrence.

In the interim, Europeans must become far more radical in promoting a truly deep joint strategic (and aggressive) form of defence public–private partnership built on strategic technologies over which the Allies must have complete control from concept to completion. Perhaps the apogee of such a relationship can be found across the Atlantic in the historical example of Lockheed Martin and its so-called Skunkworks during the 1950s. The

Skunkworks was a highly classified 'sensitive industrial relationship' with the US government that produced and operationalized some of the most advanced technologies of its day. Some Skunkworks products had a genuinely revolutionary strategic effect, such as the SR-71 (Blackbird) which was designed in the 1950s and remains to this day the fastest air-breathing manned aircraft ever built. The U-2/TR-1 platform of the same era is still in service undertaking high-altitude, edge-of-the-atmosphere reconnaissance, whilst the F-117 stealth attack fighter-bomber that crushed Saddam's Soviet-built integrated air defence system during the 1991 Gulf War led to today's advanced F-22 air defence fighter and the F-35 strike aircraft. None of these platforms could have been built by the US government alone, nor could they have been built by industry without the US government providing both the requirements and the early investment. This kind of advanced partnership still exists in the US, particularly regarding the development of advanced technologies. Again, Europe?

Interestingly, the Trump administration has failed to capitalize on the power of the US government and the tech industry to further exploit the necessary synergy and capacity for a truly world-beating future force. It is a failure that is most evident in the lack of a real alternative to Chinese 5G technology that is able to compete globally on both price and quality. This should worry Europeans. Such a lack of cohesion and coherence between Washington and its major defence contractors is one factor that is enabling a far more coherent China to compete effectively against US tech giants, although perhaps not as yet challenge the capacity of integrated US/tech to maintain a hyperwar edge into the future if properly organized to such an end. For how long, though, remains a moot point.

There are also other lessons for Europeans from the American future war defence-industrial experience. In-Q-Tel is a flagship US public–private partnership. In-Q-Tel is also a CIA asset. It concentrates on horizon scanning for candidate businesses that could support the US strategic interest and then helps interesting start-ups to scale up, thus accelerating promising technologies and companies. The lesson for Europe is threefold. First, Europeans should create something akin to the US Defense Advanced Research Projects Agency or DARPA, which is at the very cutting edge of defence technology and capability development. A Euro-DARPA would be charged with identifying, capturing, and developing emerging or advanced technologies vital to Europe's future war defence. Second, an EU/Euro version of In-Q-Tel would help close the gulf in Europe between the public defence sector and much of the private sector supply chain and could thus critically assist business in start-ups, scale-ups, and acceleration of defence capability acquisition. Third, an EU/Euro (or Transatlantic) Infrastructure Development Bank could parry, blunt, or block the attractiveness of Chinese strategic investments designed to 'cherry-pick' Europe's best tech companies. Indebtedness to China is a strategic risk that traps European states and their industries into a series of 'bilateral' (one-way) investment relationships with the Chinese at the expense, and to the detriment, of the EU, NATO, and the broader transatlantic relationship.

Critically, developments in disruptive technologies will fundamentally change the character of war with the most profound implications for the defence of Europe. Unlike in the past, it is the private sector and not the traditional defence-industrial sector that is driving much of the future-fast technological change across this sector. The European military response to such change has been extremely slow, as has that of the European defence sector as a whole, which lags far behind developments taking place in the US, China, and Russia. It is vital Europeans collectively develop a new and radical concept of military-technology (mil-tech) development to better understand the role and application of such technologies and incorporate them quickly into strategic defence and force planning.

Crafting the future NATO–EU strategic partnership

The future NATO–EU strategic partnership will be the pillar upon which the future defence of Europe will stand or fall.

The EU has a vital role to play if a future strategic public–private partnership worthy of the name is ever to be generated. This is not least because of the European Commission's growing importance as a mechanism for funnelling national taxpayers' money towards advanced defence-tech projects. The European Defence Agency (EDA) could play a vital role in developing and coordinating projects if it was given the necessary mandate and resources. Given the pressing need, a true test of the EU–NATO strategic partnership is whether it can be applied where politics and investment are most sensitive. For example, Europeans would better harmonize national security and defence requirements within a joint EU–NATO framework. Again, the EDA could play a vital enabling role by providing a specific framework for EU member-states to pragmatically and practically drive forward requirement and specification, promote more effective and efficient project management, and ensure rigorous delivery regimes and timetables. Critically, any such effort would need to take place in close conjunction with NATO's Defence Investment Division and the NATO Support and Procurement Agency. Sadly, in the continued absence of a functioning joint structure, the possibility of at least one real EU–NATO strategic partnership for defence procurement and acquisition at the level of emerging technologies looks bleak. Unfortunately, too many vested national interests continue to block such efforts.

Above all, Europeans need mechanisms in place that can enable them to make the right technology decisions together. Critical to any such process will be the ability to incorporate new technology thinking in defence planning and do it constantly and consistently. New thinking means challenging orthodoxy, which in turn means systematic, independent, and robust 'red-teaming' with institutions not only strong enough to cope with challenge, but confident enough to exploit it. New thinking and innovative thinkers in defence are always disruptive precisely because they tend to be focused on radical defence outcomes and the outputs that must be generated, rather than the 'steady as we decline' inputs beloved of Establishments under pressure from a raft of competing domestic demands.

European strategic enablers will be central to any enhanced European defence. Operations over Libya as early as 2011 revealed the extent to which even Europe's most capable military actors lack such enablers. PESCO and the promotion of pooling and sharing, as well as NATO's Smart Defence and the Connected Forces Initiative, indicate some efforts are underway to close these dangerous gaps in Europe's capability. However, they are too slow and too modest. As a matter of urgency, NATO's Defence Investment Pledge should be reinforced by an EU–NATO Capability Action Plan, with the EU and NATO together seeking to act as defence investment 'brokers' to better forge synergies, harmonization, and efficiencies into the relationship between suppliers and end-users.

If Europeans properly embrace innovation, they could in time build a defence of Europe that is worthy of the name. However, such a defence would require a step-change in strategy, organization, structure, and investment that seems very unlikely in the current circumstances. However, even if the aim of Europeans is to only share a legitimate burden of their own defence, they must, as a matter of urgency, grip ground-breaking defence developments in technology, such as AI, deep learning, the military application of nano- and bio-technologies, the developing and changing threat posed by chemical, biological, and radiological weapons, as well as missile and other kinetic delivery systems and weapons. That will also require of Europeans significant changes over the next decade. What of the here and now? At the very least, NATO and the EU need to do far more together to enhance the military mobility of forces across Europe, which on the eve of a possible future war would be critical to the maintenance of credible deterrence. The good news is that military mobility is one of the thirty-four main PESCO projects, with the Netherlands in the lead. The bad news is that, as with so many such projects, investment in military mobility also suffers from a lack of resources. Indeed, there is (again) a danger that Europeans will set the threshold of defence 'success' low enough to satisfy political rather than strategic needs. If that is the case, any such effort will fail. Even enhanced military mobility requires grand strategic thinking and a strategic public–private partnership because much of Europe's critical infrastructure is these days is privately owned.

Next steps? There are three immediate steps the EU and NATO could take together. First, an audit should be undertaken by both the EU and NATO to better understand what Europeans need, where the real shortfalls can be found, and the level of resource-waste caused by redundant fixed assets and duplication of effort. Second, a Current Assets Framework should be established that would purposively focus on the more efficient use of existing assets and capabilities. Third, a Future Requirements Framework would identify the operational capability the Europeans need and how best to obtain them by 2030.

Sharpening the spear-tip of NATO

NATO will remain critical to Europe's future war defence because NATO is essentially a warfighting, defensive alliance. However, if Europeans are serious about a future war European defence, they will need an alliance able to act not just as a strategic force hub, but also as a responsive force generator, coalition-builder, and force facilitator. Consequently, Europeans need to test themselves against two fundamental future defence questions. What NATO capacity is needed for Europeans to move, fight, and stay fighting during a major emergency against a high-end peer competitor within the European theatre, and quite probably beyond? What further NATO

capacity is needed to integrate quickly large follow-on forces from continental North America?

At the very least, the implicit ambition in both questions would mean
furnishing the Alliance with the ability to reinforce quickly in mass and
move quickly across both the Atlantic and Europe in security. Defender
Europe 20 should have been a beginning, but COVID-19 put paid to that,
revealing yet another vulnerability. In any case, it will be necessary for the
Alliance to go far further than Defender 20 and re-create, in effect, the
twenty-first-century equivalents of massive past NATO exercises such as Big
Lift in 1963, as well as the REFORGER and LIONHEART series of
exercises during the 1970s and 1980s.

The importance of effective exercising and training cannot be overstated.
NATO forces must train as they mean to fight. For too long, NATO
exercises have seldom tested the Alliance to failure because permitting
such failure has been deemed too politically and/or bureaucratically sensitive
for both the member nations and the Alliance. If the Alliance is to be re-
tooled to command and fight future war, it will thus need credible future
warfighting forces, and a collective European future force constructed
without compromise with such an aim in mind. Indeed, the existence of
such a force will be central and pivotal to the credibility of future Alliance
defence and deterrence. The exercising and training of such a force will also
be an essential part of Alliance strategic messaging to deter any imaginable
opponent. Far more 'snap exercises' are also needed to foster a 'fight tonight'
mentality. Too many NATO exercises are devoted to successful visits by
distinguished visitors (DV Days). Whilst such visits are not unimportant, the
urgent need is to test principles and practice in much the same way as then
Soviet and now Russian practice. There is a particularly pressing need for
full-scale European theatre-wide integrated air and missile defence exercises.

NATO also needs a new nuclear strategy and posture. At present, there is
a 'don't ask, don't tell' attitude in many European countries with regard to
American, British, and French nuclear weapons. Worse, German ambivalence over the presence of US nuclear weapons on German soil threatens to
undermine NATO's still critical nuclear policy.[7] Many European leaders

---

7. In May 2020, the US Ambassador to Germany, Richard Grenell, accused Berlin of refusing to
   support NATO's policy on nuclear deterrence. This followed calls by Rolf Mutzenich, the SPD
   leader in the *Bundestag*, for Germany to insist upon the removal of US nuclear weapons from
   German soil. Allied to recent Pew research, it suggests growing German ambivalence about the
   wider transatlantic relationship, Trump or no Trump. President Putin then increased the

recall the mass anti-nuclear demonstrations during the Euromissiles crisis of the 1970s and 1980s. However, new Russian systems, some of which breach the now-deceased 1987 Intermediate Nuclear Forces Treaty, threaten again to cleave a dangerous gap between NATO's conventional and nuclear deterrence, and possibly decouple the US from the defence of Europe. The Alliance's decision-making processes are being streamlined to better cope with such change, and the readiness and survivability of dual-capable conventional-nuclear strike aircraft are being enhanced, particularly now that the F-35 Lightning 2 is being deployed by European forces. Theatre nuclear weapons are also being modernized, with declaratory policy sharpened, and conventional and nuclear exercises strengthened. However, a much more comprehensive and robust concept of nuclear exercises is also needed to underpin the future credibility of nuclear deterrence in Europe. This particular goal will only be achieved by integrating conventional and nuclear forces across the CBRN (chemical, biological, radiological, nuclear) spectrum. Critically, such exercises will also need to involve senior European politicians, as in the past, who might be called upon *in extremis* to make the most extreme decision any politician could ever make. The Alliance critically needs to become far more deterrence-smart by systematically exploring the role of new technologies in deterrence with the goal of creating a new and seamless continuum across the hybrid-cyber-hyperwar mosaic.

Above all, and in the wake of COVID-19, the Alliance critically needs to better understand the nature of future war and the ability of Allied command structures to adapt and operate to effect across cyber warfare, information operations, hybrid threats, and high-end kinetic warfare. This will place particular importance on the ability of the Alliance to make very fast command decisions if it is to respond quickly to short-warning and often ambiguous hybrid attacks, as well as engage an enemy effectively on a new escalation ladder of violence from information warfare to, heaven forbid, nuclear warfare.

Such real adaptation (as opposed to the pretend adaptation in which the Alliance is engaged) will not be easy. NATO is simply the sum of its nations and it is those nations that must give the Alliance the tools to do the job. NATO is an essentially small organization which suffers from a profound inner tension between the ends it is charged with delivering and the ways

political pressure on Germany by announcing that Russia might resort to a first-strike nuclear policy in the event of a conventional military attack on Russia.

and means at its disposal. NATO also makes much about being a 360-degree alliance, and its aim must be to become just such an alliance. Indeed, even whilst the Alliance considers how best to deter, defend, and, if needs be, fight a future war, it must also be able to engage a host of wider missions, most notably responding to catastrophic terrorism or assisting civilian authorities respond to threats such as COVID-19. NATO's role in Rapid Air Movement during the COVID-19 crisis again demonstrated the flexible utility of the Alliance.

In reality, today NATO is three 90-degree alliances—north, east, and south, with the Americans the only really 360-degree force element. Therefore, if NATO is to successfully fight terrorism (and there is an important debate to be had about exactly what role NATO could or should play therein) and manage crises beyond NATO's borders, as well as prepare to engage in high-end future war, it will at the very least need a far greater capacity to generate disparate forces that are able to move fast, fight hard, stay longer, and stabilize large areas. NATO will also have to add a further dimension—digital.

Furthermore, the Alliance's challenge to Europe's south must not be underestimated, much of which remains decidedly analogue. NATO is called upon to help train the forces of partners, build capacity and professionalism into those forces, and thus project stability. Given the dangerous mix of instability and suffering across the Middle East and North Africa and Sub-Saharan Africa, which COVID-19 has only made worse, and with climate change possibly leading to between 10 and 50 million climate refugees by 2070, this whole concept of projecting stability also needs to become far more ambitious than it is today. The long-term effect of climate migration could well become *the* greatest threat to Europe and its society. Given that strategic context, just how could the Alliance strike the series of balances such a range of threats demand, given that all of them are resource-hungry?

An enduring dilemma for European defence will be how to generate and pay for the forces and resources needed to meet the pan-security and defence challenge Europe faces. In short, the Alliance and its leaders are going to have to make hard choices. Indeed, if NATO is ever to refocus on its core warfighting competence and thus maintain credible defence and deterrence, limits to Alliance action will also need to be set. Such trade-offs again point to the EU–NATO strategic partnership even if both institutions are resourced by many of the same states. The EU is far better placed to bear much of the burden of promoting long-term stability in and around Europe, but only if it begins to match deeds with words.

The post-Cold War peace is over. Only by refocusing the Alliance on its core mission of defence and deterrence will NATO work to effect. Whilst effective Alliance planning will go a long way to solving many of the problems caused by an expanding NATO task-list, the limited forces and resources available to it mean that choices now have to be made. Therefore, rather than loading ever more missions and tasks onto NATO, the Alliance should start considering which ones could be abandoned. Critically, the Alliance needs to become far more rigorous, robust, and responsive across a wide range of future war contingencies and begin the process of preparing for them.

Given the nature of future war, NATO must in an emergency delegate significantly more command authority to the pinnacle of NATO's military chain of command—Supreme Allied Commander Europe (SACEUR). Democracies, for very understandable constitutional and proprietary reasons, prefer to limit the decision-making senior military officers are permitted. However, given the almost incestuous complex strategic relationship between hybrid war, cyber war, and hyperwar and the speed of command it will take, a new command mandate and structure will be needed that goes significantly beyond the recent NATO Command Structure reform if the credibility of NATO defence and deterrence is to be preserved.

Even relatively low-level crisis management exercises reinforce the need for early delegation of command authority in an emergency. This is especially so in the case of short-warning and ambiguous hybrid attacks. If not, given the nature and escalatory speed of 5D warfare, there is a danger that the Alliance could see political leadership, the supreme command authority, quickly decapitated. Indeed, without such reform the effective use of nuclear coercion and other forms of blackmail could present NATO leaders with a fait accompli, all because the Alliance was unable to come to decisions quickly enough about what course of action to take.

Effective strategic communications will thus be a critical enabler of such a defence. Such communications will also be central to the growing range and variety of strategic partnerships, including between the Alliance and the private sector. In this information age, when data richness and data security are so vital to any institution, the secure broadcasting of mission-critical data is already the *sine qua non* of success. Resiliency against ever more sophisticated and dangerous cyber-attacks is not a luxury, but a core defence requirement, and not just for the Alliance. National European military and civilian systems, particularly those of critical private sector partners, also need to become far more robust and far better integrated into the Alliance and its command structures, given the changed nature of information flows that will be generated by future war.

Perhaps the greatest mind-set change that will be needed is for Europeans to realize that for all the centrality of the Americans to NATO, the future Alliance is dependent on choices Europeans make. Indeed, to realize a properly adapted NATO, the European Allies will need to play a far larger role in non-Article 5 missions as well as begin preparations for a future war Article 5 defence. Only NATO could deliver such a force because it is, and will continue to be, the conduit for American military power in support of European defence. Indeed, the only way for NATO to remain credible, and with it the future war defence of Europe, is for North American and European forces to move closer together, even if at the same time Europeans also slowly become both more strategically responsible and autonomous from the US. Counterintuitively, a more responsible, autonomous Europe would probably also become a better ally of the US. A truly strategically autonomous Europe would likely be a Europe far more willing to back words with forces and resources and build a full-spectrum military Europe, COVID-19 or no.

Future war will also demand of NATO and its European members the ability to jointly protect the so-called Global Commons, in the air, at sea, in cyber space, and in outer space, because future war will be fought in all of those domains. Again, only NATO could provide the necessary synergy with US forces that, unless there is a step-change in European thinking (and action), will undoubtedly lead such efforts. For the Americans, a European capability at this level of military engagement would also help maintain US strength in domains that are equally vital to America's security. The political utility of such a force would thus match its military utility, and reinforce a vital sense amongst the American people that Europeans were finally and willingly prepared to share burdens equitably.

NATO's ability to act as a force multiplier and coalition-generator would also be vital. For over seventy years the Alliance has developed a unique understanding of and capacity for the generation and command of complex coalitions. This experience was demonstrated to good effect between 2001 and 2015 in Afghanistan where a range of non-European democracies used NATO Standards to do coalition business. Finland and Sweden have also adopted NATO Standards, whilst beyond Europe's borders, Middle Eastern partners, such as Jordan and the United Arab Emirates, and Australia, Japan, New Zealand, and South Korea in the Indo-Pacific, have all by and large done the same to ensure military coalitions function.

However, NATO's most compelling reality is the one many Europeans find hardest to accept: the future defence of Europe will ultimately rest on Europeans. NATO's future war spear-tip will thus need to be a European spear-tip forged by a deep joint European future force that balances strategy, capability, technology, and affordability and is able to operate at the high end of conflict across the multi-domains of air, sea, land, space, cyber, information, and knowledge, and is both projectable and protectable. Such a force would have the necessary mass and hyper-manoeuvrability necessary to fight a high-end future war in and around Europe, and to operate closely and effectively with the future US future force. To that end, such a combined European force would probably look not unlike the multinational Anglo-American-led force that emerged during World War Two, when Allied forces operated under the command of Supreme Headquarters Allied Expeditionary Force or SHAEF.[8] Indeed, SHAEF provided the blueprint of what eventually became SHAPE (Supreme Headquarters Allied Powers Europe), which first stood up in 1950.[9] Interestingly, both headquarters were first commanded by US General, later President, and Supreme Allied Commander Dwight D. Eisenhower, which also provided essential continuity of effort and purpose. The key to the effectiveness of SHAEF was the speed and fairness of command between the Allies, even if the forces in the field remained firmly under American or British command. This approach was underpinned by an enlightened US approach towards its

---

8. Stephen E. Ambrose, in his excellent 1994 study on D-Day, wrote, 'Thanks to the clear-cut command authority, a single-minded clarity of purpose pervaded Supreme Headquarters Allied Expeditionary Force (SHEAF), in sharp contrast to the situation at OB West and Army Group B. A factor in creating unity at SHAEF was Eisenhower's relationship with his immediate subordinates, which contrasted sharply with Rommel's command structure'. The danger today is that NATO's command structure is more akin to that of Rommel than Eisenhower. Stephen E. Ambrose (1994) *D-Day, June 6, 1944: The Climactic Battle of World War II* (London: Simon & Schuster), p. 69.

9. The transition from SHAEF to SHAPE was not at all seamless. As an insightful 2013 Lawrence Kaplan analysis reveals, it took four years between the 1949 creation of NATO and the 1953 establishment of SHAPE, driven mainly by the lack of Allied command unity during the 1952–4 Korean War. See Lawrence Kaplan (2013) *NATo before the Korean War* (Kent, OH: Kent State University Press).

junior British partner embodied and personified by Eisenhower.[10] Relations between the Americans, British, and others were never easy and such tensions helped create the political conditions for military disasters, such as the British-led Operation Market Garden in September 1944, which was as much about intra-allied politics as ending the war in Europe quickly. And yet it prevailed.

A European future force would doubtless suffer more because there would be no one dominant power. However, President Macron's idea of the collective European Intervention Initiative offers a possible template for an intergovernmental solution to such a dilemma. And, whilst a common European force would be more efficient in theory, such a collective force would be more practical in reality. In the short term, Europeans should focus on defence synergies that help better integrate combat support and combat support services, so-called 'tail' formations, whilst leaving 'teeth' formations essentially national in nature.[11] Over the medium term, the goal must be the European future force. NATO's future depends on it, and so does the future war, future defence of Europe.

Future war and the defence of Europe

This book has six core messages: COVID-19 is likely to accelerate change and magnify existing systemic tensions; the global balance of military power is shifting fast and eroding America's strategic dominance; technology is fast changing the character of warfare and will make it easier for Europe's adversaries, large and small, to exert complex strategic coercion on it; NATO is not a military EU—it is a warfighting defensive alliance that must refocus on its core task of defence and deterrence; NATO must better use its extensive defence planning to prepare to fight a hi-tech future war throughout the hybrid war, cyber war, hyperwar mosaic; and NATO and the EU should be organized around three 'dual'-tracks. These are: first, to enable a new and effective model of comprehensive security so that

---

10. Eisenhower's role as honest broker between US and British interests and commanders did not always work. Perhaps the main reason for the failure of the ambitious Operation Market Garden in September 1944 was that Eisenhower refused to commit the weight of forces the operation needed to succeed, particularly at the spear-tip in Arnhem. He was under intense pressure from Washington, and his fellow American Generals Bradley and Patton, to support the push by US Third Army further south in Belgium.

11. Combat support provides fire and operational support to forces in combat, whilst combat service support sustains forces directly engaging an enemy.

post-COVID-19 human (health) security and national defence can both be strengthened; second, to realize a new balance between the military power projection upon which future defence will be mounted with enhanced people protection through greater resilience and redundancy of systems; and third, to engage Russia with both defensive strength and engaged and sustained dialogue. In the wake of the COVID-19 crisis, Americans and Europeans need to wean their critical supply chains off dependence on China and identify strategic technologies over which the Allies have complete control, from concept to completion. To that end, Europe's technological and industrial base must be exploited across the civil and military spectrum to better prepare NATO for a future war defence.

The driver of defence policy will be a new European agenda. Such an agenda would necessarily range across a raft of instruments and conclusions: the need for a vital new comprehensive balance between human security and European defence in the wake of the COVID-19 crisis; the recognition that strategic autonomy will only come as a consequence of strategic responsibility; collective action, not common action, is the way forward; the need for Europeans to construct a first, fast-response, high-end future force able to operate to effect across the multi-domains of future war in and around Europe to enable Europeans to grip twenty-first-century high-end warfighting; and, above all, a recognition that European leaders must lead.

On the eve of World War Two, British historian Edward Hallett Carr wrote in his seminal work, *The Twenty Years' Crisis, 1919–1939*, that,

> We can describe as utopian in the right sense (i.e. performing the proper function of a utopia in proclaiming an ideal to be aimed at, though not wholly attainable) the desire to eliminate the element of power and to base the bargaining process of peaceful change on a common feeling of what is just and reasonable. But shall we also keep in mind the realist view of peaceful change as an adjustment to the changed relations of power; since the party which is able to bring power to bear normally emerges successful from operations of peaceful change, we shall do our best to make ourselves as powerful as we can. In practice, we know that peaceful change can only be achieved through a compromise between the utopian concept of a common feeling of right and the realist conception of a mechanical adjustment to a changed equilibrium of force. That is why a successful foreign policy must oscillate between the apparently opposite poles of force and appeasement.[12]

---

12. E.H. Carr (1964 edn) *The Twenty Years' Crisis, 1919–1939* (New York: Harper & Row), pp. 222–3.

This book is not a call to militarize Europe; far from it. Indeed, much of the effort will be diplomatic, such as seeking to normalize relations with Belarus so it can fend off some future union with Russia which would further tip the regional military-strategic balance in Russia's favour. Rather, and in the wake of the COVID-19 crisis, it is a call for a new European realism allied to newly grounded American strategic modesty. Both Americans and Europeans need to understand together that great forces of change are underway, much of it good, but like all such big change it has a big, dark side too. Therefore, if a new peace-bearing equilibrium, the motherlode of peace, is to be found and mined, it will be by Americans and Europeans together striking a new balance between defence and diplomacy. For that to happen, Europeans need to abandon the dangerous 'utopia' that covenants without reasonably relevant swords are of any use, whilst Americans need to finally abandon any romantic notions of isolationism and/or unilateralism as the shortest route to an American peace in what was once meant to be the American century.

In March 1946, Winston Churchill said, 'When American military men approach some serious situation they are wont to write at the head of their directive the words "over-all strategic concept." There is wisdom in this, as it leads to clarity of thought. What then is the over-all strategic concept which we should inscribe today? It is nothing less than the safety and welfare, the freedom and progress, of all the homes and families of all the men and women in all the lands'.[13] That simple statement made all those years ago has stood the test of time and encapsulates the future war, future defence dilemma of Europe's challenge today.

The defence of Europe is not quite yet at peril, although the Baltic States may wish to disagree. A claim one hears in Brussels from time to time is that Europeans are more willing to live with risk than Americans. That may also be so, but how much risk is it reasonable to ask European citizens to endure, even in their blissful ignorance? When does risk become threat? When is 'living with risk' simply ignorance of threat? Is ignorance a defence? Perhaps the most important question is thus: is the level of risk to Europe manageable, or is the future of Europe again being gambled with?

In a way the tragedy, or perhaps the tragedy to come, is that too much of Europe's defence has been words—past, present, future. NATO and its

---

13. https://winstonchurchill.org/resources/speeches/1946-1963-elder-statesman/the-sinews-of-peace.

members need to go far beyond current planning. Even if the 2014 Wales, 2016 Warsaw, and 2018 Brussels Summit are successfully operationalized, NATO could in time fail because of the exigencies of COVID-19 as political resolve weakens and the military power (capability, capacity, and technology) of illiberal states and groups outstrips that of Europe's liberal states. Critically, if the EU is to help properly organize the European effort into something akin to strategic responsibility, it will need to end its own PESCO fantasy that ever more ambition with ever less money will ever realize the security and defence Europeans need and deserve. If such practice continues, Europeans will simply be deluding themselves that they are safe until one day, as so often before in Europe, that terrible day of shock arrives. Is that European strategic autonomy? The ultimate paradox for Europeans and their future defence is thus: even if the US remains critical to the future defence of Europe, as it does, and only when Europeans themselves learn again to stop fearing their own hard power and once again carry a sufficiently big and legitimate military stick will the defence of Europeans be properly assured.

Therefore, for Americans and Europeans together to fulfil the future war, future defence mission in the twenty-first-century security environment, across the hybrid war, cyber war, hyperwar mosaic, the transatlantic relationship must remain central even if it must also evolve and reform if it is to survive and flourish. To that end, Europeans will, at the very least, have to devote far larger means in pursuit of far greater strategic ends via far more integrated civil and military ways. In other words, Europeans need a grand strategy to match the future defence of Europe against the future war that is coming. That, in turn, will demand a profound change of the European strategic mind-set, and an even more profound shift in Europe's strategic assumptions. It will also need European leaders with the political vision and courage to rediscover their first duty to their respective citizens—safety and security.

Ultimately, future war is hyperwar: war at the level of such speed of strategy, technology, and destruction that its effects could be worse than World War Two. Humans must remain at the centre of decision-making, but make no mistake that if decision-making is dependent on them, defence could well fail. Human-augmenting 'intelligent machines' are the future of warfare, whether Europeans like it or not. European leaders need to be confronted with this dangerous reality, and properly educated about what it means for their respective security and defence policies, above all for the peoples for whom and to whom they are responsible. They need urgently to understand something else, for all that technology will afford Europeans any such defence, it will ultimately fall again to the airmen, sailors, and soldiers who will remain the first and last lines of defence. Too many Europeans have abandoned or are abandoning the warfighting ethos, including the ethos of close combat, vital to the successful conduct of war. The profession of arms is not an adjunct to management consulting, or a branch of IT. It is about fighting and winning, but, above all, it is about preventing war—future war. It is about gaining and winning the Hard Yards.

In 1919 the British government established the so-called Ten-Year Rule by which Britain could assume safely in the wake of the victory in World War One that for a decade the country would not need to wage major war. In 1932, on the eve of Hitler's rise to power, the Committee of the Chiefs of the Imperial Staff scrapped the Ten-Year Rule, and in February 1934, in spite of Britain still being mired in economic depression, London began the great rearmament programmes that six years later were to stave off defeat and laid the foundations for Britain's role in the eventual defeat of the Nazis. Too many of Europe's contemporary leaders are locked into a virtual Ten-Year Rule, believing falsely that another major war in Europe is impossible. They are wrong, and dangerously so.

Professor Sir Lawrence Freedman once made a distinction between 'wars of choice' and 'wars of necessity'. He wrote,

> 'necessity' refers not so much to the actual decision but to the need to make a decision, between situations when there are doubts about whether there is any reason to consider military action and situations so dire that consideration is unavoidable. There are clearly some wars that can be considered more on a 'take it or leave it' basis, in which the most vital national interests are not engaged, although these are matters of degree. In such circumstances, 'discretionary wars' capture the issue. The element of discretion means that inherent costs and dangers of any war are viewed against different standards to wars in which the issue is self-evident.[14]

Imagine a war that takes place simultaneously across a spectrum from discretion to existence, from disease to mass destruction, from hybrid war to hyperwar, via cyber war. Imagine a war in which a disease like COVID-19

---

14. Sir Lawrence Freedman (2017) 'Force and the International Community: Blair's Chicago Speech and the Criteria for Intervention', *International Relations*, vol. 31/2 (London: Sage), p. 111.

has been deliberately employed as a prelude to war. Then, it is future war that is being imagined.

Above all, if Europeans need Americans, Americans need Europeans. As China and Russia contest American leadership, Washington's need for capable allies will increase, not diminish. The European allies will remain at the forefront not just of American strategic concerns, but also American strategic partnerships. And, even on a practical level, the advantages afforded US strategic posture by having forces and resources pre-positioned in Europe will remain vital for access to, and intelligence of, a host of regions critically important to US security and defence.

Europe's future war bottom line? European defence and deterrence will rest on the ability of Europeans to again generate a twenty-first-century heavy force, armed with a suite of twenty-first-century force projection and power protection enablers, with assured access and a robust capacity established to receive American and Canadian forces back into the European theatre. Like it or not, and given the diverse threats posed by COVID-19 and future war, this is just one of those moments in European history when Europeans are going to have to pay heed to all their security and defence needs, and spend far more on them.

Think big, Europe. Future war big. Your future defence depends on it because no European can any longer be sure that a major war could not again happen in Europe. If nothing else, it is time for Europeans to scrap the virtual Ten-Year Rule too many of them observe. For, as Niccolo Machiavelli once said, 'All courses of action are risky. So prudence is not in avoiding danger (it is impossible) but calculating risk and acting decisively. Make mistakes of ambition, not mistakes of sloth. Develop the strength to do things, not the strength to suffer'.[15]

15. Niccolo Machiavelli (2008 edn) 'The Prince', edited by Maurizio Viroli (Oxford: Oxford University Press).

Scenario 2

Europe defended

COVID-29

It all started with COVID-29. Early in 2030 a new pandemic had spread across the world. It was similar to COVID-19, which had locked Europe down in 2020 and brought healthcare systems close to collapse, only worse. This particular strain of pandemic was extremely contagious. Strangely, Russian forces seemed unaffected. There was a reason. Even more surprising was how little Allied forces were affected. There was also a reason.

It was mid-April 2030 when Jim had received a text message during leave to report back immediately to Fort Hood. For days now he had been recovering from a mild dose of COVID-29, having contracted the illness during an exercise with British forces in late 2029, but against which he had received a cocktail of anti-virals and a new, experimental vaccination. Since COVID-19 the US, in conjunction with Britain's Defence Science and Technology Laboratory, had been working on a range of vaccines to combat possible engineered mutations of COVID-19. They were not perfect but at least they enabled a sufferer to function. However, Jim had other things on his mind. Unlike COVID-19, COVID-29 also affected young people in huge numbers. It did not kill them, but it laid them low and he worried for his wife and kids.

As a front-line combat soldier, and an experienced non-commissioned officer, Jim also knew that in another European emergency he would be one of the first to go overseas, possibly alongside the US Marines of Regimental Combat Team 2, which was being hastily assembled at Camp Lejeune, North Carolina, and with which Jim's team had been working up for some time. Jim was a very proud member of the elite US Army's 'Ironhorse' Brigade, and had twice been deployed to Europe as part of an armoured Brigade Combat Team (BCT), the spear-tip of American fighting power.

Jim left his worried wife with the usual assurances that it was just another scare and that he would be home in no time. But this was different. When he got back to Fort Hood it was clear he was walking into a full-blown crisis. There was none of the usual 'let's tick the box and go through the motions' stuff. This was for real. Very quickly, Jim's force had been joined by other BCTs which had been earmarked for trans-shipment to Bremerhaven, Germany. Jim quickly learnt that having arrived in Germany, the plan was to travel across Europe by rail, which worried him. From past experience Jim knew that Europe's rail system was simply not up to the task of getting his force forward-deployed quickly or securely enough. Military mobility?

The decision had also been taken by the 'brass' to use requisitioned civilians' ships and escort them across the Atlantic, such was the parlous state of US fast military sealift. With tensions so high, Jim also knew this was risky. The US Navy was dangerously overstretched, with the bulk of its forces in the Indo-Pacific theatre. Jim felt better after leaving Norfolk as his convoy had been met by an impressive escort, composed of the latest USN air, surface, and sub-surface units, many of them unmanned autonomous escorts operating above and below the water. There was also an advanced Allied unit composed mainly of European warships, together with British and French nuclear attack submarines.

The Task Group had been designated NTG2 (NATO Task Group 2), albeit firmly under US command. As NTG2 crossed the Atlantic at around 30 knots, fast jets, helicopters, and drones from two escorting carriers, the USS George H.W. Bush and the French carrier, Charles de Gaulle, criss-crossed the air all around them. The force was armed with the latest anti-submarine and air defence capability, much of it driven by the artificial intelligence (AI) packages that been fitted to Allied ships over the past year, all of which were designed to defend just such a large and vital convoy against some of Russia's latest weapons, including the long-range hypersonic missiles that Jim had read about. The Russians may even have tried to penetrate the perimeter defence that surrounded him, but Jim saw and heard nothing.

Once embarked and underway, Jim and his men settled down into a sort of routine during which constant weapons checks and exercising on deck were interrupted only for ORPs (operation ration packs) and fitful sleep. They engaged in friendly and at times not-so-friendly banter with the Marines on board. 'Dumb bastards!' Jim had thought, ' . . . but brave bastards'. Still, Jim could smell the apprehension. Some men talked too much, whilst others talked too little.

In fact, the voyage to Bremerhaven went surprisingly smoothly. They had taken the northern route and sailed close to Cape Wrath at the very tip of Scotland. As they approached the UK, more aircraft had arrived, affording Jim additional protection, this time launched from the land away to Jim's south and from Norway to his east. Jim *noticed something else he had never seen before: swarms of drones far out to sea which seemed to track NTG2. As they approached Europe there would be an explosion every now and then, but to Jim it was as though NTG2 was within a bubble, a bubble that moved with him.*

As they arrived at Bremerhaven, they were quickly disembarked. They had landed alongside a powerful British strike force. The British 'yanked Jim's chain'. 'Nice to see you yanks. On time for a change?' one British officer had quipped. Pompous jerk. To Jim, the offloading process seemed a well-oiled machine as they quickly boarded special trains which, to Jim's surprise, took advantage of Europe's high-speed rail network to move fast to the east. Throughout their journey Jim repeatedly noticed those strange swarms of drones and aircraft off in the medium distance seemingly tracking him. It was as though he had his own personal protection. Jim was not aware of the major AI and cyber war underway to protect the infrastructure upon which his progress depended. Nor was he aware of the impressive, just completed German-led investment in Europe's critical infrastructure, including the hardened railways upon which he travelled that enabled fast military mobility across Europe in an emergency, and which had helped drive Europe out of the post-COVID-19 economic slump.

Like all soldiers on the eve of combat, there was anticipation, a tightening of Jim's stomach . . . and a firming of resolve. This was mixed with boredom, uncertainty as to what lay ahead, and the adrenalin-edged smelly expectation that fear generates. Would it happen? Could it happen? Will I survive? What about my family? Above all, will I let myself and the boys down? Over and over again Jim's mind mulled the eternally mullable. It was a relief simply to go through another drill or to again check weapons as Germany merged into Poland. Every now and then he would linger for a nostalgic moment on the last images he had of his wife and kids, but he found it better to simply shut 'normal' life out of his mind. In any case, there had been little 'normal' about life since 2020 and COVID-19.

Salafist chaos: resisted and restored

In March 2029 suicide bombers had attacked Athens, Madrid, and Rome Fiumicino airports. Some one hundred Jihadis had then opened fire on the faithful and tourists in the Vatican, murdered the Swiss Guard, and then sealed off the Holy See from the rest of Rome. Semtex explosives smuggled into the Vatican in backpacks had been placed in the Basilica and detonated, bringing down the mighty dome of St Peters. A little-known Salafist calling himself Abdul al-Adel claimed he was the cousin of now dead one-time al-Qaeda leader Said al-Adel (real name Mohammed Ibrahim Makkawi, a former colonel in the Egyptian Army), who had announced in St Peters the creation of the Islamic State of Europe. Bizarrely, he had spoken with a southern English accent, before he had begun to publicly behead hostages in front of the shattered Basilica, starting with captured clergy.

Al-Adel had hoped to inspire a Salafist uprising across Europe. However, there was a fundamental flaw in his plan: the mistaken belief that many millions of Muslims across Europe, both citizens and refugees alike, would support him. The massive majority of European Muslims were simply appalled.

Muslim citizens also worked with hard-pressed European police and intelligence services to help construct a picture of the situation, specifically to identify those actively involved in the attacks, and those at risk of being subverted by them. The COVID-19 crisis had actually improved inter-communal relations, assisted by the changed attitude of many European governments. In 2021, the EU and its member-states had created 'safe channels' for migrants to enter Europe, so by 2029 those with a right to stay were housed, whilst those with no right to stay were humanely deported with the recipient countries offered aid and support. Migrants were also treated with respect, and seen to be so, whilst other Europeans were reassured that migration was being properly managed.

The EU also moved to support the so-called front-line states by adapting Permanent Structured Cooperation (PESCO) to strengthen FRONTEX. A major new European counter-insurgency force (EUROCOIN) was created from Europe's many gendarmerie-type forces and trained to deal with threats to European stability short of all-out war. Europe's criminal and military intelligence services had also been reorganized and now acted through an EU intelligence brokerage based in Brussels which was called EURODOMINT. The new agency offered critical support to the front-line states by helping them to better understand the scale of the threats they faced, and more critically how best to deal with them.

A new European war?

Russia had hoped that China would support their ambitions in Europe. However, whilst the United States was still mired in tensions with China, the threat of a systemic conflict in the Indo-Pacific theatre had receded. After a shaky start, China had adopted a more conciliatory and constructive posture in the wake of COVID-19. In 2021, Beijing had finally acknowledged that COVID-19 had originated in Wuhan and that it was making wholesale changes to animal welfare practices to ensure it did not happen again. In 2022, the US and China had normalized trade relations which helped lift the world economy out of a sharp, post-COVID-19 'V'-shaped recession. Many Western companies based in China had still 're-shored' back to either the US or Europe, but globalization had become a more reciprocal set of economic relationships than prior to 2020. Washington's concerns about military overstretch had also been eased by the performance of its European Allies and the ongoing programme of defence reform that had been organized by and around the UK, France, and Germany. A revitalized EU–NATO Strategic Partnership had also strengthened European defence and, in spite of COVID-19, Europeans had not only fulfilled their commitment to increase their defence spending to 2 per cent, with 20 per cent investment spent annually on modernization, but Europe's much-heralded 'Strategic Public–Private Partnership' was already paying dividends. Europe's use of defence modernization to help avoid a post-COVID-19 economic slump had worked, even if many European states remained mired in public debt.

Equipment and weapons systems bought from the Americans were steadily being reinforced with advanced European 'kit' that for the first time was being 'fielded' rapidly. The relationship between human security and national defence in Europe had also become more seamless as new technologies increased both the efficiency and effectiveness of both, whilst significantly reducing the cost. In the political arena, Brexit had finally been resolved by a new political settlement with the UK so that by 2029 Europe was far more politically and strategically cohesive than it was during the 'teens'. Europe's enhanced defence investment was also leading towards some European strategic autonomy, helped by the improved pooling and sharing of European strategic air and sea lift, and allied to new legal requirements on European airlines and ship-owners to provide aircraft and ships in an emergency. Regular deployments of European forces in support of robust US 'freedom of navigation' exercises in the Indo-Pacific theatre had also reinforced a growing sense that the US-led 'West' was no longer a place, but an idea built on solidarity between democracies the world over. It was a triumph not just of European strategic realism, but of American statecraft.

Critically, for seven years European forces had been gearing up to act as effective fast, first, high-end responders in the event of a major attack on Europe. That attack had now come. With President Putin's health failing, and the Kremlin riven by a power struggle between two factions—one with links to the FSB and the other with its roots in the Army—Russia had become dangerously unpredictable. A post-COVID-19 economic crash had been caused by the collapse of the oil price, but the regime had refused to scale back the security state, the cost of which was ruinous, and the Russian economy simply never recovered. Unable to reform either the economy or society for fear of what it might lead to, the Kremlin faced internal chaos. The Kremlin was now lashing out in the desperate hope of shoring up the failing regime by invoking Russian nationalism.

In July 2029 Russia had moved a large formation of naval infantry (Marines) to Pechanga, close to Russia's short border with Norway, and strengthened its forces facing Finland and Sweden. Alarmed, Helsinki, Oslo, and Stockholm had jointly called on the Alliance for support. Tensions had also increased in the Baltic Sea, as more and more reports came in of Russian forces close to the strategically vital Swedish island of Gotland. On 10 August, as tensions had increased, and by way of response, the North Atlantic Council had ordered the Supreme Allied Commander Europe (SACEUR) to take all necessary steps to demonstrate to Moscow the Alliance's determination to defend its borders, and key partners.

And then came North Cape. NATO Task Group 1 (NTG1) had been working up to full operating capability for some years and was despatched by SACEUR to demonstrate NATO's resolve and intent and to deter Russia's still powerful Northern Fleet from attempting to interdict Allied reinforcements as they crossed the Atlantic. NTG1 was organized around two British heavy aircraft-carriers, the command ship, HMS Queen Elizabeth, and HMS Prince of Wales, both armed with the latest Sea Ceptor 2B, Britain's hypersonic ship defence system. NTG1 included ships, aircraft, and submarines from the UK, Canada, France, Germany, the Netherlands, and Norway. Critically, NTG1 was also supported by the Zumwalt-class 'stealth' destroyer, USS Lyndon B. Johnson, which acted as a form of 'picket ship' some way from the fleet, and yet was still able to protect and assure it. NATO-assigned Global Hawk maritime surveillance drones monitored threats operating across the bandwidth spectrum, whilst RAF and Royal Norwegian Air Force Boeing 'Poseidon' P8 maritime patrol aircraft, armed with an array of intelligent anti-submarine systems, offered a further layer of forward-deployed force protection. Beneath the fleet two French Navy Barracuda-class nuclear attack submarines, the Duquay-Trouin and Tourville, acted as sub-surface sentinels, able to operate both as part of NTG1 or wholly independently from it. On this occasion, the two submarines were also acting as platforms and command nodes for fully automated 'defence-bots', reinforced by US AI-powered autonomous combat submersibles which acted as submarine 'pickets' for the NATO force above. They were also capable of launching an array of smart torpedoes and AI-powered autonomous aerial combat vehicles—super-drones.

The Second Battle of North Cape

At 0430 hours on 15 August, the Second Battle of North Cape began. Weapons and defence systems on board HMS Queen Elizabeth, driven by a range of AI defence packages, had suddenly surged into life, as the Russians tried and failed to breach the cyber-defences of NTG1.

At 0431 hours, an autonomous Russian underwater stealth platform launched a swarm of intelligent, autonomous, flying armed 'attack-bots'. Immediately, the Task Group put up an automated layered defence, whilst the on-board super-computers launched a counter-swarm of 'defence-bots', reinforced by the latest missile and 'goalkeeper' defence systems.

At 0432 hours, the commodore commanding NTG1 ordered the fleet to engage full, automatic defence. Interlocking, digitally networked systems on board all the ships engaged the enemy, creating a multi-domain 'defence sphere' around the fleet, on, above, and below the water, as well as in the cyber domain. At the same time, autonomous underwater bots began to systematically search for the source of the Russian attack.

At 0433 hours, using 'block sonar/radar technology', a hi-def 3D virtual picture of the fleet and its surrounds emerged, and two Russian Yasen-class nuclear attack submarines were identified, together with a Sevastopol-class unmanned underwater launch platform. They had been hiding in a cold layer of water that would in the past have afforded them silent anonymity. No longer.

At 0434 hours, now fully technology-autonomous, NTG1 launched a wave of intelligent attack-bots, the twenty-first-century descendants of World War Two torpedoes and depth charges. Several 'pods' were also launched by the two French nuclear attack submarines.

At 0434 hours, HMS Queen Elizabeth scrambled 809 Squadron, Fleet Air Arm, whilst HMS Prince of Wales scrambled the embarked US Marine Corps Squadron VMA-542 'Tigers' and their F-35B Lightning II5 (ER) fighters to provide top cover against any possible Russian manned air incursion. Both ships also deployed some thirty EH-101 Merlin 7 helicopters, together with a host of data-link and weapons drones. In fact, the manned systems were little more than back-up for increasingly sophisticated, long-range, AI-autonomous systems, a further layer of defensive redundancy . . . just in case.

At 0437 hours, three enormous underwater explosions were registered to the north and west of the Task Group. All a now shocked and alarmed Moscow heard was silence . . . as NTG1 forged forward.

Land war

As HMS Queen Elizabeth came under attack off North Cape, a series of ongoing Russian Army exercises underway in and around Kaliningrad and Belarus, on the

Ukrainian border, and in the Black Sea suddenly intensified and expanded. 'Little Green Men' were reported in the Baltic States seizing vital installations. The 10,000 NATO troops in the Enhanced Forward Presence battlegroups reacted, together with their Estonian, Latvian, and Lithuanian allies. Then, what the Russians call non-linear warfare began to turn into real warfare, as the equivalent of four army corps, or some 120,000 troops, in the Western Military Oblast moved into the Baltic States.

Two weeks prior, the North Atlantic Council (NAC) had put both the Very High Readiness Joint Task Force (VJTF) of some 15,000 troops and the enhanced NATO Response Force (e-NRF) of some 60,000 troops on two days' Notice to Move, and ordered the nine High Readiness Force (HRF) headquarters to stand by, including the British-led Allied Rapid Reaction Corps. For the first time, SACEUR and his staff were given devolved command authority to act further. This act alone strengthened NATO's response and had enabled Alliance forces to begin moving quickly to reinforce NATO's forward presence, whilst another 180 battalions across Europe had also begun to move. Many of these units had been re-equipped since 2020 with critical fires and logistics packages, and by an exercising and training regime that kept them at a level of readiness that enabled them to move quickly in an emergency.

NATO had also finally begun to realize its goal of a 360-degree alliance. Whilst many of the forces of the southern Allies had their eyes firmly fixed on the south of the Mediterranean, Alliance leaders were confident new EU policing capabilities would further assist them in any such crisis in Strategic Direction South, enabling the Alliance to focus on the high-end crisis with Russia. In any case, the new ACO Heavy Mobile Force provided a powerful reserve and was able to quickly move and support forces to the east and south.

Suddenly, Russian forces seized land either side of the Lithuanian and Polish borders between Kaliningrad and Belarus along the so-called Suwalki Corridor, over some 65 kilometres in length. Moscow cited the failure of both Vilnius and Warsaw to agree to guaranteed Russian land access to Kaliningrad. The Russian force build-up in the Baltic States also continued. The NAC again met in emergency session and, at Poland and Lithuania's request, issued an ultimatum: unless Russian forces were withdrawn from NATO territory in twenty-four hours, the Alliance would declare a breach of Article 5 of the Washington Treaty and invoke collective defence. Russia immediately responded by putting Iskandr M and Kalibr 'short'- and medium-range nuclear weapons on full alert, thus threatening a nuclear attack on European cities. In the wake of the NAC meeting the Kremlin also cited a 'vital' Russian need to consolidate a 'peace buffer' between Russia and a 'clearly aggressive NATO'. Russian Spetsnaz, naval infantry, and airmobile forces also moved to seize vital areas of the three Baltic States.

But then the tide turned. The Russian Navy suffered a major and surprising defeat off Norway's North Cape at the hands of a mainly European force, which unsettled the Kremlin. Estonian, Latvian, and Lithuanian forces, together with their NATO Allies, put up an effective delaying action in the woods of all three countries and Russian forces were also unable to penetrate the force protection of the VJTF and the eNRF as they moved into place, Vitally, heavy US reinforcements made their way quickly and securely to Europe. The speed and strength of the NATO response surprised the Kremlin. By 2029 Allied deterrence comprised layers of advanced, automated conventional and air defence systems, deeply embedded in offensive and defensive cyber forces. Indeed, the Alliance had, in effect, reinvented the concept of deterrence.

Crash and counter-crash!

As HMS Queen Elizabeth and her Task Group were defeating the Russian Navy, the electricity grid crashed across much of Europe. A few minutes' later internet and phone systems—fixed and mobile—also crashed. At first people were bemused, almost resigned, but confident that in a short time their lives would be restored to normalcy. Their confidence was not misplaced. In the early 2020s European leaders had quietly established a Europe-wide structure to cope with just such an emergency. NATO and the EU had also created a 'fused' big, data-based intelligence analysis centre which had given European leaders forewarning of the combined cyber and terrorist attacks that were being coordinated from Moscow. A European AI-powered comprehensive coord- inated intelligence analysis mechanism also provided clear indications of final prepar- ations for a series of attacks some time before they had been launched by the Internet Research Agency in St Petersburg.

As the attacks unfolded, European counter-terrorism and law enforcement agencies swung into action as AI-enabled systems countered each strike simultaneously. After the initial shock, an overarching, comprehensive, coordinated European cyber defence not only absorbed each of Russia's offensive cyber strokes, but began to inflict serious damage on Moscow's own cyber domain as European offensive cyber capabilities attacked Russian cyber units and Russian proxy cyber criminals. Moreover, since early 2025 the entire European power grid had been future-proofed against just such an attack with algorithms designed to protect and adapt specific nodes, first isolating them and then re-routing power around a hardened network with redundancy the DNA of the system. The sparring in cyber space between European and Russian cognitive AI cyber security systems for control of the European electrical grid ended with Europeans firmly in control of their cyber environment . . . and much of Russia's.

As the attack began to falter, European citizens were also advised to activate the civil defence protocols they had been trained to undertake in the wake of COVID-19. Ultimately, it was Europe's prepared people who were key to Europe's resilience; lessons had been learned from both the Cold War when civil defence was nationally based but locally focused, and COVID-19 during which local volunteers had proven decisive in helping their respective communities recover from a catastrophic disinformation and disruption attack. Their skill-sets ranged from establishing signals networks, undertaking heavy and light rescue, and fire-fighting to the provision of medical aid and the maintenance of civil cohesion. They could also be employed to meet a host of emergency contingencies using local knowledge to provide reassurance, alternative sources of power, communications, and catering and administrative assistance in support of professional emergency services. All such efforts were underpinned by a robust strategic communications network able to resist the attacks which, after a couple of hours, began to update citizens.

Thereafter, nationally administered civil defence rapidly restored power and some transportation and food distribution networks. Local civil defence cells also quickly moved to establish need, going from household to household, whilst regional medical centres deployed personnel and trained civilians to ensure the provision of aid and assistance, and counter any spike of COVID-29 cases. Police units, reinforced by specially trained and sanctioned civilians, reassured the population and helped restore effective government.

The future war, future defence of Europe has held

Faced with a far longer war than expected, the Russian attack stalled. Russia's much-vaunted 5D warfare and its use of complex strategic coercion had failed to cause the chaos across the rest of Europe that Moscow hoped would forestall a robust Allied response. Critically, when it came to war, Beijing refused to back Moscow and the Kremlin quickly realized it had disastrously miscalculated. A chastened President Putin picked up the telephone to the White House and several European leaders. He apologized to them for what he called 'rogue elements within the Russian Armed Forces', and promised to do all in his power to root out the 'traitors'.

Jim? Jim had heard rumours about the Kh-47M2 Kinzhal hypersonic missile that had tried to kill him and destroy his column, but it had been downed by an AI-enabled drone which formed part of the bubble that had protected him and his entrained Bradley Armoured Fighting Vehicle.

For a few days Europe had teetered on the edge of disaster. Jim had seen that in the face of the people: the stress, the fear, that 'nowhere to run, nowhere to hide' hopelessness of the trapped. However, facing defeat, Russian forces quickly withdrew from those parts of the three Baltic States they had briefly occupied, although not without killing a lot of people and destroying several towns.

A few weeks later Jim began to make his way home. Europeans cheered him as he and his colleagues made their way back across Europe. Actually, Jim felt a bit of a cheat, as to his mind he had done nothing, fought no-one. Jim could not be more wrong. His very presence, the speed of his deployment, and the inability of Russian forces to kill him had, in effect, averted World War Three.

Deterrence achieved, collective defence confirmed, future war averted.

John R. Allen, F. Ben Hodges, and Julian Lindley-French
January 2021

Bibliography

Strategy and Threat

Barnett, Thomas, P.M. (2004) *The Pentagon's New Map: War and Peace in the Twenty-First Century* (New York: Berkley).

Bergen, Peter L. (2001) *Holy War Inc: Inside the Secret World of Osama Bin Laden* (London: Weidenfeld and Nicolson).

Berkowitz, Bruce (2003) *The New Face of War: How War Will Be Fought in the 21st Century* (New York: Free Press).

Biddle, Stephen (2004) *Military Power: Explaining Victory and Defeat in Modern Battle* (Princeton, NJ: Princeton University Press).

Bobbit, Philip (2003) *The Shield of Achilles: War, Peace and the Course of History* (London: Penguin).

Bracken, Paul (2013) *The Second Nuclear Age: Strategy, Danger and the New Power Politics* (New York: St Martin's Press).

Brenner, Joel (2011) *America the Vulnerable: Inside the New Threat Matrix of Digital Espionage, Crime, and Warfare* (New York: Penguin).

Bryant, William D. (2015) *International Conflict and Cyberspace Superiority: Theory and Practice* (New York: Routledge).

Byman, Daniel (2015) *Al-Qaeda, the Islamic State, and the Global Jihadist Movement* (Oxford: Oxford University Press).

Chesterman, Simon, Ignatieff, Michael, and Thakur, Ramesh (2005) *Making States Work: State Failure and the Crisis of Governance* (Tokyo: UN Universities Press).

Codevilla, Angelo M. (2005) *No Victory, No Peace* (Lanham, MD: Rowman & Littlefield).

Coker, Christopher (2015) *Future War* (Cambridge: Polity).

Cooper, Julian (2016) 'If War Comes Tomorrow: How Russia Prepares for Possible Armed Aggression', Whitehall Report, 4–16 (London: RUSI).

Cooper, Julian (2016) *Russia's State Armament Programme to 2020: A Quantitative Assessment of Implementation 2011–2015* (Stockholm: FOI).

Cordesman, Anthony H. (2019) 'China's New 2019 Defense White Paper: An Open Strategic Challenge to the United States, but One Which Does Not Have to Lead to Open Conflict' (Washington, DC: CSIS).

Cornish, Paul and Donaldson, Kingsley (Eds.) (2017) *2020: World of War* (London: Hodder and Stoughton).

Covington, Stephen R. (2016) *The Culture of Strategic Thought Behind Russia's Modern Approaches to Warfare* (Cambridge, MA: Belfer).

Deitchman, Seymour (2000) *On Being a Superpower: And Not Knowing What to Do About It* (Boulder, CO: Westview).

De Wijk, Rob (2004) *The Art of Military Coercion: Why the West's Military Superiority Scarcely Matters* (Amsterdam: Mers & Schildt).

De Wijk, Rob (2015) *Power Politics: How China and Russia Reshape the World* (Amsterdam: Amsterdam University Press).

European Union (2004) *A European Security Strategy* (Paris: EU-ISS).

Fishman, Brian (2016) *The Master Plan: ISIS, Al Qaeda, and the Jihadi Strategy for Final Victory* (New Haven, CT: Yale University Press).

Forbes, Felix (2020) "Five Things We Learnt from This Week's Sophy Ridge on Sunday", news.sky.com/story/five-things-we-learnt-from-this-weeks-sophy-ridge-on-Sunday-12127574

Frederick the Great (2020) "Diplomacy without Arms: If Britain Wants a Central Role in World Affairs It Needs to Fund Defence Properly", *The Times*, February 1, 2020.

Friedman, George (2010) *The Next 100 Years: A Forecast for the 21st Century* (New York: Anchor).

Galbraith, J.K. (1975) *Money: Where it Came, Where It Went* (New York: Houghton Mifflin).

Garton-Ash, Timothy (2004) *Free World: Why a Crisis of the West Reveals the Opportunity of Our Time* (London: Allen Lane).

Goodhart, David (2017) *The Road to Somewhere: The Populist Revolt and the Future of Politics* (London: Hurst).

Guisnel, Jean and Tertrais, Bruno (2016) Le President et al bombe' (Paris: Odile Jacob).

Haaland Matlary, Janne and Heier, Tormonds (Eds.) (2016) *Ukraine and Beyond: Russia's Strategic Security Challenge to Europe* (London: Palgrave Macmillan).

Haukkala, H. and Popescu, N. (Eds.) (2016) *Russian Futures: Horizon 2025* (Paris: EUISS).

Heuser, Beatrice and Shamir, Eitan (2017) *Insurgencies and Counterinsurgencies: National Styles and Strategic Cultures* (Cambridge: Cambridge University Press).

HM Government (2011) *Prevent Strategy* (London: Cabinet Office).

Hoffman, Frank (2016) *Foresight into 21st Century Conflict: End of the Great Illusion* (Philadelphia, PA: Foreign Policy Research Institute).

Hoffman, Frank G. and Mattis, James N. (2005) 'Future War: The Rise of Hybrid War'. *Naval Institute Proceedings*, vol. 132 (November), p. 11.

Hopkinson, W. and Lindley-French, J. (2017) *The New Geopolitics of Terror* (London: Routledge).

Huldt, Bo et al. (Eds.) (2005) *Strategic Yearbook 2005* (Stockholm: Swedish National Defence College).

Huldt, Bo et al. (Eds.) (2006) *Strategic Yearbook 2006* (Stockholm: Swedish National Defence College).

Ignatieff, Michael (2001) *Virtual War: Kosovo and Beyond* (London: Vintage).

Kaplan, Robert D. (2002) *Warrior Politics: Why Leadership Demands a Pagan Ethos* (New York: Random House).

Kilcullen, David (2016) *Blood Year: The Unravelling of Western Counterterrorism* (Oxford: Oxford University Press).

Kilcullen, David (2019) *The Accidental Guerrilla: Fighting Small Wars in the Midst of a Big One* (New York: Oxford University Press).

Kissinger, Henry (2001) *Does America Need a Foreign Policy? Towards a Diplomacy for the Twenty-First Century* (New York: Touchstone).

Kupchan, Charles A. (2002) *The End of the American Era* (New York: Alfred A. Knopf).

Labara, Erick (2004) *Pre-emptive War* (Washington, DC: Global Security Press).

Lake, Anthony (2000) *Six Nightmares* (Boston, MA: Little, Brown and Co.).

Lawrence, T.E. (2011 edn) *Seven Pillars of Wisdom: A Triumph* (Blacksburg, VA: Wilder).

Liddell Hart, Basil (1967) *Strategy* (London: Faber & Faber).

Lindley-French, Julian (2002) *Terms of Engagement: The Paradox of American Power and the Transatlantic Dilemma Post-11 September* (Paris: EUISS).

Lindley-French, Julian (2005) 'Euronukes?' *Aspenia*, no. 27–28 (Rome: Aspen).

Lindley-French, Julian (2010) *Britain and France: A Dialogue of Decline?* (London: Chatham House).

Lindley-French, Julian and Algieri, Franco (2005) *Why Europe Needs to Be Strong . . . and the World Needs a Strong Europe* (Gutersloh: Bertelsmann).

Lo, Bobo and Shevtsova, Lilia (2012) *A 21st Century Myth: Authoritarian Modernization in Russia and China* (Moscow: Carnegie Moscow Center).

Lukes, Steven (Ed.) (2004) *Power* (Oxford: Blackwell).

Luttwak, Edward (2012) *The Rise of China versus the Logic of Strategy* (Cambridge, MA: Harvard University Press).

Marlowe, Christopher (2001) 'Doctor Faustus', in Charles W. Eliot, LLD (Ed.), *The Harvard Classics: The Shelf of Fiction* (New York: Bartleby.com).

Mearsheimer, John J. (2001) *The Tragedy of Great Power Politics* (New York and London: Norton).

Merom, G. (2003) *How Democracies Lose Small Wars* (Cambridge: Cambridge University Press).

Myers, Steven Lee (2015) *The New Tsar: The Rise and Reign on Vladimir Putin* (New York: Knopf).

Nye, Joseph, S. (2005) *Soft Power: The Means to Success in World Politics* (New York: Public Affairs).

Nye, Joseph S. (2010) *Cyberpower* (Cambridge, MA: Harvard Kennedy School).

O'Hanlon, Michael, E. (2019) *The Senkaku Paradox: Risking Great Power War Over Small Stakes* (Washington, DC: Brookings).

Pejsova, Eva (Ed.) (2016) 'Sense and Sensibility: Addressing the South China Sea Disputes' (Paris: EUISS).

Rid, Thomas (2013) *Cyberwar Will Not Take Place* (Oxford: Oxford University Press).

Schmitt, Michael N. (Ed.) (2017) *The Tallinn Manual 2.0 on the International Law Applicable to Cyber Operations* (Cambridge: Cambridge University Press).

Shirreff, General Sir Richard (2016) *2017: War with Russia—An Urgent Warning from Senior Military Command* (London: Hodder).

Smith, General Sir Rupert (2005) *The Utility of Force: The Art of War in the Modern World* (London: Allen Lane).

Stansfield, Gareth (2013) 'The Remaking of Syria, Iraq and the Wider Middle East: The End of the Sykes-Picot State System', Briefing Paper (London: RUSI).

Stewart, Patrick (2011) *Weak Links: Fragile States, Global Threats, and International Security* (New York: Oxford University Press).

Strachan, Hew and Schieppers, Sibylle (Eds.) (2011) *The Changing Character of War* (Oxford: Oxford University Press).

Tardy, Thierry (Ed.) (2005) *Peace Operations after 11 September, 2001* (London and New York: Frank Cass).

Van Crefeld, Martin (2017) *More on War* (Oxford: Oxford University Press).

Waltz, Kenneth, N. (1979) Man, *the State and War* (New York: Columbia University Press).

World Health Organization (Ed.) (2006) *SARS: How a Global Epidemic Was Stopped* (Geneva: World Health Organization).

Zaborowski, Martin (Ed.) (2006) *Friends Again? EU-U.S. Relations after the Crisis* (Paris: EUISS).

Eu and Nato

Allen, John R., Breedlove, Philip, Lindley-French, Julian, and Zambellas, George (2017) *Future War NATO* (Bratislava: GLOBSEC).

Allin, Dana, H. (2002) 'NATO's Balkan Intervention', IISS Adelphi Paper 377 (Oxford: Oxford University Press).

Binnendijk, H., Gompert, David, C., and Kugler, R. (2005) 'A New Military Framework for NATO'. *Defense Horizons*, vol. 48 (May) (Washington, DC: NDU).

Biscop, Sven (Ed.) (2005) *E Pluribus Unum? Military Integration in the European Union* (Brussels: IRRI-KIIB).

Biscop, Sven (2019) *European Strategy in the Twenty-First Century* (London: Routledge).

Brimmer, Esther (Ed.) (2002) *The EU's Search for a Strategic Role* (Washington, DC: CTR).

Cordesmann, Anthony, H. (2018) *The U.S., NATO and the Defense of Europe: Underlying Trends* (Washington, DC: CSIS).

Czulda, Robert and Los, Robert (Eds.) (2013) *NATO: Towards the Challenge of a Contemporary World* (Brussels: NATO).

Czulda, Robert and Los, Robert (Eds.) (2015) *Newcomers No More? Contemporary NATO and the Future of the Enlargement from the Perspective of 'Post-Cold War' Members* (Brussels: NATO).

David, Charles-Phillipe and Levesque, Jacques (Eds.) (2005) *The Future of NATO: Enlargement: Russia and European Security* (Montreal and Kingston: McGill and Queens University Press).

Forster, Antony (2006) *Armed Forces and Society in Europe* (Basingstoke: Palgrave).

Hamilton, Daniel S. (2004) *Transatlantic Transformations: Equipping NATO for the 21st Century* (Washington, DC: Center for Transatlantic Relations/Johns Hopkins University).

Harmon, C., Pratt, A., and Gorka, S. (2011) *Towards a Grand Strategy against Terrorism* (New York: McGraw-Hill).

Herd, Graeme P. and Kriendler, John (2013) *Understanding NATO in the 21st Century: Alliance Strategies, Security and Global Governance* (London: Routledge).

Hopkinson, W. (2001) 'Enlargement: A New NATO', Chaillot Paper 49 (Paris: WEU-ISS).

Howorth, Jolyon (2007) *Security and Defence Policy in the European Union* (Basingstoke: Palgrave).

Howorth, Jolyon and Keeler, John T.S. (2003) *Defending Europe: The EU, NATO and the Quest for European Autonomy* (New York: Palgrave Macmillan).

Kaplan, Lawrence S. (1999) *The Long Entanglement: NATO's First Fifty Years* (Westport, CT: Praeger).

Kaplan, Lawrence S. (2013) *NATO before the Korean War* (Kent, OH: Kent State University Press).

Kay, Sean (1998) *NATO and the Future of European Security* (Lanham, MD: Rowman & Littlefield).

Lasconjaras, G. and Larsen, J.A. (2015) *NATO's Response to Hybrid Threats* (Rome: NDC).

Lindley-French, Julian (2002) 'In the Shade of Locarno: Why European Defence Is Failing'. *International Affairs*, vol. 78, no. 4 (London: Chatham House).

Lindley-French, Julian (2003) 'My End Is Going Down . . . Iraq and the Transatlantic Political-Security Mess'. *American Foreign Policy Interests*, vol. 25, no. 6 (New York: NCAFP).

Lindley-French, Julian (2015) *NATO: The Enduring Alliance* (London: Routledge).

Lindley-French, Julian and Algieri, Franco (2000) *Enhancing the European Union as an International Security Actor* (Gutersloh: Bertelsmann).

Lindley-French, Julian and Algieri, Franco (2004) *A European Defence Strategy* (Gutersloh: Bertelsmann).

McKenzie, Mary M. and Loedel, Peter H. (Eds.) (1998) *The Promise and Reality of European Security Cooperation* (Westport, CT Praeger).

Missiroli, Antonio (2015) *Towards an EU Global Strategy: Background, Process and References* (Paris: EUISS).

Moens, Alexander, Cohen, Lenard J., and Sens, Allen G. (2003) *NATO and European Security* (Westport, CT: Praeger).

Papocosma, Victor S., Kay, Sean, and Rubin, Mark R. (Eds.) (2001) *NATO after Fifty Years* (Wilmington, DE: Scholarly Resources).

Parkes, Roderick (2016) 'People on the Move', Chaillot Paper 138, June (Paris: EUISS).

Rynning, Stan (2019) 'Atlantic Futures: The Atlantic Alliance between Power and Purpose', Research Paper 2, March (Rome: NDC).

Schmidt, G. (Ed.) (2001) *A History of NATO: The First Fifty Years* (London: Praeger).

Serfaty, Simon (Ed.) (2005) *The United States, the European Union and NATO: After the Cold War and Beyond Iraq* (Washington, DC: CSIS).

Tardy, Thierry (Ed.) (2009) *European Security in a Global Context* (London: Routledge).

Voyger, Mark (Ed.) (2019) *NATO at 70 and the Baltic States: Strengthening the Euro-Atlantic Alliance in an Age of Non-Linear Threats* (Tartu: BDC).

History

Albright, Madeleine (2003) *Madam Secretary: A Memoir* (London: Macmillan).

Ambrose, Stephen E. (1988) *Rise to Globalism: American Foreign Policy since 1938* (New York: Penguin).

Ambrose, Stephen E. (1994) *D-Day June 6, 1944: The Climactic Battle of World War II* (New York: Simon & Schuster).

Baker, James A. III (1995) *The Politics of Diplomacy: Revolution, War and Peace 1989–1992* (New York: Putnam).

Beevor, Antony (2009) *D-Day: The Battle for Normandy* (New York: Viking).

Biscop, Sven and Whitman, Richard (2013) *The Routledge Handbook of European Security* (London: Routledge).

Boccaccio, Giovanni (2008 edn) *The Decameron*, edited by Jonathan Usher (Oxford: Oxford University Press).

Carr, E.H. (1964 edn) *The Twenty Years' Crisis, 1919–1939* (New York: Harper & Row).

Clark, Wesley, K. (2001) *Waging Modern War* (New York: Public Affairs).

Clinton, Bill (2004) *My Life* (New York: Alfred A. Knopf).

Cornish, Paul (1996) *British Military Planning for the Defence of Germany 1945–50* (London: Macmillan).

Dimbleby, Jonathan (2015) *The Battle of the Atlantic: How the Allies Won the War* (London: Penguin).

Freedman, Lawrence (1989) *The Evolution of Nuclear Strategy, Second Edition* (London: Macmillan).

Freedman, Lawrence (1998) 'The Revolution in Strategic Affairs', IISS Adelphi Paper 318 (Oxford: Oxford University Press).

Freedman, Lawrence (2013) *Strategy: A History* (Oxford: Oxford University Press)

Freedman, Lawrence (2017) *The Future of War: A History* (London: Allen Lane).

Fukuyama, Francis (1992) *The End of History and the Last Man* (London: Hamish Hamilton).

Gaddis, John Lewis (1989) *The Long Peace: Inquiries into the History of the Cold War* (Oxford: Oxford University Press).

Garthoff, Raymond L. (1985) *Détente and Confrontation* (Washington, DC: Brookings).

Gibbon, Edward (1996 edn) *The History of the Decline and Fall of the Roman Empire* (London: Penguin).

Gnesotto, N. (Ed.) (2004) *European Security and Defence Policy: The First Five Years 1999–2004* (Paris: EUISS).

Gordon, Andrew (2005) *The Rules of the Game: Jutland and British Naval Command* (London: John Murray).

Gray, Colin S. (2005) *Another Bloody Century: Future Warfare* (London: Weidenfeld & Nicolson).

Grehan, John (2019) *The Berlin Airlift: The World's Largest Ever Air Supply Operation* (Barnsley: Pen and Sword).

Grosser A. (1980 edn) *The Western Alliance: European-American Relations since 1945* (London: Macmillan).

Hackett, John (1982) *The Third World War: The Untold Story* (New York: Macmillan).

Halliday, Fred (1989 edn) *The Making of the Second Cold War* (London: Verso).

Handel, Michael I. (Ed.) (2001) *Masters of War: Classical Strategic Thought, Third Edition* (London: Routledge).

Hart, Peter (2008) *1918: A Very British Victory* (London: Phoenix).

Herman, Arthur (2004) *To Rule the Waves: How the British Navy Shaped the Modern World* (London: Hodder & Stoughton).

Howard, Michael (2000) *The Invention of Peace* (London: Profile).

Hughes, Daniel J. and Bell, Harry (1993) *Moltke and the Art of War* (New York: Presidio Press).

Huntingdon, Samuel J. (1996) *The Clash of Civilisations and the Remaking of World Order* (New York: Simon and Schuster).

Hurd, Douglas (2010) *Choose Your Weapons: The British Foreign Secretary 200 Years of Argument, Success and Failure* (London: Weidenfeld and Nicolson).

Ikenberry, John G. (2001) *After Victory* (Princeton, NJ and Oxford: Princeton University Press).

Jenkins, Roy (2001) *Churchill* (London: Pan).

Kampfner, John (2003) *Blair's Wars* (London: Simon and Schuster).

Keegan, John (2005) *The Iraq War* (Ottawa: Vintage Canada).

Kennedy, Paul (1987) *The Rise and Fall of the Great Powers: Economic Change and Military Conflict from 1500 to 2000* (New York: Random House).

Kennedy, Paul (1993) *Preparing for the Twenty-First Century* (London: Harper Collins).

Kennedy, Paul (2004 edn) *The Rise and Fall of British Naval Mastery* (London: Penguin).

Kissinger, Henry (1994) *Diplomacy* (New York: Touchstone).

Kissinger, Henry (2014) *World Order: Reflections on the Character of Nations and the Course of History* (London: Allen Lane).

Konstam, A. (2009) *The Battle of North Cape: The Death Ride of the Scharnhorst, 1943* (Barnsley: Pen and Sword).

Kotkin, Stephen (2001) *Armageddon Averted: The Soviet Collapse 1970–2000* (Oxford: Oxford University Press).

Kuklick, Bruce (2006) *Blind Oracles: Intellectuals and War from Kennan to Kissinger* (Princeton, NJ: Princeton University Press).

LaFeber, Walter (1991) *America, Russia and the Cold War 1945–1990, Sixth Edition* (New York: McGraw-Hill).

Massie, Robert K. (2007) *Castles of Steel: Britain, Germany and the Winning of the Great War at Sea* (London: Vintage).

McNamara, Robert (1990) *Out of the Cold: New Thinking for American Foreign and Defence Policy* (London: Bloomsbury).

Meyer, C. (2005) *DC Confidential* (London: Weidenfeld and Nicolson).

Priest, Dana (2003) *The Mission: Waging War and Keeping Peace with America's Military* (New York: Norton).

Rapaport, Anatol (Ed.) (1968) *Carl von Clausewitz: On War* (London: Penguin).

Reid, Walter (2013) *Empire of the Sand: How Britain Made the Modern Middle East* (Edinburgh: Birlinn).

Ruane, Kevin (2000) *The Rise and Fall of the European Defence Community: Anglo-American Relations and the Crisis of European Defence* (London: Macmillan).

Thayer Mahan, Alfred (1897 edn) *The Influence of Sea Power upon History* (London: Sampson, Low, Marston and Rivington).

Tyerman, Christopher (2006) *God's War: A New History of the Crusades* (London: Penguin).

Military Technical

Adams, Gordon, Ben-Ari, Guy, Logsdon, John, and Williamson, Ray (2004) *Bridging the Gap: European C4ISR and Transatlantic Interoperability* (Washington, DC: GWU).

Arquilla, John and Ronfeldt, David (1993) 'Cyberwar Is Coming!' (Santa Monica, CA: RAND Corporation), https://www.rand.org/pubs/reprints/RP223.html.

Arreguin-Toft, Ivan (2001) 'How the Weak Win Wars: A Theory of Asymmetric Conflict'. *International Security*, vol. 26, no. 1, pp. 93–128.

Blair, Bruce G. (1985) *Strategic Command and Control: Redefining the Nuclear Threat* (Washington, DC: Brookings).

Bronk, Justin (2018) 'Next Generation Combat Aircraft: Threat Outlook and Potential Solutions', Occasional Paper, November 2018 (London: RUSI).

Citino, Robert. M. (2004) *Blitzkrieg to Desert Storm: The Evolution of Operational Warfare* (Lawrence, KS: University of Kansas Press).

Cooper, Julian (2016) *Russia's State Armament Programme to 2020: A Quantitative Assessment of Implementation 2011–2015* (Stockholm: FOI).

CREST (2000) 'Coalition Military Operations: The Way Ahead Through Co-operability', Report of a French-German-UK-US Working Group (Washington, DC: US CREST).

CREST (2002) 'Future Military Coalitions: The Transatlantic Challenge', Report of a French-German-UK-US Working Group (Washington, DC: US CREST).

Di Paola, Giampaolo and Lindley-French, Julian (2017) *Affording and Equipping the Alliance* (Bratislava: GLOBSEC).

Dobbins, James, Jones, Seth G., Runkle, Benjamin, and Mohandas, Siddarth (2009) *Occupying Iraq: A History of the Coalition Provisional Authority* (Santa Monica, CA: RAND).

Dunlap, Charles J. (2011) 'Lawfare Today . . . and Tomorrow', in Raul A. Pedrozo and Daria P. Wollschlaeger (Eds.), *International Law and the Changing Character of War* (Newport, RI: US Naval War College, International Law Studies).

Dupuy, Trevor (1992) *Future Wars* (London: Sidgwick & Jackson).

Flournoy, Michele A. (Ed.) (2001) *QDR 2001: Strategy Driven Choices for America's Security* (Washington, DC: NDU).

Flournoy, Michele A. and Smith, Julianne (Eds.) (2005) *European Defense Integration: Bridging the Gap between Strategy and Capabilities* (Washington, DC: CSIS).

Glaser, Charles, L. (1990) *Analyzing Strategic Nuclear Policy* (Princeton, NJ: Princeton University Press).

Gompert, David C., Binnendijk Hans, and Bonny, Lin (2014) *Blinders, Blunders, and Wars* (Santa Monica, CA: RAND).

Gompert, David C., Kugler, Richard L., and Libicki, Martin C. (1999) *Mind the Gap: Promoting a Transatlantic Revolution in Military Affairs* (Washington, DC: NDU).

Guehenno, Jean-Marie (2015) *The Fog of Peace: A Memoir of Peacekeeping in the 21st Century* (Washington, DC: Brookings).

Hagman, Hans-Christian (2002) 'European Crisis Management and Defence: The Search for Capabilities', IISS Adelphi Paper 353 (Oxford: Oxford University Press).

Heisbourg, Francois (Ed.) (2000) 'European Defence: Making It Work', Chaillot Paper 42 (Paris: WEU-ISS).

Holmes, Richard (2006) *Dusty Warriors: Modern Soldiers at War* (London: Harper).

Hooker, Jr, R.D. (2017) 'How to Defend the Balkans' (Unpublished).

Hope, Ian C. (2015) *A Scientific Way of War: Antebellum Military Science—West Point and the Origins of American Military Thought* (Lincoln, NE and London: University of Nebraska Press).

Husain, Amir (2017) *The Sentient Machine: The Coming Age of Artificial Intelligence* (New York: Scribner).

Husain, Amir and Allen, John R. (2017) 'On Hyperwar', Naval Institute Proceedings, July 2017.

Husain, Amir and Allen, John R. (2019) *Hyperwar: Conflict and Competition in the AI Century* (Austin, TX: SparkCognition Press).

Johnson, Andrew (Ed.) (2014) *Wars in Peace: British Military Operations since 1991* (London: RUSI).

Khalil, J. and Zeuthen, M. (2015) 'Countering Violent Extremism and Risk Reduction: A Guide to Programme Design & Evaluation', Whitehall Paper, 2–16 (London: RUSI).

Kilcullen, David et al. (2016) *A Great Perhaps? Conflict and Convergence* (London: Hurst).

King, Anthony (2011) *The Transformation of Europe's Armed Forces: From the Rhine to Afghanistan* (Cambridge: Cambridge University Press).

Krause, Joachim and Bruns, Sebastian (Eds.) (2016) *Routledge Handbook of Naval Strategy and Security* (London: Routledge).

Lavrov, Anton (November 2018) *Russian Military Reform from Georgia to Syria* (Washington, DC: CSIS).

Ledwidge, F. (2011) *Losing Small Wars: British Military Failure in Iraq and Afghanistan* (New Haven, CT: Yale University Press).

Lutz, Rachel Anne (2001) *Military Capabilities for a European Defence* (Copenhagen: Danish Institute of International Affairs).

Malis, Christian (Ed.) (2009) *Guerre et Manoeuvre* (Paris: Economica).

Neal, Derrick J. and Wells, Linton (2011) *Capability Development in Support of Comprehensive Approaches: Transforming International Civil-Military Interactions* (Washington, DC: NDU Press).

Nuno, Frank and Standley, Vaughn (2018) 'Bolt Out of the Blue: Nuclear Attack Warning in the Era of Information and Cyber Warfare', *War on the Rocks*, 14 June, https://warontherocks.com/2018/06/bolt-out-of-the-blue-nuclear-attack-warning-in-the-era-of-information-and-cyber-warfare.

O'Hanlon, Michael (2000) *Technological Change and the Future of Warfare* (Washington, DC: Brookings).

O'Hanlon, Michael E. (2013) *The Science of War: Defense Budgets, Military Technology, Logistics, and Combat Outcomes* (Princeton, NJ: Princeton University Press).

O'Hanlon, Michael E. (2015) *The Future of Land Warfare* (Washington, DC: Brookings).

Olsen, John Andreas and van Creveld, Martin (Eds.) (2011) *The Evolution of the Operational Art: From Napoleon to the Present* (Oxford: Oxford University Press).

Osinga, Frans (2005) *Science, Strategy and War: The Strategic Theory of John Boyd* (Delft: Eburon).

Persson, Gudrun (Ed.) (2016) *Russian Military Capability in a Ten Year Perspective* (Stockholm: FOI).

Roberts, Peter and Hardie, Andrew (2015) 'The Validity of Deterrence in the Twenty-First Century', RUSI Occasional Paper, August (London: RUSI).

Rostek, Michael and Gizewski, Peter (Eds.) (2011) *Security Operations in the 21st Century: Canadian Perspectives on the Comprehensive Approach* (Kingston, ON: McGill-Queens University Press).

Sarotte, Mary-Elise (2001) 'German Military Reform and European Security', IISS Adelphi Paper 340 (Oxford: Oxford University Press).

Schroeer, Dietrich (1984) *Science, Technology and the Nuclear Arms Race* (New York: John Wiley).

Terriff, Terry, Osinga, Frans, and Farrell, Theo (Eds.) (2010) *A Transformation Gap? American Innovation and European Military Change* (Stanford, CA: Stanford University Press).

Thomas, James P. (2000) 'The Military Challenges of Transatlantic Coalitions', IISS Adelphi Paper 333 (Oxford: Oxford University Press).

Till, Geoffrey (2013) *Seapower: A Guide for the Twenty-First Century* (London: Routledge).

United States Institute for Peace (USIP) (2009) *Guiding Principles for Stabilization and Reconstruction* (Washington, DC: USIP and US Army Peacekeeping and Stability Operations Institute).

US Department of State (January 2009) *US Government Counterinsurgency Guide* (Washington, DC: State Department).

Wells, L., Hailes, T.C., and Davies, M.C. (2013) *Changing Mindsets to Transform Security: Leader Development for an Unpredictable and Complex World* (Washington, DC: NDU Press).

Reports and Declarations

'2015 Russian National Security Strategy' (Moscow: Russian Federation).

'2017 National Security Strategy of the United States' (Washington, DC: USG).

'2018 National Defense Strategy of the United States' (Washington, DC: USG).

'Active Engagement, Modern Defence: Strategic Concept for the Defence and Security of Members of the North Atlantic Treaty Organization' (2010) (Brussels: NATO).

Allen, John R., di Paola, Giampaolo, Langheld, Wolf, Lindley-French, Julian, Valasek, Tomas, Vershbow, and Alexander (2017) *The GLOBSEC NATO Adaptation Report* (Bratislava: GLOBSEC).

'A European Defence Strategy' (2004) Venusberg Group (Gutesloh: Bertelsmann).

'Defending Europe: Scenario-Based Capability Requirements for NATO's European Members' (April 2019) (London: International Institute for Strategic Studies (IISS)).

'EU, a Secure Europe in a Better World: European Security Strategy' (12 December 2003) (Brussels: EU).

'EU, Shared Vision, Common Action, a Stronger Europe: A Global Strategy for the European Union's Foreign and Security Policy' (29 June 2016) (Brussels: EU).

'Global Strategic Trends: The Future Starts Here, Sixth Edition (2018) (London: Cabinet Office).

'Joint Declaration on European Defence: Joint Declaration Issued at the Franco-British Summit', St Malo (4 December 1998).

Marrione, Alessandro, de France, Olivier, and Fattibene, Daniele (2016) 'Defence Budgets and Co-operation in Europe: Developments, Trends and Drivers', Istituto Affari Internazionale (Rome: IAI).

'National Security Strategy and Strategic Defence and Security Review 2015: A Secure and Prosperous United Kingdom' (London: TSO).

Persson, Gudrun (2017) *The War of the Future: A Conceptual Framework and Practical Conclusions—Essays on Strategic Thought* (Rome: NDC).

'Security Britain in an Age of Uncertainty: The Strategic Defence and Security Review' (2010) (London: TSO).

'The Notification on Permanent Structured Cooperation (PESCO) to the Council and to the High Representative of the Union for Foreign Affairs and Security Policy' (June 2017) (Brussels: EU).

'The Strategic Defence Review' (1998) (London: TSO).

'The Strategic Review of Defence and National Security: Key Points' (2017) (Paris: French Republic), p. 2.

Theory

Bayliss, John and Rengger, N.J. (1992) *Dilemmas of World Politics: International Issues in a Changing World* (Oxford: Clarendon).

Bowker, Mike and Brown, Robin (1993) *From Cold War to Collapse: Theory and World Politics in the 1980s* (Cambridge: Cambridge University Press).

Buzan, Barry (1991) *People, States and Fear, Second Edition* (New York: Harvester Wheatsheaf).

Feldner, Denise (2020 Ed.) *Re-designing Institutions: Concepts for the Digitally Connected Society* (Berlin: Springer).

Gilpin, Robert (1981) *War and Change in World Politics* (Cambridge: Cambridge University Press).

Hollis, Martin and Smith, Steve (1991) *Explaining and Understanding International Relations* (Oxford: Clarendon).

Hughes, Daniel J. (Ed.) (1993) *Moltke on the Art of War: Selected Writings* (New York: Presidio Press).

Machiavelli, Niccolo (2008 edn) *The Prince*, edited by Maurizio Viroli (Oxford: Oxford University Press).

Morgenthau, Hans J. (2005 edn) *Politics Amongst Nations: The Struggle for Power and Peace* (New York: McGraw-Hill).

Sheehan, Michael J. (1988) *Arms Control: Theory and Practice* (Oxford: Blackwell).

Tuck, Richard (Ed.) (1991) *Hobbes' Leviathan* (Cambridge: Cambridge University Press).

Wiener, Antje and Thomas, Diez (Eds.) (2003) *European Integration Theory* (Oxford: Oxford University Press).

Reference

Haines, Jean-Yves (Ed.) (2003) 'From Laeken to Copenhagen: European Defence—Core Documents' (Paris: EUISS).

International Institute for Strategic Studies (2015) *The Military Balance 2015* (London: IISS).

International Institute for Strategic Studies (2019) *The Military Balance 2019* (London: IISS).

International Monetary Fund (April 2016) 'Report for Selected Country Groups and Subjects' (PPP Valuation of Country GDP), World Economic Outlook Database, https://www.globalfirepower.com/countries-listing.asp.

Korteweg, Rem (2005) *The Discourse on European Defence* (The Hague: Clingendael).

Lindley-French, Julian (2007) *A Chronology of European Security and Defence 1945–2005* (Oxford: Oxford University Press).

Lindley-French, Julian and Boyer, Yves (Eds.) (2014) *The Oxford Handbook of War* (Oxford: Oxford University Press).

Meijer, Hugo and Wyss, Marco (2019) *The Handbook of European Defence Policies and Armed Forces* (Oxford: Oxford University Press).

Oxford University Press (1982) *The Oxford Concise English Dictionary* (Oxford: Oxford University Press).

Rutten, M. (Ed.) (2001) 'From St Malo to Nice: European Defence—Core Documents', Chaillot Paper 47 (Paris: EUISS).

Rutten, M. (Ed.) (2002) 'From Nice to Laeken: European Defence—Core Documents', Chaillot Paper 51 (Paris: EUISS).

Articles

'After the UK Leaves the EU, 80 Percent of NATO Spending Will Come from Outside the EU', George Allison, 22 February 2018, https://ukdefencejournal.

org.uk/uk-leaves-eu-80-percent-nato-spending-will-come-outside-eu-says-alliance-head.

'A Marriage of Convenience: The Future of Italy-Russia Relations', Angelantonio Rosato, European Council on Foreign Relations, 16 July 2016, https://www.ecfr.eu/article/commentary_a_marriage_of_convenience_the_future_of_italyrussia_relations.

'Army Restructures to Confront Evolving Threats', 1 August 2019, *Army News*, https://www.army.mod.uk/news-and-events/news/2019/08/army-restructures-to-confront-evolving-threats.

'As America Changes, Some Anxious Whites Feel Left Behind', Michele Norris, April 2018, https://www.nationalgeographic.com/magazine/2018/04/race-rising-anxiety-white-america.

'As Trump Rattles NATO, 42 Percent of Germans Now Want U.S. Troops Out of the Country', Rick Noack, 12 July 2018, *The Washington Post*, https://www.washingtonpost.com/news/worldviews/wp/2018/07/12/as-trump-rattles-nato-42-percent-of-germans-now-want-u-s-troops-out-of-the-country/?noredirect=on.

'Boris Is No Churchill, but If He Saves Us from the EU Empire This Will Be His Finest Hour', William Shawcross, 11 August 2019, *The Sunday Times*, https://www.thetimes.co.uk/edition/news/boris-johnson-is-no-churchill-but-if-he-saves-us-from-the-eu-empire-this-will-be-his-finest-hour-3wmg09khd.

'Britain's Parallel Army of Cyber-Warriors', Lucy Fisher, 17 August 2019, *The Times*, https://www.thetimes.co.uk/article/britains-parallel-army-of-cyberwarriors-gzkzzdnvh.

'Britain Pulls Out of EU Defense Force', Tom McTague and David M. Herszenhorn, 20 March 2018, *Politico*, https://www.politico.eu/article/theresa-may-uk-military-britain-pulls-out-of-eu-defense-force.

'British Army Chief: Russia "Far Bigger Threat Than IS"', 24 November 2019, *BBC News*, https://www.bbc.com/news/uk-46327046.

'China Owns US Debt, but How Much?', https://www.investopedia.com/articles/investing/080615/china-owns-us-debt-how-much.asp.

'China's Defense Budget', 6 March 2019, GlobalSecurity.org, https://www.globalsecurity.org/military/world/china/budget.htm.

'Cyber Attack on NHS Would Trigger Full NATO Response, Says Alliance's General Secretary', Robert Mendrick, 27 August 2019, *Daily Telegraph*, www.telegraph.co.uk/news/2019/08/27/cyber-attack-nhs-would-trigger-full-nato-response-says-alliances.

'Defending Our Data: Huawei, 5G and the Five Eyes', Bob Seely MP, Dr Peter Varnish OBE, and Dr John Hemmings (London: Henry Jackson Society).

'Dunford: Leaders Mull First NATO Military Strategy in Decades', Paul McCleary, 30 May 2019, *Breaking Defense*, https://breakingdefense.com/2019/05/dunford-first-nato-strategy-okd-in-decades.

'Eisenhower's "Military-Industrial Complex" Shrinks to 1% of Economy', Loren Thomson, 8 May 2017, *Forbes*, https://www.forbes.com/sites/lorenthompson/2017/05/08/eisenhowers-military-industrial-complex-shrinks-to-1-of-economy/#9d931dbed1f2.

'European Defence Spending: The New Consensus', Lucie Beraud-Sudreau, 15 February 2018, *The Military Balance Blog*, IISS, https://www.iiss.org/blogs/military-balance/2018/02/european-defence-spending.

'Former MI6 Boss: Brexit Would Make Britain More Secure', Agnes Chambre, 24 March 2016, *Politics Home*, https://www.politicshome.com/news/europe/eu-policy-agenda/brexit/news/73111/former-mi6-boss-brexit-would-make-uk-more-secure.

'France Calls for EU-Russia Reset', Andrew Rittman, 10 September 2019, *EU Observer*, https://euobserver.com/foreign/145886.

'Franco-German Treaty of Cooperation and Integration [Aachen Treaty]', 22 January 2019, *European Sources Online*, https://www.europeansources.info/record/treaty-of-franco-german-cooperation-and-integration-aachen-treaty.

'French Armed Forces Chief Quits After Clash with Emmanuel Macron Over Budget Cuts', Lizzie Dearden, 19 July 2017, *The Independent*, https://www.independent.co.uk/news/world/europe/emmanuel-macron-pierre-de-villiers-head-of-french-armed-forces-quits-france-budget-cuts-army-resigns-a7848186.html.

'German Parliamentary Report Identifies Continued Bundeswehr Equipment Shortages', Nicolas Fiorenza, 30 January 2019, *Janes 360*, https://www.janes.com/article/86062/german-parliamentary-report-identifies-continued-bundeswehr-equipment-shortages.

'Germany's Lack of Military Readiness "Dramatic", Says Bundeswehr Commissioner', 20 February 2018, *DW*, https://www.dw.com/en/germanys-lack-of-military-readiness-dramatic-says-bundeswehr-commissioner/a-42663215.

'Global Zero: Obama's Utopian Pathway to a Nuclear-Free World', 6 May 2010, *DW*, https://www.dw.com/en/global-zero-obamas-utopian-pathway-to-a-nuclear-free-world/a-5538827-0.

'Here's How the Russian Military Is Organizing to Develop AI', Samuel Bendett, 20 July 2018, *Defense One*, https://www.defenseone.com/ideas/2018/07/russian-militarys-ai-development-roadmap/149900.

'In Military-Civil Fusion, China Is Learning Lessons from the United States and Starting to Innovate', Elsa B. Kania, 27 August 2019, https://www.realcleardefense.com/articles/2019/08/27/in_military-civil_fusion_china_is_learning_lessons_from_the_united_states_and_starting_to_innovate_114699.html.

'ISIS's Second Comeback: Assessing the Next ISIS Insurgency', Jennifer Cafarella, with Brandon Wallace and Jason Zhou, http://www.understandingwar.org/report/isiss-second-comeback-assessing-next-isis-insurgency.

'Islamism, Salafism, and Jihadism: A Primer', Shadi Hamid and Rashid Dev, 15 July 2016, https://www.brookings.edu/blog/markaz/2016/07/15/islamism-salafism-and-jihadism-a-primer.

'Massive NATO Wargame Seeks to Shore Up Fraying Alliance', Paul McCleary, 14 October 2019, *Defense News*, https://breakingdefense.com/2019/10/massive-nato-wargame-acquisitions-seek-to-shore-up-fraying-alliance.

'Merkel Says Franco-German Treaty a Step Towards European Army', 22 January 2019, RTE.ie, https://www.rte.ie/news/brexit/2019/0122/1024688-france-germany-treaty.

'MH17: Read the Full Report by the Dutch Safety Board—Investigators Found That a Warhead Fired from a Buk Missile System Caused the Crash in July 2014', Lizzie Dearden, 13 October 2015, *The Independent*, https://www.independent.co.uk/news/world/europe/mh17-read-the-full-report-by-the-dutch-safety-board-a6692591.html.

'(More) Gerasimov on Future War', 30 March 2018, *Russian Defence Policy*, https://russiandefpolicy.blog/2018/03/30.

'Netanyahu's Bizarre PowerPoint Presentation on Iran: Israel's Leader Says Iran Cheated on the Nuclear Deal, Adding Doubts about the Agreement's Survival. But He Mostly Described Past Programs', Khrishnadev Calamur, 30 April 2018, *The Atlantic*, https://www.theatlantic.com/international/archive/2018/04/netanyahu-iran-nuclear-deal/559250.

'On Hyperwar', Amir Husain and John R. Allen, July 2017, *Naval Institute Proceedings*, https://www.usni.org/magazines/proceedings/2017/july/hyperwar.

'Our Enemies Aren't Drinking Lattes', Max Boot, 5 July 2006, *Los Angeles Times*, https://www.latimes.com/archives/la-xpm-2006-jul-05-oe-boot5-story.html.

'Putin's Prepared Remarks at 43rd Munich Security Conference on Security Policy', 12 February 2007, *Washington Post*, http://www.washingtonpost.com/wp-dyn/content/article/2007/02/12/AR2007021200555.html.

'Recommendations on 5G and National Security', James Jones, Atlantic Council, Scowcroft Center for Strategic and Security, Strategic Insights Memo No. 3, 11 February 2019.

'Russia "Could Cut Undersea Internet Cables", Defence Chief Warns', Arj Singh, 14 December 2017, *The Independent*, https://www.independent.co.uk/news/uk/home-news/russia-attack-uk-cables-underwater-sea-protection-a8111536.html.

'Russian Military Reform from Georgia to Syria, Anton Lavrov, November 2018 (Washington, DC: CSIS).

'Russian MoD: First LHD Amphibious Assault Ship to Be Built in Russia by 2022', 29 May 2017, https://navyrecognition.com/index.php/news/defence-news/2017/may-2017-navy-naval-forces-defense-industry-technology-maritime-security-global-news/5235-russian-mod-first-lhd-amphibious-assault-ship-to-be-built-in-russia-by-2022.html.

'Russian Nuclear Sub Successfully Test-Launches Intercontinental Ballistic Missile, Government Claims', Nicole Darrah, 30 October 2019, *Fox News*, https://www.foxnews.com/world/russia-submarine-icbm-nuclear-test-missile.

'Russia's New Amphibious Assault Ships to Join Fleet in 2025', 24 June 2019, https://defence-point.com/2019/06/24/russia-s-new-amphibious-assault-ships-to-join-fleet-in-2025.

'Russia Wants to Unplug Its Internet from the Rest of the World. Is That Even Possible?', Sabra Ayres, 4 March 2019, *LA Times*, https://www.latimes.com/world/europe/la-fg-russia-internet-20190304-story.html.

'Saudi Arabia and Iran: The Cold War of Islam', Susanne Koelbl, Samiha Shafy, and Bernhard Zand, 9 May 2016, *Der Spiegel*, http://www.spiegel.de/international/world/saudia-arabia-iran-and-the-new-middle-eastern-cold-war-a-1090725-2.html.

'Saudi-Led Airstrikes Intensify in Yemen as Possible Coalition Land Attack Looms', Ali al-Mujahed and Hugh Naylor, 28 March 2015, *Washington Post*, https://www.washingtonpost.com/world/saudi-arabia-evacuates-diplomats-as-attacks-intensify-in-yemen/2015/03/28/627dc24a.

'Science, Science, and Science: Gerasimov's 2018 Speech', Christoph Bilan, April 2018, http://sipol.at/en/2018/04/10/gerasimov2018.

'The Battle of the Military Theorists: Clausewitz v Sun Tzu', Mark McNeilly, 25 January 2015, *History News Network*, https://historynewsnetwork.org/article/158123.

'The EU-Turkey Refugee Agreement: A Review', 18 March 2003, *DW*, https://www.dw.com/en/the-eu-turkey-refugee-agreement-a-review/a-43028295.

'The Fourth Industrial Revolution: Opportunities and Challenges', Min Xu, Jeanne David, and Suk Kim, 2018, *International Journal of Financial Research*, vol. 9, pp. 90–5.

'The Future of All Arms Warfare in the Twenty-First Century', Homeland Security Digital Library, https://www.armed-services.senate.gov/imo/media/doc/Deptula_03-15-17.pdf.

'The General Theory of Employment', John Maynard Keynes, *The Quarterly Journal of Economics*, vol. 51, no. 2, 1 February 1937.

'The Geographical Pivot of History', Halford Mackinder, *The Geographical Journal*, vol. 23, no. 4, April 1904.

'The Legacy of Obama's "Pivot" to Asia', Michael J. Green, 3 September 2016, *Foreign Affairs*, https://foreignpolicy.com/2016/09/03/the-legacy-of-obamas-pivot-to-asia.

'Theodore Roosevelt: Foreign Affairs', Sidney Milkis, https://millercenter.org/president/roosevelt/foreign-affairs.

'The Paradox of the EU-Turkey Refugee Deal', Elizabeth Collett, March 2016, The Migration Policy Institute, https://www.migrationpolicy.org/news/paradox-eu-turkey-refugee-deal.

'The Revenge of Hard Power Politics', Andrew A. Michta, October 2018, *The American Interest*, https://www.the-american-interest.com/2018/10/16/the-revenge-of-hard-power-politics.

'The Russian National Security Strategy', 31 December 2015, http://www.ieee.es/Galerias/fichero/OtrasPublicaciones/Internacional/2016/Russian-National-Security-Strategy-31Dec2015.pdf.

'The Untold Story of Notpetya: The Most Devastating Cyberattack in History', Andy Greenberg, 22 August 2018, *Wired*, https://www.wirEd.com/story/notpetya-cyberattack-ukraine-russia-code-crashed-the-world.

'The US Army Is Preparing for Major Changes to Force Structure', Jen Judson, 5 March 2019, *Defense News*, defensenews.com/land/2019/03/06/major-army-force-structure-changes-afoot.

'The US Military Is Preparing for a New War', Michael T. Klare, 5 June 2019, *The Nation*, thenation.com/article/us-military-is-preparing for new-wars-china-russia.

'Ursula von der Leyen: "We Are Building a European Defense Union"', Michalis Tsikalas, ekstherimerin.com, http://www.ekathimerini.com/238679/article/ekathimerini/news/ursula-von-der-leyen-we-are-building-a-european-defense-union.

'"US Defense Budget Not Much Bigger Than China, Russia": Gen. Milley', Sidney J. Freeberg, Jr, 25 May 2018, *Fact.International*, http://fact.international/2018/05/us-defense-budget-not-that-much-bigger-than-china-russia-gen-milley.

'US Expects Record Domestic Oil Production in 2019, 2020', David Koenig, 12 February 2019, https://www.usnews.com/news/best-states/new-mexico/articles/2019-02-12/us-expects-record-domestic-oil-production-in-2019–2020.

'US Fires INF-Busting Missile, First Test since Treaty Signed', Paul McLeary, 19 August 2019, *Defense News*, https://breakingdefense.com/2019/08/us-fires-inf-busting-missile-first-test-since-treaty-signed.

'Vladimir Putin: Russia and the Changing World', 15 February 2015, GlobalResearch.com, https://www.globalresearch.ca/vladimir-putin-russia-and-the-changing-world/5477500.

'War and PEACE on China's Digital Silk Road', Jonathan Hillman, 16 May 2019 (Washington, DC: CSIS).

'War Clouds on the Horizon', Paul Cornish, September 2019, The Alphen Group, https://thealphengroup.home.blog.

'We Want a Better Deal, Not War with Iran, Says Envoy Turning the Screw for Donald Trump', Josh Glancy, 12 May 2019, *The Times*, https://www.thetimes.co.uk/article/we-want-a-better-deal-not-war-with-iran-says-envoy-turning-the-screw-for-donald-trump-7rbjllgsm.

'What Does China Really Spend on Its Military?' (2019) (Washington, DC: CSIS), https://chinapower.csis.org/military-spending.

'What Is Extraterritoriality?', Kallie Szczepanski, 29 January 2019, https://www.thoughtco.com/what-is-extraterritoriality-194996.

'What's in Japan's Record 2018 Defense Budget Request?', 28 August 2017, *The Diplomat*, https://thediplomat.com/2017/08/whats-in-japans-record-2018-defense-budget-request.

'"Whoever Leads in AI Will Rule the World", Putin to Russian Children on Knowledge Day', 1 September 2017, *RT*, https://www.rt.com/news/401731-ai-rule-world-putin.

'Xi Jinping's Chinese Dream', Robert Lawrence Kuhn, 4 June 2013, *New York Times*, https://www.nytimes.com/2013/06/05/opinion/global/xi-jinpings-chinese-dream.html.

Communiques, Fact–Sheets, and Official Statements

'2018 European Deterrence Initiative (EDI) Factsheet', U.S. European Command Public Affairs Office, https://nl.search.yahoo.com/search?fr=mcafee&type=E211NLoG0&p=European+Defense+Initiative.

'Active Engagement, Modern Defence: Strategic Concept for the Defence and Security of Members of the North Atlantic Treaty Organization', Lisbon, November 2010 (Brussels: NATO), https://www.nato.int/strategic-concept/pdf/Strat_Concept_web_en.pdfThe European Union.

'D-Day Facts and Stats', Stephen Ambrose Historical Tours, https://stephenambrosetours.com/d-day-facts and 'Ten Things You Need to Know About D-Day', Imperial War Museum, https://www.iwm.org.uk/history/the-10-things-you-need-to-know-about-d-day.

'Defence Ministers to Agree NATO Readiness Initiative', 7 June 2018, https://www.nato.int/cps/en/natohq/news_155348.htm.

European Defence Agency (2014) 'Defence Data 2014 (2014 Estimates)' (Brussels: EDA), p. 4, https: www.eda.europa.eu/docs/default-source/documents/eda-defencedata2014-final.

External Action, 'The Joint Comprehensive Plan of Action', https://eeas.europa.eu/headquarters/headquarters-homepage_be/8710/Joint%20Comprehensive%20Plan%20of%20Action.

'Global Strategic Trends: The Future Starts Here, Sixth Edition' (2018) (London: Cabinet Office).

NATO Brussels Summit Declaration, 11 July 2018, https://www.nato.int/cps/en/natohq/official_texts_156624.htm.

NATO Communiqué, 18 November 2018, https://www.nato.int/cps/en/natohq/news_160671.htm?.

'Press Conference by NATO Secretary General Jens Stoltenberg Following the Meeting of the North Atlantic Council (NAC) in Defence Ministers' Session', 7 June 2018, https://www.nato.int/cps/en/natohq/opinions_155264.htm?selectedLocale=en.

'The National Risk Register of Civil Emergencies' (2017) (London: Cabinet Office).

'The NATO Wales Summit Declaration', https://www.nato.int/cps/en/natohq/official_texts_112964.htm.

'Treaty between the United Kingdom of Great Britain and Northern Ireland and the French Republic for Defence and Security Co-operation', London, 2 November 2010 [The Treaty entered into force on 1 July 2011] (London: Cabinet Office).

'Washington's Farewell Address', USHistory.org, http://www.ushistory.org/documents/farewelladdress.htm.

Online Sources

Brookings Institution: www.brookings.edu

Charles de Gaulle Archive: www.charlesdegaulle.org

CNN: www.cnnstudentnews.com

Council on Foreign Relations: www.cfr.org

European Defence: www.european-defence.com

European Defence Agency Data Portal: www.eda.europa.eu

European Navigator: www.ena.lu/mce.cfm

European Union: www.europa.int

European Union Council of Ministers: www.ue.eu.int

Eurotreaties: www.eurotreaties.com

globalEdge: www.globalEdge.com

Globalfirepower.com: www.globalfirepower.com

GlobalResearch.com: www.GlobalResearch.com

Heritage Foundation: www.heritage.org

Human Rights Watch: www.hrw.org

Keesings Online Archive: www.keesing.com

NATO: www.nato.int

Source Watch: www.sourcewatch.org

Statista: www.statista.org

WarontheRocks: www.warontherocks.com

Western European Union: www.weu.int

Yale University: www.yale.edu

Index

For the benefit of digital users, table entries that span two pages (e.g., 52–53) may, on occasion, appear on only one of those pages.